WQ037943

WSQ: Women's Studies Quarterly, a peer-reviewed, theme-based journal, is published in Summer and Winter by The Feminist Press at The City University of New York, The Graduate Center, 365 Fifth Avenue, Suite 5406, New York, NY 10016; 212-817-7926.

WEB SITE
http://www.feministpress.org/wsq

EDITORIAL CORRESPONDENCE
Cindi Katz and Nancy K. Miller, *Women's Studies Quarterly*, The Feminist Press at The City University of New York, The Graduate Center, 365 Fifth Avenue, Suite 5406, New York, NY 10016; 212-817-7926; wsqeditorial@gmail.com.

SUBSCRIPTIONS
Subscribers in the United States: Individuals—$40.00 for 1 year; $90.00 for 3 years. Students—$28.00 for 1 year. (Student subscribers must provide a photocopy of current student identification.) Institution—$60.00 for 1 year; $144.00 for 3 years. *Subscribers outside the United States:* Add $15 per year for surface delivery; add $45 per year for airmail delivery. To subscribe or change an address, contact Customer Service, *Women's Studies Quarterly,* The Feminist Press at The City University of New York, The Graduate Center, 365 Fifth Avenue, Suite 5406, New York, NY 10016; 212-817-7925; sales@feministpress.org.

FORTHCOMING ISSUES
The Global and the Intimate, edited by Geraldine Pratt, *University of British Columbia,* and
  Victoria Rosner, *Texas A&M University*
Envy, edited by Patricia Clough, *The Graduate Center, City University of New York,* and
  Jane Gallop, *University of Wisconsin–Madison*

RIGHTS & PERMISSIONS
Fred Courtright, The Permissions Company, Tel. (570) 839-7477, Email: fhowe@gc.cuny.edu

SUBMISSION INFORMATION
For the most up-to-date guidelines, calls for papers, and information concerning forthcoming issues, write to *Women's Studies Quarterly* at The Feminist Press at The City University of New York or visit our Web site.

ADVERTISING
For information on display ad sizes, rates, exchanges, and schedules, please write to *WSQ Marketing,* The Feminist Press at The City University of New York, The Graduate Center, 365 Fifth Avenue, Suite 5406, New York, NY 10016; 212-817-7925; wsqeditorial@gmail.com

Printed in the United States of America by Sheridan Press.

ISSN: 0732-1562   ISBN: 1-55861-512-1 $22.00

WOMEN'S STUDIES QUARTERLY

VOLUME 33   NUMBERS 3 & 4   FALL/WINTER 2005

An Educational Project of the Feminist Press at the City University of New York and the Center for the Study of Women and Society at The Graduate Center, City University of New York

TABLE OF CONTENTS

With this issue, we are delighted to assume the general editorship of *WSQ* (formerly *Women's Studies Quarterly*). For the first time in ten years, the journal will be edited under the same roof as the editorial offices of our publisher, The Feminist Press at the City University of New York, located in The Graduate Center where we both teach. We look forward to the creative synergy that this cohabitation will allow.

WSQ will continue to offer a stimulating interdisciplinary mix of scholarly articles, creative writing, and pedagogical resources for feminist research and practice, but the journal will also add several features. Along with our new name and look, *WSQ* will include interviews with leading feminist theorists, a "classics revisited" section where scholars reconsider a pivotal text in women's studies in the light of contemporary concerns, an expanded book section featuring review articles as well as individual reviews, and an endnotes column titled, "Alerts and Provocations," dealing with pressing political issues. We are also committed to publishing more visual work and to developing thematic issues that cut across the disciplines in ways that expand and remap the contours of women's studies.

Each volume is guest edited and structured around a theme embodying topical concerns about women, gender, and sexuality. For this, our first issue, we are excited to have worked with Deborah Nelson, author of *Pursuing Privacy in Cold War America*, on the themes of gender, culture, and society in the 1950s. Forthcoming themes include "The Global and the Intimate," edited by Geraldine Pratt and Victoria Rosner, and "Envy," edited by Patricia Clough and Jane Gallop. Calls for papers are posted on a broad array of listservs and are available on the *WSQ* Web site. Information about the journal, submission guidelines, our editorial and advisory boards, and recent and forthcoming issues can also be found on our Web site, www.feministpress.org/wsq.

We are pleased to introduce a newly appointed editorial board of feminist scholars, critics, writers, and artists whose work and expertise give *WSQ* a broad interdisciplinary profile. We have also created an

[*WSQ: Women's Studies Quarterly* 33: 3 & 4 (Fall/Winter 2005)]

advisory board to help bring the journal to a wider audience of readers in the United States and around the globe. We are inspired by the generosity of our board members and the uninterrupted history of the journal—from four-page newsletter in 1972 to its present double-issue format—as we take on the challenge of remaking *WSQ*'s profile at the threshold of a new century.

Cindi Katz
Professor of Geography in Environmental Psychology
The Graduate Center, City University of New York

Nancy K. Miller
Distinguished Professor of English and Comparative Literature
The Graduate Center, City University of New York

INTRODUCTION

DEBORAH L. NELSON

The untitled photograph by Sylvia Plachy on the cover of this issue is identified in her magnificent collection, *Signs and Relics*, as "Barbie Convention, Niagara, NY, 1992." In the photograph, a woman's shapely legs, emerging at the thighs from the right side of the photograph, angle to her black high-heeled shoes across the tiled walkway of a pool. Sitting erect on her crossed knees is a Barbie doll dressed in a black and white striped bathing suit, the doll's shapely legs and black-and-white high-heeled shoes angled in symmetry with the woman's. With nothing more than her plastic hands to stabilize her perch on the uneven surface of a bent knee, Barbie seems to exhibit both poise and self-possession—indeed, because we see her face and not her owner's, perhaps more than the woman on whom she rests. Plachy's photograph wittily asks the question: Who is imitating whom? Is the doll copying the woman, or the woman the doll?

Plachy captures the iconicity of the 1950s with a more complex irony than we typically find in the endless recycling of images from that decade. On refrigerator magnets and birthday cards; in film and in television programming and commercials; in print advertising and on book covers—the 1950s are everywhere a part of contemporary visual culture. However, displaying an image that is recognizably "fifties" without some degree of sarcasm has become a rarity. Mere citation seems to produce irony, with caption or without. The refrigerator magnet or birthday card reproduces the 1950s to register incredulity that such an image could ever have been taken seriously. Ironically embracing the earnestness of the image, which is the hallmark of camp, the reproduction (or imitation) suggests that the fifties, however ubiquitous, remain zip-locked in a sensibility that lies safely in the past. Plachy's photograph refines this irony by tempering its distancing effect. The sheer beauty of the visual rhyme between human and doll suggests that the 1950s continue to shape the culture of gendered self-fashioning, even

[*WSQ: Women's Studies Quarterly* 33: 3 & 4 (Fall/Winter 2005)]

in parody. Plachy's photograph (and the Barbie convention itself) indicates that the 1950s remain serious, though not humorless, business.

Thinking about the 1950s has always been serious business in gender studies because "the fifties" has been used in American political debate to signify ideologies of home and nation that require women to relinquish their participation in the public world in order to fulfill their obligations to family. Nearly all scholars working on the 1950s in the United States make a distinction between their own critical revisions of the decade and mainstream nostalgia for the fifties as a time of prosperity, family togetherness, and national strength. Against the massive edifice of this ideal, a revisionary account has been mounted, primarily from the political Left and in the realms of gender and sexuality studies. This account, which began with Betty Friedan's *The Feminine Mystique* in 1963, redescribed the 1950s as an era of oppressive normalization, anxiety, depression, and simmering dissent. When Elaine Tyler May's 1988 *Homeward Bound: American Families in the Cold War Era* linked the domestic ideology first described by Friedan to Cold War politics, the metaphor of "containment" provided a frame wide enough to draw together a variety of social, political, and aesthetic phenomena into a powerful counternarrative of the period. Indeed, *Homeward Bound* remains the most often cited work on gender in the 1950s.

The best work in gender studies produced in the 1990s, Joanne Meyerowitz's *Not June Cleaver: Women and Gender in Postwar America, 1945–1961* (1994), sought to complicate both the nostalgic idealization of the 1950s and the by then canonical narrative of containment. Meyerowitz was among the first to recognize that even the alternative vision of the 1950s had calcified into a form of conventional wisdom. Her own contribution to that volume revises the first revision of the 1950s, Friedan's *The Feminine Mystique*. While Meyerowitz called *Not June Cleaver* part of an "on-going revisionist endeavor" (2) more than ten years ago, few of the volumes that followed took her lead in subjecting both stories of the 1950s to critique. Joel Foreman in *The Other Fifties* has even suggested that this "critical effort . . . needs to be sustained into the indefinite future" because it has yet to "bring about more than minimal changes in the thinking of large audiences outside of academe" (1–2). Despite a wide nonacademic readership for such critical efforts as Wini Breines's *Young, White, and Miserable: Growing up Female in the 1950s*, Stephanie Coontz's *The Way We Never Were: American Families and the Nostalgia Trap*, and even David Halberstam's *The Fifties*, scholars keep insisting that the idealization of the fifties remains so dominant that it crowds out the alternative.

This issue of *WSQ* participates in the spirit of revision that marks the history of scholarly reflection on the 1950s, but does so under the sign of "Barbie Convention." Plachy's shrewd balance of wit and seriousness in her treatment of one of the decade's most famous icons offers an important insight into how the 1950s might best be approached. Pop culture parody of the ideal fifties may too vehemently deny its continuing influence on contemporary culture, but too much insistence that we remain in thrall to that ideal ignores the corrosive effects of its ironization. That is, the idealization of the 1950s, no matter what its provenance, cannot continue to exert the same pressure on history or memory when it has to compete with its own parody. The ironic view of fifties culture is part of a transition, part of the gap that opens when memory and history part ways. And as this gap opens, we can no longer assume that the idealization of the fifties is the proper context for thinking about the decade.

Likewise, the counternarrative of the 1950s, the line from Friedan to May and forward, is bound to change alongside the idealized image. Logically, this counternarrative can never entirely supplant the idealization of the 1950s because that idealization is fully embedded in it. The fifties trying to be "the fifties," to paraphrase Michael Wood, is precisely the oppressive normalization that accounts for the anxiety and depression that stands at the center of the containment account.[1] As the "happier" and "simpler" "fifties" become laden with scare quotes, the counternarrative begins to look a bit more paranoid. Moreover, as the "on-going revision" goes on and on, now for more than a decade, young scholars are at least as familiar with the revision as with the idealization. To judge from the submissions to this issue, what they have found surprising, and therefore worthy of exploration, are the examples of complex thinking about gender and sexuality that the decade supplies in limited, if still salient, amounts.

Though I have marked a generational shift in this volume, I do not wish thereby to emphasize a generational divide. The younger scholars included here were trained by feminist scholars committed to a form of revision that has been supremely important in revamping our understanding of the decade. Equally important, the issue itself includes contributions from scholars and artists from a wide spectrum of ages, sensibilities, methodologies, and disciplinary and interdisciplinary investments. If the transition out of the binary narratives of the 1950s has opened up new questions, it has also elicited powerful work fretting out the relationship between memory and history. Feminist criticism, history, and art have long insisted on attending to the personal experience that shapes the history-making process, and the issue includes work in the best of this tradition.

What new stories emerge and what new questions are asked when the dominant narratives and counternarratives of the period no longer have the same influence? And how do these new stories and questions fit into the already well-established histories? These are some of the questions that are provisionally answered in this volume. But the final and most pressing question might be: Why continue to think in terms of the 1950s, whether defined as "the fifties" or as the "long 1950s" (1945–1961), a designation preferred by many scholars? What are the advantages and disadvantages to this frame? On the one hand, because the decade has been a Rorschach test for U.S. political memory, "the fifties" tends to elicit a predominantly U.S. focus. This is certainly true of this issue. On the other hand, a simple library search using "1950s" provides an index of cultural ferment around the globe, a sample of which includes Chinese film, South African popular music, Cuban and Puerto Rican drama, Taiwanese poetry, television in Great Britain, opera in Australia, and method acting in Indonesia. The decade designation provides what Paula Rabinowitz, following Foucault, calls the "synchronic slice," the term she uses to brilliant effect in her syllabus "Fifty Years After." Using the decade as a "synchronic slice" permits more than a comparison across various organizing rubrics for the period: the Khrushchev years in the USSR, the Cold War in the United States, the Communist ascendancy in China, decolonization in Africa, the postwar, the postcolonial, and sometimes the postmodern. It generates a productive disorganization, a flattening of hierarchies, a scrambling of inside and outside, centers and margins, that opens space for multiplicity, contradiction, and experimentation. This issue provides some working material for such a comparativist or transnational approach, beginning to make good on the aspirations of a synchronic slice.

The energy behind the interest in the fifties, particularly in gender studies, has always been as much about the present as it is about the past. As Rachel Brownstein asks in her review of Kate Walbert's *Our*

Kind: "Is it the current repressive regime and the consequent fear of losing the gains of the sixties and seventies that is provoking anxious glances back toward the fifties?" There is every good reason for feminists to look back to a period before the massive social changes produced by second-wave feminism—the period that, as many have argued, produced second-wave feminism itself. But anxiety is not felt uniformly by the contributors to this issue. Some, more optimistically, seem to be searching out modes of survival in periods of feminist retrenchment and international containment. If the fifties no longer mean what they once meant, there might be less political advantage in staking a claim to what they "really" were, but considerable historical advantage in clearing the field for new thinking.

The thematic body of the issue is divided into four sections: "Articles," "Arts and Archives," "Feminist Classics," and "Reviews."[2] While the first and fourth categories need no explanation, the new sections require a word of description. "Arts and Archives" is this issue's version of a section traditionally called "Creative" in *WSQ*. We sought to gather not only creative pieces that worked imaginatively with the 1950s, but archival material from the decade that needed exposure or further reflection. We also folded the traditional "pedagogy" section into "Arts and Archives" because of the provocative ways Paula Rabinowitz assembles her archive in the course "Fifty Years After." "Feminist Classics" is another new addition to the journal. Featuring a pivotal feminist work *from* the fifties, Mirra Komarovsky's *Women in the Modern World* (1953), rather than a landmark work *about* them, seemed like a good strategy in light of the interventions this issue wishes to make.

To describe these interventions is more difficult. This collection addresses a miscellany of interests in the 1950s, which I take to be symptomatic of the waning influence of the two master narratives of the decade. Moreover, it actuates an array of approaches to gender studies. Indeed, gender and sexuality, either or both of which is a major consideration of each piece, do not always occupy the central point of argument—a measure of the assimilation of gender studies into the traditional disciplines. The wealth of topics is exhilarating, but organizing them into lines of common concern can only be provisional. Rather than following the order of the different sections or the more obvious connections of subject matter, which I trust readers to discover for themselves, this description of the issue will cross over the boundaries between creative work, scholarship, and reviews to suggest patterns of intervention. Shuffling the order would produce equally interesting juxtapositions and I urge readers to crisscross at will.

I want to begin with Alicia Ostriker's review of both the new facsimile edition of Sylvia Plath's *Ariel* and Diane Middlebrook's *Her Husband*, a sophisticated reinterpretation of the Plath/Hughes marriage, because it reframes the Plath legend, both in art and life. Reinterpreting potent fifties myths, both from and about the decade, constitutes one type of intervention in this issue. Several of these essays revisit fifties myths by creating new continuities between the fifties and other moments in the twentieth century. Refusing the idea of fifties exceptionalism—the various "ends" (as in ideology) or "declines" (as in culture)—these essays recast the decade in ways that shed new light on contemporary politics and twentieth-century aesthetics. Andrew Hoberek's "Liberal Antiliberalism: Mailer, O'Connor, and the Gender Politics of Middle-Class *Ressentiment*," for example, locates in the 1950s the origins of our own red state/blue state conflicts over the social wage and the traditional family. In a complex merging of literary and political analysis drawn from both fifties and contemporary sources, Hoberek tells the story of the proletarianization of the middle class, its declension from property owners to wage laborers with its concomitant loss of agency. Rereading the decade's familiar sociological account of the loss of masculine autonomy in organized society (*The Organization Man* and *The Lonely Crowd*, for example) by tracing another version of this anxiety submerged and displaced in fifties fiction, Hoberek understands the scenes of violent comeuppance in O'Connor's stories as a displaced version of middle-class self-hatred. In the conservative logic of middle-class *ressentiment*, he argues, "relocating the realm of feminized dependency from the home to the state, enables some women to move into the public sphere by mounting a rhetorical defense of the very family structure that is being undermined." Flannery O'Connor, he says, is the precursor to Ann Coulter.

Coming to the 1950s from the first half of the twentieth century, Evan Brier produces a materialist history of the book industry to link *Peyton Place*, the book that for fifties reviewers marked the decline and fall of American civilization, with *Ulysses*, the book that was a pinnacle of modernist literary excellence. "The Accidental Blockbuster:

Peyton Place in Literary and Institutional Context" reconsiders feminist arguments about the novel's status as part of feminized and feminizing mass culture. Brier instead argues that conceding the separate spheres of culture can only take us so far in understanding the way books create their own publics. Because *Peyton Place* and *Ulysses* were marketed by the same people and achieved commercial success by way of scandal, publishing history tells a different story about the transformation of American culture at midcentury, one that puts modernism and mass culture on intimate terms.

Looking across the twentieth century, Lubna Najar seeks to redraw African American literary history in "The Chicago Poetry Group: African American Art and High Modernism at Midcentury." Sandwiched between two periods of great visibility—the Harlem Renaissance and the Black Arts Movement—the 1950s have been conspicuous for their absence in narratives of twentieth-century African American writing. In the "Arts and Archives" section, Najar offers two poems from the archives of the South Side Community Art Center, where a group of African American writers and artists collaborated across a range of media. Known best for its nurturing of Gwendolyn Brooks, the South Side Community Art Center produced a number of artists significant not only for their work but for their promotion of black arts in the city of Chicago. Margaret Danner Cunningham, both a poet and an associate editor at *Poetry* magazine (the signature journal of American poetic modernism), offers an intriguing link between modernist poetry and postwar African American literature.

In the "Feminist Classics" section, Shira Tarrant and Natalie Kampen both reflect on the work of the 1950s premier feminist sociologist, Mirra Komarovsky. Tarrant's "When Sex Became Gender: Mirra Komarovsky's Feminism of the 1950s" argues against the historical convention of organizing feminism into "waves," arguing that feminists miss important continuities with the 1950s by ignoring evidence of its "constrained" but "continuing feminist project." Positioning Komarovsky as an early social constructionist, Tarrant reveals her persistent questioning of women's roles as they were dictated not only by Cold War ideology, but also by functionalist sociology. Natalie Boymel Kampen, in a more personal reflection, "Mirra Komarovsky: Another Appreciation," revisits Komarovsky's crucial role in nurturing women's studies at Barnard College before and during the feminist movement, attesting to her contributions at the institutional level in securing a place for feminist scholarship in the academy.

Sarah Glazer's review of *Beyond the Gray Flannel Suit* by David Castronovo frames a second line of inquiry, one that shares Tarrant's insistence on recovering the continuities with feminist work in the fifties. Castronovo's book reproduces as "great" American literature what could be called a "fifties" view, since it duplicates the argument of Leslie Fiedler's *Love and Death in the American Novel* (1960): American literature is defined by rebellion against society and conformity, which is also the flight from domesticity and from women. Castronovo writes, Glazer argues, as if feminism had never happened. However, we might wonder whether feminists themselves have inadvertently collaborated in creating this blind spot. While it is easy enough to believe that Castronovo is unfamiliar with feminist literary criticism on the 1950s, there is probably less of such criticism to recommend than on any other decade of the century.

Several essays in the volume seek to fill that gap. Ann Peters's "A Traveler in Residence: Maeve Brennan and the Last Days of New York" reclaims the work of Brennan, the *New Yorker* essayist and short story writer, by resituating her in the context of midcentury urban development, suggesting that Brennan was a scrupulous observer of the destruction of New York's residential hotels, one of the few refuges of single women and women artists in the city. Rather than a demure suburbanite enjoying the milder pleasures of city life, Brennan becomes a part of the larger protest carried out primarily by women, most notably Jane Jacobs, against Robert Moses's creative destruction of New York public life.

In a similar move of recovery, William Orchard and Yolanda Padilla reconstruct the career of a Chicana novelist, playwright, and screen writer in "Lost in Adaptation: Chicana History, the Cold War, and the Case of Josephina Niggli." Tracking Niggli's adaptation of her novel *Mexican Village* for the film *Sombrero*, Orchard and Padilla show that by eliminating her meditation on the Mexican Revolution under pressure of Cold War anxieties about Communism, she deprived the film of the novel's coherence and critique. Without this political subtext, *Sombrero* became a loose collection of sentimental folk elements, rather than an intricate reworking of folk culture that expressed her belief in the democratic possibilities of the revolution. Reimagining

Niggli's commitment to the ideals of the Revolution makes her an important figure for Chicana/o studies, which has been hesitant to embrace her, but unable to omit her from its history. Orchard and Padilla provide a rubric under which to re-examine the work of Niggli and other Chicana intellectuals of the midcentury.

These examples of recovery suggest that returning to the archive is a fruitful priority for scholarship on gender and culture in the 1950s. Not only are new works still emerging that test the ways we have of understanding the decade, but new interpretations of familiar stories keep existing paradigms open and fluid. Exceptional and surprising cases make the history of the decade more uneven than it has appeared to be. Diane Middlebrook's review of *De Kooning: An American Master* takes up one such case. Rather than focusing on Willem de Kooning himself, Middlebrook mines the biography for what it says about the women in his life and their unusual domestic arrangements with him. Exploring its mixture of prestige and companionship, intellectual gratification and sexual stimulation, work and comfort, Middlebrook understands Elaine and Willem's rarely cohabitative marriage not as a convenience but as a bending of the institution to their needs. Attending to the couple's gratifications in their unconventional pact, Middlebrook's review reminds us that *Homeward Bound* was similarly open to the variety of individual experience in marriage. Far from presuming that politicians, marketers, and experts spoke for married couples, May's paradigm-making study attended carefully to the stories people told of their own experience of marriage, as contradictory as these stories often were.

Restoring complexity to the containment metaphor is the work of several essays here. May's central term lies at the heart of two essays that begin by contrasting American Cold War domestic ideology with its counterparts in the Soviet Union and Mexico, but use the comparison to introduce new twists and openings. Natasha Kolchevska cites the model of *Homeward Bound* in her article "Angels in the Home and at Work: Russian Women in the Khrushchev Years," ironically disrupting the Cold War fiction of the diametric opposition between the USSR and the United States Kolchevska brings together the memoir of a survivor of the gulag, Eugenia Ginzberg, and Vladimir Menshov's 1979 film *Moscow Doesn't Believe in Tears*, which returned to the 1950s to think about women's lives in the Khrushchev era. Using the aesthetic rendering of objects in both works, Kolchevska reads the material changes to women's lives during the thaw, a period in which private life was made a state priority without abrogating women's duties to the collective. Kolchevska shows that "a dissident artist could incorporate *kul'turnost'* and consumption into narratives that were critical of the Soviet system, and conversely, that a mainstream director could use the dual discourses of domestic mastery and public competence to reassure his audience that the Soviet society is progressing to middle-class afflu-ence and good taste."

Likewise, Soledad Loaeza begins with Elaine Tyler May to describe the situation of women in Mexico during the anti-Communist crusade. In "Mexico in the Fifties: Women and Church in Holy Alliance," Loaeza argues that traditional roles for women as guardians of tradition and continuity were resurrected to counteract the massive changes wrought by the Mexican Revolution in the first half of the century. Describing the religious dimension of Mexican anti-Communism fol-lowing World War II, influenced as much by the Vatican and Franco's Spain as by the United States, Loaeza also traces the longer history of Mexican women in the Catholic Church. Loaeza asks feminist histori-ans to imagine ways of understanding women's social history when the narrative runs between empowerment and oppression. Women's exalted role in the family was both a way of conscripting them for the maintenance of the home and engaging them in national service. This double service to home and nation explains the missionary zeal with which certain Mexican women carried out their social duties during the Cold War. The piece makes clear the national political stakes of women's contradictory domestic roles.

Also linking religion and domesticity, Arissa Oh's article, "A New Kind of Missionary Work: Christians, Christian Americanists, and the Adoption of Korean GI Babies, 1955–1961," offers an extension of domestic ideology in the context of the Korean War. Coining a new term, "Christian Americanism," Oh demonstrates the interpenetration of religious and patriotic ideals as they came together to foster an adop-tion movement for Korean war orphans, many of whom had been fathered by American GIs. Oh tracks the publicity campaign to win sympathy for these orphans and explains the unusual bending of racial prejudice in the evangelical families who adopted these mostly mixed-race children. Since one of the central claims of the adoption movement was the kinship between the United States and South Korea as two Christian nations, Oh's important contribution reminds us of the still undertheorized and underhistoricized place of religion in gender and ethnic studies.

Stacy Wolf's review of Christina Klein's *Cold War Orientalism: Asia in the Middlebrow Imagination, 1945–1961*, and Bruce McConachie's *American Theater in the Culture of the Cold War: Producing and Contesting Containment, 1947–1962*, demonstrates how Oh's essay takes part in a more general rethinking of the period: the revamping of the containment metaphor in light of U.S. foreign policy in Asia. Wolf argues for the importance of Klein's new metaphor, that of "integration," which more fully incorporates the sentimental vein of U.S. foreign policy and middlebrow cultural production that, taken together, generated a discourse of racial tolerance. Both metaphors, however, have proven inadequate to understanding the complex sexual history of the 1950s, as several of the contributions to this issue indicate. Frederick Whiting, for example, positions his innovative reading of masculinity, race, and sexuality between the poles of May's containment and Klein's integration paradigms in "Stronger, Smarter, and Less Queer: 'The White Negro' and Mailer's Third Man," arguing that each requires the suppression of same-sex desire and unconventional forms of masculinity. Reading "The White Negro" in the context of Mailer's essays and fiction from *Advertisements for Myself* (1959), Whiting notes the long silence by Mailer's critics on his fascination with passivity. Rather than a negativity or absence, passivity for Whiting signals a form of receptivity, "a preparedness to recognize the rich combinatorics of individual sexual experience as well as the proximity of kinds of experience that we have perhaps too rigidly segregated." Whiting's "masculine passive" contributes another complication to the burgeoning area of masculinity studies, a major source of new work in the field of gender studies.

Similarly, in "Patriotic Perversions: Patricia Highsmith's Queer Vision of Cold War America in *The Price of Salt, The Blunderer*, and *Deep Water*" Victoria Hesford examines masculinity under the containment rubric that Highsmith explodes in her domestic thrillers. Finding that Highsmith's novels *The Blunderer* (1954) and *Deep Water* (1957) exhibit a fear of "Americanness" rather than the un-American, Hesford explores "heteronormative domesticity" as "a space of dehumanization in which people are made into effigies of a controlled and functional masculinity and femininity." Ending with Highsmith's lesbian pulp classic, *The Price of Salt* (1952), Hesford shows Highsmith's investments in other geographies—the road, the city—that relieve the pressure of American domesticity.

Not all discussions of sexuality fall into the realm of domestic relations; indeed, sexuality outside the home was one of the 1950s most polarizing topics. Tiffany Gilbert's "American Iconoclast: *Carmen Jones* and the Revolutionary Divadom of Dorothy Dandridge" examines Dandridge's ground breaking performance in *Carmen Jones*, which provided Dandridge with the diva status thitherto reserved for white stars. Gilbert argues that the film's aesthetic mixture of opera and film cleverly exploited the high culture status of opera to permit Dandridge more leeway in pursuing an aggressive sexual autonomy. Diverting the stereotypes of black sexuality onto the supporting cast (Harry Belafonte and Pearl Bailey), the film created a space for Dandridge to explore an aggressive sexuality that could be coded neither black nor white.

Mixing both personal reflection and archival research, Karen Winkler visits the Kinsey Institute in her roles as psychotherapist, sex researcher, cultural critic, and single mother. "Kinsey, Sex Research, and the Body of Knowledge: Let's Talk about Sex" explores the treasure of the Kinsey archive not only the interviews for which Kinsey is famous but also for the art he collected, some of which is included in the essay. Reviewing the recent film of Kinsey's life and the current state of sex research, Winkler reflects on the effect of Kinsey's work on national culture, which is still struggling to assimilate his findings; in her field, which has fallen under the chilling effect of "sexual McCarthyism"; and in her own home, where she tries to teach her daughter a relationship to the body that Kinsey would have appreciated.

The wonderful generic elasticity of Winkler's essay—part social analysis, part criticism and review, part personal essay—represents the kind of creativity that we hoped to solicit for the "Arts and Archives" section. Two final pieces, a chapter of Alice Jardine's forthcoming novel, *BOOMING*, and a photo-essay by Lorie Novak, exhibit similarly innovative strategies for contending with the history of the 1950s. Each of these last pieces plays with time in illuminating ways, exploring not only the relationship of past and present, but also past and future. In Alice Jardine's *BOOMING*, a multigenre novel, equal measures detective story and science fiction picaresque, the title refers to her main character's ability to "negotiate time and space effortlessly." As a "virtual girl" and "antenna," Baby surfs through history, "inhabiting/speaking/ listening to those who have lived in other conjunctions of space-time, whether those historical conjunctions take place in books, movies or . . . 1950s TV." For this issue, Jardine has contributed one of the middle chapters, "The Game Show," a quiz-show-cum-revenge-fantasy that features "a gang of notorious blondes" who test Philip Wylie, Norman Vincent Peale, Hugh Hefner, and Talcot Parsons on their knowledge of the 1950s. The rollicking and sadistic fun of the chapter belies the seriousness of the facts that the blondes reveal to their unwitting contestants, facts about back-alley abortions and single motherhood, surgical menopause and electroshock therapy.

The photographer Lorie Novak offers a photo-essay that meditates both on her compositional practices in three installation projects and on the interplay of personal and public history that has become the center of her work. Beginning with a collection of her own family's snapshots from the 1950s, Novak reflects on the conventions of the family photograph and its combination of straightforward message and unintended mystery. She builds on them in the essay (as she does in her larger projects) toward an account of her stunning installation featuring Ethel Rosenberg. Superimposing photographs of Ethel Rosenberg, the children deported by Klaus Barbie, and her family snapshots, Novak becomes "the recipient of the weight of her cultural past," but also opens a space in which those histories might have been lived differently. The brilliance of the installation lies in its unpredictability, which Novak achieves by blurring foreground and background. Each new viewing reframes the past by recombining its elements and their respective weights.

I'd like to conclude by thinking back on the issue by way of Jardine's time travel and Novak's superimpositions. Both techniques produce a fluid relationship with time, juxtaposing past, present, and future in ways that help to defamiliarize a period with which we have assumed a too-comfortable intimacy. This fluidity is something this *WSQ* seeks to keep alive. It does not so much look to banish the narratives with which the 1950s have become familiar, but to superimpose new knowledge on them, altering the picture, restructuring the timeline, and offering the future a different past.

DEBORAH NELSON is an associate professor in the department of English at the University of Chicago. Her first book, *Pursuing Privacy in Cold War America*, was published in the Gender and Culture series at Columbia University Press. She is currently at work on *Tough Broads: Suffering in Style*, a book about women intellectuals in the mid–twentieth century. A chapter from this book, "Suffering and Thinking: The Scandal of Tone in Eichmann in Jerusalem," appears in *Compassion: The Culture and Politics of an Emotion*.

NOTES

1. From his foreword to the 2000 edition of Peter Biskind's *Seeing is Believing*, ix.
2. Part V, "Alerts and Provocations," another new feature of the redesigned *WSQ*, will present topical essays solicited close to press time on current events unrelated to the thematic focus of the issue.

WORKS CITED

Biskind, Peter. *Seeing is Believing: How Hollywood Taught Us to Stop Worrying and Love the Fifties*. New York: Henry Holt, 2000.

Breines, Wini. *Young, White, and Miserable: Growing Up Female in the 1950s*. Boston: Beacon Press, 1992.

Coontz, Stephanie. *The Way We Never Were: American Families and the Nostalgia Trap*. New York: Basic Books, 1992.

Foreman, Joel, ed. *The Other Fifties*. Urbana: University of Illinois Press, 1997.

Friedan, Betty. *The Feminine Mystique*. 1963; reprint, New York: Dell, 1983.

Halberstam, David. *The Fifties*. New York: Villard Press, 1993.

May, Elaine Tyler. *Homeward Bound: American Families in the Cold War Era*. New York: Basic Books, 1988.

Meyerowitz, Joanne, ed. *Not June Cleaver: Women and Gender in Postwar America, 1945–1961*. Philadelphia: Temple University Press, 1994.

LIBERAL ANTILIBERALISM: MAILER, O'CONNOR, AND THE GENDER POLITICS OF MIDDLE-CLASS *RESSENTIMENT*

ANDREW HOBEREK

It is safe to say that Norman Mailer's 1957 essay "The White Negro" has achieved canonical status in accounts of post–World War II American masculinity.[1] In what follows, I want to complicate this now automatic use of Mailer's essay to describe postwar masculinity by locating a similar dynamic in the fiction of Flannery O'Connor. O'Connor, like Mailer, is drawn to alienated outsiders who wreak real and symbolic violence against the postwar social order. Morris Dickstein's account of the Misfit in O'Connor's 1953 story "A Good Man Is Hard to Find" as "a violent bearer of unpleasant truths to foolish people" applies equally well to many of O'Connor's characters.[2] In O'Connor's fiction, however, such representatives of "rebellion, neurosis, and madness as forms of lucidity"[3] tend to be not urban black men or their hipster epigones but rather poor white Southerners. And while these regional rather than racial figures are often men, O'Connor deploys them in ways that cannot be understood solely—or even primarily—as models for the compensatory reassertion of troubled white masculinity. Rather, O'Connor's decidedly Maileresque obsession with middle-class characters' humiliation (and worse) at the hands of their imagined social inferiors reveals a concern with class that she in fact shares with Mailer.

Thomas Schaub has linked Mailer and O'Connor, along with other authors, in a shared framework of Cold War–era resistance to what they perceived as the historically discredited rationalism of Marxist intellectuals and their fellow travelers.[4] In what follows, however, I discuss this aspect of their writing as a product of the postwar transformation of class, exploited but not generated by Cold War politics. I argue elsewhere that postwar writing, so far from eschewing questions of class and economics, actually displays an occluded but fundamental concern with the long transformation of the American middle class from small property owners to white-collar employees.[5] This investment is difficult

[*WSQ: Women's Studies Quarterly* 33: 3 & 4 (Fall/Winter 2005)]

to see, however, because such writing tends—amid the economic well-being underwritten by the postwar boom and a strong welfare state—to displace apprehensions about middle-class proletarianization onto worries about abstract individualism. O'Connor and Mailer both participate in such transformative misreadings of class, although in ways that, I will argue in this essay, have less to do with Marxism than with forms of populist *ressentiment* currently being exploited by the Right. O'Connor's fiction in particular serves as an engine for the transformation of class anxiety into the regional articulation of universal values associated with (but not strictly geographically bound to) the so-called red states. If Thomas Frank is correct to argue that red-state rhetoric highjacks the ideas and investments traditionally associated with class struggle, locating dispossession not in the operations of capitalism but rather in the perverse hegemony of a coastal elite deaf to mainstream values,[6] then O'Connor becomes—in direct contradiction of her reputation as an author whose theological interests epitomize postwar fictional unworldliness—the most culturally central author of the 1950s.

I am thus suggesting that the scenes of aggression that link O'Connor and Mailer have at least as much to do with class as they do with gender. In "The White Negro" Mailer does not just turn to black men to remake white men. He also turns to lower-class men—economically marginal hipsters—to remake middle-class men or, as he calls them, "Square cell[s], trapped in the totalitarian tissues of American society, doomed willy-nilly to conform if [they are] to succeed."[7] In a long parenthetical, Mailer writes:

> (It can of course be suggested that it takes little courage for two strong eighteen-year-old hoodlums, let us say, to beat in the brains of a candy-store keeper, and indeed the act—even by the logic of the psychopath—is not likely to prove very therapeutic for the victim is not an immediate equal. Still, courage of a sort is necessary, for one murders not only a weak fifty-year-old man but an institution as well, one violates private property, one enters into a new relation with the police and introduces a dangerous element into one's life. The hoodlum is therefore daring the unknown, and so no matter how brutal the act, it is not altogether cowardly.) (593)

This is self-evidently a scene of remasculinization through violence, but it is also a story of violence directed against the middle class
as embodied by the storekeeper. O'Connor's characters act out similar
dramas of middle-class violation outside the context of intramasculine
aggression with which we normally associate Mailer. The Misfit, for
instance, carries out or orders the murders of an entire family that
O'Connor has been at pains to establish as middle-class stereotypes: a
stiff-necked, angry father; a silent, slacks-wearing mother; bratty kids;
and a grandmother who wears "white cotton gloves" and mourns the
time when "children were more respectful of their native states and
their parents and everything else."[8] Much of O'Connor's fiction, as I
demonstrate herein, mobilizes similar—if less dramatic—forms of anti-
middle-class violence.

In initially deemphasizing gender, however, I do not wish to turn
away from it entirely, but rather to draw our attention to late–twentieth-century reorganizations of gender that go far beyond the normative
ascription of white masculinity with which critics of "The White
Negro" have by and large been concerned. Reading a much larger sampling of Mailer's work, Sean McCann has recently demonstrated how
Mailer's "distrust of liberal institutions," and his efforts to imagine an
alternative social order grounded in violent assertions of masculine
authority, lay the groundwork for an "intensely private obsession with
patrimony and heritage" and a narrowed focus on "the isolated family"
in more recent writing.[9] McCann's assertion that the family takes on
such importance with "de-federalization and the decline of the welfare
state" (331) resonates with recent feminist critiques of the resurgence of
the patriarchal family as coercive ideal alongside the triumph (real and
ideological) of the market. Thus Gwendolyn Mink argues that attacks
on welfare have sought "to induce poor single mothers to conform to
patriarchal conventions" while undermining such women's ability to
participate in alternative family forms,[10] while Rebecca Dingo shows
how neoliberalism has turned to the patriarchal family to "provide a
scapegoat for the bad economy, the amoral market, and the decline of
national cultural values *and* a sense of individual agency to change one's
personal economic or social position."[11] This is not simply a case, however, of some sort of "return" to the family. As Wendy Brown has
shown, liberalism has traditionally defined its version of political and
economic selfhood in constitutive—and not just accidental—opposition

to women's subordination and dependence within the family.[12] The "movement of 'women's work' into the market" thus "subjects 'the family' to new and ultimately untenable pressures, and generally undermines the spatially organized sexual division of labor on which liberalism is premised" (144). Under these pressures, Brown suggests, "liberal conventions of feminine positioning and concerns" are simultaneously "subvert[ed]" and "reiterate[d]," "both reaffirming and decentering masculinist liberal discourse" (165).

Between them, Mink and Dingo point to two poles of the reconstitution (with a difference) of liberal gender roles within late modern society. On one hand, Mink illuminates the way in which the welfare mother has replaced the angel in the home as the characteristic figure of subordinated gender, implicitly replacing dependence on a man with dependence on the state as the mark of deindividualization. Dingo, meanwhile, discusses the way in which right-wing Christian women have employed the rhetoric of family values as a source of authority within public debates, thereby entering a public sphere now open to some women at the price of symbolically affirming traditional gender roles. In both cases, a now largely phantasmatic ideal of the family not only covers for but indeed drives the dissolution of the family in the face of market forces and of what Brown calls "the classificatory, individuating schemes of disciplinary society" (69). Welfare reformers, in Mink's account, employ the rhetoric of family values to defund state support for poor women's work as mothers and thereby drive these women into the low-paying service economy, while more privileged women, in Dingo's scheme, use the same rhetoric to leverage their participation in the public sphere. Gender becomes cross-cut with class in a way that does not simply reflect but in fact produces a state of affairs in which "middle- and upper-class" women are able to "'purchase' their liberty, personhood, and equality through child care and 'household help' provided by women earning a fraction of their boss's wage" (Brown, 164–5). But on an even more fundamental level, gender becomes partially defixed from actual gendered bodies, as liberal discourse preserves its dialectic of feminized dependence and masculine autonomy by relocating the former in those (including some men) associated with the state and extending the latter to those (including some women) charged with the defense of the family in crisis.

Insofar as this political formation preserves the form of classical liberalism by attacking more recent liberal efforts to use the state to soften the worst effects of capitalism, I refer to it by the only seemingly paradoxical name of "liberal antiliberalism." Liberal antiliberalism is liberal in Brown's sense—the nineteenth-century sense and perhaps the ontological one—of positing a masculine realm of agency against a feminized, naturalized realm of dependency, while it is antiliberal in McCann's sense—the Progressive/New Deal sense—of understanding the state as a buffer zone between individuals and capitalism. Proponents of liberal antiliberalism are antiliberal in the same dialectical way that modernist authors such as Pound and Eliot were antimodernist, their conservatism produced as a means of navigating the contradictions embedded within the nature of modern society. In what follows, I locate the origins of liberal antiliberalism in the work of postwar authors such as Mailer and O'Connor, who misread the crisis of the middle class in ways that anticipate contemporary forms of *ressentiment* directed against the welfare state, its employees, and its agents.

As I suggested earlier, the postwar reorganization of the middle class around white-collar employment can be understood as a form of structural proletarianization in which the ownership of small property that had traditionally defined middle-class status in the United States is replaced by the sale of (mental) labor to large corporations. The actual effects of such proletarianization were, of course, only imminent in the postwar period, when the middle class enjoyed what is still imagined as a golden age of prosperity and cultural influence. But they have since come home to roost in the form of downsizing, overwork, and deskilling, and in the general evisceration of middle incomes in an economy increasingly divided between the wealthy and the poor.[13] Ironically, given what Paul Krugman has identified as the postwar middle class's dependence on a strong welfare state,[14] this class displaced its anxiety about such developments onto a largely privatized (and, given the demographics of work in this period, masculinized) discourse of deindividualization within large organizations.

Two elements of this discourse in particular anticipate contemporary political rhetoric. On one hand, its neo-Weberian distrust of large institutions—sundered, to be sure, from the attention to the corporate world it receives in a book like William H. Whyte's 1956 *The Organization Man*—becomes the basis of the antigovernment rhetoric honed over the course of several decades of attacks on the welfare state. Less immediately obvious, however, but perhaps even more significant, is the debt that current pro-market pieties owe to postwar writers' tendency to romanticize the free market as the site of vanished middle-class agency.[15] This tendency appears in the work not only of right-wing figures like Ayn Rand and F. A. Hayek but also of a leftist like C. Wright Mills, whose *White Collar* (1951) understands the transformation of the middle class both as a form of proletarianization contingent on "the centralization of small properties" *and* a shift in American character from "the independent individual" of the past to "the little man" of the present day.[16] It is in this latter mode that Mills celebrates a putative middle-class golden age:

> Since few men owned more property than they could work, differences between men were due in large part to personal strength and ingenuity. The type of man presupposed and strengthened by this society was willingly economic, possessing the "reasonable self-interest" needed to build and operate the market economy. He was, of course, more than an economic man, but the techniques and the economics of production shaped much of what he was and what he looked forward to becoming. He was an "absolute individual," linked into a system with no authoritarian center, but held together by countless, free, shrewd transactions. (9)

It is with this passage in mind that we might return to Mailer's parable of the candy store owner to see it—*pace* Mailer's own self-glossing—as an attack not so much on the "institution" of "private property" per se as on the middle-class declension figured by property's possession by "a weak fifty-year-old man." Here too we can note that Mailer describes the hipster in contrast to his conformist "Square cell" as "a frontiersman in the Wild West of American night life" (585), and that he figures the world of the hipster as a sort of bohemian analog of laissez-faire capitalism governed by "the competition for pleasure" (595). In this world, he writes, "there is not nearly enough sweet for everyone. And so the sweet goes only to the victor, the best, the most, the man who knows the most about how to find his energy and how not to lose it" (595). As Schaub suggests, "the hipster's affinities with classic economic liberalism make him something of a philosophe as gangster, physiocrat as urban entrepreneur."[17] The hipster's oscillation between black and white in Mailer's essay figures, in this regard, his divided character as at once a non-middle-class other and a nostalgic representative of the heroic middle-class past.

This nostalgia for the middle-class past, which is ultimately no less central to the failure of Mailer's critical project than his racial minstrelsy, springs from his effort to confront those "characteristics of late modern secular society" that, according to Brown, generate *ressentiment* (69). The "incitement to *ressentiment*" springs, Brown argues, from individuals' subjection to "global configurations of disciplinary and capitalist power of extraordinary proportions" at the same time that they find themselves "nakedly individuated, stripped of reprieve from relentless exposure and accountability for themselves" (69). The demise of the welfare state, to frame Brown's argument in the terms with which we have been dealing, does not signal the end of disciplinary regimes as such but only, perhaps, those most concerned with protecting individuals from capitalism. The hyperinvestment in normative models of the family subjects individuals to enormous constraints at the same time that they face "the increased fragmentation, if not disintegration, of all forms of association not organized until recently by the commodities market," including families (Brown, 68–9). Mailer confronts half this problem, posing his "American existentialist—the hipster" against a world in which "our collective condition is to live with instant death by atomic war, relatively quick death by the State as *l'univers concentrationnaire*, or with a slow death by conformity with every creative and rebellious instinct stifled" (584). It is in this respect that Mailer, stressing hipsters' Nietzschean efforts "to create a new nervous system for themselves" (Mailer, 591), anticipates Brown's call for contemporary intellectuals and activists to eschew the retreat into *ressentiment* and the fetishization of pain and powerlessness in politicized identity and to instead take on the Nietzschean task

> of formulating oneself as a creator of the future and a bridge to the future in order to appease the otherwise inevitable rancor of the will against time, in order to redeem the past by lifting the weight of it, by reducing the scope of its determinations. (Brown, 72)[18]

But this Nietzschean, utopian side of Mailer's work—which is also, we might add, the proto-queer side that turns to sexuality as the most intensely policed site of the social normativity he seeks to overthrow[19]—is blunted by his typical postwar tendency to cast the problem in terms of a threat to masculine individualism. Mailer, to a far greater extent than Nietzsche himself in Brown's description, "privileg[es] individual character and capacity over the transformative possibilities of collective political invention" (Brown, 74), in ways that foretell the collapse of his progressive tendencies into the masculinist antiliberalism that McCann describes. In this respect we can understand the narrative of anti-middle-class violence in "The White Negro" as an attempt at utopian renewal that fails because it remains bound to middle-class nostalgia for a lost form of market individualism. Mailer's "response to conformity," Schaub argues, "tended all too often merely to underline the rhetoric of Wild West individualism" in a way that not only implicitly buttressed postwar capitalism but also "touted a new masculinity that confirmed the prevalent repression of the feminine, which in political terms meant the weak: minorities, women, and young people."[20]

I will return to this suggestive delinking of femininity from actual women shortly, although I want to do so by way of O'Connor. O'Connor's work repeatedly stages similar confrontations between a weakened white-collar middle class and agents of violent renewal who are at once non-middle class and representatives of the middle class's heyday. Her 1960 novel *The Violent Bear It Away*, for instance, describes the life-long conflict between the pedantic, ineffectual psychology teacher Rayber—referred to throughout the novel as "the schoolteacher"[21]— and the unbending, self-styled prophets of God both named Tarwater. Rayber is the nephew of the elder Tarwater, who had briefly kidnapped him and sought to raise him in his strict version of evangelical Protestantism. Rayber, in reaction, becomes self-consciously secular and modern, and the two joust when Tarwater comes to live with his nephew: Rayber turns Tarwater into a case study for a journal article, and Tarwater in turn kidnaps the nephew whom Rayber has been raising. At the start of the novel, the elder Tarwater's death frees the younger to find and commence a similarly antagonistic relationship with Rayber, before eventually taking up the mantle of prophet himself. If Rayber responds to what he sees as the madness in his bloodline with "a rigid ascetic discipline" that transforms him into an ineffectual organization man—"All his professional decisions were prefabricated and did not involve his participation" (402)—then the elder Tarwater, who proclaims "Called myself!" (341), represents the autochthonous middle class translated into the terms of the poor, white, religious South. This was O'Connor's characteristic solution to the problem of the organization man: as she writes in a letter, "the prophet is a man apart. He is not typical of a group."[22] Thus it should come as no surprise to see O'Connor asserting in another letter that "The modern reader will identify himself with the school teacher, but it is the old man who speaks for me."[23]

But it is not simply the novel's mobilization of religion as a realm transcending the bureaucratized world of the organization—"Yours not to grind the Lord into your head and spit out a number!" old Tarwater tells Rayber (351)—that anticipates the red-state rhetoric of the contemporary Right. Just as importantly, the regional identity through which O'Connor channels this logic already contains in the 1950s a fully developed form of the antigovernment sentiment then only nascent in Mailer and U.S. mainstream culture.[24] This antigovernment sentiment cohered, of course, around resistance to integration, a framework that O'Connor invokes throughout the novel. Thus she pointedly has the younger Tarwater reflect, in terms whose resonance would have been inescapable in the era of massive resistance, that "he would dislike to have to kill [Rayber] but if he came out here, messing in what was none of his business except by law, then he would be obliged to" (351–52). What makes O'Connor so forward-looking, however, is the way in which her predominantly theological interests lead her to graft such antigovernment sentiment onto a religious framework that would ultimately prove more enduring than white Southern racism. It is in this respect crucial to note that she identifies Rayber with a "welfare-woman" (380) who accompanies him on his failed mission to rescue the younger Tarwater from the elder Tarwater's efforts to "instruct . . . the boy . . . in the hard facts of serving the Lord" (332). At this moment in the novel, with the twin figures of the ineffective intellectual and the intrusive, feminized state turned aside by the somehow admirably inflexible believer, we are not too far from the forces that shaped the 2004 presidential election.

What these readings of Mailer and O'Connor should suggest is that red-state politics are middle class and *not* working class in origin. Or more accurately, they are the politics of the U.S. middle class on its way to becoming working class in the Marxist sense of selling its labor. Red-state politics acknowledge this transformation affectively, to the extent that they are organized around an emotional analog of class conflict. But they misrepresent this conflict, as Thomas Frank describes, by understanding the class enemy in cultural rather than economic terms. There is a danger here of seeing this structure of feeling as crude false consciousness, in which people are fooled into believing that some interests are more fundamental than those of class. Mailer and O'Connor help us avoid this error, however, by suggesting that red-state politics are never simply cultural, but rather contain a refracted version of the class transformation that produces them. Simply put, the elitist enemy is always a grotesque version of those qualities (mental labor, commitment to organizations) with which the middle class identifies its declension, while the figure of the people is always characterized by those elements of agency and autonomy that the middle class has lost. The figure of the non-middle class other through which this middle class discourse acts out its self-hatred is a figure of action severed from intellection. Mailer's hoodlums "act" in vivifying opposition to what he elsewhere in "The White Negro" describes as "the committee-ish cant of the professional liberal" (603), while the elder Tarwater distinguishes himself from Rayber by proclaiming that "It was me could act . . . not him. He could never take action. He could only get everything inside his head and grind it to nothing" (379).[25] There is, of course, a proto-fascist or at least authoritarian element here whose appeal has been realized in the marketing of George W. Bush as a man of convictions, no matter what they are or where they lead.[26] Less dramatically but perhaps even more significantly in the long term, the middle class, by buying into this celebration of unthinking action, cuts its own throat, denigrating precisely those activities (mental labor) and institutions (higher education, the welfare state, etc.) through which it exercised its agency in the period between the late nineteenth and late twentieth centuries.[27]

With this in mind we can return to O'Connor's fiction to consider how this class phenomenon simultaneously produces and depends on what I have suggested is the late modern reorganization of gender roles. While O'Connor's 1955 story "Good Country People" might initially seem like a parable of the restoration of traditional gender roles, reading it in terms of the gap between characters and author reveals a more complicated picture. "Good Country People," in which an itinerant Bible salesman named Manley Pointer turns out to be far less "simple" than a middle-class mother–daughter duo suspects, offers yet another narrative of middle-class violation and humiliation at the hands of a non-middle-class other. For the mother Mrs. Hopewell, another representative of residual Southern female gentility like the grandmother in "A Good Man," Pointer is "good country people . . . just the salt of the earth."[28] Her self-consciously modern, Northern-educated daughter Joy-Hulga, meanwhile, thinks of him as a "child" (275) whom she will seduce and then move "into a deeper understanding of life" (276). By story's end, however, Pointer has stolen Joy-Hulga's artificial leg and left her trapped in the second story of a barn, telling her, "I may sell Bibles but I know which end is up and I wasn't born yesterday and I know where I'm going!" (283). As he departs, Mrs. Hopewell recognizes him in the distance as "that nice dull young man that tried to sell me a Bible yesterday" (283). "I guess the world would be better off," she tells her hired helper Mrs. Freeman, "if we were all that simple" (283). Mrs. Freeman, of course, is not fooled: "'Some can't be that simple,' she said. 'I know I never could'" (284). But while the story makes fun of both Mrs. Hopewell's and Joy-Hulga's fantasies about the salesman, it employs him against them in a revenge scenario acted out not on the part of real poor white Southerners but of a third middle-class position: O'Connor's own unformulated one outside the story.

This splitting—in a letter O'Connor described Joy-Hulga as a more "primitive" "projection of myself"[29]—makes clear the way O'Connor's fiction, like "The White Negro," displaces what might otherwise be an economic account of the American middle class's fate onto a form of middle-class self-hatred. Such self-hatred objectifies not only the non-middle-class agents of its aggression but also the other, bad middle class that becomes its target. O'Connor's own analysis of "Good Country People" from another letter suggests some of the lineaments of this bad middle-class other. Joy-Hulga, she writes,

> is full of contempt for the Bible salesman until she finds he is full of contempt for her. Nothing "comes to flower" here except her realization in the end that she ain't so smart. It's not said that she has never had any faith but it is implied that her

fine education has got rid of it for her, that purity has been over-ridden by pride of intellect through her fine education.[30]

As this makes clear, "Good Country People" reproduces the scenario of comeuppance that I have already located elsewhere in Mailer's and O'Connor's work: an overintellectualized, feminized avatar of the middle class is humiliated and punished by a non-middle-class figure characterized by the ability to act. Even more clearly than she does with Tarwater in *The Violent Bear It Away*, however, O'Connor links Pointer's motives to a form of *ressentiment* directed against Joy-Hulga's intellectual elitism. "And I'll tell you another thing, Hulga," he says in his parting words to her—"using the name," O'Connor specifies, "as if he didn't think much of it"—"you ain't so smart. I been believing in nothing ever since I was born!" (283).

That O'Connor uses exactly the same formulation ("ain't so smart") in glossing the story suggests her closeness to the Bible salesman at this moment. If this split identification with her characters (she is at once Joy-Hulga and Manley Pointer) bears out the argument that the drama of anti-middle-class violence is itself a middle-class product, it also complicates what we might otherwise see as the story's simple parable of femininity restored. To sketch this parable, "Good Country People" depicts Joy-Hulga as defeminized by her intellectual proclivities, and not only in the eyes of her more traditional mother who pities "the poor stout girl in her thirties who had never danced a step or had any *normal* good times" (266; O'Connor's emphasis). Her compound name stems, for instance, from her effort to replace her more conventionally feminine childhood name, which Mrs. Hopewell still insists on using, with the new one that she at first adopts "purely on the basis of its ugly sound" only to realize "the full genius of its fitness" in "a vision of the name working like the ugly sweating Vulcan who stayed in the furnace and to whom, presumably, the goddess had to come when called" (266–67). If, as this classical allusion suggests, Joy-Hulga understands her artificial limb as her symbolic link to the masculine realms of agency and technical mastery (and perhaps the possibility of same-sex desire), then the theft of the limb by the unsubtly named Manley Pointer functions not only as class but as gender revenge. Showing her "that she ain't so smart" also means violently restoring her to conventional femininity.

The way in which "Good Country People" treats Joy-Hulga, how-ever, must be distinguished from the masculine position that O'Connor adopts through her identification with Pointer. In crossing the divide separating the story's treatment of Joy-Hulga from its composition by O'Connor, I want to suggest, we also cross between the two poles of liberal antiliberalism. The story's content, that is, is antiliberal in the vernacular sense that it enacts Joy-Hulga's violent restoration to tradi-tional gender roles. But its form is, broadly speaking, liberal in that this restoration underwrites the contrasting agency of Pointer and—as a product of the late modern reorganization of gender—O'Connor her-self. As I suggested earlier, this reorganization, by relocating the realm of feminized dependency from the home to the state, enables some women to move into the public sphere by mounting a rhetorical defense of the very family structure that is being undermined. Brown implies this when she suggests that the true heir of Jean-Jacques Rousseau and John Stuart Mill in asserting the liberal principle "that women in the family are the seat of moral restraint in an immoral world" is Phyllis Schlafly (147). It is a truism that the major female fiction writers of the postwar period—O'Connor on the highbrow end of the spectrum and Ayn Rand on the popular—produce work that problematizes some forms of feminist analysis through its self-conscious adoption of gen-derless or masculine perspectives. This is no accident, insofar as it becomes possible at precisely the moment that masculine public author-ity, threatened by the putatively feminizing regime of organizational life, becomes available even for male authors like Mailer only as a fan-tasy of old middle-class agency relocated in non-middle-class bodies.

This quality in the work of O'Connor and Rand, moreover, directly anticipates the more political expressions of liberal antiliberalism prac-ticed by figures like Schlafly and Ann Coulter, whose writing combines masculine themes and rhetoric with the seemingly contradictory assertion of traditional gender roles. Coulter's tribute to Schlafly, "Call Her Mrs.," exemplifies this combination on multiple levels. Schlafly, Coulter argues, addressed important public issues while feminists remained subject to a stereotypically feminine obsession with ephemera. "As the feminists spent 20 years engaged in a death-match debate over whether it is acceptable for feminists to wear lipstick," Coulter writes, "Schlafly was writing 10 books, most of them on military policy." At the same time, Coulter's Schlafly gives up a rare chance to attend Harvard

Law School in the era before it admitted women in order to marry and raise children. Coulter's essay, furthermore, reproduces the combination of masculine rhetorical authority and fealty to traditional gender roles allegorized by Schlafly's career. "Soon feminists took up the issue of girl-firemen," Coulter writes,

> demanding to know what possible arguments there were, pray tell, for women not to be firemen. (A short list: their inability to pick up the hose, their tendency to cry and panic when confronted with dangerous situations, the effect on families whose homes are on fire when they open the door and see the female equivalent of Michael Dukakis in a tank.)[31]

Here Coulter—in ways made all the more obvious by her characteristic hectoring frat-boy tone—adopts precisely the same position that O'Connor does in "Good Country People," her own authority secured by reasserting traditional femininity on the would-be transgressive women about whom she writes.

That the reorganization of gender on which Coulter's exercise of public authority depends has not become completely normalized is attested by the results of a Google search for the terms "Ann Coulter" and "adam's apple." Yet the idea that Coulter must be a (former) man, no less than her own portrayal of feminists as not overly masculinized but overly feminized, makes clear the extent to which her public persona depends on her structurally masculine counterassertion of a realm of feminized dependency. What distinguishes these gender politics from those of classic liberalism, however, is that for Coulter, as her tell-tale reference to Dukakis makes clear, the realm of feminized dependency is no longer located in the family, but in the institutions associated with the welfare state: government, of course, but also academia and other organizations whose inhabitants are presumed not to work for a living. (Hence Saul Bellow's *mot* in *The Dean's December* that "a professor when he gets tenure doesn't *have* to do anything. A tenured professor and a welfare mother with eight kids have much in common.")[32] One effect of this move is to reopen the family as a site of agency, especially insofar as the family is reimagined not as a banal retreat from the market but rather as a battleground in the conflict with the welfare state. Thus Coulter can imagine Schlafly's voluntary return to the family not as stereotypically feminizing, like feminist concerns about makeup, but continuous with the real world of military policy. At the same time, gender partly frees itself from actual gendered bodies insofar as the welfare state replaces the family as the site of dependence and femininity. Government bureaucrats and tenured professors don't work but rather subsist on the wealth earned by others, just like women in the terms of classical liberalism—except that, like welfare mothers, they don't provide their benefactors with any reciprocal benefits. Thus the answer to the riddle, "What's the female equivalent of Michael Dukakis in a tank?" is, on some crucial level, "Michael Dukakis in a tank."

Liberal antiliberalism thus certifies some women to speak in the public sphere while circumscribing the ways in which men and women alike can do so. In this respect Mailer's and O'Connor's project is not all that discontinuous with the concerns of confessional poetry, which among other things mapped the process whereby "categories of citizens—women or homosexuals—rather than unlucky individuals were banished to the deprivation, rather than the liberation, of privacy."[33] As I have argued, we need to understand this process not (as we are wont to do with all contemporary conservative politics) as a reaction to the 1960s, but as a product of the reorganization of the middle class that preoccupied the 1950s. O'Connor's 1961 rewriting of "Good Country People" as "Everything That Rises Must Converge" provides, in this respect, both a coda to the elaboration of middle-class *ressentiment* in the fifties and an anticipation of the shape such *ressentiment* would begin to assume in the sixties. "Everything That Rises" carries over the earlier story's theme of intergenerational middle-class comeuppance, although with the daughter transformed into a sexually suspect son and with the poor white Manley Pointer transformed into urban black bus riders. The son, Julian, a would-be writer who lives with his mother and sells typewriters, is feminized in the classic terms of postwar Momism, rendered "weak and passive" by his overprotective mother.[34] "Everything That Rises" comes closer than most of O'Connor's fiction to acknowledging the transformation of the middle class, insofar as Julian's downwardly mobile white-collar work is balanced by the nostalgia, which he shares with his mother, for the ancestral home lost through their predecessors' "reduced circumstances."[35] Within the story, however, Julian's participation in his mother's nostalgia serves less to implicate him in what he thinks of as her "struggle to act like a Chestny without the Chestny goods" (491) than it does to undermine his mistaken belief that "he was not dominated by his mother" (492).

Rather than making him vulnerable to seduction by Communism, as it would have several years earlier,[36] Julian's Momism instead serves to render his liberal antiracism as a kind of erotic perversion. Julian is already the demonized liberal with which we are familiar from contemporary discourse, "too intelligent [in his own estimation] to be a success" (491) and condescending to the African Americans whose status he claims he wants to change but on which he feeds his elitism. "It gave him a certain satisfaction to see injustice in daily operation. It confirmed his view that with a few exceptions there was no one worth knowing within a radius of three hundred miles" (492). Julian's questionable sexuality thus limns the story's treatment of his politics not as a form of public engagement but rather as a private pathology. Cruising a black man on the bus with whom he is anxious to speak by asking for a match even though he has no cigarettes, he is met with "an annoyed look" (493). So far from a critique of white Negroism, this is in fact an instance of O'Connor's right-wing version of it: the black man, on to Julian in the same way that Manley Pointer was on to Joy-Hulga, serves as O'Connor's agent in undermining Julian's liberal pretensions.

Rather than seeing "Everything That Rises," then, as a product of O'Connor's softening on racial issues under the influence of her more liberal friend Maryat Lee,[37] I want to claim that on some level O'Connor is uninterested in concrete racial politics to the same degree and for the same reason that Mailer is in "The White Negro." The story climaxes when a black woman, angry that Julian's mother has tried to give her child a penny, hits the white woman with her pocketbook and brings on a stroke. In this scene, Patricia Yeager suggests, "O'Connor invents a black giantess to bring down an inanimate white aristocracy."[38] But if this scene thus resonates with the "violent politics opposing the nonviolent strategies of groups such as SNCC [Student Nonviolent Coordinating Committee] in the early sixties,"[39] this isn't the case because O'Connor has any sympathy with such politics: she isn't *that* much like Norman Mailer. Rather, O'Connor uses the black woman as another of the figures through which she attacks not an "inanimate white aristocracy" but an inanimate white middle class. Julian's response is, typically, to deliver a speech:

"Don't think that was just an uppity Negro woman," he said. "That was the whole colored race which will no longer take your condescending pennies. That was your black double. . . . What all this means," he said, "is that old world is gone. The old manners are obsolete and your graciousness is not worth a damn." He thought bitterly of the house that had been lost for him. "You aren't who you think you are," he said. (499)

It is only when he realizes that his mother is truly ill that he begins to comprehend the story's point: that his true responsibility is to his family and that reality is not something apprehended by thought but is rather "the world of guilt and sorrow" toward which he finds himself propelled at the story's end (500).

This "world of guilt and sorrow" is related to the memorialization of suffering that Brown sees as fundamental to contemporary *ressentiment*, although in its partial difference it bears out Brown's somewhat under–argued contention that such *ressentiment* is the property not of identity groups but of late modern liberal subjects more generally.[40] In "Everything That Rises" such guilt and sorrow serve not (or not only) as a source of collective identity but rather as a ground of authenticity from which to oppose the over–intellectualism that taints not only early sixties racial liberalism but the postwar middle class more generally.

This world of guilt and sorrow reappears in the book that I would like to conclude with by briefly describing it as the heir of Mailer's and O'Connor's fiction, Philip Roth's *The Human Stain* (2000). As Ross Posnock has pointed out, Coleman Silk's story of remaking himself as a white man only to have his career ruined late in life by a fatally misunderstood classroom remark invokes both the mid-twentieth-century Jewish intellectual milieu and the heroic age of American individualism.[41] Indeed, this is no accident, since postwar fascination with Jewish American writing derived at least in part from the way in which Jewish upward mobility in this period constituted a kind of last reiteration of the American middle class's favorite story about itself.[42] Coleman is a classic figure of American autogenesis whose career is prefigured by the middle-class virtues of self-discipline and self-motivation that he brings to his early stint as a boxer. In the ring,

Coleman thought, and the same way that he thought in school or in a race: rule everything else out, let nothing else in, and immerse yourself in the thing, the subject, the competition, the exam—whatever's to be mastered, become that thing. He could do that in biology and he could do it in the dash and he could do it in boxing.[43]

Although Silk eventually becomes a professor of classics he remains an outsider in the academy, eventually becoming dean of faculty and incurring his colleagues' ire for running the college, as the saying goes, "like a business": shutting down the journal they use to puff up their vitas, "rul[ing] . . . faculty meetings by fiat" (9), and insisting on merit as the sole criterion for promotion. Coleman's professional disgrace and eventual death thus symbolize the passing of a kind of intellectual career, and behind that a form of middle-class identity, in the process of dying out. Silk's chief adversary Delphine Roux—who participates in his professional disgrace and then harasses him over his affair with a younger woman who works on the campus's maintenance staff—likewise fulfills the pattern that Mailer and O'Connor would lead us to expect. Michael Gilmore notes that "Roux . . . is the least rounded characterization in the novel, and Roth comes uncomfortably close to ascribing her witch-hunting to sexual frustration,"[44] although to note what is old (and typically Rothian) about her as a figure of gender is to miss what is truly innovative about her as a figure of class. Roux is not only a bad woman compared to Silk's lover Faunia Farley—an "icon . . . for id-like animality"[45] that would do Mailer proud—but is also a figure of the alienated white-collar-worker-cum-academic. "Brimming . . . with intellectual self-importance" despite the fact that she is "virtually without experience outside schools" (184), Roux's intellectual work is determined by fashion—"Every ultra-cool Yale graduate student is working on either Mallarmé or Bataille" (188)—and her "credentials" consist in Silk's mind of "the sort of prestigious academic crap that the Athena students needed like a hole in the head but whose appeal to the faculty second-raters would prove irresistible" (190). Roux is a hodge-podge of anti–academic stereotypes, although to see this as an aesthetic failure is to miss the way in which Roth uses stereotype to distinguish between good characters and bad. Thus Silk's other adversary, Faunia's husband, is a stereotypical traumatized Vietnam vet (who even more than Roux seems like a refugee from a less ambitious novel), while the admirable characters are distinguished by interiority in the form of secrets (Silk's passing, Faunia's disavowed literacy).[46] In this way, the novel remains locked in the fundamental literary problem of the 1950s: how to represent individuals in a time of conformity. I have suggested that this was a problem generated by the transformation of the middle class, and indeed Roux points us in this direction through the way in which her stereotype is grounded in work. To the extent that, in precise opposition to Silk, her success depends not on merit but on appearance and consensus, she might well have stepped from the pages of *The Organization Man*.

What makes her different is, of course, the fact that she is an organization woman, and it is here, and in the fact that she is an academic, that we can gauge what Roth gains by addressing fifties concerns about individuality at the end of the nineties. Whereas Mailer and O'Connor had to turn to non-middle-class figures to oppose the middle-class ills messily dispersed, in books like *The Organization Man*, across the world of white-collar employment, *The Human Stain* inherits several decades of political work designed to quarantine these ills in the institutions of the welfare state and thereby to resanctify the business world as a site of masculine agency. The specific *way* that Roux values appearance over substance—during her job interview with Silk she frets over her "schoolgirl's uniform" (185)—functions (recall Coulter's criticism of feminists) to render the institution she represents a site not of masculine agency but of feminine preening. Against Roux, and against the world of the academy that shares her taint, Silk emerges as a representative, albeit a dying one, of American middle-class individualism. Ironically—although not uncharacteristically for someone writing in the post-Reagan era—Roth locates the heroic age of individualism in the fifties, precisely the decade when authors such as Mailer and O'Connor saw such individualism as threatened.

The fact that Roth's depiction of Silk revives such individualism only to again figure it as threatened points us, finally, to the element of repetition that Brown notes is central to the politics of *ressentiment*. But this is repetition mobilized not to memorialize a group identity but rather to disavow downward class mobility, to pose the crisis of the middle class as a problem not of economics but—in classically liberal terms—as one of individual character. In order to disavow the class character of its dilemma, I have argued, the middle class must deny the concrete sources of its own collective agency, including most dramatically thinking itself. Thus it is no accident that Delphine Roux sends Coleman Silk an anonymous letter referring to his affair with Faunia Farley that begins, "Everyone knows" (38), or that the novel takes on itself the task of denying this potential credo of a middle class cognizant of its own sources of agency. In a lonely mood, Roth's frequent narrator Nathan Zuckerman goes to a concert at Tanglewood and has a revelation similar to Julian's encounter with the world of guilt and sorrow, seeing the crowd of "elderly tourists" (205) as "an entity of sensate flesh and warm red blood, separated from oblivion by the thinnest, most fragile layer of life" (206). Of course Zuckerman's morbid turn of mind is shaped by his recovery from prostate cancer in the novel, although that does not dictate the moral he draws from this vision, thinking,

> Because we don't know, do we? *Everyone knows* . . . How what happens the way it does? What underlies the anarchy of the train of events, the uncertainties, the mishaps, the disunity, the shocking irregularities that define human affairs? Nobody knows, Professor Roux. "Everyone knows" is the invocation of the cliché and the beginning of the banalization of experience, and it's the solemnity and the sense of authority that people have in voicing the cliché that's so insufferable. What we know is that, in an unclichéd way, nobody knows anything. (208–9; Roth's emphasis and ellipsis)

If the institutions of the welfare state have become coded as the realm of feminized dependency, then the masculine agency that seeks to define itself in opposition to this realm must perhaps inevitably embrace not knowing as its credo.[47] *The Human Stain* is self-consciously a book of the late Clinton years, in which knowing or wanting to know too much is associated with the Monica Lewinsky scandal that might have been forestalled, the novel's Maileresque "chorus" (151) suggests, by properly masculine behavior on Bill Clinton's part: "If Clinton had fucked her in the ass, she might have shut her mouth" (146). Roth's recent criticism of the Bush administration, however, gives one hope that he—like all of us—has begun to grasp the problematic nature of not knowing as a basis for action.[48]

ACKNOWLEDGMENTS

Thanks to Pat Chu for sharing her seemingly unlimited knowledge of the state and gender; anything I get wrong is, of course, my own fault. Thanks also to the students in my winter 2005 contemporary fiction seminar for helping me to think through a number of the works I discuss in this essay.

ANDREW HOBEREK is an associate professor of English and peace studies at the University of Missouri-Columbia, where he teaches courses in twentieth-century literature and culture, and the author of *The Twilight of the Middle Class: Post–World War II American Fiction and White-Collar Work* (Princeton, 2005). He has recently begun work on a study of American fiction and international development policy since 1960.

NOTES

1. Mailer's piece lies both figuratively and literally at the center of Eric Lott's frequently cited essay "White Like Me: Racial Cross-Dressing and the Construction of American Whiteness," *Cultures of United States Imperialism*, ed. Amy Kaplan and Donald E. Pease (Durham: Duke University Press, 1993), 474–95, where it emblematizes the "virtual impersonation of black manhood" (484) on which white masculinity grounds itself. In the anthology *Race and the Subject of Masculinities*, ed. Harry Stecopolous and Michael Uebel (Durham: Duke University Press, 1997), Gayle Wald reads jazz musician Mezz Mezzrow's 1946 autobiography *Really the Blues* as an example of emergent "'white Negro' masculinity" (119); Lee Medovoi uses Mailer's essay to illuminate the cross-racial dynamics of Richard Brooks's 1955 juvenile delinquent movie *Blackboard Jungle* (154–6); and Deborah McDowell describes contemporary white suburban rap fans as "this generation's incarnation" of Mailer's subjects (379). These examples attest to the canonical status of "The White Negro" through their use of its title as shorthand for a sociological phenomenon they imagine to exist outside of and to both pre- and postdate Mailer's actual text. James Naremore's *More Than Night: Film Noir in Its Contexts* (Berkeley: University of California Press, 1998) likewise positions Mailer as discoverer rather than inventor, contending that in many noirs "black extras or bit players . . . give the protagonist an aura of 'cool,' so that he resembles what Norman Mailer once described as the 'White Negro'" (240). As Andrea Levine has suggested in her essay "The (Jewish) White Negro: Norman Mailer's Racial Bodies," *MELUS* 28.2 (Summer 2003): 59–81, Mailer's essay "often serves to name a whole U.S. tradition of interracial desire and fantasy, from nineteenth-century blackface minstrelsy and the white romance with Harlem Renaissance 'primitivism,' to Elvis Presley and the countless interracial male 'buddy' films that Hollywood continues to

produce" (59). But if the concept of white Negroism thus defies historical specificity, it also remains bound in our minds to the era of rock 'n' roll, the Beats, and the nascent Civil Rights movement. It has become, along with the Cold War and suburban consumerism, one of the handful of concepts by which we currently comprehend the culture of the 1950s, and—as the masculine equivalent of feminine domesticity—a lynchpin for our understanding of the operations of gender in this period.

2. Morris Dickstein, *Leopards in the Temple: The Transformation of American Fiction, 1945-1970* (Cambridge: Harvard University Press, 2002), 140.

3. Ibid.

4. Thomas Hill Schaub, *American Fiction in the Cold War* (Madison: University of Wisconsin Press, 1991), 116–62, passim.

5. For two accounts of postwar fiction that, despite fundamental interpretive differences, foreground the shift away from class and economic concerns, see Schaub, *American Fiction*, and Dickstein, *Leopards*. I argue against this reading of postwar fiction in my book *The Twilight of the Middle Class: Post–World War II American Fiction and White-Collar Work* (Princeton: Princeton University Press, 2005).

6. Thomas Frank, *What's the Matter with Kansas? How Conservatives Won the Heart of America* (New York: Metropolitan, 2004).

7. Norman Mailer, "The White Negro: Superficial Reflections on the Hipster," *The Portable Beat Reader*, ed. Ann Charters (New York: Penguin, 1992), 585; hereafter cited parenthetically.

8. Flannery O'Connor, "A Good Man Is Hard to Find," *Collected Works* (New York: Library of America, 1988), 138, 139, 137–53 passim.

9. Sean McCann, "The Imperiled Republic: Norman Mailer and the Poetics of Anti-Liberalism," *ELH* 67.1 (Spring 2000): 298, 331, 293–336 passim; hereafter cited parenthetically. Given the longstanding interest of female authors like Toni Morrison and Marilynne Robinson in the family, McCann's argument implicitly describes the extension of its thematics into the work of male authors. McCann's example of such family-focused writing is Mikal Gilmore's reworking of the materials Mailer had used in *The Executioner's Song* (1979) for his own *Shot in the Heart* (1994), but his argument convincingly anticipates the recent turn to the family on the part of self-consciously ambitious male authors like Jonathan Franzen and Dave Eggers.

10. Gwendolyn Mink, *Welfare's End* (1998; rev. ed. Ithaca: Cornell University Press, 2002), 35, passim.

11. Rebecca Dingo, "Securing the Nation: Neoliberalism's U.S. Family Values in a Transnational Gendered Economy," *Journal of Women's History* 16.3 (2004): 176, 173–86 passim.

12. Wendy Brown, *States of Injury: Power and Freedom in Late Modernity* (Princeton: Princeton University Press, 1995), 135–65; hereafter cited parenthetically.

13. See, in addition to the newspaper, Jeffrey Madrick, *The End of Affluence: The Causes and Consequences of America's Economic Dilemma* (New York: Random

House, 1995), and Paul Krugman, "For Richer," *New York Times Magazine* 20 October 2002: 62–7, 76–8, 141–42.

14. Krugman, "For Richer."

15. In this respect, the 1950s constitute a crucial moment in what Christopher Newfield describes as the American middle class's "war with itself over its response to the market." See Newfield, *Ivy and Industry: Business and the Making of the American University, 1880–1980* (Durham: Duke University Press, 2003), 13, passim.

16. C. Wright Mills, *White Collar: The American Middle Classes* (1951; New York: Oxford University Press, 2002), xiv, xii; hereafter cited parenthetically.

17. Schaub, *American Fiction*, 154.

18. For Brown's critique of identity politics see especially 66–76.

19. See, in this regard, Shelly Eversley's important attempt to parse the progressive dimensions of Mailer's and Kerouac's fascination with interracial sex in her essay "The Source of Hip," *minnesota review* 55–7 (2002): 257–70.

20. Schaub, *American Fiction*, 160.

21. O'Connor, *The Violent Bear It Away, Collected Works*, 329–479; hereafter cited parenthetically.

22. O'Connor, "To Sister Mariella Gable (4 May 63)," *Collected Works*, 1183.

23. O'Connor, "To John Hawkes (13 September 59)," *Collected Works*, 1108.

24. Derek Nystrom provides a fascinating and detailed account of the articulation of Southernness and middle-classness in the films of the 1970s in his forthcoming book on class identity in 1970s American cinema.

25. On O'Connor's investment in the ineffable, see John Burt, "What You Can't Talk About," *Flannery O'Connor*, ed. Harold Bloom (New York: Chelsea House, 1986), 125-43. On Mailer's "avowed contempt for rational argument" and his Wilhelm Reich–inspired turn to "instincts and impulses" see Schaub, *American Fiction*, 141, 162.

26. As Bush said in Italy several months before world events gave him the chance to put his theory into practice, "I know what I believe. I will continue to articulate what I believe and what I believe—I believe what I believe is right." See Brian Williams, ed., "The Bottom Line," *The Courier-Mail* (Queensland, Australia), http://web.lexis-nexis.com/universe (accessed August 28, 2004).

27. See Newfield, *Ivy and Industry*.

28. O'Connor, "Good Country People," *Collected Works*, 274; hereafter cited parenthetically.

29. O'Connor, "To A. (30 September 55)," *Collected Works*, 959.

30. O'Connor, "To A. (24 August 56)," Collected Works, 999–1000.

31. Ann Coulter, "Call Her Mrs." (18 July 2002), FrontPageMagazine.com: Accessed 16 April 2005 http://www.frontpagemag.com/Articles/ReadArticle.asp?ID=1961. Compare Coulter's discussion of Schlafly in *Slander: Liberal Lies About the American Right* (New York: Crown, 2002), 35–41.

32. Saul Bellow, *The Dean's December* (New York: Penguin, 1982), 303; Bellow's emphasis and ellipsis.

33. Deborah Nelson, *Pursuing Privacy in Cold War America* (Columbia University Press, 2002), xiii, passim.

34. See Elaine Tyler May, *Homeward Bound: American Families in the Cold War Era* (New York: Basic, 1988), 74.

35. O'Connor, "Everything That Rises Must Converge," *Collected Works*, 488; hereafter cited parenthetically.

36. May, 116–17; Robert J. Corber, *In the Name of National Security: Hitchcock, Homophobia, and the Political Construction of Gender in Postwar America* (Durham: Duke University Press, 1993), 196–7.

37. Sarah Gordon, "Maryat and Julian and the 'not so bloodless revolution,'" *The Flannery O'Connor Bulletin* 21 (1992): 25–36. Interestingly, Gordon wants to make this point but continually returns to O'Connor's use of Julian to parody liberalism.

38. Patricia Yeager, *Dirt and Desire: Reconstructing Southern Women's Writing, 1930–1990* (Chicago: University of Chicago Press, 2000), 183.

39. Ibid.

40. Brown, 52–76.

41. Ross Posnock, "Purity and Danger: On Philip Roth," *Raritan* 21 (Fall 2001): 85–101. Posnock argues that the novel also engages a second version of American individualism, critical of the more familiar "proprietary logic" (88) I discuss herein—a claim that in a longer discussion would necessarily complicate my reading of the book.

42. See Hoberek, *Twilight*, 70–94.

43. Philip Roth, *The Human Stain* (New York: Houghton Mifflin, 2000), 100; hereafter cited parenthetically.

44. Michael Gilmore, *Surface and Depth: The Quest for Legibility in American Culture* (New York: Oxford, 2003), 175.

45. Ibid.

46. Posnock asserts that Les Farley does have a secret (killing Silk and Faunia), although this information is not, unlike their secrets, something that Roth's narrator Nathan Zuckerman provisionally withholds from the reader. Moreover, in Zuckerman's encounter with Farley at the end of the novel the latter refers to himself as "a guy with a subconscious mind full of PTSD" (360)—that is, as someone whose interiority is colonized by an externally produced and defined syndrome.

47. Gilmore offers a different reading of the novel's concern with "occultation within disclosure" (176) in *Surface and Depth*, 174–7.

48. See, for instance, Roth, "The Story Behind 'The Plot Against America,'" *New York Times Book Review* 19 September 2004: 10.

THE ACCIDENTAL BLOCKBUSTER: *PEYTON PLACE* IN LITERARY AND INSTITUTIONAL CONTEXT

EVAN BRIER

Chapter 19 of Book 2 of Grace Metalious's scandalous 1956 novel *Peyton Place* describes Peyton Place's annual Labor Day carnival, "The Show of 1,000 Laffs." The carnival's original owner was a "true 'carny'" named Jesse Witcher, and while Metalious doesn't explain what it is that makes a carny "true," Witcher's authenticity seems to be tied to the one detail that Metalious does tell us about him, the fact that he "liked his whiskey and woman . . . a helluva lot more than he enjoyed paying his bills" (257). As a carny, in other words, Witcher was an indifferent businessman, his authenticity signified by his inability or refusal to turn his carnival into a viable commodity. By the time the carnival is described in the novel, September 1939, the bank has foreclosed on it. Mill owner and bank chairman Leslie Harrington has assumed owner-ship, eager to turn his employees into paying customers on their state-mandated day off.

Compared to the novel's more salacious moments, what happens at the carnival is mild: Kathy Ellsworth, the daughter of one of Harring-ton's mill workers, loses her arm in a grotesque funhouse accident that is the result of Harrington's negligence. But while far from scandalous, the carnival episode resonates in the context of old and new attempts to define the novel's place in both book history and literary history—attempts that, as I discuss in this article, have dominated the intermit-tent critical conversation about *Peyton Place* since it was published. The brief description of the change in the carnival's ownership captures in miniature something of an inevitable shift in the ownership of enter-tainment in the twentieth century: the movement away from "popular" culture toward something like what historian Michael Kammen calls "proto–mass culture," now owned not by "the people" but by larger businesses with commercial interests.[1] Kathy's carnival injury can be seen as a sign of what is lost with this shift in ownership, and when she

[*WSQ: Women's Studies Quarterly* 33: 3 & 4 (Fall/Winter 2005]

loses her lawsuit against Harrington despite his obvious culpability, the sinister degree to which Peyton Place's nascent culture industry is in league with the town's larger power structure is revealed. "It would have been impossible," Metalious explains, "to find twelve people in Peyton Place who neither worked at the mills nor owed money on mortgaged property at the . . . [b]ank where . . . Harrington was chairman of the board" (287).

Harrington is, to put it in terms appropriate to the 1950s, the most powerful of the town's power elite, and the novel's carnival episode thus functions as an unlikely allegory of the commodification and decline of culture. Versions of this narrative of cultural decline were often told in the fifteen years after World War II, in the face of the emergence of television, comic books, and paperbacks as commercial and cultural forces. These narratives, by otherwise strange bedfellows like Theodor Adorno, T. S. Eliot, and Dwight Macdonald, among many others, express anxiety about the fate of "high" culture in an age of mass literacy and emergent mass culture.[2] The problem with commodified "mass" culture, Macdonald explained in 1953, is that it is "imposed from above. It is fabricated by technicians hired by businessmen" (60). As Peyton Place's chief businessman, Leslie Harrington is ideally suited to the role of the owner who ruins what had been a cultural activity, fabricating, to use Macdonald's term, a carnival that was, when owned by Witcher, "authentic."

What makes Metalious's version of the narrative of cultural decline unlikely is the fact that the novel in which it appears is sometimes itself seen as a sign and site of processes of commodification, fabrication, and decline similar to those both she and Macdonald describe: the growth and much-lamented consolidation of the American publishing industry in the second half of the twentieth century, and the development of relations between it and the larger world of mass media industries; the movement away from popular culture toward mass culture; and the death of a kind of authentic culture at the hands of big business institutions. This notion of the 1950s as a turning point towards cultural decline has persisted, albeit in less apocalyptic terms than those used by Macdonald and his midcentury peers, in recent assessments of the twentieth-century book trade. In his mammoth history of the American publishing industry, for example, John Tebbel deems the period from 1920 to 1950 the industry's "golden age," implying the decline to follow; Jason Epstein, a longtime editor at Random House, recently noted that during the postwar era of consolidation and corporatization, "book publishing has deviated from its true nature by assuming, under duress from . . . the misconceptions of remote managers, the posture of a conventional business" (4).[3]

As I show in the next section of this essay, *Peyton Place* has been viewed, almost (but not quite) from the moment of its publication in 1956 until very recently, as a symbol of and turning point toward the cultural decline described in the 1950s by Macdonald and Clement Greenberg and in retrospect by Tebbel and Epstein. This perception, a product of the fact that the novel achieved unprecedented commercial success at the moment that anxiety about the fate of high culture was at its apex, was no doubt fed by the gendered subtext of much of the modernist disdain for mass culture. As Andreas Huyssen has argued, critics of mass culture dating back to the mid-nineteenth century frequently posited it as feminine, in opposition to superior (male) modernist culture: "[C]onnotations of mass culture as essentially feminine . . . remain central to understanding the historical and rhetorical determinations of the modernism/mass culture dichotomy" (Huyssen, 48). This gendering has taken multiple forms; in some cases, it is the masses themselves that are associated with femininity, while in others it is the producers and arbiters of a culture deemed inferior that are linked to a notion of femininity that in and of itself connotes artistic inferiority. In whatever way mass culture has been linked to femininity, *Peyton Place* seems to fit: not only was the novel authored by a woman and largely about women and presumably read by women, it was also produced in hardcover and paperback editions by publishing houses headed by women. Thus the gendered subtext of the modernism/mass culture debate seems particularly relevant to a discussion of the novel's reception, and the novel itself seems an obvious symbol of the problem that a feminized mass culture represented to postwar intellectuals.

That subtext has been brought to light in recent reassessments of *Peyton Place*, which have argued persuasively that the rejection of the novel by the male literary establishment is tied to its defiant representation of independent women and its focus on, in Ardis Cameron's words, "female sexual agency, hypocrisy, social inequities, and class privilege" (x).[4] These studies have brought welcome attention to *Peyton Place*'s merits as a novel, but as I show, even as they have recovered the novel, they have largely left unchallenged the story of cultural decline in which it has figured. This article argues that the story of *Peyton Place*'s success constitutes a challenge to the paradigmatic narrative of 1950s cultural decline that the novel has been said to embody. It does so by shining a light on unexamined aspects of the otherwise familiar story of *Peyton Place*'s publication and promotion: specifically, the novel's wholly neglected connections to publishing's purported "golden age." In fact, there are substantial genealogical links between the institutions that produced *Peyton Place* and those that produced the most celebrated modernist texts of the 1920s and 1930s, texts wholly endorsed by the male literary establishment that rejected Metalious's novel. Far from being either a symbol of Huyssen's great divide between (male) modernism and (female) mass culture or the "first blockbuster" (as recent sympathetic accounts of the novel characterize it), *Peyton Place* is an unlikely symbol of institutional continuity and as such a challenge to an enduring narrative of 1950s cultural rupture and decline.

I. FROM NOVEL TO SENSATION

At a time when first novels typically sold a total of 2,000 copies, *Peyton Place* sold 60,000 copies in the first ten days of its official release and 104,000 copies in its first month. It was the second-best-selling novel of 1956 despite not arriving in bookstores until September 24 of that year, and it went on to be the best-selling novel of 1957 as well, spending a total of fifty-nine weeks at the top of the *New York Times* best-seller list. That this is, in a sense, only the first part of the story of *Peyton Place*—it was soon followed up by various multimedia attempts to capitalize on its fame that, in terms of audience, dwarfed the success of the novel itself—should not obscure the extent of this popularity. *Peyton Place* became, for its time, the best-selling novel of the twentieth century, with more than ten million copies sold (Cameron, viii).

With unprecedented success came, perhaps inevitably, efforts to interpret and then reinterpret that success. As early as January 1957, three months after the novel arrived in bookstores and before any of these nonliterary spinoffs, it was written that "the decline and fall of the American novel predicted by the pessimists had one corroboration in the sensation of the year, Grace Metalious's *Peyton Place*" (Butcher, 35). Given the well-documented pervasiveness of narratives of cultural decline in the fifteen years after World War II,[5] the sentiment is surely not surprising, but perhaps it *is* surprising that the comment appeared not in *Partisan Review* or even in, say, the *New Yorker*—publications that were in the business of culture, ensconced in what Bourdieu calls the "field of cultural production"—but in *Publishers Weekly*, a trade magazine that at the time was not even in the business of reviewing novels and that was, as the very nature of a "trade magazine" suggests, in the business of business, entrenched in the larger economic world.[6]

Strictly speaking, *Publishers Weekly*'s assessment is not merely a book review, if it is one at all; the badness of *Peyton Place* is only implicit (as though so obvious that it does not need to be elaborated) in the idea that it corroborates a far-reaching and unspecified decline of the novel.[7] The idea that a single bad novel could be evidence of a widespread decline in the quality of all novels is specious on its face, because novels deemed bad have been written every year: even assuming that an objective rating of novels were possible, the only evidence for such a decline would be the absence of good novels rather than the presence of bad ones, much less a single bad one. But it is notable that *Peyton Place* is, in fact, not identified as a novel in *Publishers Weekly*'s assessment, a designation that would in itself signal an aesthetic achievement. Instead it is called a "sensation"—a term that not only denies the novel its status as such but also insists on viewing it in the context of its popularity, as a kind of constructed media event. The problem that *Peyton Place* represents is found, in other words, in the relationship between its badness and its popularity, the number of people willing to spend their time and money on something so bad. James Baldwin noted in the symposium eventually published as *Culture for the Millions*, another seminal document of the postwar debate over mass culture, that he was "less appalled by the fact that *Gunsmoke* is produced than . . . by the fact that so many people want to see it" (121). Something similar is at play in *Publishers Weekly*'s designation of *Peyton Place* as a sensation rather than a novel.

One striking aspect of *Publishers Weekly*'s assessment is how far removed it is from the fairly good reviews *Peyton Place* received when it was published just three months earlier. As Emily Toth notes in her biography of Metalious, while *Peyton Place* did not receive raves, it was not unkindly reviewed in such mainstream publications as the *New York Times*, the *Chicago Tribune*, *Time*, and the *San Francisco Chronicle*. "She has humor, heart, vigor, a feeling for irony," wrote Phyllis Hogan in the *San Francisco Chronicle*. "She captures a real sense of the temper, texture, and tensions in the social anatomy of a small town," according to *Time*. "The pace is swift, for Mrs. Metalious has great narrative skill," said Edmund Fuller in the *Chicago Sunday Tribune* (quoted in Toth, 135). These comments convey the seriousness with which Metalious's novel was treated when it was first published.

Publishers Weekly's own original capsule description of the novel is striking for how different it is from the same publication's assessment of *Peyton Place* just three months later.

> Another very promising first novelist has written a rather grim but powerful study of a small town in New Hampshire in which there is considerable illicit sex, murder, and suicide. Before the final page, however, most of the characters are happy and properly married. Messner plans a $10,000 advertising campaign. (916)[8]

The description of Metalious as a "very promising first novelist" is particularly telling, all the more so because it is an idea that was echoed even in critical moments of other reviews. After hailing Metalious as literary kin to revolt-from-the-village luminaries like Sherwood Anderson and Sinclair Lewis, for example, Carlos Baker concluded in the *New York Times Book Review* in late September 1956 that "Metalious is a pretty fair writer for a first novelist . . . if Mrs. Metalious can turn her emancipated talents to less lurid purposes, her future as a novelist is a good bet" (4).

What is notable in these passages, surprising in retrospect if hardly so in context, is how Metalious's output is described in terms of possibility and potential; her career is considered a literary one, and it is on those grounds that she succeeds or fails. As *Publishers Weekly*'s January 1957 dismissal indicates, however, within months—and well before the novel gave way to a movie, an inferior literary sequel, and a television show—*Peyton Place*'s literariness had already been erased. As early as January 1957, in other words, *Peyton Place* already was what it has remained in most critical conversations to this day: not so much a novel, good or bad, that can be talked about in terms of literary success or failure, but instead something nebulous called a "sensation," and, as such, a symbol in an often-told narrative of cultural decline.

II. FROM SENSATION TO BLOCKBUSTER

Scholars who have in recent years challenged this denigration of the novel's aesthetic merits—this erasure of the novel *as* a novel—have confronted a paradox that has gone unacknowledged. Both Toth and Ardis Cameron, in her introduction to Northeastern University Press's 1999 reissue of the novel, argue that *Peyton Place* is a novel of neglected literary merit—and that its merit has been missed in part because of the entrenched sexism of the literary establishment and in part because of that establishment's knee-jerk disdain for the popular, the tendency toward what Cameron aptly calls "the conflation of well-liked with badly written, of pop with trash" (xvii). What has not been addressed in the reevaluation of the novel as literature is the way that it necessarily alters our understanding of the novel's place in book history, and indeed our understanding of the development of the book trade in the second half of the twentieth century. If *Peyton Place* is a novel of literary merit, then the narrative of cultural decline in which it has previously figured needs either to find a new symbol or to be revised. If it is a novel of literary merit, its claim to an important place in the history of the book trade is suddenly ambiguous. As *Peyton Place* gains in literary status, in other words, its place in the history of the book trade, and along with it the narrative we tell about the postwar book trade, becomes more of a cipher.

Some of this ambiguity is encapsulated in the designation with which Cameron describes the novel's place in book history. Citing its massive sales, she calls it "the first 'blockbuster'" (viii). But the term "blockbuster" is undefined, and its usefulness is an open question. The idea that *Peyton Place* is the "first" of anything suggests first of all that the blockbuster means something more than "great bestseller," because great bestsellers long predate Metalious's novel, and second that its emergence either causes or follows an unseen rupture in cultural history. Indeed, Cameron writes that the novel "transformed the publishing industry" (viii). But the exact nature of this transformation, and exactly why *Peyton Place* is responsible for it, have yet to be explained.[9]

In one sense, at least, Cameron's notion of the blockbuster seems connected to the meaning ascribed to the term by Thomas Whiteside in his earlier study *The Blockbuster Complex*. What Whiteside calls a blockbuster is the product of, among other things, the postwar expansion and consolidation of the book trade and its developing links to mass culture institutions. "The upshot" he writes of these developments, "is that the entire economy of trade-book publishing seems to have become focused on the pursuit of 'the big book'—the so-called blockbuster" (19). Whiteside's is a more concrete version of the postwar narrative of cultural decline previously told by Dwight Macdonald, and it is clearly also linked to Epstein's account, quoted earlier, of postwar change in the publishing industry. In Whiteside's formulation, with its emphasis on not just success but on the "pursuit" of that success, blockbusters are not merely books that happen to prove enormously popular, they are books *designed* to be popular—the product, that is, of the publishing industry's awareness of the possibility of a certain level of mass commercial success. That success, moreover, includes not just book sales but also movie and maybe even television show tie-ins, the likelihood—if not, as was and is often the case, the certainty—of which is built into the decision to publish the book in the first place. To call a novel a blockbuster according to this definition is both to make a negative literary judgment and to observe a new set of institutional relationships among publishers, Hollywood studios, and television networks; it is, moreover, to cite the latter as the cause of the former in a narrative of cultural decline not unlike the narrative of the decline of the *Peyton Place* carnival. When big business enters the picture, the culture suffers.

Peyton Place was published at the moment of the transformation of the book trade to which Cameron presumably alludes, but it does not fit Whiteside's definition of the blockbuster; old and new literary judgments aside, it fails the institutional test. The novel was not the product of corporate calculation; as Cameron and Toth emphasize in their retellings of the story, it was produced and promoted not by a multi-media conglomerate but rather by a modest publishing house called Julian Messner, Inc. And even by Messner's modest standards, *Peyton Place*'s $10,000 advertising budget was not a major investment. That same year, another Messner novel, this one by Francis Parkinson Keyes, was backed with an advertising campaign that cost $25,000.[10] In short, there is little evidence to suggest that *Peyton Place* was published with mass success in mind.

The institutional origins of cultural products are essential to prevailing narratives of cultural decline; thus the question of what Messner was, if not a multimedia conglomerate, is crucial to any effort to locate the novel in cultural history. As noted earlier, both Toth and Cameron emphasize the fact that when it was published, Messner was run by

Julian Messner's ex-wife, Kitty Messner, then one of only two women in America in charge of a publishing house.[11] The other, both note, was Helen Meyer at Dell, which published the paperback edition of *Peyton Place*. This emphasis has been designed less to fix the novel's place in book history than to help reframe it as a feminist text, the value of which was seen by the independent women who ran these two houses but not by the otherwise male literary establishment. According to Cameron, *Peyton Place* and its readers rebel not just against a notion of "high culture" traditionally gendered as male, but also against guardians of a relatively new form of middlebrow culture that, as Janice A. Radway shows in *A Feeling for Books*, were repeatedly gendered female by their critics.[12] To read *Peyton Place* in the repressed 1950s, Cameron argues, was to "traverse the borders of middlebrow culture and taste" (vii), and the novel's institutional origins with Messner and Dell are used to support a reading of it as "a powerful political commentary on gender relations and class privilege" (xiii) appreciated by women and rejected by the male literary establishment.

My aim here is neither to deny the salience of the fact that Messner and Meyer, unlike their male counterparts in publishing, recognized *Peyton Place*'s merits, nor to take issue with Cameron's persuasive reading of the novel as a feminist text. However, Cameron's interpretation of the story of the novel's publication—both the notion that it is the first blockbuster and the emphasis on the gender of its publishers—risks reinforcing the notion that the novel was produced in a sphere of culture separate and apart from the sphere that produced "high culture"— on the other side, as it were, of a cultural divide. This perspective obscures what I will now argue are Messner's and thus the novel's significant connections to American publishing's past. And it is these connections that illuminate the novel's otherwise murky place in cultural history and more specifically offer the strongest challenge to the narrative of cultural decline in which the novel has long been said to figure. To recover these links we need to reconsider Messner from a genealogical perspective, from which *Peyton Place* is best seen not as the first blockbuster—not as something new, not as something that follows or causes an unseen break or rupture in cultural history—but rather as an end, a culmination of a distinctly commercial success story that dates back to the early twentieth century.

III. GENEALOGY

That story properly begins in New York City's Greenwich Village, and it might be said to start with the founding of the Washington Square Book Shop in 1911. The shop was founded by two brothers, Albert and Charles Boni, and it quickly became a meeting place for Greenwich Village artists and activists including John Reed, Emma Goldman, Edna St. Vincent Millay, and Max Eastman. The Boni brothers, somewhat like Witcher, Metalious's "true carny" in Peyton Place, were true believers in art but poor businessmen. Their bookstore failed to turn a profit while they were running it—in part because they loaned rather than sold books to their friends and neighbors—and their stated reason for entering the publishing business was not to turn a profit but to over-come "the philistine attitude of the American public toward the arts" (Satterfield, 17). They were, according to Harry Scherman, their friend and later the founder of the Book-of-the-Month Club, "bitten by the idea of being publishers of *avant garde* things" (quoted in Satterfield, 17). Their first publishing venture was the Little Leather Library, which they cofounded with Scherman in 1915: a set of low-cost reprints of short classics and abridgements of longer ones including works by Shakespeare, English Romantic poets, Shaw, Ibsen, and Tolstoy. The Little Leather Library proved to be a commercial success, but the Bonis never enjoyed it: financial problems at the bookstore forced them to sell their share of the Library before it hit its stride.

In 1915, after he had sold his share in the Washington Square Book Shop, Albert Boni met Horace Liveright and together they developed the idea of the Modern Library: inexpensive reprints of the best modern literature. Liveright had socialist sympathies and capital to invest; Boni was the artistic soul with a passion for avant garde books. Early Modern Library authors included Strindberg and Ibsen, Nietzsche and Schopenhauer. As Jay Satterfield describes it in his recent study of the Modern Library, Boni and Liveright initially aimed for "titles that exuded a scandalous air" that would appeal to their audience of bohemians (20). This is a recipe for commercial success that, in a way, would be repeated with the publication of *Peyton Place*, and the connec-tions between the two are more than analogous.[13]

The Modern Library's success having proven the existence of an audience for literature advertised as "modern" and "avant garde," Boni and Liveright soon founded a publishing house called Boni and Liveright that would produce original books. As this house, which published Eugene O'Neill, William Faulkner, and Sherwood Anderson, among others, is forever associated with the Greenwich Village art scene of the 1910s and 1920s, with modernism and a golden age of American literature, linking it with *Peyton Place* might seem a strange move. But that perception of strangeness, a product of what recent scholarship insists is a misguided tendency to link modernism with the rejection of commerce, is part of the point.[14] First, for all of its deservedly privileged place as disseminator of American modernism, Boni and Liveright's legacy is as much commercial as it is literary. The company functioned as a kind of training ground for some of the most successful American publishers of the twentieth century; onetime Boni and Liveright salesmen Richard Simon and Bennett Cerf went on to found Simon & Schuster and Random House, respectively. More importantly, as much recent scholarship has discussed, some of the savviest and most sophisticated marketing efforts of the early twentieth century were for modernist novels.[15]

There is, moreover, a clear but as yet unnoted line connecting the marketing of those novels and the eventual marketing of the scandalous *Peyton Place*. When Cerf and Simon worked in Boni and Liveright's sales department, their manager was Julian Messner. Messner's role at Boni and Liveright was considerable. In addition to managing the sales department, Messner was, Tom Dardis notes in his biography of Liveright, the company's "general factotum," who Liveright intended would assume the role in the company held by the Boni brothers after they left in July 1918 (67). It is said that when Cerf bought the Modern Library from Liveright (who was, in his storied profligacy, also not unlike Witcher the carny), Messner pleaded with Liveright to reconsider.[16] Messner remained loyal to Liveright after the sale, which, along with his drinking, triggered Liveright's demise, and he was at Liveright's bedside when he died in 1933.

The company Messner formed that same year, when he set out on his own, was to remain considerably smaller than Random House and Simon & Schuster. In 1956, for example, Messner published forty-five books, compared to Random House's 146 and Simon & Schuster's 180. Emily Toth suggests that this modesty was intentional:

[Julian and Kitty Messner] wanted to publish books that most interested them, including juvenile books; their adult list would be small, so they could give each book individual attention . . . [F]or the first few years, Kitty and Julian did everything. He was president and in charge of sales; she was secretary, treasurer and all-around clerk . . . Both did editorial work, and except for the advertising—handled by Aaron Sussman from the start—Kitty could do any job in the publishing firm. (101)

Aaron Sussman is rarely more than a footnote in accounts of *Peyton Place*, but he might be the unlikely key to its place in American book history. Among other things, Sussman is credited (by Toth) with rejecting Metalious's original title for her novel, *The Tree and the Blossom*, and suggesting *Peyton Place* as an alternative. But what Sussman did for the novel is probably less important than where he came from. Prior to working for Messner, Sussman had been in charge of advertising for Boni and Liveright; he later established his own agency, which continued to handle advertising for the Modern Library and for Random House.[17] Thus, among many other ads, Sussman wrote for Random House in 1934 the famous "How to Enjoy James Joyce's Great Novel *Ulysses*" ad, which originally appeared in the *Saturday Review* and was (and still is) hailed as a landmark in the marketing of modernism to the general reading public.[18] Almost unknown to twentieth-century literary history, Sussman has the unique distinction of having helped sell both the most celebrated literary novel published in English in the twentieth century, a high point of high modernism and high culture, and one of the most reviled, the purported symbol of that culture's decline.

The connections between *Peyton Place* and *Ulysses* go beyond the fact of Sussman's involvement. In the attempt to revive interest in *Peyton Place* as a novel of literary merit, it has been common to note thematic similarities between it and more celebrated literary novels like *Lolita*.[19] However, as the story of Sussman's involvement suggests, another perhaps more fruitful set of connections can be found by comparing the marketing of *Peyton Place* to that of more celebrated literary novels. This requires rethinking *Ulysses* rather than rethinking *Peyton Place*. We are not accustomed to thinking of Joyce's novel as a great commercial success, but that is just what it was (and, needless to say, what it continues to be). Bennet Cerf, who knew better than anyone, notably and accurately described *Ulysses* as "a big commercial book" (94), "our first really important trade publication" that was not a reprint (94), and "a great best seller" (95). The advertisement Sussman designed was no small part of that success: a coupon attached to it was redeemed for purchase of the novel 25,000 times (Turner, 210). Like *Peyton Place*, moreover, and like early Modern Library texts, *Ulysses* sold in large part on the basis of scandal.

In fact, two things link *Ulysses* to *Peyton Place*: the exploitation of a scandal that preceded publication and Aaron Sussman. *Ulysses*'s scandal was more or less genuine—the novel had famously been banned in America for obscenity. *Peyton Place*'s prepublication scandal, on the other hand, was a contrivance—marketers exploited a perhaps untrue story that Metalious's husband was fired from his job because of the novel that was about to be published.[20] But this suggests, more than anything perhaps, that over the course of the century, lessons about the value of scandal had been learned from previous marketing triumphs. There are, in fact, reasons to think that those lessons were learned from *Ulysses* itself: As Turner argues convincingly in *Marketing Modernism*, well before Random House published *Ulysses*, Sylvia Beach had made the scandal surrounding it the center of her marketing campaign for the limited edition of the book. One of her techniques, soon to be borrowed for *Peyton Place*, was to create advertisements made up of headlines and attacks.[21] Scandal, and the potential of scandal to lead to strong sales, was no doubt part of the reason Cerf wanted to publish *Ulysses* in the first place. When he announced that Random House was going to publish it, an advertising agent wrote to him that the novel was "the most talked about book since the bible" (quoted in Turner, 175). Prior even to publication, in short, the novel was what *Peyton Place* would be twenty-three years later: a sensation. Cerf, moreover, was not under the illusion that *Ulysses* sold solely on the basis of literary merit: "[P]erhaps," he wrote, "many did read the last part to see the dirty words; in 1934 that sort of thing was shocking to the general public" (95). This speculation matches the recorded reactions by shocked readers of *Peyton Place* in 1956, the reactions that Ardis Cameron documents in her introduction to the reissue edition of the novel.[22]

The links between *Ulysses* and *Peyton Place* are institutional rather than literary, and what they suggest is that the commercial success of the one is not that different from the commercial success of the other—a truth obscured in the prevalent narratives of 1950s cultural decline that have dominated discussions of *Peyton Place*'s place in book history. Those narratives of decline notwithstanding, no great institutional divide separates *Ulysses* from *Peyton Place*; they are products of the same book trade. Both novels, that is, were commodities marketed to great success by the same people using many of the same techniques. Ironically, when viewed in its institutional context, the story of *Peyton Place* has more to tell us about the marketing of literary novels that preceded it—about the great savvy with which they were sold as both works of art and commodities, as well as about the impressive growth and modernization of the American publishing industry in the first half of the twentieth century, more generally—than it does about postwar cultural decline, the consolidation of the book trade, and the literary value (or lack thereof) of the blockbusters that came after.

IV. GREENWICH VILLAGE AND PEYTON PLACE

Boni and Liveright's Greenwich Village makes an unlikely appearance in Metalious's novel. *Peyton Place* is, among other things, a portrait of the artist—Allison MacKenzie—as a young woman. Until Allison leaves Peyton Place for New York City, New York City functions for her in a way familiar to those versed in the story of Boni and Liveright and the Washington Square Book Shop. It is a kind of ideal escape from the combination of hypocrisy and conventional morality that characterizes Peyton Place, and it is a symbol of artistic and personal freedom, bound up in Allison's twin desires to become a writer and to avoid conventional married life. Midway through the novel, speaking to Kathy Ellsworth, who wants to marry and have babies and is soon to be a victim of Harrington's carnival, Allison says, "'I'm going to move away . . . as fast as ever I can after I finish high school . . . to New York City'" (222). Later, she notes: "New York . . . that's where all the writers go to get famous," and Kathy replies: "Maybe we could go together and be bachelor girls in an apartment in Greenwich Village, like those two girls in that book we read" (213). In Allison's imagination, which Metalious frequently reminds us is naïve, New York City is the anti–Peyton Place, a haven of authenticity and artistic freedom. Her decision to leave Peyton Place for New York is in part motivated by her unhappiness after Kathy's injury at the corrupt carnival.[23]

The events in New York City, told in a flashback after Allison returns home to Peyton Place for Selena's trial, have been called the least interesting and least convincing part of the novel, but like the carnival episode they are noteworthy in the context of attempts to locate the novel in both literary history and the history of the book trade. When Allison arrives in New York City in the early 1940s, she finds that the literary world is not what she thought it was. It is an unforgiving business in which concepts like literary merit are complicated by the presence of middlemen and the need to sell books. This fallen, compromised world is embodied in the love triangle in which Allison becomes enmeshed. On one side of it is David Noyes, an ambitious writer of the sort, presumably, that would have been at home at the Bonis' bookstore: "David was twenty-five," Metalious writes, "and had been hailed as a brilliant new talent by the critics on the publication of his first novel. He wanted to reform the world" (356). On the other side is Allison's literary agent, Brad Holmes, a married man who seduces her, and whom, she quickly learns, she needs in order to get published. Noyes is an artist, but Holmes, the unscrupulous businessman, is necessary for a career: "she never would have begun to be successful without Holmes" (353). This portrayal of the 1940s book trade, while maybe an unconvincing product of Metalious's 1950s imagination, nonetheless aptly suggests that changes to that trade that have been attributed to the emergence of postwar mass culture and the success of *Peyton Place* itself in fact predate that success. If literary culture was in decline in 1956, it was not because of *Peyton Place*.

EVAN BRIER is assistant professor of English at Louisiana State University in Shreveport. His most recent publication is "Constructing the Postwar Art Novel: Paul Bowles, James Laughlin and the Making of *The Sheltering Sky*" (forthcoming, *PMLA*). This essay is drawn from his current book project on the relationship between mass culture's emergence and the making and marketing of American novels in the 1950s.

NOTES

1. Kammen deems the period from 1908 to 1938 the era of "proto–mass culture," the somewhat clumsy term intended to correct the indiscriminate use of the term "mass culture" to describe forms of culture that do not in fact reach the masses and

are distinctly different from what would be called mass culture after World War II. See chapter 1 of *American Culture*, "Coming to Terms with Defining Terms."

2. See Macdonald, *Against the American Grain*; Horkheimer and Adorno, especially their chapter "The Culture Industry: Enlightenment as Mass Deception"; and Eliot.

3. See the fourth volume of Tebbel's history of American publishing, *A History of Book Publishing in the United States*, and Epstein's *Book Business*.

4. See, especially, Ardis Cameron's "Open Secrets: Rereading *Peyton Place*," included as the introduction to the 1999 reissue of the novel. See also Emily Toth's biography of Metalious, *Inside Peyton Place: The Life of Grace Metalious*.

5. See Michael Kammen, *The Lively Arts* for one look at the fears of postwar mass culture. See also Brantlinger.

6. Pierre Bourdieu, "The Field of Cultural Production, or: the Economic World Reversed," in his book *The Field of Cultural Production*. ed.

7. Who, specifically, were "the pessimists" to which *Publishers Weekly* referred? Writing about New Critics and New York Intellectuals in the 1950s, Schaub asserts that "the most dramatic and consequential agreement among these critics was their uniform dismissal of most recent and contemporary American fiction" (41). This idea had filtered into mainstream magazines, where laments over the state of the novel became more common.

8. The passage is notable for what it gets wrong. There are no murders in the novel (Selena Cross is acquitted of the charge of murdering her stepfather) and there is only one suicide.

9. If any great best-seller is a blockbuster, why is Margaret Mitchell's *Gone With the Wind* (1936), the best-selling novel prior to *Peyton Place*, not the first? For that matter, why not Harriet Beecher Stowe's *Uncle Tom's Cabin* (1852)?

10. The source for this is an advertisement that appeared in the front of the December 31, 1956 issue of *Publishers Weekly*.

11. Cameron notes that Messner "staffed the firm almost entirely with women: women were the editors, sales directors, publicity agents, readers, and editorial assistants, as well as the company's typists and secretaries. What seems to have turned off other publishing houses fired the imagination of Messner and her staff" (xix).

12. See especially chapter 6, "Automated Book Distribution and the Negative Option," in Radway's *A Feeling for Books: The Book-of-the-Month Club, Literary Taste, and Middlebrow Desire*.

13. For more on Boni and Liveright, see Tom Dardis, *Firebrand: The Life of Horace Liveright*.

14. The best study of the tendency to link high modernism with the rejection of commerce is Andreas Huyssen's *After the Great Divide*.

15. See, in addition to other critical studies of the selling of modernism cited in this article, Rainey's *Institutions of Modernism*. Rainey focuses on the strategic marketing efforts of high modernist writers Eliot, Joyce, Pound, and H. D., and those who helped them produce their works.

16. Dardis puts it this way: Messner was "horrified and outraged at the prospect of the firm's losing, without a word of warning, its chief asset and glory as well as its bulwark against future bad times. Under no circumstances could Horace do something so monstrous!" (229).

17. Sussman receives a single mention in *At Random*, Bennett Cerf's memoir: "Aaron has been invaluable to us" (123).

18. Catherine Turner devotes a chapter to this advertisement specifically and the selling of *Ulysses* in America generally in her study *Marketing Modernism Between the Wars*. See chapter 6, "How to Enjoy James Joyce's Great Novel *Ulysses*."

19. See Wood's *Lolita in Peyton Place*. As Wood notes, Metalious's and Nabokov's novels share a plot element: a quasi-incestuous relationship between a stepfather and his unwilling, underage stepdaughter.

20. See Toth, 120–5.

21. Toth, 130.

22. See Cameron, vii–viii.

23. The primary cause of Allison's decision to leave is no doubt the revelation that her father had been married to a woman who was not Allison's mother when Allison was conceived. But Metalious suggests that the carnival incident and its aftermath were also factors in her decision to move to New York by having Tomas Makris, the novel's most brutally honest character, express the idea: "her determination [to leave] took on form . . . after Kathy Ellsworth's accident, during the trial" (273).

WORKS CITED

Baker, Carlos. "Small Town Peep Show." Review of *Peyton Place*. *New York Times Book Review*. 23 September 1956: 4.

Baldwin, James. "Mass Culture and the Creative Artist: Some Personal Notes." In *Culture for the Millions: Mass Media in Modern Society*. Ed. Norman Jacobs. Boston: Beacon Press, 1971.

Bourdieu, Pierre. *The Field of Cultural Production: Essays on Art and Literature*. Ed. Randal Johnson. New York: Columbia University Press, 1993.

Brantlinger, Patrick. *Bread and Circuses: Theories of Mass Culture and Social Decay*. Ithaca: Cornell University Press, 1983.

Butcher, Fanny. "A Selection of Outstanding Books That Were Published in 1956." *Publishers Weekly*. 21 January 1957: 34–7.

Cameron, Ardis. "Open Secrets: Rereading *Peyton Place*." In *Peyton Place*, by Grace Metalious. Boston: Northeastern University Press, 1999.

Cerf, Bennett. *At Random: The Reminiscences of Bennett Cerf*. New York: Random House, 1977.

Dardis, Tom. *Firebrand: The Life of Horace Liveright*. New York: Random House, 1995.

Eliot, T. S. *Notes Toward the Definition of Culture*. New York: Harcourt, 1949.

Epstein, Jason. *Book Business: Publishing Past, Present, and Future*. New York: W. W. Norton, 2001.

Horkheimer, Max and Theodor W. Adorno. *Dialectic of Enlightenment*. New York: Continuum, 2001.

Huyssen, Andreas. *After the Great Divide: Modernism, Mass Culture, Postmodernism*. Bloomington: Indiana University Press, 1986.

Kammen, Michael. *American Culture, American Tastes: Social Change and the 20th Century*. New York: Basic Books, 1999.

———. *The Lively Arts: Gilbert Seldes and the Transformation of Cultural Criticism in the United States*. Oxford: Oxford University Press, 1996.

Macdonald, Dwight. *Against the American Grain*. New York: Random House, 1962.

———. "A Theory of Mass Culture." In *Mass Culture: The Popular Arts in America*. Ed. Bernard Rosenberg and David Manning White. New York: The Free Press, 1957.

Metalious, Grace. *Peyton Place*. 1956; reissue. Boston: Northeastern University Press, 1999.

Radway, Janice A. *A Feeling for Books: The Book-of-the-Month Club, Literary Taste, and Middle-Class Desire*. Chapel Hill: University of North Carolina Press, 1997.

Rainey, Lawrence. *Institutions of Modernism*. New Haven: Yale University Press, 1998.

Satterfield, Jay. *The World's Best Books: Taste, Culture, and the Modern Library*. Amherst: University of Massachusetts Press, 2002.

Schaub, Thomas Hill. *American Fiction in the Cold War*. Madison: University of Wisconsin Press, 1991.

Tebbel, John. *A History of Book Publishing in the United States*. Vol. 2. New York: Bowker, 1981.

Toth, Emily. *Inside Peyton Place: The Life of Grace Metalious*. Jackson: University Press of Mississippi, 1981.

Turner, Catherine. *Marketing Modernism Between the Two World Wars*. Amherst: University of Massacusetts Press, 2003.

Whiteside, Thomas. *The Blockbuster Complex: Conglomerates, Show Business and Book Publishing*. Middletown: Wesleyan University Press, 1981.

Wood, Ruth Pirsig. *Lolita in Peyton Place: Highbrow, Middlebrow, and Lowbrow Novels of the 1950s*. New York: Garland, 1995.

A TRAVELER IN RESIDENCE: MAEVE BRENNAN AND THE LAST DAYS OF NEW YORK

ANN PETERS

In 1965, Tom Wolfe published an article in the *New York Herald Tribune* as the first installment of a two-part attack on the *New Yorker* magazine. In it, he dubbed the magazine the "laughingstock of the literary community," lampooned its editor, William Shawn, and mocked the "whichy thickets" of its prose. He also accused the *New Yorker* of having packed up and moved to the suburbs. Catering to "educated women with large homes and solid hubbies" and a fondness for "expensive things," the magazine had become just another example of the "sentimental bourgeois," a "totem" of good breeding in the "good green world of Larchmont, Dedham, Grosse Point, Bryn Mawr, Chevy Chase" (Yagoda, 339). Wolfe also noted the abundance of stories by women in the magazine, stories in which lady writers reminisce about growing up in "curious rural bourgeois settings" or describe "domestic animals they have owned" (Yagoda, 336).[1]

Ben Yagoda, in his comprehensive study of the magazine, makes a similar observation—and in similarly disparaging terms. He remarks that the "fiction that predominated from 1952 to 1962 was reminiscence, the locale Irish (followed by English, and then American southern), the authorial gender female." Women-writing-for-women may have led to an increase in sales,[2] but, in Yagoda's opinion, it also resulted in "gentility bordering on blandness." Gone were the "vigorous" short stories and "tight objective sketches" that characterized the magazine under Harold Ross. In their stead was prose weighed down by a "deliberate long-windedness" and not "infrequent excursions into the out-and-out dull" (282).[3]

On first glance, Maeve Brennan, a short story writer and "Talk of the Town" contributor at the *New Yorker* from 1949 through the early 1970s, seems the very epitome of the ethos that Wolfe and Yagoda deride. The bulk of her *New Yorker* stories take place in the dark parlors and damp

[*WSQ: Women's Studies Quarterly* 33: 3 & 4 (Fall/Winter 2005)]

bedsits of her native Ireland: Dublin, Wexford, and Coolnaby. She also wrote a number of stories about American suburban life, most based on her experiences living in Sneden's Landing, a town along the Hudson in upstate New York.[4] There are even several stories about domestic animals—a few about Bluebell, her dog, and one story, "I See You, Bianca" (1966), told from the point of view of a cat. It was under the byline of "The Long-Winded Lady" that Brennan wrote her "Talk of the Town" pieces from 1953 through the late 1960s. In many of these, especially the early ones, she pretends to be a suburbanite, just down in the city for lunch. "The Long-Winded Lady," Angela Bourke explains, was intended to be a "two-dimensional figure," a woman seemingly "supported by a private income, and venturing forth only to shop" (191). Brennan's daily excursions around New York often record a bounded and familiar terrain, a landscape in which any woman in town from Dedham or Larchmont might feel right at home: a lunch at Longchamps, a view of a raucous party of sightseers in the Waldorf lobby, an afternoon martini at Le Steak de Paris.

Brennan also seems an ideal figure to appeal to a suburban woman hoping to catch a glimpse of midcentury urban glamour. "[T]o be around her was to see style being invented," recalls her friend and editor, William Maxwell. She painted the ceiling of her office at the *New Yorker* a Wedgwood blue, knew the difference between the colors "bone" and "taupe," and early in her career had worked as a copyeditor at *Harper's Bazaar*. The photographs of Brennan that appear to be most regularly on book jackets or in magazines support this image. They appear to be from one sitting taken the year before she began working at the *New Yorker*. Brennan sits or stands, a sleek Holly Golightly look-alike, in a room filled with "expensive things." She is dressed all in black, the ash of a cigarette dangerously long, her hair pulled back. A fire is in the fireplace, and roses are in a vase; there are stacks of books, a smoky mirror, a cut glass ashtray to catch the ash.

This past year, Angela Bourke published the first biography of Brennan, of which I received an advance copy. On the cover was the familiar photograph of Brennan in black. Inside, the publisher had inserted a publicity notice sprayed with a heavy dose of what was supposedly Brennan's favorite perfume: Russian Leather. Even here was an appeal to some kind of nostalgia for midcentury glamour. I left the book on my desk, next to my ashtray, and for days a combination of perfume and cigarettes lingered, invoking recollections of a great-aunt who, while the tenant of a much shabbier apartment in Milwaukee, bore a permanent scent of what, it seemed to me as a child, was big-city sophistication. Like those ladies in Larchmont, my aunt was the kind of woman whose subscription to the *New Yorker* never ran out.

Yet all these images—the genteel Irishwoman, the fashionable magazine writer, the lady-who-lunches—are not the whole story. For one thing, the jacket photograph on the Brennan biography is all smoke and mirrors; it was taken in the borrowed apartment of a wealthy friend, the Irish American theater critic Quinn Curtiss. Brennan did not own expensive things and rarely had a long-term address. She often lived in short-lease apartments—usually with no kitchen and usually with a stray cat. More regularly, Brennan lived in hotels. After a brief hiatus in Sneden's Landing in upstate New York—coinciding with an equally brief marriage to the *New Yorker* writer St. Clair McKelway in the mid-fifties—she lived at the Hotel Earle, the Royalton, the Iroquois, the Prince Edward, the Algonquin, the Westbury, the Lombardy, and the Holley Hotel on Washington Square. Gardner Botsford remembers that when Brennan moved, she could, "like the Big Blonde in the Dorothy Parker story, . . . transport her entire household, all her possessions and her cats—in a taxi." (220).

By the early sixties, Brennan seemed to drop the suburban persona altogether, to reveal herself as a "traveler in residence," a flâneur of daily life in midcentury New York, who had, in the words of John Updike, "brought New York back to *New Yorker*" (Bourke, 249). Brennan also began to seem less interested in shopping sprees than in a city under siege. Her story, "I See You, Bianca," is not really about a "domestic pet"; it is about an apartment, a floor-through on West Fourth and Twelfth Streets about to be torn down (*Rose Garden*, 250). In one of her "Talk of the Town" pieces, "The Last Days of New York" (1953), Brennan describes a view from the window of her hotel room on Washington Square: down below is a "narrow gap" in place of the Holley Hotel, the residential hotel she had inhabited years before. Beneath her window, "brand-new, drearily uniform apartments" take up one corner of the north side of the square, and beneath her feet, the floor of her hotel room is "already shivering under the wrecker's boots" (*Long-Winded Lady*, 87).

The New York depicted in Brennan's essays from the fifties and sixties is a "capsized" one, its inhabitants clinging "to the island that is their life's predicament" (*Long-Winded Lady*, 1). In many of the essays, however, the shipwrecked appear merely as ambience, backdrop to what is most important: the island itself; the restaurants, bookstores, department stores she and her readers frequent, even if only in their imaginations; and the threat that at any moment it all might vanish. Read together, her *New Yorker* pieces take the reader on an extended walking tour with Brennan as umbrella-toting guide—a tour that is not intended for sightseers, but for those who know the city only too well, the purpose being not discovery, but elucidation: the casting of fresh, attentive eyes on the everyday. See your walls, lest they someday be forgotten. One essay relates the rescue of a two-hundred-year-old wooden farmhouse from imminent destruction and its removal from York Avenue to Charles Street downtown in the Village. Others written in the fifties and sixties wax nostalgic about what has already been destroyed—Stern Bros. department store, Schrafft's restaurants, Wanamaker's.[5] Another mourns the Eighth Street bookstores that have moved or closed because of the high rents imposed in the sixties. Of all the spaces in the city, though, the one that holds the most significance and the one she regrets most consistently is the space connecting all the others—the New York hotel.

One might argue that in pining for Wanamaker's, Brennan was writing just the kind of middle-class reminiscence that Wolfe and Yagoda deride, or even that in detailing the ravages of urban development, she was providing her readers—the women of Larchmont and Dedham—confirmation of what they perhaps already believed: the city had gone to seed. Yet, if Brennan's essays and stories provided confirmation of why women might want to leave the city, they also reminded her readers why, in the past, they might have wanted to stay. Hers is a story of a woman traveling through the city, often preferring to eat alone in restaurants and live in hotels. Her work also reflects a tradition at midcentury of women fighting to save the city. It was often middle-class women, in the years following the destruction of Penn Station, who would be some of the most vocal opponents of the policies of Robert Moses: armed with baby carriages, the women of the Upper West Side march to save the playgrounds of Central Park, for instance, or join together, under the leadership of urban activist Jane Jacobs, to oppose Moses's plans to build a highway through the West Village.

Brennan's essays, criticized as demure and two-dimensional, were in fact addressing some of the most significant issues affecting urban life at midcentury: the rupture of neighborhoods in the era of Moses and Jacobs, the plight of New Yorkers losing their homes to the bulldozer, and the demise of the residential hotel. Brennan's work addresses the significance of the hotel for women in the first half of the twentieth century—census reports from 1920 show that for the first time in American history women made up almost half of its long-term inhabitants, a trend that continued into the thirties—and points to the destruction of hotels as one more example of the cultural shift at midcentury toward the reinstallation of women within the home. Her work also foretells, however unwittingly, the homeless crisis of the 1980s. Amid the rubble of the fifties and sixties lay not just the remains of the middle- and upper-class hotels—the Astor, the Brevoort, the Lafayette, the Savoy, the Murray Hill, the Hotel Imperial, and so many others[6]—but boarding houses, cubicle hotels, and single room occupancy hotels (SROs) as well. The destruction of so many hotels in the sixties—as well as the conversion of many residential hotels into tourist accommodations or co-op apartments in the seventies—would be one of the core factors contributing to the housing crisis that would devastate so many lives in the decades to come.

In his book about the forces of New York real estate, urban historian Max Page argues that the central dynamic of urban development in New York City is the relentless cycle of what-goes-up-must-come-down. "It will be a great place," O. Henry wrote of Manhattan, "once they finish it." Any street corner on any day in New York drives this fact home. Take this one: the corner of Thirty-fourth Street and Fifth Avenue. As I write this, I am in the library of a university building, which was once a department store, seated on the spot—I like to think—where once stood a display rack of ladies' hats.[7]

Although change and the endless tearing down of the familiar are permanent qualities of Manhattan, the fifties and sixties were a particularly traumatic moment in the city's history. In the years following World War II, New York saw the burgeoning of the service industry and a dramatic escalation of office construction.[8] "The Great Manhattan Boom" was what *Time* magazine called the commercial building fever of the 1950s: "Manhattan, written off long ago by city planners as a dying city because of its jammed-in skyscrapers and canyonlike streets, has defied and amazed critics with a phenomenal postwar building boom" (Wallock, 89). All across the city new homes were being built—large-scale, high-density, low- and middle-income housing projects—while others were crumbling, cleared away to make way not only for the new public housing complexes and office buildings, but for expressways and civic centers. The building of the new Cross Bronx Expressway had cut a wide and devastating swath through the East Tremont neighborhood in the Bronx; down came the tenements of Hell's Kitchen to make way for the Coliseum on Fifty-ninth Street, for Lincoln Center, for Fordham's midtown campus; whole neighborhoods were razed under the National Housing Act's Title I provisions for slum clearance, providing new homes for some but forcing many, mostly minorities, to seek affordable housing elsewhere.[9]

In "The Last Days of New York," Brennan writes of watching a demolition from her office on the twentieth floor of a midtown building—presumably the *New Yorker* offices on Forty-third Street. "In the afternoon, when I went to lunch, I found a whole block of Sixth Avenue gone" (218). She experiences the bewilderment common to anyone who has lived, even if only for a short time, in New York City: the missing of the taken-for-granted, the loss of what you never knew you had. "It is very disconcerting to have a gap suddenly appear in a spot where you can't remember ever having seen a wall" (218).

Later, in her hotel room, Brennan looks down from her window in her Greenwich Village hotel on Washington Square. She describes the square lovingly, the ice cream cart with its striped umbrella, a solitary woman feeding pigeons, the flight of the birds through the trees. And then, briefly, she alludes to talk of Robert Moses's plan to build an expressway: "I heard lately—it is only a rumor, I suppose—that there is talk of cutting an underpass through Washington Square. I suppose that means that part of the square anyway, will be dug up. It will hardly look the same after that."

As she sits in her hotel room, playing with a pack of cards, Brennan looks around her room and notes the brightly painted walls. She thinks "they should be even brighter, with more blue in them, so that they'd really assert themselves" (17). Perhaps then, she muses, when the hotel comes down, "as it is bound to do," the tenants of the new apartment buildings across the street will remark on its color: "I can't afford to start wondering every time I have the place painted if the walls will speak up after the room has been laid open." In a city fast becoming gaps where once there were walls—a city where homes were being forfeited and forgotten by everyone but their former inhabitants—Brennan asks her readers to follow her example: build houses of cards that will last, "paint their walls in noisy colors to astonish the tenants of high buildings all around" (56).[10]

Eight floors above the park—with even taller buildings looming above—Brennan also stands between street and skyscraper, and as such, between the two antagonistic forces of urban development at midcentury. Morris L. Ernst, the famous lawyer and supporter of the preservationist cause in New York, based his campaign on the notion that "[p]eople cannot take root when they live more than six or eight stories off the ground," a position that according to New York historian Robert Stern would "run as a continuous thread through virtually all discussions of housing and urban redevelopment in the city as a whole" (*New York 1960*, 222). The fight to save the Village was very much a fight to save the street, a fight that at the time revolved around two pivotal figures in the history of Manhattan's urban planning: Robert Moses and Jane Jacobs. Marshall Berman would see them as representing the two poles of modernity: Moses, the Faustian lover of progress; Jacobs, the believer in the integrity of street life and neighborhood.

As New York City Parks Commissioner and as chairman of the Triborough Bridge and Tunnel Authority and the New York State Power Authority, Robert Moses had long been hailed as New York's urban savior—the man responsible for the planning of two World's Fairs and for the building of innumerable parks, beaches, bridges, expressways, stadiums, and tunnels. In his capacity as chairman of the Mayor's Committee on Slum Clearance, he was also the man behind the Title I policies, which cast roughly 500,000 New Yorkers from their homes. And as chairman, he was the man behind the proposed flattening of huge sections of the southeast Village to make way for a new residential high-rise enclave called Washington Square South, a plan that included the call for a new roadway cutting through Washington Square. By the time of Maeve Brennan's piece in the *New Yorker*, some of the city's inhabitants were beginning to alter their opinion of Moses, viewing him less as urban messiah—blueprints raised heavenward, Moses commands: "Here we shall build"—and more as bully of the bulldozer. Writing of the annihilation of his Bronx neighborhood, a vibrant community torn apart by the building of the Cross Bronx Expressway, Marshall Berman would liken

Moses to the figure of Moloch in Allen Ginsberg's poem *Howl*: "Moloch whose eyes are a thousand blind windows! Moloch whose skyscrapers stand in the long streets like endless Jehovahs" (310).

If in Berman's eyes Robert Moses seemed to represent one principle of modernism—progress at all costs—then Jane Jacobs in her classic work, *The Death and Life of Great American Cities*, offered a "source of life and energy and affirmation that was just as modern as the expressway world, but radically opposed to the forms and motions of that world" (316). Moses believed highways and cars could rescue city-dwellers from the dirt, noise, and crowded conditions of the street; Jacobs believed highways and cars were destroying the diverse vibrant neighborhood. Moses revered the philosophy behind Le Corbusier's Radiant City; Jacobs longed to overthrow the "holistic urbanism" that had dominated city planning since the publication of Le Corbusier's *Urbanisme* in 1929. Moses saw no value in old buildings; Jacobs, who fought for landmark preservation, believed older buildings were as important to the vitality of neighborhoods as new ones. Moses wanted to build the Lower Manhattan Expressway through the West Village; Jacobs led the campaign to stop it.

Jacobs's argument in *The Death and Life of Great American Cities* is that most urban planners who had grown up with the Le Corbusier model were, in fact, antiurban. They wanted to build slum suburbs in the sky, towers that bred crime and isolated people from the street life below. She wanted a return to the diversity and vibrancy of the neighborhood, what she called "the ballet of the city sidewalk" (50). To illustrate her point, she traces a day in her life on Hudson Street, and does so, as Marshall Berman explains, with a "deceptive modesty." She is "just talking about her everyday life" and in prose "that often sounds plain, almost artless" (315). She observes the children leaving for school, mothers making their way to the corner grocery store, old women on their stoops, shopkeepers sweeping the sidewalk, secretaries on their way to work, the myriad sights and views of one street on one particular day.

Brennan's stories about New York are characterized by a similarly "deceptive modesty" and a similar detailing of daily life. She describes a drugstore on Tenth Street and Sixth Avenue, a crowd gathered outside the New Criterion Theatre on Times Square, two lovers walking down Sullivan Street, trucks backed up on Forty-eighth Street, a couple having lunch at the University Restaurant on Eighth Street, a tourist riding a bus down Fifth Avenue, people looking out the window of the Village Smoke Shop. She has a reporter's eye for details of the street, and at times her prose meanders, following the contours of a city stroll. Often, her descriptions also have a kind of writing-exercise quality about them: describe a dress from top to bottom; describe a woman from hat to shoes. (In an interview with *Time* in 1974, she explains that "if you are writing about people in the street, you have to describe their clothes, all of them. Clothes tell a lot.") She does the same with public spaces: describe a walk from start to finish; describe a street from end to end. Her renderings of the city are marked by a fixation with the specificity of the landscape—the corners and landmarks of the city—as if she is safe in the assumption that her reader knows the city well.

Yet as someone who was perpetually "scurrying out of buildings before the wreckers," Brennan also writes on a darker note. Her matter-of-fact observations of street life often give way to elegy. In her story, "I See You, Bianca," the owner of an apartment on Fourth Avenue lives in a "neighborhood with too many buildings half up and half down, and too many temporary sidewalks, and too many doomed houses with big X's on their windows" (*Rose Garden*, 250). Nicholas, the owner, builds bookshelves and cabinets and fixes the furnace, hoping to create a "permanent refuge" he knows is bound to fail: "his house is to be torn down." Looking out his window, he observes what Jacobs called the "ballet of the city sidewalk" down below:

> They stand outside their apartment houses on summer nights and during summer holidays. They stand around in groups or they sit together on the front steps of their buildings, taking the air and looking around at the street. Sometimes they carry a chair out, so that an old person can have a little outing. They lean out of their windows, with their elbows on the sills, and look into the faces of their neighbors at their windows on the other side of the street, all of them escaping from the rooms where they live in and that they are glad to have but not be closed up in. It should not be a problem to have shelter without being shut away. (256)

The desire for "shelter without being shut away" illustrates the underlying anxiety found in so many of Brennan's essays and stories. It is a double anxiety: on the one hand, the fear of being forced out of a home, a plight shared by thousands of New Yorkers at the time, and, on the other, the fear of being forced into one, the threat of being shut away, distanced from the activities of the street, sealed up in one of those brand-new beehive cement blocks high above—or obliged to leave the city for good. The desire for "shelter without being shut away" speaks to Jacobs's conviction that the rise of the large-scale apartment buildings—suburban slums in the sky—was destroying the "ballet of the street." It also nearly perfectly describes one reason why so many women in the first half of the twentieth century chose to live in hotels.

Of the many popular themes found in essays and stories about New York City, two perhaps carry the most resonance: that of the jubilant newcomer, gazing like Fitzgerald's Nick Carraway on the "fresh green breast of the new world" (182), and that of the longtime resident, stirring her walking companions (or her readers) with a poignant account of what was here before. Essays like "The Last Days of New York" belong to a tradition, the best of which is probably *The American Scene* (1907), the travel journal in which Henry James observes his native city after a twenty-one-year absence. James also sees gaps where once there were walls. He too finds New York diminished, and at the same time, new and enlarged. What figured in his youth as the biggest is now, in 1904, overshadowed by the even bigger: Trinity Church has been "cruelly overtopped," squeezed between those "triumphant payers of dividends," the tall buildings (60). Genteel Fifth Avenue has become a dress parade of ornate mansions; his boyhood home on Washington Square has disappeared. *The American Scene* reads something like a child's waking from a nightmare to find that the vista has been transformed into a vacant lot, the banister along which he slid stripped of its polish.[11]

This nostalgia and Rip Van Winkle disorientation characterize Brennan's essays as well.[12] Yet there are interesting differences. Most significantly, James depends on the space Brennan loved best to describe the ills of New York. For James, the two images marking the end of a way of life—the end of tradition, solidity, sanctity of home and hearth—were the looming new buildings overshadowing the spires of Trinity Church and the bustling lobby of the modern hotel. For Maeve Brennan, what marks the end of her way of life—and the loss of her home—is not the rise of the hotel, but rather its annihilation. James, "the visionary tourist," mourned the "extinction of Trinity"; Brennan, the "traveler in residence," mourned the "execution of the Hotel Astor" (*Long-Winded Lady*, 67). In one essay, she describes what was once the grand entrance of a turn-of-the-century hotel, now a darkly lit lobby, a third its original size, with an old orange leatherette sofa and a badly working elevator. Her hotels, if not destroyed, have been eclipsed, as architectural space and cultural idea, by the slabs of office buildings and apartment complexes erected all around.

James also identifies the hotel with women, who seemed to dominate the hotel lobby. Having exchanged the quiet, intimate interior for the peacock's parade, they now find in the interiors of the grand hotel the very "firesides and pathways of home" (81). Yet this transformation of public space into private space is what many women liked about hotel living. In "Snowy Night on 43rd Street," Brennan describes a street where she lived—a back street in a neighborhood bordering Times Square. (Brennan called it "The Latin Quarter," but it is commonly known as Hell's Kitchen.) Simply a description of her street and of an evening alone observing the regulars at a small restaurant, the Café Etoile, the story ends with Brennan alone in the hush of her hotel room down the street. The story illustrates one of the benefits of hotel living: the ease with which one can move between private and public space. Hotel life fulfills both the need for a room of one's own and the need to socialize down below—in the lobbies, cafés, restaurants, and bars. James may have criticized women for turning the public space of the Grand Hotel lobby into the "firesides and pathways of home," but Brennan calls the "small, inexpensive restaurants" the "home fires" of true New Yorkers (*The Long-Winded Lady*, 2).

James was not alone in identifying the hotel with the modern woman of leisure. In fact, between 1900 and the mid-1930s, the debate over the larger implications of women living in cities seemed to have found expression in the cultural tussles over the rented room. Charlotte Perkins Gilman saw the hotel as heralding the feminist utopia to come. "From the most primitive caravansary up to the square miles of floor space in the Grand hotels," Gilman writes, "the public house has met the needs of social evolution as no private house could have done" (187). She believed that not only would the modern hotel free the urban working women, the typists and clerks, from domestic tasks (instead of slaving away in the kitchen, they could live together in communal sisterhood, sharing the burdens of childcare and cooking), but that it would also liberate middle- and upper-class women from another form of demeaning labor: interior decoration. In an article, "I Like a Hotel," published in the *Sunday Worker* in 1939, Elizabeth Gurley Flynn, a Wobbly activist in the thirties, writes of seeing "lots of old ladies in hotels. People pity them. It's quite unnecessary. They enjoy it immensely. It's a sort of 'sit-down strike!'" As she puts it,

> When a committee puts me up at a hotel, I don't say "Bourgeois," scornfully. Not me! I luxuriate, because it doesn't happen often. I think "Well, this is a sample of the future, what every woman ought to have, a room to herself and release from domestic tasks." (Baxendall, 245)

Some critics, though, saw women's life in the public house as the end of harmonious family life. In his 1936 sociological study, *Hotel Life*, Norman Hayner would claim that the transient existence was a menace to family values, transforming industrious homemakers into blurry-eyed victims of the department stores, releasing throngs of precocious children, little Eloises, into the public dining rooms, and leaving men to fume in the smoking lounge. While Hayner admits that the growing number of the "other sex" in cities and hotels "may be thought of as an aspect of the general movement among women against slavish drudgery and towards the freedom of self-expression," most, he believes, are nothing more than "mental rovers" who "have gained their freedom but lost their direction" (87).

For some women, hotel living was a sit-down strike; for others, it meant greater access to street life; and for still others, it provided safety and respectability. In the nineteenth century, hotels were disreputable—no nice girl would be seen in one.[13] In the twentieth century, the residential hotel often signaled respectability, a safe haven. Downtown artists could find cheap (and decent) lodgings at the Vanderbilt or the Murray Hill; single working women, widows, and divorcées found refuge in the apartment hotels on the West Side and Upper East Side. There were also the women's residences, which catered solely to women, and, like the doorman building today, provided parents the reassurance—probably never *wholly* justified—that their daughter was out of harm's way.[14] Often, too, they were the only affordable housing for single women. Rosalind Rosenberg points out that "[a]side from these residences, living on your own in New York was impossible to afford" in the late twenties and early thirties "because even women who were college graduates were limited to low-paying jobs" (Byron, A1).

If the hotel itself provided a sense of safety, the network of Manhattan hotels also gave women a city bounded by a safe and familiar landscape. Maeve Brennan's hotels, for example, signify a connect-the-dots red line that maps a city delimited by the hotel world of three neighborhoods. She writes the backstreet hotel world of "The Latin Quarter"; she writes the hotels and inexpensive restaurants of Greenwich Village, often tracing the same route from the Hotel Earle to the University Restaurant; and she writes the upscale midtown hotels. She wonders whether she should go along to the Algonquin, "which is so small and familiar, or to walk a little farther, and east, to the Biltmore, which is so large and familiar" (8). Her New York is a narrow one: she "has never felt the urge that drives people to investigate the city from top to bottom. Large areas of city living are a blank" (*Long-Winded Lady*, 6).

The novelist Dawn Powell, whose work Edmund Wilson once described as one long story of the days of Manhattan's "small, cheap and decent hotels" (530), also delimits a woman's urban map by recording the movement from hotel to hotel. In her case, the map records a journey of urban exploration and sexual freedom. In one of her satirical novels about New York, *Angels on Toast* (1940), the heroine, Ebie Vane, takes a nostalgic tour of Greenwich Village. She starts at the Vanderbilt, "where you could lunch with one man and see over the balcony rail the man you were going to dine with that night." She moves on to the Murray Hill Hotel, where she remembers "in the dining room, publishers, agents, traveling salesmen" and "a pleasantly out-of-town flavor to it that made you able to guess the type of man he was if he suggested this restaurant" (145). In one of the older hotels, she ends up visiting her mother—a "New Woman" of an earlier era—who, along with the other "old birds," finds the hotel bar a space where she can be out in the world without having to leave the front exit.

The hotel was also an important space for writers.[15] For nearly twenty years, Dawn Powell frequented the café at the Hotel Lafayette on Ninth Street and University Place and wrote one novel, *The Wicked Pavilion*, based on the social world of the hotel café. Writing to her editor, Powell explained that with the passing of the Washington Square hotels like the Lafayette and the nearby Brevoort, both of which had popular cafés where tourists mingled with artists and writers, "went an entire way of life," one that she recognized as "almost a necessity" for "writers, artists and people who work alone all day."

> In our work we can't plan a social life too definitely—we never know but what we may get going good just when we're expected at a dinner. We do not know that we'll want to see somebody—anybody, sometimes—after being locked up with ourselves all day but we daren't risk tying ourselves down any more than we have to. So we depend on running into friends by chance when we're through work—stay a little while or for hours as we like—feeling that, in spite of the isolation y our work demands of you, you are in touch with the world. (*Letters*, 215)

Other artists felt the same, although for some the hotel's attraction lay less in the possibility for social contact than in the freedom to focus on their work. Georgia O'Keeffe preferred the Shelton Hotel to an apartment because the hotel, with its maid service and public dining room, left her unhampered. Dorothy Parker lived at the Algonquin because "among institutional furnishings she felt free and organized" (Meade, 123). Even Dawn Powell ended up appreciating not just the social life afforded by the café, but the pleasures of living upstairs. After being kicked out of her apartment on Ninth Street, she moved with her husband to the Madison Square Hotel at Madison and Twenty-sixth Street (now demolished)—which, though "in the suburbs" above Fourteenth Street, was "a good place to live" because it was a "restful and practical way to live and enormously economical" (*Letters*, 261).

Because the hotel was central to many women's experience of New York in the first half of the twentieth century, it is not surprising that women (and women writers) were often the most outspoken in recording and regretting its destruction. (Women were also, as Robert Caro points out, some of the most outspoken and earliest critics of Robert Moses and his development plans. The fiction writer Fanny Hurst, one of Moses's most vocal foes, was involved in the first fight to save the playgrounds of Central Park.)[16] Ruth Wittenberg, a longtime Greenwich Village activist widely credited with being the most important force behind the successful effort to grant large portions of the Village landmark status in the fifties, recalls that there were "two spots in the Village that everybody in our crowd knew, the Brevoort and the Lafayette, which were the centers of political and writing activities." The destruction of these hotels "really changed the Village. The physical aspects of it have a real effect on the population. People weren't isolated in apartment houses where they didn't know what was going on next door. They collected in small cafés" (Baxendall, 442–43).

The same year Brennan published "The Last Days of New York," Eudora Welty wrote a short skit entitled "Bye Bye Brevoort," to be performed as part of an off-Broadway production in 1956.[17] In the skit, three "old relics" (Millicent Fortescue, Violet Whichaway, and Agatha Chrome) throw a tea party in their room upstairs at the Brevoort, not yet reached by the wreckers dismantling the building. Fitted with hearing aids, they remain unaware that the building is being torn down around them. Portraits are falling, tea tables shaking, and still the women continue to think it merely "modern times!" "The noise is frightful," says Fortescue: "The vehicles! I can't think why they don't make vehicles go around the island!"—a fitting complaint, considering that Robert Moses couldn't think why the city didn't make the vehicles go across it. The skit ends with the wreckers carrying the shrieking ladies, still in their rocking chairs, out onto the street.

The closing scene of Dawn Powell's *The Wicked Pavilion*, written the year before "The Last Days of New York" and "Bye Bye Brevoort," tells a similar story. After a farewell banquet in the Café Julien dining room, made up of "real estate men commemorating their grief in selling the Julien to a mysterious concern rumored to be about to change it into apartments," the wreckers arrive. Two of the hotel café regulars stand in the street and watch the Julien come crashing down, gouging another gap in the familiar landscape and casting its regular patrons—writers, painters, and hangers-on—permanently back onto the street. The description of the gutted-out interior echoes Brennan: "[I]t was disconcerting to look through the paneless café windows straight into the open garden," the canopy "a tumbled pile of rags," the letters "Café Julien" "almost indiscernible under rubble," and the laurel vines "a great heap of gleaming green leaves," still "breathing and quivering with life" (178).

For Powell, the destruction of these hotels marks the end of a social world, the end of her subject: café society in Greenwich Village. Yet, the final scene also records the effect of the wrecking ball on the people who reside upstairs. Along with the artists and writers watching the Julien come down, there is also a "rouged and dyed old lady elaborately dressed in the fashion of World War One," dabbing at her "mascaraed eyes with a lacy handkerchief" (320). She has come not only to watch what had been her home for more than thirty years transformed into rubble, but to guard the welfare of her birds, who had made a nest outside her upstairs window, right above the café. One of the workmen in the demolition team makes his own observation: These women, the "old birds," were being sighted, looking lost and confused, everywhere around the Village. One could see a whole "nest of them" feeding the pigeons in Washington Square Park.

In eulogizing the New York hotel, writers like Brennan and Powell record not only the end of a period of voluntary homelessness for women in the city, but also the beginning of a period of enforced homelessness for thousands of New Yorkers. The dramatic depletion in the number of residential hotels, SRO buildings, and rooming houses in the sixties and seventies would ultimately be a root cause of the homeless crisis of the eighties. Since the turn of the century, residential hotels had been one of the main housing options for poor single adults and childless couples. In the seventies, when New York began to adopt its policy of "deinstitutionalization," the YMCAs and SROS and cubicle hotels became a resource for discharged patients of state psychiatric hospitals. Yet as the seventies passed, more and more homeless people were on the street, and a principal cause of this was that the affordable residential hotel was becoming obsolete.

One of the problems was that residential hotel life depended on old constructions. After 1930, almost no new residential hotels were built, partly because the "sheer primacy and publicly secured profits of suburban single-family houses overshadowed most notions of investing in downtown apartments or residential hotels" (Groth, 9). The single-room housing stock also became increasingly regulated; in 1955 changes in housing codes barred the conversion or construction of new for-profit single-room housing.[18] In the sixties, many older residential hotels were destroyed to make way for office buildings, and by the seventies, those that were left were swiftly being converted into higher-cost housing, especially in areas that were gentrifying, like the Upper West Side.[19] Between 1972 and 1982, 100,000 SRO units disappeared.[20] The only option, then, for many of the urban poor was the street or the shelter.

Brennan's phrase, "It should not be a problem to have shelter without being shut away," seems eerily prescient of what would happen to so many New Yorkers in the seventies and eighties. It was also eerily prescient of what would happen to her. By the late seventies she began experiencing psychotic episodes. Gardner Botsford recalls that she began to listen obsessively to Billie Holliday records and called him from Yaddo, the writers' colony, convinced that the people there were engaged in a plot to harm her. At one point, she was found sleeping in the ladies room at the *New Yorker*. She was institutionalized for a period, then released. For a time, she seemed to be taking her medication, but when she went off it, she stopped speaking to her friends at the *New Yorker*. She disappeared until in the early eighties she was sighted by one of her colleagues at the magazine near Rockefeller Center among a group of homeless people, feeding the pigeons, just like one of the ladies she had described from her window in "The Last Days of New York," and like one of those old birds Powell describes adrift in Washington Square. Although no one knew for sure, it was thought that the "traveler in residence" may have been homeless. A receptionist at the *New Yorker* noticed a "bag lady" in the waiting room one afternoon but had no idea who the woman was, and only later realized that the woman was once a glamorous staff writer for the magazine. Brennan briefly returned to Dublin to live with relatives, but then with no warning called a taxi and moved into a hotel. She did the same in Chicago, after another brief period living with her brother. Every once in a while, there would still arrive at the *New Yorker* a "Talk of the Town" piece, with no one sure where it had been written or where she was. Maeve Brennan died in a nursing home in 1993, with no recollection that she had either lived in New York or written for the *New Yorker*.

ANN PETERS is an assistant professor of English literature at Yeshiva University. She lives in Brooklyn.

NOTES

1. Wolfe admitted to wanting to have "a little fun" with the magazine by writing what he called an "anti-parody." Lurid and littered with exclamation points, the two pieces published in the *New York Herald Tribune* in April 1965 were entitled "Tiny Mummies! The True Story of the Ruler of 43rd Street's Land of the Walking Dead" and "Lost in the Whichy Thicket: The *New Yorker*—II." As

expected, the articles horrified the *New Yorker* staff. One of the complaints was that Wolfe had neglected to fulfill a basic tenet of good journalism: he got his facts wrong. But one fact he did get right. In the late fifties, there were more women living in the suburbs and more women reading the magazine than ever before. By 1954, they made up 55 percent of the readers and would continue to outnumber men for the next ten years (Yagoda, 311). There were also more women writing for the magazine. A 1958 survey of the contents of the magazine records that more than half the stories and short essays were by women (Yagoda, 282). That women writing for women should connote a slippage in quality, however, is not a matter of fact, but of taste. Alice Munro considers the fiction published in the magazine at midcentury, next to Chekhov, the most significant influence on the development of her short story style. The writer she recalls by name is Maeve Brennan. Brennan's short story "The Springs of Affection," published in the *New Yorker* in 1972, was an "all-time favorite" of Munro's. What Munro liked about Brennan was that she "wrote about the same things— about emotions and places" (1). In her 1988 essay about her years working at the *New Yorker* in the sixties, Frances Kiernan remembers defending the magazine against similar attacks, often by people who had not read the magazine in years. She writes: "if you believe that fiction at its best can enrich or even change our lives, mustn't you constantly bear in mind that women have lives too?" (90).

2. Yagoda points out that in the fifties and early sixties the circulation of the *New Yorker* grew 40 percent and that its advertising pages increased by more than 70 percent. He explains the success partly as a result of the increase of the female readers living in the suburbs who were "flocking to the *New Yorker*" as "one of the few ways they could exercise—and in some cases advertise—their learning and culture" (Yagoda, 311).

3. It should be noted that the rise in the number of women readers and writers was not the only explanation Yagoda gave for the decline in the quality of the writing. In the case of nonfiction stories, he blames the "whichy sentence" on the magazine's "labyrinthine editorial procedure" and its "scrupulousness in matters of fact, grammar, and style," which had become "fetishized under Shawn" (327). In the case of fiction, he points to the decline in the popularity of the short story form and the fact that many writers had abandoned the *New Yorker* for Hollywood (283). The suggestion, although never stated, is that the only fiction writers available and willing were women.

4. Brennan's stories can be divided geographically: Sneden's Landing, Long Island, Ireland, and Manhattan. The suburban stories, otherwise known as the Herbert's Retreat Stories, are mainly collected in *The Rose Garden* (2000) and were originally published in the *New Yorker* in the early- and mid-fifties. There are also a number of stories set in the Hamptons, where Brennan sometimes lived in the winters, borrowing summer houses from friends like Sara and Gerald Murphy. The stories of Ireland were published throughout her career, although most reviewers consider her final stories, published in the late sixties and early seventies, to be her best. Most of these were republished in *The Springs of Affection: Stories of Dublin*

in 1997. Of the Manhattan stories, there are two kinds. The early ones, which seem very much in the tradition of Dorothy Parker, are somewhat brittle, quaintly urbane: a couple buys a tie, a man is given a hot water bottle for a gift. And then there are the later New York stories, which I discuss here, most of which are about solitary life in the city and the transformation of the urban landscape.

5. In December 1954, Wanamaker's, occupying the entire block bounded by Broadway, Fourth Avenue, Ninth and Tenth Streets, closed in order to concentrate on its suburban operations. In the *New York Times*, journalist Meyer Berger wrote that New Yorkers "had come to love the place, its soft-spoken salespeople, its suave—but not too suave—floor walkers, its mellow indoor bells, the concerts in the great Wanamakers Auditorium, the air of quiet gentility that always lay, sort of reverent and hushed, over its well-stocked counters." In 1956, a plan was announced to tear down the store—one of the greatest achievements of cast-iron architecture in New York—and replace it with two nineteen-story apartment buildings. On July 14, 1956, shortly after demolition had begun on the store, a fire broke out in the building, one of the worst in New York's history, burning out of control for nearly twenty-four hours. Much of the building's cast-iron façade remained intact; still "there were no second thoughts about the building's future, and it was demolished" (*New York 1960*, 22-4).

6. The Hotel Astor, a landmark hotel since its completion in 1909, was demolished in 1966. In its place was built One Astor Plaza, or the W. T. Grant Building, a large office building. One Astor Plaza marked the "dramatic acceleration in the shift from Times Square's principal role as a nighttime world of entertainment to its hitherto secondary daytime role as an office district" (*New York 1960*, 443). In recent years, Times Square has swung back again as a center of entertainment, this time for Walt Disney. The space that was once the Hotel Astor is now the headquarters for MTV. The year Brennan published "The Last Days of New York," demolition began on the Brevoort, off Washington Square. It had closed down in 1949, but its famous dining room and sidewalk café remained open until 1953, when it was demolished, along with the Lafayette, to make way for a gigantic fourteen-story apartment house of 301 units and a restaurant "whose promise to recapture the culinary glory and atmosphere of the old hotel's dining room and café were not fulfilled" (*New York 1960*, 223). Along with these, many other hotels were being destroyed in the fifties and sixties, including some of the grand hotels, like the Savoy. The Manhattan Hotel on Forty-second Street and Madison Avenue was torn down in 1961, replaced by a forty-one-story office building. The Dauphin, on the west side of Broadway between Sixty-sixth and Sixty-seventh Streets, went down in 1961. For more on the many upscale hotels that disappeared, see *New York 1960*, 1104.

7. The B. Altman Department Store, originally opened in 1906, was closed in 1989. In August 1999, The Graduate Center of the City University of New York moved in, another example of a trend in the last twenty years of converting large department stores. See Collins B1.

8. See the *New York Times*, 29 March 1954, 21 March 1956, 19 January 1954.

9. Instead of eradicating slums, the Title I policies ultimately created new ones. Because those evicted under the policy—largely black, Hispanic, and poor— were not given adequate provisions for relocation, many ended up crowding into other neighborhoods, thereby creating new slums. See Caro, 777–78, 966–79.

10. This image of the building stripped of its exterior, the walls painted in bright colors is found in other depictions of New York at midcentury. In Jane Bowles's *Two Serious Ladies*, there is a long passage that describes the same image to night- marish effect. On a visit to the city, Miss Goering sees from her kitchen a build- ing about to be destroyed and replaced by an apartment building. One wall "had already been torn down. The rooms were still partially furnished and rain splat- tered the wallpaper. The wallpaper was flowered and already covered with dark spots, which were growing larger." In typical Bowles fashion, horror is magnified through the dryly observant manner in which it is told. At the same time, we are invited to laugh. When Mrs. Copperfield hears the story, she responds: "How amusing, or perhaps it was depressing." Miss Goering then tells of seeing a man come into the room who "walking deliberately over to the bed, took up a coverlet which he folded under his arm" and then "walked around the room aimlessly for a bit" before standing at the edge and "looking down into the yard with his arms akimbo. I could see him more clearly now, and I could easily tell that he was an artist. As he stood there, I was increasingly filled with horror, very much as though I were watching a scene in a nightmare." Mrs. Copperfield asks, "Did the man jump?" No, replies Mrs. Goering: the man "just remained there for quite a while looking down" with an "expression of pleasant curiosity on his face" (17). In a sense, this is what Brennan does throughout: horror is magnified through the understated manner in which she tells of the city's destruction: "I suppose that means that part of the square anyway, will be dug up. It will hardly look the same after that."

11. The shock recorded in *The American Scene* was not just about the transformation of the landscape but also about the changes in the city's demographic that occurred while he was away as well. The child's nightmare could be described another way: a grown man has suddenly awakened to find wild elephants stomping in the nursery, dirty boots tracking mud on the carpet, strangers in possession of the house. On a visit to Ellis Island, he observes the throngs of Ital- ian and Jewish immigrants and is left with a sense of having "seen a ghost in his supposedly safe old house" (66). A walk through the Lower East Side elicits an eruption of class prejudice: the immigrants on the fire escapes are described as "human squirrels and monkeys," clinging to the cages of "some great zoological garden" (102). There is no escape uptown either. Here, James is accosted by the ill manners of the parvenus. If Brennan's pen leads us like the tourist guide with her umbrella, James wields his pen much the way a man caught in a crowd of unruly children might swing his walking stick: with a wave, he longs for them to disappear. Fifty years later—when Brennan was writing her New York nos-

talgia trip—immigrants were once again pouring into the city, this time Puerto Ricans and blacks rather than the Irish, Jews, and Italians of James's day, while the white middle class, a class comprising the offspring of James's "aliens" of 1904, were flocking to the suburbs. Brennan, however, makes little comment about these changes in the urban population.

12. It is worth noting, too, that at the same time that Brennan was writing many of the nostalgic essays about New York, she was writing stories of women returning to their childhood homes in Ireland, where she finds the landscape (and people) of her youth unsettlingly altered. See especially her novella *The Visitor*, written in the forties and posthumously published in 2000.

13. Throughout the nineteenth century, the title "hotel lady" was shorthand for prostitute. It signaled the unseemly, such that middle-class and upper-class hotels built separate ladies' lounges so that "respectable" women could be shielded from the potentially licentious influence of the public rooms as well as from the implications that went along with hotel dwelling.

14. For the upper-class girls, fresh out of Vassar or Smith, there was also the more luxurious "clubhouse hotel." The most famous of these, the Barbizon on Lexington and East Sixty-third Street, offered a dormitory feel—Vassar extended—and breathtaking views on an eighteenth-floor roof deck with lounges, a restaurant, and a solarium (*New York 1930*, 191). There were also a number of men's hotels designed on the club model in the twenties, but most of these failed because, as Robert Stern points out, they were considered "faintly Victorian." Women's hotels fared much better, a more sophisticated version of the old-fashioned boarding house: a step forward, not a step backward. Nearly all were built in the late twenties. Along with the Barbizon there was the women's club residence at 18 Gramercy Park South, built in 1927; the Allerton on Fifty-seventh Street built the same year; and The American Women's Association Building at 353 West Fifty-seventh Street, built in 1929. Containing 1,257 bedrooms and a 1,200-seat theater, as well as a cafeteria, lounge, indoor swimming pool, and bowling alleys, the AWA building was the largest and "aimed to duplicate the success of the Barbizon with a lower-class market" (*New York 1930*, 195).

If in the early days the clubhouse hotels seemed to represent the chic, modern city girl—albeit a privileged one—by the fifties they came to symbolize something antiquated and repressive. And dull. The heroine of Sylvia Plath's *The Bell Jar*, for example, wins a magazine scholarship and is put up at the "Amazon." Modeled on Plath's own memories of living at the Barbizon, *The Bell Jar* tells a story of suffocation and of "girls at posh secretarial schools like Kay Gibbs, where they had to wear hats and stockings and gloves to class . . . and were waiting to get married to some career man or other" (4). The experience nearly pushes the heroine off the roof deck's edge. Dan Wakefield, in his memoir of New York in the fifties, describes his courtship of a girl at the Menemsha Bar in the Allerton House, noting condescendingly that it is "a residential hotel where girls just off the train to New York could stay and be protected while they learned how to fend off the evils of the big city," a place that he, as a recently arrived Greenwich Villager, deemed both "suburban" and "bourgeois" (212). There are few residential hotels left: the Gramercy Women's Residence (or the Parkside Evangeline) is still in existence, owned and operated by the Salvation Army. So too is the Webster Hotel on Thirty-fourth Street, founded in 1923 by a Macy's executive for the department store's employees. While no longer associated with Macy's, the residence continues to offer the same services to single working women: full maid service; breakfast and dinner; a patio deck; and "the beau parlor," a room to entertain male visitors. The Webster still aims to be affordable: a room costs $213 a week. Men may visit until midnight. There is also El Carmelo Residence (owned by the Carmelite Sisters) on West Fourteenth Street, and the Markle Memorial Residence on West Thirteenth Street—for women only.

15. After stepping off their trains at Grand Central or Pennsylvania Station, it was often a hotel where artists in the twenties and thirties landed and would remain, sometimes for years—Nathaniel West at the Hotel Sutton; Willa Cather at the Grosvener on Fifth Avenue; Edna Ferber at the Hotel Majestic on Seventy-seventh Street; Dorothy Parker at the Algonquin; Dylan Thomas and Virgil Thompson at the Chelsea; Georgia O'Keeffe and Alfred Stieglitz on the penthouse floor of the Shelton; and Dawn Powell, a self-proclaimed "permanent visitor" to New York, playing hostess down at the Lafayette.

16. Moses's 1956 plan to build a parking lot for Tavern on the Green in place of a playground in Central Park was one of the first of his actions to incite a citywide uproar. The fight to save the park was instigated by a number of Upper West Side mothers and a number of well-known residents living on Sixty-seventh Street, including those who lived in the "literarily oriented residence hotel, the Hotel des Artistes" across the street from the park. Living at the hotel at the time was Howard Chandler Christie, the artist, and Mae Murray, the "Merry Widow" who "had once been Hollywood's most glamorous star." She lived in an "attic formerly a chambermaid's room" at the top of the hotel. On the same street also lived the now elderly Fanny Hurst. As Robert Caro explains, the fight to save the park was successful partly because it had harnessed the support of so many well-known artists and writers and show-business people living in the neighborhood. Fanny Hurst wrote the original petition against the parking lot. She would become as identified with the fight to save the park as the mothers with their baby carriages lined up at the edge of the construction site. Moses, when speaking to reporters, even referred to her: "Oh, who are these critics anyway?" he demanded. "Troublemakers. A small, noisy minority. You have Mr. Isaacs and the Citizens Union and these childless women howling about their non-existent children. Take a woman like Fanny Hurst. Where are all her children? I've never heard of her having any children." This attack would lead the *Post* to respond with its own comment: "It had not previously occurred to most Americans that they had to give birth before disputing Robert Moses." See Caro, 985, 1001.

17. "Bye Bye Brevoort" was one of the skits in "The Littlest Revue," which opened

at the Phoenix Theatre in New York City on May 22, 1956. The play was not published at the time, although in 1980, Palaemon Press put out a limited number for the subscribers of the New Stage Theater in Jackson, Mississippi.

18. See O'Flaherty, 175–6.

19. In the seventies, with New York City teetering on bankruptcy, the city did a number of things to try to attract and hold the middle class. One of these incentives was the real estate abatement program (J51), which provided real estate tax abatements for ten or fifteen years on the conversion of older buildings into residential use—the conversion of rental units into co-op apartments. While this had benefits—a rise in home ownership in the inner city—it also meant that many SRO hotels on the Upper West Side, mid-Manhattan, and downtown Brooklyn were converted. See O'Flaherty, 57–9, 48–51; and Hoch, 239–40.

20. In his study of SRO hotels, Anthony Blackburn records that the number of single-room units fell from about 129,000 in 1960 to 25,000 in 1978. By the late seventies, the erosion of hotel life was especially dramatic. A 1979 study of "lower-priced hotels," including SROs and facilities like the YMCA, shows that the number of residents in these kinds of lodging places had fallen from 35,000 to 23,000 from 1975 to 1979, a dramatic decline in only four years. See Blackburn, 1–8.

WORKS CITED

Baxendall, Rosalyn Fraad. *Words on Fire: The Life and Writing of Elizabeth Gurley Flynn*. New Brunswick: Rutgers University Press, 1987.

Bennett, Charles G. "Major Drop in Manufacturing." *New York Times*. 21 March 1954.

Berman, Marshall. *All That is Solid Melts into Air: The Experience of Modernity*. New York: Simon and Schuster, 1982.

Blackburn, Anthony J. *Single Room Occupancy in New York City*. New York: Department of Housing Preservation and Development, 1986.

Botsford, Gardner. *A Life of Privilege, Mostly*. New York: St. Martin's Press, 2003.

Bourke, Angela. *Maeve Brennan: Homesick at* The New Yorker. Washington, D.C.: Counterpoint, 2004.

Bowles, Jane. *Two Serious Ladies. My Sister's Hand in Mine: An Expanded Edition of the Collected Works of Jane Bowles*. New York: Ecco, 1978.

Brennan, Maeve. *The Long-Winded Lady: Notes from* The New Yorker. 1969; New York: Mariner, 1998.

———. *The Rose Garden*. Washington, D.C.: Counterpoint, 2000.

Byron, Ellen. "Rooms for Rent: Maid Service, Hot Meals, No Men." *The Wall Street Journal*. 31 August 2004, A1.

Caro, Robert. *The Power Broker: Robert Moses and the Fall of New York*. New York: Knopf, 1974.

"City's Future is Bright in Zeckendorf's Opinion." *New York Times*. 19 January 1954.

Collins, Glenn. "In Aisle 3: Medieval Studies." *New York Times*. 5 April 2000, B1.

Fitzgerald, F. Scott. *The Great Gatsby*. New York: Scribner, 1925.

Gilman, Charlotte Perkins. *Women and Economics: A Study of the Economic Relation Between Men and Women as a Factor in Social Evolution*. 1898; Berkeley: University of California Press, 1998.

Groth, Paul Erling. *Living Downtown: The History of Residential Hotels in the United States*. Berkeley: University of California, 1994.

Hayner, Norman S. *Hotel Life*. Chapel Hill: Univeristy of North Carolina Press, 1936.

Hoch, Charles, and Robert A. Slayton. *New Homeless and Old: Community and Skid Row*. Philadelphia: Temple University Press, 1989.

Jacobs, Jane. *The Death and Life of Great American Cities*. 1961; New York: Vintage, 1992.

James, Henry. *The American Scene*. 1907; Ed. John Sears. New York: Penguin, 1994.

Kiernan, Frances. "Fiction at *The New Yorker*." *American Scholar*, September 1998: 81–91.

Kisseloff, Jeff. *You Must Remember This: An Oral History of Manhattan from the 1880s to World War II*. New York: Schocken, 1989.

Maxwell, Robert. "Introduction." *The Springs of Affection: Stories of Dublin* by Maeve Brennan. Boston: Houghton Mifflin, 1997.

Meade, Marion. *Dorothy Parker: What Fresh Hell Is This?* New York: Penguin, 1988.

Munro, Alice. "Interview with Cara Feinberg." *Atlantic Monthly Online*: 14 December 2001. Accessed 3 July 2003. http://www.theatlantic.com/doc/200112u / int2001-12-14.

O'Flaherty, Brendan. *Making Room: The Economics of Homelessness*. Cambridge: Harvard University Press, 1996.

Page, Max. *The Creative Destruction of Manhattan: 1900–1940*. Chicago: The University of Chicago Press, 1999.

Plath, Sylvia. *The Bell Jar*. London: Faber and Faber, 1963.

Powell, Dawn. *Angels on Toast*. 1940; South Royalton: Steerforth Press, 1996.

———. *Selected Letters of Dawn Powell: 1913–1965*. Ed. Tim Page. New York, Henry Holt, 1999.

———. *The Wicked Pavilion*. 1954; South Royalton, VT: Steerforth Press, 1996.

Stern, Robert A. M., Thomas Mellins, and David Fishman. *New York 1960: Architecture and Urbanism Between the Second World War and the Bicentennial*. New York: Monacelli Press, 1995.

———., Gregory Gilmartin, and Thomas Mellins. *New York 1930: Architecture and Urbanism Between the Two World Wars*. New York: Rizzoli, 1987.

Wakefield, Dan. *New York in the Fifties*. Boston: Houghton Mifflin, 1992.

Wallock, Leonard, ed. *New York: Culture Capital of the World, 1940–1965*. New York: Rizzoli, 1988.

Welty, Eudora. "Bye Bye Brevoort." Jackson, Ms.: New Stage Theater/Palaemon.

Wilson, Edmund. "Dawn Powell: Greenwich Village in the Fifties." *The Bit Between My Teeth: A Literary Chronicle of 1950–1965*. New York: Farrar, Strauss and Giroux, 1965, 526–33.

Yagoda, Ben. *About Town*. New York: Da Capo, 2001.

LOST IN ADAPTATION: CHICANA HISTORY, THE COLD WAR, AND THE CASE OF JOSEPHINA NIGGLI

WILLIAM ORCHARD AND YOLANDA PADILLA

In 1953, Metro Goldwyn Mayer released *Sombrero*, a film based on Josephina Niggli's 1945 novel *Mexican Village*. Niggli was a stable writer for MGM and, with director Norman Foster (then best known for directing installments of the Charlie Chan series), adapted the novel for the big screen, becoming the first Mexican American woman to earn a writing credit on a major studio production. Upon its publication, *Mexican Village* received wide acclaim: it was reviewed in high-profile publications like the *New York Times* and *Yale Review* and was repeatedly singled out as one of the best novels of the year.[1] MGM attracted the attention of the press when it announced that it had purchased the rights to the acclaimed novel as a vehicle for its rising star Ricardo Montalban.[2] Jack Cummings, the nephew of Louis B. Mayer and producer of many of the studio's most successful musicals, produced the film and enlisted the talent of such high-profile stars as Pier Angeli, Cyd Charisse, Yvonne de Carlo, and Vittorio Gassman. This assemblage of talent sustained the interest of the press, which profiled the production as it was filming on location in Tepoztlán, Mexico.[3] Optimistic about the prospects of the film, MGM commissioned Foster to prepare a sequel, based on other parts of the novel, even before the film was released.[4] However, the sequel stalled after *Sombrero* was panned by critics. Referring to the film "as a squashy sort of picture, as massive as the garment for which it is named," Bosley Crowthers, writing for the *New York Times*, acknowledged Niggli's talents as a novelist while lamenting that the "stories [in the film] are told so poorly and the jointing is so curious and confused, in a clumsy staggered fashion, that the sum is a jumbled tedious blob."[5] In later years, Niggli herself would wonder how so many talented individuals could make "such a stinker."[6]

The story of *Sombrero* is more than a story of a bad adaptation. We argue that *Sombrero* is representative of a crisis in the cultural production

[*WSQ: Women's Studies Quarterly* 33: 3 & 4 (Fall/Winter 2005)

and political rhetoric of Mexican Americans in the 1950s. In the 1920s and 1930s, Mexican Americans found themselves responding to the political upheavals resulting from the Mexican revolution of 1910. In Mexico, the cultural arm of the revolution at once promoted its ideologies and helped a previously fragmented nation imagine itself as whole. Similarly, Mexicans in the United States who had previously identified with such local affiliations as *californio* or *tejano* began to understand themselves, through the Revolution's doctrines and media, as part of a totality.[7] In the fiction and drama of Niggli, most of which was written before 1950, the Mexican revolution becomes a vehicle to conceptualize and consider the obligations and demands of civic life and modernity. In the 1950s, Mexican Americans found themselves adapting to a radically shifting United States political climate that, with the commencement of the Cold War, more emphatically insisted on the pliant "Americanness" of its citizens. Cold War politics and the rise of McCarthyism in the United States necessitated the suppression of the revolution as a topic in both literature and politics. The loss of the revolution as an option for thinking and imagining political life turns the more coherent narratives of Mexican American life before World War II into something like the "jumbled tedious blob" that Crowthers discovered in his viewing of *Sombrero*.

The story of *Mexican Village*'s adaptation into *Sombrero* is about more than the loss of the Mexican Revolution as a vehicle for thought. It is also a story of the loss of the 1950s in Chicana history. As the Chicano movement valorized "the history of class struggle and its impact on the mass of men and women who participated in these struggles," the "exceptional men and women" who were part of the middle class and achieved visibility in their moment were erased to bring the laborer and his and her concerns into the fore.[8] To be sure, Niggli was an exceptional individual and unusual in Chicana literary history. She did not write *Mexican Village* in the borderlands but in the hills of North Carolina; she secured the University of North Carolina Press and Holt, Rinehart to publish her works at a time when few Chicanas were published; she wrote love scenes for many Hollywood productions; and she finished her years as a professor of literature and chair of the theatre department at Western Carolina University. Our argument here is not that she is exceptional but that her exceptional achievements bring into view certain typical features of the moment that allow us a more complete understanding of the experience of Chicanas in the 1950s. The Chicana writers of this period have been read by scholars of Chicano literature as perpetuating a romanticized view of Mexico and the southwestern United States that was in vogue in the larger U.S. culture at that time.[9] Our reading contests this view by situating Niggli in her historical moment and seeing her cultural production not as complicit with the appetites of the consumer market but as marked by the impossible political contradictions facing Mexican Americans at midcentury.

FOLK WISDOM AND REVOLUTIONARY INTELLIGENCE

This is not to suggest that Mexican Americans did not feel the pull of two allegiances in the period leading up to World War II. In order to understand the way Cold War politics reshaped Chicano political discourse one must gain a sense of how Mexican Americans negotiated the twin demands placed on them by U.S. perceptions of Mexicans and Mexican nationalism's attempts to redefine the national culture. Niggli's *Mexican Village*, written alongside her folk drama in the 1930s and 1940s, adapts Mexican literary forms and political thought to a U.S. audience, while also imagining how a selective and judicious schooling in U.S. modernity could revive both Mexico and Mexican Americans. Niggli's novel cannily exploits a common term in U.S. and Mexican discourse about Mexican Americans to produce a bivocal text, one aimed, on the one hand, at teaching and delighting a U.S. public and, on the other, at thinking about the consequences and aftermath of the Mexican Revolution on its subjects at home and abroad.

The common term that Niggli works with and through is the "folk." Despite a general agreement about the folk base of Chicano literature, Chicano literary critics have been dismissive of Niggli's use of folk history and traditions.[10] In contrast to the *corrido* (border ballad) tradition that became a repository of Chicano countermemory, one that could be recovered by the folklorist or the ethnographer, Niggli's "folk" seemed too manufactured. In this view, it too easily accommodated the tastes of U.S. artists and intellectuals who were looking to Mexico and the "Hispanic" Southwest to escape the dehumanizing effect of an increasingly modern, machine-driven society. As Genaro Padilla explains, these artists and thinkers often essentialized Mexicans and Indians as they "mystified and mythified their cultural practices, reduced their social history, and ignored their individuality."[11]

Niggli's training as a writer was suffused with a general view that American drama should mine its folk history to produce indigenous and authentic materials. In 1935, she joined the University of North Carolina's renowned drama troupe, the Carolina Playmakers, already well established as one of the premier drama organizations in the country. The Playmakers made their name through their innovative stagings of "folk plays," which they defined as plays that dealt with "the folkways of our less sophisticated people living simple lives not seriously affected by the present-day, complex social order . . . The term 'folk' . . . applies to that form of drama which is earth-rooted in the life of our common humanity."[12] This definition of the "folk" largely conforms to the way the concept was understood in other U.S. contexts, such as the ones Padilla describes. These representations of the folk were meant to provide an escape from the dehumanizing aspects of urban modernity. Located in village spaces, folk cultures were considered to be static, outside of time, a view expressed in Charles Lummis's romanticized tribute to the American Southwest:

> Sun, silence, and adobe—that is New Mexico in three words. Here we see the land of *poco tiempo*—the home of "Pretty Soon." Why hurry with the hurrying world? The "Pretty Soon" of New Spain is better than the "Now! Now!" of the haggard States. . . . Let us not hasten—*mañana* will do.[13]

Such representations were popular among large segments of the U.S. population, who were taken with the idea of the Southwest and Mexico as unspoiled, premodern, potentially generative entities.

Details from Niggli's work leave her vulnerable to the charge that she not only fed the appetite for romanticized versions of the folk, but that she was herself the promoter of such a view of the Southwest. *Mexican Village*, for instance, contains an abundance of *dichos* (proverbs), the obligatory *curandera* (folk healer or witch doctor), and detailed descriptions of Mexican food, clothing, and courtship rituals. These are all hallmarks of a folk style that at times reduces characters to what Richard Brodhead describes as "ethnologically colorful personifications of the different humanity produced in non-modern settings."[14] Certainly Niggli's employment of this style makes sense given the years she spent under the tutelage of the Playmakers. Yet reading her work only in the context of her training in North Carolina fails to acknowledge Niggli's equally deep immersion in modalities of the folk that were prevalent in her homeland, modalities that were central to the Mexican novel's representations of the postrevolutionary future in Mexico.

In fact, read in a tradition of Mexican letters, Niggli's novel is bold in its attempts both to produce a vision of Mexican political life, one that has repercussions for the lives of Mexicans living in the United States, and in its refiguring of the novel of the Mexican Revolution, a genre that is typically associated with men. Novelists from Mariano Azuela to Juan Rulfo to, later, Carlos Fuentes operate in the tradition of the *letrado*, a writer whose double duty is to his art and to his country.[15] Such a figure produces work of imaginative power that also has relevance for the emerging nation. Thus situated, *Mexican Village* is transformed from a work of simple autoethnography—the reportage of one Mexican on the lives and customs of her people—into a work that uses the figure of Mexican village life to imagine new utopian horizons that are in many ways conditioned by the promise of and disappointment in the Mexican Revolution of 1910.

By drawing this distinction between American and Mexican uses of the folk, our point is not to suggest that local color writers were viewed as not contributing to cultural knowledge in the United States, nor is it to claim that local color was gendered female in the United States in contrast to a masculine association with folk customs in Mexico.[16] Rather, we are interested in the decidedly feminine stamp that is impressed on local color writing by Chicano critics of the midcentury writings of such figures as Niggli, Fabiola Cabeza de Baca, Cleofas Jaramillo, and María Cristina Mena. In Niggli's case, scholars have focused most of their attention on the aspects of the text that can be read as providing both pleasure and ethnographic information for white American audiences, ignoring the bivocality that we argue is one of the novel's most crucial aspects.

Certainly Niggli herself considered her work to be politically and historically engaged. In fact, one of her primary motivations for writing about Mexico was her dissatisfaction with representations of her homeland. In a 1957 letter to Maren Elwood, Niggli wrote, "when I was a young kid, starting out as a writer, I had a shining goal. I was going to present Mexico and the Mexicans as they had never before been presented."[17] Niggli would clarify her intentions years later, asserting that "in the '20s and '30s many otherwise well-educated people in the United States really thought there was nothing more to Latin American life than the stereotypes they saw at the movies," and that the distinction she was most proud of was that her *Mexican Village* had helped end the "banana republic" view of Latin America.[18]

Niggli's comments may seem ironic to the casual reader of her work, for she was certainly complicit in the promotion of Anglo-American stereotypes of Mexicans. Niggli publicized her work with images that exploited an exoticized view of Mexicans. On the frontispiece of *Mexican Folk Plays* she appears in a *sombrero* and *serape*, while in the *New York Times* she is pictured in a *reboso*—articles of clothing that belonged to the traditional dress of the Mexican peasantry, not to the middle-class Mexican American writer. While one may read Niggli's attire as an attempt to establish an affiliation with the working and peasant classes, as Frida Kahlo did when she donned traditional garb, Niggli's performances of exoticism often seem more akin to Carmen Miranda's exaggerated *bahia* garb. What prevented Niggli from becoming a cultural caricature in the Miranda model was a dual relation to her performance and work. She at once performed the exotic and assumed the role of an ethnographer.

What ultimately moves Niggli's work beyond ethnography is her attention to Mexican political life. Because it attends to the aftermath of the Mexican Revolution, Niggli's book can be read as part of the tradition that Roberto Fernández Retamar calls "the 'other' novel of the Mexican Revolution." As Retamar and numerous other scholars have described, the tradition that begins with Mariano Azuela's *Los de abajo* (1916) is initially a descriptive one marked by a documentary style.[19] While description would continue as an aspect of novels of the revolution, the period that begins with Martín Luis Guzmán's *La sombra del caudillo* (1929) marks a shift from a documentary to an introspective mode that characterizes Retamar's "other" novel of the revolution.[20] Ironically, for all of the emphasis contemporary reviewers and recent scholars place on the "folk" and "quaint" aspects of *Mexican Village*, Niggli's book shares much more with some of the most established novels of this "other" tradition. Like Gregorio López y Fuentes's *El indio* (1935), *Mexican Village* attends to the nationalist concern of integrating the country's fragmented groups into a coherent whole. And like *El indio* and Augustín Yanez's *Al filo del agua* (1947), Niggli's narrative emphasizes the collective over the individual, highlighting the transformative power of the village itself. Perhaps most importantly, *Mexican Village* shares with Juan Rulfo's *Pedro Paramo* (1955) a preoccupation with the fall of the *patrón* or cacique system as the primary consequence of the revolution. And yet, an even more basic commonality shared by all of these texts is precisely their use of the "folk" to explore the issues thought to be of the most urgent importance to the nation.

In contrast to U.S. understandings of the "folk" and of village life, the first shots of the Mexican Revolution transformed the Mexican village into a volatile, dangerous, and politicized place. The revolution was always rural: its demands were agrarian and it most important battles were fought in the previously ignored provinces, far from the glamour of Mexico City. As Alan Knight suggests, "the revolution arose in the provinces, established itself in the countryside, and finally conquered an alien and sullen capital."[21] The impulse to represent village life is at the center of a genre, the novel of the revolution, that has much in common with "regionalist" and "local color" fiction in the United States. Known in Mexico as *costumbrismo*, folk literature is broadly defined by Alberto Millán Chivite as

> a type of minor literature . . . that dispenses with the development of plot, or whose plot is rudimentary, limiting itself instead to the painting of a colorful canvas, reflecting with charm and ease the mode of life of an epoch, popular customs, or representative types.[22]

While this definition echoes the somewhat dismissive tone that historically has characterized discussions of U.S. regional literature, studies of the Mexican novel take *costumbrismo* more seriously than do their U.S. counterparts—especially when it is considered in relation to the novel of the revolution. One reason for the weightier significance given to *costumbrismo* in Mexico has to do with the very different attitudes toward the village. Mexican writers, like those from the United States, view the village as a nonmodern space, but they also know from firsthand experience how violent, threatening, and potentially transformative that space can be. Beyond a recognition of the political potential that lay dormant in the village scene, Mexican novelists of the 1940s and 1950s, as Robert McKee Irwin notes, used *costumbrismo* to "create an autochthonous image of Mexico, free from foreign influence," one that mirrors the attempts of the Mexican muralists to form an aboriginal image of the nation through the Indians represented in their art.[23] *Costumbrismo* was not indigenous or native in any substantial way, but rather, like modernism, drew from a range of popular traditions at home and abroad.

FRAMING DEMOCRACY

Costumbrismo and the novel of the Mexican Revolution often dramatized political concerns by fixating on a character whose masculinity is somehow in crisis. The hero of such novels is typically a dispossessed male who must resolve the problem of his paternity (and, by allegorical extension, the problem of the nation). *Mexican Village* is framed by just such a hero, Bob Webster; but the film completely removes Bob from the narrative and focuses instead on a minor comic character, Pepe Gonzalez. The adaptation of the novel loses more than a character. By erasing Bob and installing Pepe as the focus, the film not only loses the novel's concerns with the politics of democracy, but also capitulates to a number of stereotypes alive in the postwar United States about Mexican Americans and their capacities for citizenship.

Like other novelists of the revolution who attempt to assess the future of Mexico in the wake of chaos, Niggli focuses on the fall of *caciquismo*. In contrast to most other practitioners of the genre, she shows Mexico as a country full of possibilities once the elite *cacique* system is dismantled. However, Niggli does not idealize the revolution; on the contrary, she devotes some of her most important early work to dispelling romantic attachments to the political upheaval. *Mexican Village* is an example of a novel of the revolution written north of the border with a different audience in mind. For her, everything points back to her "shining goal" of portraying Mexican society to U.S. audiences in a way they had never before seen. While *Mexican Village* gives a detailed portrait of Mexican customs and folk culture, it also tries to undo what she calls the "banana republic" view of Mexico by representing village life in a mode that would be legible to a U.S. audience as an indication of progress. It does so by tempering the folk culture it portrays with glimpses of an increasingly civic-minded society that values hard work and democratic process over aristocratic blood.

Bob Webster, the town quarry foreman who is haunted by his legacy as the illegitimate son of a Mexican maid and her Anglo boss, is the figure through whom Niggli endorses work over aristocratic privilege, represented in the novel by the ailing Castillo family. When Bob's Texan father rejects him because he refuses to believe that an "Indian" could be his son, Bob moves to Hidalgo, keenly feeling the need to make a connection with the culture his Mexican grandmother endlessly spoke of when he was a child. Although the townspeople initially view Bob as a "gringo," he gradually undergoes a symbolic "browning" process through which he increasingly is identified as *mestizo*—the half-Spanish, half-Indian mixture that is said to constitute the Mexican race. This transformation reaches its culminating moment when Bob rechristens himself Roberto Ortega Menendez y Castillo.

His status as a *mestizo* becomes significant when we discover that Bob's grandmother was the sister of the Castillo patriarch Don Saturnino and had run away in her youth. In this connection, Niggli shifts the novel of the revolution's concerns with patrilineal descent to issues of maternity. Traditionally, women are associated with the indigenous, an association that echoes Cortez's conquest of the nation, after which he impregnates his Aztec translator Malintzin (La Malinche), resulting in the birth of the Mexican race. While scholars debate the degree of agency Malintzin may have exerted in this sexual congress, the consensus is that she was an unwilling participant and that, consequently, the birth of the Mexican people was necessarily pained and left a long shadow on the national character.[24] The novel prepares us for a repetition of this tradition by presenting Bob as the offspring of an *india* Mexican and a white Texan. Here, the place of the conquering Spaniard has been assumed by the more immanent imperial power at the moment of Niggli's writing—the United States.

However, the grandmother's *criollo* (pure-blooded Spanish) background upsets this figuration. Her Spanishness presents a whiteness that nearly eclipses that of Bob's father and that attempts to unsettle questions of agency and consent in the production of *mestizo* subjects. In the story of the female Castillo, we witness the founding narrative in reverse: the Spanish female and Indian male unite to generate a *mestizo* who is, until the revolution has been completed, disinherited from the nation. In his transformation from an uneasy Anglo into Roberto Ortega de Menendez y Castillo, Bob not only inherits the wealth and stature of the family's legacy but also, through his Indian blood, assumes a genealogical claim to the nation.[25] In this way, he has inherited Mexico itself, embodying the passing of control from the hands of pure-blooded

Spanish *criollos* to the mixed-race *mestizo* classes. But what are we to make of Bob's American heritage? Is it entirely erased by the recuperation of the grandmother's history? Or has it rather been displaced and projected onto the new national project in which Bob has been symbolically enfolded? One place where this is manifest is in Niggli's treatment of the village's democratic practices.

The turn *Mexican Village* makes in its final chapters to questions of civic responsibility can perhaps best be understood in the context of longstanding debates in the United States that made "democracy" a racial issue. As Matthew Frye Jacobson argues, almost from its inception "[American] republicanism would favor or exclude certain peoples on the basis of their 'fitness for self-government,' as the phrase went, and some questionable people would win inclusion based upon an alchemic reaction attending Euro-American contact with peoples of color."[26] Thus, while groups such as the Irish and the Italians were "questionable" in terms of the related issues of their whiteness and their "fitness for self-government" in the nineteenth century, their status became solidified on both counts as racial formations changed over time, diminishing the perceived salience of racial difference within white communities. For Mexicans, whose racial status was perpetually in flux, the complicated U.S. relationship between race and republicanism meant that they consistently found themselves before the bar of public opinion. At times they were judged to be white enough—and consequently fit enough—to merit inclusion as full U.S. citizens, while at other times their status as racially mixed people was marshaled as evidence against liberal immigration policies that promoted the virtues of the "melting pot" ideal. Madison Grant, whose *Passing of the Great Race* was among the most influential expressions of the rising eugenic view of immigration in the 1920s, argued that the true achievement of the "melting pot" was best exemplified by "the racial mixture we call Mexican, and which is now engaged in demonstrating its incapacity for self government."[27]

Mexican Village answers these prejudices with numerous scenes that emphasize democracy as an important element of village life. Passing references to such entities as the building committee and the saloon committee abound, underscoring the importance of the group over the individual when decisions must be made. These references run counter to the idea of Mexico as a premodern society too hampered by racial impurity to organize itself around a system of democracy. The most striking example of this comes in a passage about the town's beauty contest. The young women of Hidalgo submit photos of themselves that are judged by the men:

> The judging of pictures was handled in an easy manner. Anyone who cared to vote could do so, writing his preferences on a slip of paper and pushing it into a locked ballot box. Don Nacho put Don Ricardo to guard the box so that there could be no ballot stuffing. All the town's men voted, first examining each picture as minutely as though it were the quality of the camera work and not the beauty of the sitter that impressed them. . . . The voting was laborious, requiring much wetting of lead pencils and scratching of ears, but finally the last ballot had been thrust into the box, and it remained for the committee to sort and count them. To keep from showing any hint of favoritism, Alejandro had invited three of his Monterrey friends to make up the committee. (313)

Strikingly, while the contest's primary function in the novel is to introduce the love story between Alejandro, a member of the town's great Castillo family, and María of the River Road, an orphaned woman whom the town regards with distrust, Niggli also uses it as an opportunity to describe the voting process in detail. She explains that the only qualifications a man needs in order to vote is the desire to do so, and she emphasizes the lengths the village goes to in its efforts to ensure that not even the slightest hint of fraud can mar the integrity of the outcome. Here, the villagers are not only dedicated participants in democratic action, but they also are attuned to the way technology and media may inadvertently misrepresent the appearance of things.

Niggli further illustrates the still-precarious but important place of democracy in the village in the scene in which the votes are counted. The committee members react with horror when they realize that María has won by a landslide, knowing that the entire valley will be outraged to learn that a woman of questionable background has been judged the most beautiful. In an attempt to avoid this situation, the committee members plead with Alejandro to disregard the results of the vote and to name instead a "reputable" woman as the winner.

"No," Alejandro said thickly. "This María won the contest. Her name shall be declared as the winner in Hidalgo. The counting of the votes will be kept secret . . . You were asked to count the votes and that was all. I am chairman of the committee. We shall simply announce that María won the majority of the votes." (315)

In *Sombrero*, Niggli makes Alejandro's protests even more pointed. When asked to ignore María's victory, Alejandro responds, "María's photograph was properly entered according to your own rules. If we disqualify her, every town in the valley will think we don't know what democracy means." When the mayor continues to complain, Alejandro snaps, "What is the difference between you and María? She was voted most beautiful just as you were voted mayor."[28] Certainly Alejandro is not a disinterested party; he is in love with María and wants her to occupy what he already believes to be her rightful position as the most beautiful woman of Hidalgo. However, rather than simply assert his will by virtue of his standing in the village as one of the great Castillos, he appeals to the democratic process as the final arbiter of justice. The villagers similarly transcend the restrictions of tradition and local propriety by using the technology of voting to unleash themselves from entrenched social prejudices that would have excluded María.

If Alejandro's objection finds crisper articulation in the movie version of the voting episode, the movie also blunts the force of this moment in several significant ways that correlate with the changing political climate that Mexican Americans faced in the 1950s. Most significantly, the voting episode lacks the grand framing of the novel. While the novel, as we have explained, is framed by the entrance and transformation of Bob Webster, the movie opens with a different framing, one that immediately moves into the previously mentioned voting episode, a scene that occurs in the final third of the novel. In the first moments of *Sombrero*, a taco-eating constable, the village's Jesuit priest, a professor, and a doctor are on the trail of "that finger-nail of Satan" and "son of a cheese maker," Pepe Gonzalez, who has drawn moustaches on the pictures of the women who entered the beauty contest. While the authorities are unable to discover Pepe in the opening episode, the camera does. Pepe—played by the movie's biggest star, Ricardo Montalban—addresses the camera as he conspiratorially promises to entertain his audience with his antics. Although Pepe is a minor character in the novel, he emerges in the film as the principle character, whose romance must be resolved before the movie can end. Using Pepe rather than Bob to frame the narrative has implications for how readers or viewers interpret the voting scene. With Bob as the figure of primary interest, the voting scene becomes part of the evolving Mexican national imaginary that develops after the dismantling of the *cacique* system in the wake of the revolution. As Bob becomes more Mexican, the village takes on some attributes of American political life that he symbolically imports. In *Sombrero*, the revolution is not mentioned, obscuring any sense of the nation reconstituting itself politically. Indeed, the locale seems to be out of time, and it is jarring when a scene set in Mexico City reveals skyscrapers and mass transit. Instead, Pepe conveys many of the stereotypes about Mexicans as unfit for democracy. In addition to Pepe's defacing of the voting process, the priest, doctor, professor, and policeman in the opening scene all prove ineffectual checks on Pepe's delinquency. Mexico thus both produces and is incapable of policing delinquent subjects.

Such a view of Mexican political life corresponds with a wartime and postwar U.S. cultural climate in which Mexicans and Mexican Americans were continually being produced as delinquent subjects. Standing in stark contrast to the 1920s and 1930s, when an appetite for Mexican folk artifacts and culture could result in commissions for murals that baldly criticized their capitalist patrons, Mexicans and Mexican Americans were consistently presented in the 1940s and 1950s as dangerous to the American way of life. The most renowned of these depictions were the Sleepy Lagoon case of 1942 and the Zoot Suit riots of 1943, in which young Mexican males were cast as delinquents.[29] At the same time, Mexican workers were being imported through the *bracero* program to provide labor to support the wartime economy. Between 1942 and 1947, more than 200,000 workers came to the United States.[30] Beginning in 1949 and systematically after the implementation of "Operation Wetback" in 1953, however, Mexican workers were rounded up and deported in droves as the border became increasingly militarized.

Mexican "delinquency" was often linked to un-American activities or the Communist Party. The Sleepy Lagoon Defense Committee, for example, was accused of "Communist leanings."[31] Similar charges were waged against Mexican activists, effectively inscribing democratic reform and labor activism within the same realm of the delinquent as the zoot suiter. The pro-labor Asociación Nacional México-Americana (ANMA), an important precursor to the Chicano movement, was the subject of scrutiny, although, as Ernesto Chávez notes, the organization was far from "un-American": "it promoted reform of American society, not revolution, and the reform it sought was protection of the constitutional rights of all."[32] Chávez further notes that "what they did not quite appreciate was that the Cold War era was not a good time to emphasize anything that could even remotely be construed as denigrating or attacking 'American democracy.'"[33]

With its references to revolution and to democracy and its concern for Mexico, Niggli's *Mexican Village* hits on many of the sensitive issues of the early Cold War period and would have been an object of scrutiny. The examination would have been multiplied when the novel was adapted into a film. As Seth Fein notes, "[F]ilm was the key mass medium undergirding U.S.-Mexican sociocultural relations" in the period coincident with *Sombrero*'s production and release, surpassing even elite communications between national officials.[34] By the time of *Sombrero*'s release, the United States Information Agency had made cinematic propaganda a key weapon in the Cold War management of relations with Mexico.[35] As a stable writer for MGM, Niggli was intimately familiar with the review of Hollywood by the House Un-American Activities Committee. Rosaura Revueltas, the actress who played the crucial role of the *curandera* Tía Magdalena in *Sombrero*, was deported by HUAC after her starring role as a striking mine worker in Herbert Biberman's *Salt of the Earth* (1953). Reflecting on her participation in *Salt of the Earth*, Revueltas provides a rationale for doing the role that sounds strikingly similar to the project that Niggli announced in her letter to Maren Elwood:

> From the day I became an actress I longed to play a role that would honor my people. And now such a role had been offered to me—for these miners were my people, even though they lived across the border. . . . I can only conclude that I was "dangerous" because I had been playing a role that gave stature and dignity to the character of the Mexican-American woman.[36]

Niggli left Hollywood shortly after *Sombrero* failed to meet expectations. She stopped writing and turned to teaching. To friends, she said that her decision to teach was influenced by a heartfelt conversation with Lionel Barrymore about her future in Hollywood after the failure of her film, but one can't help but think that the heightened vigilance of the Cold War effectively silenced her by restricting engagement with those very topics—Mexico, the revolution, and democracy—that had been so crucial in *Mexican Village* and in her folk plays. In an unsigned eulogy in her papers at Western Carolina University, the eulogist recounts a story Niggli told about appearing before the House Un-American Activities Committee. When asked whether she had been or was a Communist, she replied, "No darling, I'm a Catholic." In many ways, her statement is troubling: Mexican Americans were estranged from Catholic leadership in Los Angeles because of the Church's anti-labor stances. But Niggli was an extravagant fabulist, embroidering the truth of her life with stories that established a larger-than-life persona. Although we have been unable to locate evidence of her testimony, the fact that she felt compelled to account for it reveals the large place it occupied in the history of her life. If the political trauma of the Mexican Revolution set her to writing, the political drama of the HUAC investigation may have halted her flow of words.

THE HAUNTED HOUSE OF CHICANO STUDIES

While Anglo-American audiences may have regarded Pepe Gonzalez as an embodiment of their suspicions about Mexican Americans' inability to participate in civic life and democratic processes, Mexican American audiences would have recognized Pepe as a familiar character from working-class entertainments. This alternative interpretation of Pepe helps us understand how the Mexican American working class was exerting hegemony over Mexican American cultural experience. The interests and concerns of the working classes were often at odds with or indifferent to the intellectual investments in Mexico and the revolution expressed in the works of a writer like Niggli. Although the Mexican American working class was often in conflict with the dominant culture of the United States, the two opposing forces nonetheless colluded in silencing Mexican American writers. Thus, while Pepe Gonzalez's usurpation of Bob Webster's place as the narrative's framing character can be seen as a depoliticization of the novel in the face of U.S. Cold War ideologies, it can also be viewed as a capitulation to the working-class tastes of the increasingly proletarian Mexicans living in the United States.

In a recent examination of Mexican American film culture in Los Angeles, Curtis Márez argues that the classical Hollywood paradigm was in some ways "a reaction formation opposed to the possible uses of film by Mexican immigrant cultures." Mexicans incorporated film into a variety-show format that was familiar from *carpas* (traveling performance groups) that originated during the period of the revolution. For Mexican audiences in the 1930s, film would be one of many entertainments (and often not the featured one) offered in a variety show. This variety tradition consisted of several kinds of performance—songs, comedy, musical performance, and dance—and featured the singular figure of the *pelado*.[37] The *pelado* (literally, "the plucked one") occupies a position below the urban proletariat and commands his own dialect that is rife with sexual allusions and a demotic verbal dexterity.[38] An archetype of the Mexican national character, the *pelado* is marked by his hypermasculinity. The most famous *pelado* is Cantinflas, the creation of Mario Moreno Reyes, an icon of Mexican cinema who is often compared to Charlie Chaplin.[39]

Pepe Gonzalez—especially as played by the charismatic Ricardo Montalban—displays many of the characteristics of the *pelado* and could be read as a domestication of that figure in mainstream U.S. cinema. Through splendid displays of verbal dexterity and bravado, Pepe resists the authority of the village officials who symbolically represent the juridical, religious, educational, and scientific communities whose dominance correlated more with the old national order than with the new. Beyond this, the film is organized as a variety show, which is perhaps one reason Bosley Crowthers felt justified in dismissing it as a "jumbled tedious blob." While the film is framed by Pepe's romantic exploits, it also contains an array of dance numbers that are tenuously related to the main plot line as well as numerous stock scenes involving such familiar characters as the *curandera* and the spurned lover. The film's marketing materials focused on this variety structure by arranging images of key dance scenes and musical numbers around an illustrated *sombrero* on the movie poster. Cyd Charisse's "Aztec dance" was featured in most materials, and many made special reference to the appearance of famed flamenco dancer José Greco.[40] By accommodating the popular tastes of the increasingly working-class Mexican immigrants in Los Angeles, the film distances itself from many of the novel's intellectual investments in Mexican folk culture and in the political aftermath of the revolution.

This shift toward an investment in the working classes and, by extension, such issues as labor activism and immigration became prevalent in the 1950s as the Mexican population became increasingly proletarian. In the 1930s and 1940s, many Mexican Americans promoted an assimilationist agenda. The period of Niggli's greatest creative output coincides with the appearance of the League of United Latin American Citizens (LULAC), an organization both overwhelmingly Mexican and decidedly assimilationist.[41] Yet, in its exploration of racial and ethnic difference and in its concern for democracy and Mexican civic life, Niggli's work more often expressed the political orientation of activist organizations like ANMA that were important precursors to the Chicano movement. Despite these affinities, the intellectual project that her work engaged estranged her from the emergent working-class concerns that would achieve dominance in Mexican American political and cultural life by the end of the 1960s. In the histories of the 1950s, figures who engaged working-class concerns have received the most attention. While Niggli has been marginalized in the tradition, a woman like Revueltas, who shared many of Niggli's intellectual concerns, is repeatedly invoked, largely because she identified with and portrayed a Mexican American labor leader. For a variety of reasons that speak to the gendered division of labor and the social organization of Chicano families, women have not, for the most part, fared well in these histories. Occasionally, as in Mario T. García's seminal *Mexican Americans*, a woman like Josefina Fierro de Bright, a social and labor activist and founder of the Spanish-Speaking Congress, will merit mention. More typically, the histories have focused on working-class women generally.[42]

García notes that labor is not the whole story. He devotes the final section of his study to "Mexican American Intellectuals," examining the cases of the historian Carlos E. Castañeda, educational sociologist George I. Sanchez, and folklorist Arthur L. Campa. For García, these men merit the distinction of being intellectual because they were university-based professionals. Mexican American fiction writers, García notes, "published during this era, but their work appears to have only marginally contributed to the making of what historian Richard García calls the 'Mexican American mind.'"[43] By establishing a university base as a criterion, García effectively forecloses the possibility of women intellectuals.[44] García's definition of the intellectual class also is averse to those engaged in cultural production. As we noted in our discussion

of the novel of the revolution, Mexican novelists were important contributors to the nation's intellectual and political life, operating
through the institutions of publishing rather than through institutions
like universities. García's definition, then, unintentionally exalts the
work of social scientists as it diminishes the effects that literature and
other forms of cultural production could exert on the shaping of the
"Mexican American mind." With its concern for projects of social
uplift and the redistribution of resources, this social science orientation
reflects the dominance of working-class concerns in the formation of
Chicano studies. As Kirsten Silva Gruesz has recently noted, the sociological dominance in Latino studies has resulted in a future and present
progressive orientation in the field that tends "to register only the con-
temporaneity of the immigrant situation."[45] Much of Chicana/o and
Latina/o history that lies outside of the immigration narrative gets
repressed in this figuration of the discipline.

Niggli's continual reappearance and dismissal from the canon of
Chicana/o literature can be read as a return of the repressed—the persistent return of an aspect of the Mexican American experience that the
field has been incapable of fully assimilating into its image of itself.
Appropriately, those who travel to Western Carolina University to
examine Niggli's papers at the Hunter Library Special Collections may
be surprised by a legend that involves the campus theater, which was
named after Niggli and is perhaps the only theater in the United States
named for a Mexican American woman. A ghost haunts the Niggli
Theater, and that ghost is no other than the woman herself. This story
resonates with Niggli's place in the canons of Chicana/o literature. Her
presence has haunted the field of Chicana/o studies, which has been
uncomfortable with her exclusion but hesitant to embrace her fully. If
the story of *Mexican Village*'s adaptation into *Sombrero* reveals how the
dominant culture of the United States worked to suppress references to
the revolution in the cultural production of Mexican Americans, it also
reveals how Mexican Americans themselves repressed aspects of their
community as a new political image began to form.

Niggli poses a number of challenges to scholars of Chicana/o literature. She was born in 1910 in the town of Hidalgo, just outside of
Monterrey, Mexico. Niggli's father, Ferdinand Niggli, was a Texan
who was comptroller for several Mexican factories, while her mother,
Goldie Morgan, was a Virginia-born concert violinist. The family fled

into the United States when the revolution reached their town, and they remained itinerant until 1920, when they resettled in Mexico. Niggli would once again leave for the United States in 1925 to pursue her education at Incarnate Word College in San Antonio, Texas. Although Mexican by birth, Niggli lacked the ethnic and class markers that later Mexican Americans would regard as central to their cultural identity. Often, critics view her as a crucial missing link, necessary in comprehending the development of writing by Mexican Americans but denied full membership in that group. Raymund Paredes, in an early assessment of the field, comes closest to fully incorporating Niggli into the canon of Chicano literature when he writes that *Mexican Village* "stands as a major transitional work in the development of Chicano fiction . . . [and] pointed forward to an emerging school of realism, confronting such issues as racism, the oppression of women, and the failure of the Mexican Revolution."[46] In her fine introduction to the University of New Mexico Press's 1994 reissue of *Mexican Village*, María Herrera-Sobek is less comfortable situating Niggli in a Chicana/o or Mexican American literary tradition, according her instead the sympathetic status of "border writer." Herrera-Sobek notes that Niggli's "intense interest in exploring the history, psychology, and folk ways of Mexican people and her consistent inclusion of the above vectors in her works, make her a direct precursor of Mexican American literature."[47] Similarly, in her important study of Latina contributions to U.S. drama and performance, Alicia Arrizón qualifies Niggli's identity by describing Niggli as "a privileged upper-class writer during the 1930s."[48]

The reservations voiced by these critics imply that Mexican American identity is homogeneous and prescribed. But the version of Mexican American identity that these critics are using to evaluate Niggli was in the process of being formed in precisely the moment that Niggli was writing. Arrizón's class-based reservations direct us to some of what is being repressed in *Mexican Village*'s adaptation to the screen and to some of the difficulties literary scholars face when they try to account for Chicanas prior to 1960. While men like Mario Suárez and Luis Pérez wrote fiction at the same time as writers like Niggli, Mena, and Jaramillo, it is important to note that fiction was one of a limited number of vehicles for the expression of Mexican American women's thought. To publish before the 1960s, however, a Mexican American woman had not only to possess an education but also the means to secure a publisher. Therefore, all of them came from middle- or upper-middle-class backgrounds. As working-class concerns grew to take precedence in the Chicano movement and in the institutionalization of Chicano studies in universities, scholars disidentified with these non-working-class writers, even as they found themselves occupying a social position that increasingly mirrored that of these disavowed figures.

Certainly part of this disavowal is attributable to the cultural nationalism that Chicano studies inherited from the Chicano movement. At the cusp of the twenty-first century, a postnationalist Chicano studies is in the making. The adaptation of Niggli's *Mexican Village* into the film *Sombrero* forces us to think of Mexican American experience beyond sociological models, to move beyond the simple resistance narratives of the field's nationalist phase, and to recognize that Chicano identity has been and continues to be heterogeneous and fraught with contradictions. In Niggli's Hollywood experience, we see that working-class resistance sometimes worked in concert with the power to which it opposed itself to silence and repress inconsistency or dissent. With recognitions such as the one this case offers, new horizons for thinking about the connections between Mexican American experience and the larger currents of U.S. culture become available.

WILLIAM ORCHARD is completing a Ph.D. in English at the University of Chicago.

YOLANDA PADILLA is assistant professor of English at the University of Pennsylvania. She is currently working on a book that examines the importance of Mexican political and cultural histories for Mexican American literary canons and political projects, especially from the period of the Mexican Revolution to the end of the Chicano Movement. Writers whose work she examines include Maria Cristina Mena, Josephina Niggli, Luis Perez, and Ron Arias.

NOTES

1. See, for example, "Ten Christmas Lists of Ten 'Best,'" *New York Times*, 2 December 1945: BR3. Among the other authors listed alongside Niggli were Sinclair Lewis, James Thurber, E. B. White, and Richard Wright. Betty Smith, author of *A Tree Grows in Brooklyn* (for which Niggli allegedly provided the title), declared, in a *New York Times*, advertisement, that *Mexican Village* was the

"best novel published in the past two years" and asserted that it surpassed the quality of Ernest Hemingway's *For Whom the Bell Tolls*. Display ad 363, *New York Times*, 18 November 1945: 115.

2. Thomas F. Brady, "Metro Will Film 'Mexican Village,'" *New York Times*, 5 June 1951: 49.

3. John Rothwell, "Focus on 'Sombrero' Below the Border," *New York Times*, 28 September 1952: X4.

4. Thomas Pryor, "Metro Schedules 'Mexican Village,'" *New York Times*, 2 September 1952: 19.

5. Bosley Crowthers, "Review of *Sombrero*," *New York Times*, 23 April 1953: 37.

6. Barbara Eberly, interviewed by William Orchard and Yolanda Padilla, Cullowhee, North Carolina, May 20, 2000.

7. See chapter 5, "The 'New Nationalism,' Mexican Style," in George Sánchez's *Becoming Mexican American: Ethnicity, Culture, and Identity in Chicano Los Angeles, 1900–1945* (London: Oxford University Press, 1993).

8. Rosaura Sánchez, "The History of Chicanas: Proposal for a Materialist Perspective," in *Between Borders: Essays on Mexicana/Chicana History*, ed. Adelaida del Castillo (Encino, CA: Floricanto Press, 1990), 13. One notable exception to the erasure of Chicanas in the 1950s is Josephina Fierro de Bright of the Spanish-Speaking Peoples Congress (or "El Congreso"). Her affiliation with the Popular Front and labor causes align her with the ideological aims of the kinds of history Rosaura Sánchez is committed to recuperating. For treatments of Fierro, see Mario T. García, *Mexican Americans: Leadership, Ideology, and Identity, 1930–1960* (New Haven: Yale University Press, 1989), especially chapter 6, "The Popular Front: Josefina Fierro de Bright and the Spanish-Speaking Congress"; and chapter 3, "Anarchy in the U.S.A.: The Mexican Revolution, Labor Radicalism, and the Criminalization of Marijuana," in Curtis Márez, *Drug Wars: The Political Economy of Narcotics* (Minneapolis: University of Minnesota Press, 2004).

9. For one example of this kind of reading, see José David Saldívar and Hector Calderón's introduction to the influential essay collection *Criticism in the Borderlands: Studies in Chicano Literature, Culture, and Ideology* (Durham: Duke University Press, 1991). On the craze for Mexican cultural artifacts in the 1930s and 1940s, see Helen Delpar, *The Enormous Vogue of Things Mexican: Cultural Relations Between the United States and Mexico, 1920–1935* (Tuscaloosa: University of Alabama Press, 1991).

10. The literature is voluminous but begins with Américo Paredes's seminal essay, "The Folk Base of Chicano Literature," in *Modern Chicano Writers: A Collection of Essays*, ed. Joseph Sommers and Tomas Ybarra-Frausto (Englewood Cliffs, NJ: Prentice-Hall, 1979), 4–17.

11. Genaro Padilla, "Imprisoned Narrative? Or Lies, Secrets and Silence in New Mexican Women's Autobiography," in *Criticism in the Borderlands*, 46–7. For more on the U.S. romance with the Southwest in the first half of the twentieth century, see John Chavez, *This Lost Land: The Chicano Image of the Southwest* (Albuquerque: University of New Mexico Press, 1984), 87; and Delpar, *The Enormous Vogue for Things Mexican*.

12. Frederich Koch, "American Folk Drama in the Making," introduction to *American Folk Plays*, ed. Frederich Koch (New York: D. Appleton-Century Company, 1939), xv–xvi.

13. Charles Lummis, *The Land of Poco Tiempo* (New York: New Press, 1897). Cited in Padilla, "Imprisoned Narrative," 45.

14. Richard Brodhead, *Cultures of Letters: Scenes of Reading and Writing in Nineteenth-Century America* (Chicago: University of Chicago Press, 1993), 115–16.

15. On the *letrado* tradition, see Angel Rama, *The Lettered City*, trans. John Charles Chasteen (Durham: Duke University Press, 1996).

16. Indeed, recent reappraisals of local color fiction in the United States have noted its cosmopolitan character and viewed it as instrumental in developing a transnational imaginary within the United States. See, for example, Brad Evans, "Howellsian Chic: The Local Color of Cosmopolitanism," *ELH* 71 (2004): 775–812; and Amy Doherty, "Redefining the Borders of Local Color: María Cristina Mena's Short Stories in *Century Magazine*," in *"The Only Efficient Instrument": American Women Writers and the Periodical*, 1837–1916, ed. Aleta Feinsod Cane and Susan Alves (Iowa City: University of Iowa Press, 2001).

17. *The Carolina Playmakers*. Josephina Niggli Papers, Box 1, Folder 46, Special Collections, Hunter Library, Western Carolina University.

18. Steve Eberly, "Josephina Niggli," *The Arts Journal* (May 1982): 37.

19. Roberto Fernández Retamar, "Carlos Fuentes y la otra novela de la revolución mexicana," *Casas de las Americas* 4:26 (October–November 1964): 123.

20. For example, see Silvia Lorente-Murphy, *Juan Rulfo: Realidad y mito de la revolución mexicana* (Madrid: Editorial Pliegos, 1988), 22.

21. Alan Knight, *The Mexican Revolution: Porfirians, Liberals, and Peasants* (Cambridge: Cambridge University Press, 1986), 2.

22. Alberto Millán Chivite, *El costumbrismo mexicano en las novelas de revolución* (Sevilla: Universidad de Sevilla, 1996), 19.

23. Robert McKee Irwin, *Mexican Masculinities* (Minneapolis: University of Minnesota Press, 2003), 187.

24. Accounts of Cortez and Malintzin abound. The classic—and much contested—account of how this shaped the Mexican national character is Octavio Paz's "Los hijos de la chingada," in *Labyrinth of Solitude*, trans. Lysander Kemp, Yara Milos, and Phillips Belash (New York: Grove Press, 1972), 65–88. Niggli, of course, was very familiar with the Malinche story, incorporating it into her published folk play "Azteca" and innovatively drawing on it in an unpublished historical drama about the Emperor Maximillian entitled "The Fair God."

25. In the national romances of Latin America, Doris Sommer notes, the political is often allegorized in the erotic. Sommer sees the heterosexual romances as "bind[ing] together heterodox constituencies: competing regions, economic interests, races, and religions," diffusing conflict and promoting peaceful resolution (albeit in the form of hegemonic compliance). This romantic peace serves the interest of the *criollos* who lack a genealogical claim to authority in the region (which properly belongs to the indigenous peoples of Latin America) and

instead offers a generative one. Doris Sommer, *Foundational Fictions: The National Romances of Latin America* (Berkeley: University of California Press, 1990), 7, 14–15.

26. Matthew Frye Jacobson, *Whiteness of a Different Color: European Immigrants and the Alchemy of Race* (Cambridge: Harvard University Press, 1998), 17.

27. Quoted in Jacobson, 81. On the turn toward nativism in this period, see also Walter Benn Michaels, *Our America: Nativism, Modernism, and Pluralism* (Durham: Duke University Press, 1997).

28. *Mexican Village* screenplay. Josephina Niggli Papers, Special Collections, Hunter Library, Western Carolina University, 10–11.

29. In the so-called Zoot Suit riots, young Mexican men in California engaged furloughed sailors (epitomes of a brand of Americanness against which the Mexicans would be compared) in a brawl after the sailors made unwanted advances on Mexican women whom they assumed were Tijuana prostitutes. In the Sleepy Lagoon case, zoot suiters were rounded up and put on trial for a gang murder. The case monopolized Los Angeles tabloids for much of the year.

30. Rodolfo Acuña, *Occupied America: A History of Chicanos* (Philadelphia: Harper & Row, 1988), 261.

31. Acuña, 256.

32. Ernesto Chávez, *Mi Raza Primero: Nationalism, Identity, and Insurgency in the Chicano Movement in Los Angeles, 1966–1978* (Berkeley: University of California Press, 2002), 18.

33. Ibid, 16.

34. Seth Fein, "Everyday Forms of Transnational Collaboration: U.S. Film Propaganda in Cold War Mexico," in *Close Encounters of Empire: Writing the Cultural History of U.S.-Latin American Relations*, ed. Gilbert M. Joseph, Catherine C. LeGrand, and Ricardo D. Salvatore (Durham: Duke University Press, 1998), 405.

35. Ibid, 406.

36. Rosaura Revueltas, "Reflections on a Journey," in *Salt of the Earth*, ed. Deborah Silverton Rosenfelt (New York: Feminist Press, 1978), 174, 176.

37. Curtis Márez, "Subaltern Soundtracks: Mexican Immigrants and the Making of Hollywood Cinema," *Aztlán* 29 (2004): 72 ff.

38. Joseph Spielberg, "Humor in Mexican American *Palomilla*: Some Historical, Social, and Psychological Implications," *Revista Chicano-Riqueña* 2.3 (1974): 45.

39. As Ilan Stavans notes, "Cantinflas" entered the Spanish dictionary as a verb, "cantiflear," meaning "to talk too much and to say nothing . . . To confuse, to evade reality, to use language as a weapon." Ilan Stavans, *The Hispanic Condition: Reflections on Culture and Identity in America* (New York: Harper Collins, 1995), 129.

40. Greco's performance appears to have been extraordinarily popular. In the print of the film that we were able to locate, a number of the frames during his featured dance were removed, presumably taken as souvenirs by exhibitors and resulting in a "skipping" effect when viewed now. Our thanks to Jacqueline Stewart for pointing out this practice to us.

41. Assimilation was about more than the retention of class privilege; it was also

concerned with retaining racial privilege. Within Mexico and Latin America, "whiteness" has been and continues to be associated with the higher social echelons, while the lower and working classes are seen as "dark," "*indio*," or "black." However, despite their racial and class position prior to arriving in the United States, Mexican immigrants found themselves incorporated into the United States' unfamiliar racial hierarchy, which was divided along the lines of white and black. Given that the United States defined black as consisting of even the smallest drop of African blood, it is not surprising that Mexicans, with their often mixed racial backgrounds compounded by the tincture of foreignness, were quickly racialized and subjected to Jim Crow legislation. In this context, the assimilationist agenda of LULAC was an internalization of U.S. racism, a continuation of Latin American racial thinking, and an attempt to counteract real persecution.

42. For excellent examples of work in this vein, see Vicki Ruiz, *Cannery Women, Cannery Lives: Mexican Women, Unionization, and the California Food Processing Industry, 1930–1950* (Albuquerque: University of New Mexico Press, 1987); and Emma Pérez, *The Decolonial Imaginary: Writing Chicanas into History* (Bloomington: Indiana University Press, 1999).

43. García, *Mexican Americans*, 231–2.

44. Interestingly, Niggli was offered a teaching position at the University of Texas at Austin, but she eventually chose to pursue her Hollywood dream. She would later settle at Western Carolina University after teaching at the University of North Carolina, but her inhabitation of the university environs would occur outside the historical period of García's study.

45. Kirsten Silva Gruesz, "Utopía Latina: *The Ordinary Seaman* in Extraordinary Times," *Modern Fiction Studies* 49 (2003): 56.

46. Raymund Paredes, "The Evolution of Chicano Literature," *MELUS* 5 (1978): 90.

47. María Herrera-Sobek, Introduction to *Mexican Village* by Josephina Niggli (1945; Albuquerque: University of New Mexico Press, 1994), xxi. Sadly, this edition of the novel went out of print just three years after its reissue.

48. Alicia Arrizón, *Latina Performance: Traversing the Stage* (Bloomington: Indiana University Press, 1999), 43. Arrizón begins her consideration of Niggli's writing with this terse description and qualification of Niggli's identity.

ANGELS IN THE HOME AND AT WORK: RUSSIAN WOMEN IN THE KHRUSHCHEV YEARS

NATASHA KOLCHEVSKA

Like the citizens of much of Europe, Russians were confronted with major challenges after World War II. The Soviet Union's staggering wartime losses, especially of men, were compounded by the destruction of many families as a result of Stalin's terror, which began in the mid-1930s and continued until his death in March 1953. Following Nikita Khrushchev's 1956 speech at the Twentieth Communist Party Congress about the criminal excesses of the "cult of personality," Soviet citizens also had to cope with the reality of millions dead or exiled as a result of that cult, as well as the return of the living from decades in the system of "gulags" or labor camps created on Stalin's orders. The 1950s in the Soviet Union were a period of ideological and social anxieties. The "thaw," often mentioned in connection with Khrushchev's liberalization policies, was itself a problematic and unstable phenomenon.[1] Despite some gains made during Khrushchev's years in power, he was more of a tinkerer—a "repairman" as the historian John Thompson has characterized him—than a reformer, which explains the failure of a number of his policies in the spheres of foreign and domestic affairs, including culture. My project will be to examine the transposition of some of these dissonances to the retrospective viewpoint of two different constituencies—the dissident intelligentsia and the rising middle class—as they look back at the 1950s from the vantage point of the Brezhnev era.

How does the first post-Stalin decade add up for women? Recent years have seen a surge of interest in the status of women in the Soviet Union under Khrushchev, and out of these path-breaking studies some critical facts emerge.[2] Mary Buckley has described the tension inherent in this period as one that lay "between ideological claims about the successful liberation of women under Soviet socialism and more realistic observations about women's lives" (quoted in Ilic, 1). Indeed, typically those lives diverged mightily from the glossy representations of Stalin-

[*WSQ: Women's Studies Quarterly* 33: 3 & 4 (Fall/Winter 2005)]

ist iconography. True, education for women, particularly higher and specialized education, improved, especially in the growing urban areas.[3] Yet it was also true that the war produced a critical demographic imbalance, with women significantly outnumbering men well into the 1960s. As late as 1959, almost fifteen years after the end of World War II, there were 20 million more women than men in the Soviet Union, in a population of about 210 million, creating a ratio of about 55 to 45. As Barbara Clements speculates, "the unenviable situation of unmarried women may have intensified the value Soviet women in general attached to marriage" (276). Similarly, while women's achievements were increasingly recognized and celebrated, as Melanie Ilic points out, there was also a widespread tendency to denigrate them, at home if not abroad (19).

As major contributors to the country's reconstruction effort, women were asked to perform equally at home and in public life, to both rebuild the home and family and to step into the workplace as necessary. Even before the change in leadership in 1953, living standards, especially in urban areas, were beginning to improve. When Khrushchev came to power, he addressed the severe postwar housing shortage by initiating a major push in residential construction, which produced new building projects notable for their numbers and scale if not for their quality. After decades of emphasis on the heavy industrial sector, by the late 1950s the supply of consumer goods also slowly improved, although prices were high and quality low.

Women, many of them moving from the countryside, came into the labor market in ever larger numbers, but the bulk of these new workers entered, and remained, in low-paying manual and service jobs. Often forced to give up the more challenging work they had done in wartime Russia, women were placed at the center of ambivalent Khrushchevian policies aimed at reestablishing domestic "normalcy" while also being expected to play a prominent role in the public sphere, for example, in workplace unions and in political and social organizations. In 1956, women constituted 45 percent of the Soviet labor force and were essential workers in education, healthcare, trade, public services, and light industry. Even so, the term "glass ceiling" could have been invented for Russian women in the postwar era, since they rose to top management or professional positions in only a few sectors of the economy (for example, the textile industry, the health-care sector, and education).

Restrictive Stalin-era social policies were also reversed: abortion was relegalized in 1955, divorce once again became more accessible, and longer leaves for pregnancy and childbirth were introduced. *Zhensovety* or "women's councils," eliminated in 1930 with Stalin's declaration that the "woman question" had been solved, were revived in the late 1950s and charged with improving services for women (Ilic 18). These gains were partial, however, and, in spite of official rhetoric, improvements in the quality and quantity of both social services and essential consumer goods were often mitigated by increased expectations of women's participation in public life and the regime's continued privileging of production over consumption (Reid, "Cold War," 216). Working mothers, both married and single, complained that daycare facilities did not match work schedules; traditional Russian mores expected women to spend more time on domestic and child-rearing duties; social services could not keep up with the effects on family life of men's alcoholism and domestic violence; and single women continued to suffer discrimination in housing distribution and the workplace. Hence, by the end of the decade, the "double burden" that continues to plague Soviet women beyond the existence of the Soviet Union itself was well entrenched, although not widely acknowledged. That topic would have to wait to be addressed by writers such as Elena Grekova and Natalia Baranskaia in the 1960s.

The Russian word *fortochka*, which describes a small hinged windowpane used to air out homes without fully opening a window, has been popularly used to describe the Khrushchev era. It is an apt image: the 1950s did allow a breath of fresh air into cultural and intellectual debates without permitting fundamental change, which would have to wait until the Gorbachev years. The whiff of domesticity is also apt because, as part of the rejection of official gender equality that had characterized the immediate postrevolutionary generation, concerns traditionally gendered as "women's"—domesticity, personal relationships, fashion, and grooming—now came to play a more prominent role in both the economic and cultural manifestations of an overall shift in emphasis to private life.[4] At the highest level, this is apparent from Khrushchev's shift, at least rhetorically, toward the importance of consumer goods and housing and away from heavy industry. This was most publicly (and at times comically) symbolized by the so-called Kitchen Debate that took place between Vice President Richard Nixon and

Khrushchev in a model kitchen at the American National Exhibition, a showcase for the American lifestyle—with an emphasis on consumerism—that came to Moscow in 1959.[5]

In a traditionally patriarchal society such as Russia's, revolutionary ideals and policies concerning gender equality continued their uneasy equipoise with deep-seated misogynist attitudes, and it should come as no surprise that such a heavily gendered discourse as everyday life provoked deep ambivalence in both official ideology and popular thinking.[6] The Khrushchev years saw a vigorous debate in both social and cultural spheres on this perennial question. Melanie Ilic points out that women were expected "to be fully involved in both the productive economy and the domestic sphere" (20), but this idea was countered in official speeches and debates in the popular press by the idea that women were uniquely suited to taking care of domestic and maternal matters.[7] Susan Reid provides this illuminating summary of the tension between official words and underlying assumptions:

> Far from challenging traditional gender roles, Khrushchev's speeches and policies from 1958 actually reconfirmed female responsibility for the home as the natural order of things. Despite the party's ideological commitment to equality, a number of studies have shown that it and its agents maintained stereotypical notions of gender difference: they assumed that women's biological role as mothers determined their primary responsibilities for *byt* [everyday life], and attributed to women a lower level of political consciousness and rationality. ("Women in the Home," 160)

This traditional view of women's roles is complicated by the Soviet Union's Stalinist past. Katerina Clark and others have pointed out that high Stalinism replaced the biological or nuclear family with a larger, collective one, headed by Stalin as the "wise father" of the "great family of the Soviet state."[8] In the post-Stalin years, this now-discredited model was replaced by another, headed by a mother who would not only create and nurture a healthy family but also instill in that family *kul'turnost'*—that is, the values of hygiene, etiquette, taste, and some knowledge of high culture.[9] And yet, as Catriona Kelly points out, the paradox here is that official ideology continued to assume that women, like men, were also still servants of the state (343), so that family and domestic concerns continued to defer to the official ideology that deemed these to be of secondary importance. Eventually, this would result in the expectation that women be exemplary performers both at home and in the public sphere. Indeed, as Reid, summarizing a 1959 debate that was published in *Literaturnaya gazeta*, a newspaper widely read by the intelligentsia, continues: "the gendered dichotomy of public production and private housework was not symmetrical: Khrushchevism continued to insist that a person might only become a fully valid individual through active participation in productive labour in the public sphere. . . . [and] attention to "women's" issues did not increase their opportunities for authority or real political power" ("Women in the Home," 160).

In what follows, I will examine how these conflicting discourses were internalized by two constituencies often portrayed in opposition to one another—the intelligentsia (traditionally, Russia's arbiters of high culture and moral standards) and the rising middle class of the later Khrushchev years—and their intersections as creators and consumers of cultural values.

I intend to show that a dissident artist could incorporate *kul'turnost'* and consumption into narratives that were critical of the Soviet system and, conversely, that a mainstream director could use the dual discourses of domestic mastery and public competence to reassure his audience that Soviet society was progressing toward middle-class affluence and good taste. The first case is Eugenia Ginzburg, author of *Journey into the Whirlwind*, a two-volume memoir of her years spent in the Gulag and in exile between the 1930s and the 1950s that became one of the most widely circulated memoirs to come out of dissident circles in the post-Khrushchev decades. The second is Vladimir Menshov, whose hugely popular 1979 film, *Moscow Doesn't Believe in Tears*, opened to great popular (if not critical) acclaim and has been regarded by several generations of Russians as a classic of Soviet filmmaking. We are dealing with texts that are vastly different in provenance and intention. Nonetheless, as I will argue, the two converge on several critical issues: the prominence they give to material life; the situation of their characters within the negotiation of private versus public life; and, somewhat surprisingly, the conclusion they both come to, a conclusion shared by the state, that the happy, fulfilled urban Soviet woman—the focus of attention in most cultural arenas in the 1950s and 1960s—whether of the intelligentsia or the professional class, will successfully, meaningfully, and happily merge the two. My approach to these issues is informed not only by historical studies of women and consumption in the Soviet period, but also by the theoretical work of scholars such as Bill Brown and Naomi Schor on the intersections of literary and material culture. Brown's recent study of how the distribution and consumption of things came to define a national American culture at the beginning of the twentieth century has helped me understand how the subjects of my analysis foreground objects to think about themselves in both literary and visual genres. Similarly, Schor's interrogation of the liminal spaces between the everyday and the sublime, between the domestic sphere traditionally assigned to women, with its concomitant repetitive rituals, and the masculine public sphere, with its promise of adventure, risk, and growth, in postcard representations of Paris in 1900, is germane to my own inquiry. As I suggest by my choice of *Journey into the Whirlwind* and *Moscow Doesn't Believe in Tears*, whatever their overt ideological stances in regard to political or gender discourses, these spaces were often filled in the immediate post-Stalin years by popular forms that attempted to reclaim a middle ground that followed neither official Soviet ideologies regarding the transformation of social and gender norms, nor traditional bourgeois Western models of the same.

RETURN FROM THE GULAG

The (non)publishing history of Eugenia Ginzburg's memoir is itself a reflection of the instability of the Khrushchevian thaws. Ginzburg initially began to write the first volume in the early 1950s as a memoir for her younger son, from whom she had been separated for almost twelve years. By 1956–57, that memoir had been rewritten and was circulating in dissident circles but, in spite of Khrushchev's recent "secret speech" denouncing Stalin's cult of personality, it was rejected by the government-controlled publishing houses. The volume recounts her arrest and arrival in the Gulag, as Ginzburg focuses on the gradual realization that she was caught in an illogical world. Nonetheless, she remains a loyal Communist and limits her harshest criticisms to "the evil serpent," that is, Stalin. Ginzburg tried again, with no better luck, in the wake of a reactivation of de-Stalinization policies in the early 1960s (the "third thaw"). Although several works about the Gulag did see the light of day, Ginzburg's was not one of them. Khrushchev was dismissed as First

Secretary of the Communist Party in 1964 and, as erratic liberalization gave way to Brezhnevian repression, it soon became clear that the *fortochka* for publicly examining the Stalinist era had closed. In 1967, as a result of the publication of a smuggled manuscript of the first volume, Ginzburg was expelled from the Soviet Union of Writers, which she had only recently been allowed to rejoin. In light of that reversal, she began revising the second part of her memoir, which continued with the tale of her incarceration, but also included her years of exile, rearrest, a second period of exile in the early 1950s, and finally her return to Moscow in 1956. In this volume her earlier bewilderment is largely replaced by hostility, scorn, and at times defiance. Neither volume was published in the Soviet Union until 1990.[10]

The differences between Ginzburg's two volumes—which appeared a decade or more apart—can be used as a bellwether of the mood among the intelligentsia about the promises (and disappointments) of Khrushchev's liberalization policies and their aftermath. As Ginzburg's son, the writer Vasily Aksenov, has recently observed: "When mama was writing her first volume. . . . she wanted to show that the real Communists had won, that they had kept the faith, that we would arrive at a new, brighter communism, [but] she was completely isolated. There was no one around her, she wasn't yet surrounded by a literary [or dissident] milieu. . . . When she started writing the second volume, the boundaries of the permitted had been expanded much wider [and] she herself had changed" (9).

What is of interest for my purposes is the way that the second volume merges a much more intensive level of denunciation of Stalin's crimes than the first with the author's reestablishment of a "normal" life and, eventually, of a public persona in the dissident and reformist intelligentsia communities. Ginzburg structures her two volumes of memoirs as a *bildungsroman* in which her young heroine matures during the almost twenty years that she spends in harsh Siberian labor camps and exile. Eugenia is transformed from an immature and unquestioning believer in Stalin's new order—and a beneficiary of its policies toward women and the new professional class of the 1930s—into a conscious, courageous, and ethical citizen. The distinctiveness of Ginzburg's voice lies in its two dominant components: the truth-telling, high moral position characteristic of the Russian intelligentsia; and the reconstitution of a second, more authentic family as a metonymy for the "new"

Eugenia who emerges from the experiences of incarceration and exile. Weaving together images and metaphors of domesticity and family, as well as abundant citations from a range of cultural materials—high, middle, and low—Ginzburg negotiates between nineteenth-century notions of intelligentsia women's "culturizing" mission and her own need, as a one-time consumer cut off from that material world by her address, to reestablish herself in the world of things, and not only the world of ideas that had been the old intelligentsia model.[11]

Sociologists and literary critics have both commented on the valorizing of the private sphere in the post-Stalin public domains of culture and style. Beth Holmgren sums up Ginzburg's generation well: "[T]hese women both reflect and help facilitate the movement of post-Stalin Soviet society away from public life and specific political commitment to the private sphere, personal attachments, and individual fulfillment. They replace the icon of the dedicated revolutionary with a more capacious ideal: . . . one is now 'obliged to behave in such a way as to remain a human being'"(Holmgren, "For the Good," 132). In the first volume, Ginzburg had already used a variety of specific objects and symbols from her prearrest life—from imported Ford automobiles to elite resorts and gold watches—to establish her own turn from ascetic Communist models of the 1920s to the middle-class model of high Stalinism in the 1930s.[12]

In the second volume, Ginzburg uses her (understandable) desire for a "normal" post–labor camp life not only to signal the internal shift in her consciousness but also to introduce Khrushchevian populist ideals aimed at improving everyday life. In the way that only autobiographical literature can do, she combines biographical fact with a careful selection of details and objects to relate how her new, more "conscious" life is not only morally stronger but also more aesthetic. Even while in the Gulag and in exile, Ginzburg had put together her meager resources to create ever more domestic nests. By 1955, although she is still in the remote reaches of Kolyma, the vast area of far eastern Siberia where most of the camps were located, she has re-created a family, a home, and a career. Finally, when she is allowed to return to Moscow in 1956, she focuses on the signposts of everyday life and femininity to mark her full return to normality.

Similarly, Ginzburg uses the creation of a more authentic, if more traditional, marriage with children (her biological son and a daughter she adopted while she was in exile) to show the shift away from the two previous dominant relationship modalities in her life. The first of these is her first marriage to a prominent Communist functionary, which is vertical and seemingly revolves around ideological principles and a comfortable lifestyle rather than love. The second consists of the sister-hood that she finds with her fellow inmates in the Gulag. Her move away from that all-woman community, both in prison and in exile, which had sustained her through her "unfree" life, is signified by a third modality, a perfect marriage founded on love, shared suffering, and a higher state of consciousness. Echoing tropes found in mainstream films such as the hugely popular 1957 war film *The Cranes Are Flying*, Ginzburg's memoir parallels what Alexander Prokhorov has called "the dominant narrative of homefront melodrama during the Thaw: the reconstitution of the nuclear family around the trauma of irrecoverable loss generated by war"(214). For Ginzburg, that wartime loss (of her older son, who dies during the siege of Leningrad), is, of course, adumbrated by the losses experienced in the Gulag.

To a much greater extent than was true of her ascetic nineteenth-century predecessors from the intelligentsia, Ginzburg's "culturizing" mission—the project she undertakes to inform her fellow citizens of the Gulag's injustices—always runs in tandem with her attention to her own everyday and personal needs. While earlier bluestocking and revolutionary sisters such as those who laid the groundwork for and participated in the Russian Revolution minimized traditional family and aesthetic values, Ginzburg uses them to mark her return to freedom and "normalcy." After her release from the last of a series of labor camps, for example, she welcomes the comforts of home and femininity that have not been hers for more than ten years:

> At the seventy-second kilometer [from that camp] [my dri-ver's] pal and his educated manicurist wife greeted us with the warmth one so often encounters among people who, after being wanderers on the face of the earth for so many long years, have finally settled down in their own little house. We were treated to homemade cloudberry pie. They filled a tub with boiling water for me, and I enjoyed a good soak that enabled me to get off all the dirt of the central highway. When my driver told our hosts of how upset I had been by having my

fingerprints taken, the manicurist exclaimed: . . . "Have a real good scrub at those hands of yours. Then I'll give you a manicure that will take the wind out of your enemies. When you get to Magadan they won't be able to tell you from the colonel's wife." (II, 201)

Once she does get to Magadan, the major transit center for convicts to and from the labor camps, where Ginzburg spent the remaining years of her exile (except for a two-year period of rearrest), it turns out to be a place of considerable postwar, post-Gulag enterprise. In an ironic touch, Ginzburg's first job is in the workshop of her closest friend, Julia, where she makes that quintessential item of Soviet middle-class consumerism—lampshades. Those lampshades, as both Vera Dunham and, more recently, Svetlana Boym have convincingly demonstrated, epitomized the material universe of the middle-class Soviet citizen in the postwar years. Dunham's description of the significance of everyday domestic objects in her exegesis of middle-class values in mainstream Stalinist culture could well apply to Ginzburg's use of these as well:

Often objects speak much more eloquently than people. . . . A phantasmagoric profusion of objects came not only to form the background to [postwar Stalin-era] stories, but began to play an important role. The material universe of the Soviet citizen, his house, furnishings, personal possessions, acquired its own life and began to express spiritual values. . . . A hoard of objects began to mean happiness in terms of the new sophistication, the new kulturnost. . . . The vast tacit task of deheroization and deproletarianizing signified that the postwar ideal was for the individual to become concerned with rounded-out, integral, domestic happiness. (37)

What is of interest here is Ginzburg's adoption of this mainstream imagery to document her own journey out of the Gulag as one of Stalin's victims. While references to a range of cultural texts (literary, musical, folkloric) are widespread throughout her memoir, unlike in the first volume, where her cultural heritage—and steely will—were *all* that she had to fight against her motiveless imprisonment, in the second volume of her memoir it is this foregrounding of domestic, familial, and traditionally feminist concerns that predominates. Although she was a committed Communist who wrote her memoir in the hope of reforming the party, there is a shift in the relative weight in Ginzburg's narrative from condemning Stalinist abuses to documenting the concrete changes in her personal and private life. Tellingly, she notes the end of her nomadic existence through numberless Gulags with an image of domestic stabilization. In 1955, Ginzburg moves her reconstituted family into a "two-story wooden house [that] seemed to us like the palace of Versailles." While it is true that, in a bow to the realities of housing shortages, they must share their apartment (although "there were only two other families"), Ginzburg describes her new accommodations using the "estrangement" trope much favored by Russian writers such as Tolstoy and Formalist critics alike:

> The new apartment had a good kitchen, a bathroom, and a heated lavatory. Not daring to believe our own eyes, Anton [her new husband] and I tried out the taps in the bathroom and gingerly fingered the glazed tiles of the kitchen stove. We listened to the lavatory flush as though it were a signal from the other world: we had seen all sorts of things in the last few decades, but a lavatory with all modern conveniences was emphatically not among them.
>
> The final improbable miracle of miracles was the appearance of a telephone on our table. (II, 393)

Soon after receiving this apartment, in the next step in her rehabilitation, Ginzburg is allowed to return to Moscow for the first time in eighteen years. Bad weather causes a delay in the Siberian city of Irkutsk, and our Cinderella-like heroine describes a night spent in the hotel there:

> Its public rooms were of the sort you could only associate with Count Frederick and Countess Elvira in one of the tales of high romance so beloved of the criminal riffraff. Massive, wine-colored velvet curtains hung from golden rings right down to the gleaming varnished floors. Crystal chandeliers tinkled softly. In a luxuriously upholstered armchair sat an elaborately dressed manager, busy with her paperwork. (II,400)

When, after considerable protest, they are finally given a room, Ginzburg wonders: "Could these enormous mirrors, these satin covers, this monumental wardrobe, be meant for us?" (II, 401).

Ginzburg most likely had multiple intentions for this scene: these objects strike her as coming from another planet, and they reinforce the fairy-tale quality of her memoir, but she also observes with anger that the rooms were reserved for foreign (Chinese) visitors who were delayed because of the weather. Nonetheless, as in Dunham's paradigm, the objects move to the forefront while the criticism moves *sub rosa*.

The book's final scene describes Ginzburg's return to Moscow ("my Mars, my unattainable planet!"). Again, she uses the imagery of everyday life, in its positive and negative developments, to elaborate her sense of estrangement from the birthplace she had not been allowed to visit, much less live in, for so many years. She rents a room from a "rapacious" landlady—clearly a sign of new small-scale economic entrepreneurship in the domestic sector unthinkable under Stalin—which, though a damp semibasement, has a refrigerator and television (in 1955!). Then, in a Proustian gesture, she goes to an old haunt, the Lily of the Valley Café, and eats *pirozhki* (meat pies) that taste the same as they did twenty years ago. A young man and woman, strangers, recognizing her as a returnee from "those" places, leave the café, only to return to present her with "two bunches of gladioli wrapped in cellophane." These two bunches of common flowers—a traditional gesture of either respect or commemoration—come to represent for our middle-aged protagonist her own mini-thaw, an epiphany: "[They] were the first evidence that not everyone, by no means everyone, had believed in the great lie." She proceeds to quote from Evgeni Evtushenko, a young poet just beginning his hugely popular career: "Fears are dying off in Russia," she recites (II, 407). Other everyday and familial images capture the often conflicting emotions of this ex-prisoner's return to normalcy. A sense of estrangement from her biological sister (by comparison with all of the "sisters" who had shared her cells and other cramped quarters) is balanced by the everyday life that she has walked back into. In the narrative's final scene, having overcome the panic of not finding her "rehabilitation" certificate, which reinstates her rights as a citizen, and having almost been run down by a truck driver on a busy central Moscow street, she pauses:

> Completely drained of strength, I made my way to the foun-
> tain outside the entrance to the Arbat subway station and
> collapsed on a bench, to rest with the old men bowed over
> their prerevolutionary walking sticks and the mothers of chil-
> dren playing ball beside the fountain. I took out my certificate
> and started reading it with total concentration. . . . "The case is
> closed in the absence of any *corpus delicti.*"

She reads on, ironizing about the stated reasons for her release now. "It
had taken less than twenty years for the Supreme Court to pronounce
magisterially: no *corpus delicti.*" But this cogitation is brought to an end
by a perfectly "normal" scene of everyday life and reintegration, when
two people, clearly not Muscovites, approach her, asking for directions:

> "Would you please tell us, young lady, how we get to the
> Kazan station?" This apparently trivial happening immediately
> put me in a good mood again. For one thing, they had called me
> "young lady." So, even in my late fifties, I didn't look like an
> old woman.

The final scene is even more resonant of the pleasures of everyday life:

> I remembered that while I was rummaging in my handbag,
> looking for my mislaid certificate, I had seen in the depths a
> square of chocolate. I ate it with relish and rose resolutely from
> the bench. I looked around me. The well-fed Moscow pigeons,
> which had not yet gone out of fashion, were deep in conversa-
> tion with one another. A little girl in a red dress was busily
> skipping. A constant stream of people was constantly pouring
> into the subway. I was about to join them. I would merge with
> the general stream. Could I really do that? I was just like
> everyone else! (II, 415)

Without diminishing the centrality of Ginzburg's memoir as a critique
of what she calls the Stalinist "lunacy" (I, 339 and elsewhere) of Soviet
aggressionist policies and of the vagaries of Soviet cultural politics, I
would suggest that we should consider how this critique is grounded in
both discourses of ideological ideals and the culture of "normal" every-

day human life. For Ginzburg, mundane, persistent patterns of life (little girls skipping, city pigeons flocking) mix with the new realities of post-Stalin life, including the expansion of consumer goods and living situations. The ability of her narrative, then, to bridge the gap between traditional intelligentsia discourses grounded in the "idea" and those outside of that elite circle is very much a part of that "middle ground" that I would argue characterized important, but also widely read, texts in the Khrushchev period. Here I would agree with Holmgren's assessment.

> Many writers of both sexes in the postwar period produced an effective blend of the highbrow (strong political/social message, sophisticated writing style, complex characterizations) with what we have come to term, often pejoratively, the middle-brow—a literature that furnishes . . . empathetic identification and vaguely consumerist values situated between ultra-formula-ic commercial fiction and a too rarified elite art. (Holmgren, "Writing," 233)

Moreover, I would suggest that, as a woman author, Ginzburg was not restricted by the trappings of high aesthetic movements such as modernism, and therefore was able to adopt this middle ground to her own oppositional and aesthetic purposes.

THE TURN TO CONSUMERISM

Catriona Kelly has written, "If one can speak about a 'Great Retreat' [from revolutionary values], this occurred not in the Stalin era but in the post-Stalin era. . . . [when] the quantity of possessions that were deemed appropriate in the Soviet 'cultured person,' began to expand out of all recognition" (205). Ginzburg epitomized for many (and regarded herself as a member of) the cultural elite, and in that spirit she took on the culturizing and moralizing mission that the Russian intelligentsia had traditionally adopted as its own. However, in her autobiographical reconstruction of the 1950s, we see that the culturizing model had begun to incorporate the discourses of everyday life and consumerism. An analysis of Vladimir Menshov's *Moscow Doesn't Believe in Tears* will help us understand how these values were amplified in one of the most prominent mainstream cultural artifacts of the post-Stalin period.

In contradistinction to Ginzburg's oppositionist agenda, *Moscow* is "a slice of officially sponsored social history . . . that celebrates the increasing affluence and middle-class lifestyles of Muscovites over two decades."[13] There is no question that the movie is a glossy soap opera with many of the weaknesses of the genre, as both Russian and Western critics have observed. But *Moscow*, the last and biggest of a series of *zhenskie fil'my* (women's films) that appeared in the 1970s, was not only popular, but, as I will argue, culturally significant. Not only does it convey the ideological stresses between official policy and reality, but it also reflects the de facto concern of postwar Russian citizens less with ideology than with career and possessions.[14] Although she is analyzing the prerevolutionary period, Louise McReynolds's observation is pertinent to the period under discussion as well: "By manipulating familiar cultural categories, Russia's silver screen melodramas encouraged their audiences to reflect on social and political change. The movies problematized real choices by exaggerating them, thus allowing for identification but also providing the safety of distance" (129).

The agenda of this Cinderella story that glorifies private life is apparent from the opening scene. In a long aerial tracking shot of Moscow, it is not Red Square or other official buildings that are the focus, but rather Khrushchev- and Brezhnev-era apartment buildings. Indeed, as the title suggests, in this film about urban life, housing in its various forms and uses is central to Menshov's narrative. Like Ginzburg's memoir, *Moscow* also takes the form of a *bildungsroman*. Menshov himself was born in 1939, which makes him a contemporary of his young cinematic heroines. *Moscow* consists of two approximately equal parts, the first of which, as Gillespie recognizes, is a parodic continuation of Anton Chekhov's *Three Sisters*. Unlike those forlorn late capitalist heroines with their unrequited dream of moving "to Moscow!," these three young provincial girls have actually made the move and are pursuing their varied but related ambitions. The movie picks them up in 1958, when the three—Katia, Liudmila, and Tonia—have been sharing a room in a worker's dorm as they work full time at low-skilled jobs: Katia in a factory, Liudmila in a commercial bakery, and Tonia as a journeyman painter. Katia, the most ambitious of the three, hopes to get into medical school, but we meet her just as she has learned that she has not passed the entrance exams. The ambitions of the other two are far more traditional; Liudmila repeatedly parks herself where she is most likely to meet an eligible husband, and Tonia fairly quickly marries a man similar to her in education and aspirations. The second half of the film fast-forwards twenty years, and we see that Liudmila's marriage to a popular hockey player has fallen apart (and her now ex-husband has become an alcoholic). Tonia's marriage has, predictably, turned out to be quite stable: in a telling comment on urban versus rural trade-offs, she has moved to the country and produced three sons. Katia has risen, rather improbably, to be the director of her factory and a member of the Moscow city council, and she and her daughter (the fruit of a one-night stand with an attractive but undependable television cameraman) live a comfortable, but not quite satisfying, life together. That satisfaction comes in the film's final extended episode, with the sudden appearance of a serious love interest in her life in the guise of the enlightened proletarian metalworker, Gosha.

Here we encounter the family melodrama that Prokhorov has identified as "the preeminent cinematic form during Khrushchev's thaw" (208). Moreover, as a result of the availability after World War II of captured American films, by the 1970s the Soviet film industry was quite familiar with Hollywood classics, including such icons of the genre as *Imitation of Life, Stella Dallas*, and *Mildred Pierce*. Thus *Moscow* has two narrative centers: the sisterhood that survives misunderstandings and marriages, and the rearticulation of the family melodrama that was a commonplace, in many variants, of both Stalinist and thaw literature.

Moscow's visual memory of the 1950s, the way that it uses what Louise McReynolds has called the "world of *things*" (1)—of housing, furniture, clothing, hairstyles, and consumer goods—to communicate very directly the changes and *bildung* going on in the heroines' lives, is illuminating Far more than the movie's often banal dialogue and the Hollywood values of its *mise-en-scène, Moscow* speaks through its visual (and sound) imagery, providing a wealth of telling details about Soviet life under Khrushchev for its audience to reflect on and identify with. The housing crunch forces the three women into a tight living situation, but their dorm room has been so thoroughly feminized that there is little similarity between this room and a typical (male) worker's dorm of the 1920s or, for that matter, the men's dorm that we see in *Little Vera*, another melodrama of Soviet youth, made ten years later in the much harsher light of *glasnost'*. The familiar attributes of Stalin-era domestication—the communal kitchen, the potted plants, the orange lampshade, the screen idols' pictures on the walls—all appear, but so does a new level of consumer aspiration.

Liudmila, the extravagantly accessorized social climber with big hair, wears a brightly colored, often checkered or polka-dotted new dress for every occasion and has a penchant for strawberry facial masques. The flamboyant and pleasantly scheming Liudmila is the movie's most effective vehicle for examining the tension between consumerism and its critique, as well as Menshov's essentially conventional notions of femininity. It would be a mistake to read her fantasy wardrobe as part of the larger protest begun among urban youth in the late 1950s against "the unitary aesthetic derived from the ideology of collective 'leveling' [that] codified public behavior, concepts of propriety, and thoroughly normative notions about beauty" that Ol'ga Vainshtein discusses in her article on Soviet fashion in this period (66). For example, although Liudmila is a poster child for the protest against the prevailing notion that "a single tone range" was considered the best solution, her sartorial extravagance is not about protest but rather a statement that more color will elicit more recognition from the opposite sex. Moreover, the potential rebellion of Liudmila's appearance is set off against her plumpness, which is emphasized in the movie's second half. Tonia, the least interesting dresser, is neither too fat nor too thin, and she has the most conventional life. Katia, on the other hand, the most appealing and ultimately most rounded character in the movie, is thin and has a limited but professional (subdued and elegant) wardrobe. Mindful of the advice quoted earlier, the mature Katia only wears bright colors as an accent (a dotted blouse, a patterned scarf). Only twice is she seen in anything at all gaudy: when she dons a bright red apron and yellow kerchief in the kitchen of Tonia's house in the country, and in her own home, when the patterned *khalat* (a housecoat that was worn *ad nauseum* at home by Russian women) makes several appearances.

Liudmila is the ultimate consumer in this film, but she is not the only one. In a revealing, if incongruous, sequence, Katia is asked to housesit for an uncle, a professor who lives in an opulent Stalin-era apartment. In a number of critical scenes set in that apartment, which is situated in an ostentatious Stalin-era building in central Moscow, we see the comfortable lifestyle of Stalin's "priviligentsia," or at least that of those who, unlike Ginzburg, managed to escape the Stalinist snare.

As members of a different class, they naturally are marked by the possession of a different set of goods—shelves crammed with books, a grand piano, a large study, and a vacuum cleaner! In one of the film's numerous if veiled misogynist gestures, it is the professor's wife who has a Pekinese dog adorned with a red bow.

But these two—Liudmila and the professor—are not exceptional. Even in 1958, consumerism is omnipresent in this metropolitan setting; our young protagonists stroll in front of well-lit and well-decorated store windows, and potential suitors arrive with cans of caviar and crabmeat. Katia and Liudmila discuss the pros and cons of marriage in terms of the sequencing of appliances a married couple is likely to procure.[15] However, the most pervasive marker of a newly consuming class is the television, which is seen and discussed on a number of occasions, as it appears in every desirable home to which our heroines aspire. The film's ambivalent attitude toward this premium consumer product—and sign of technological advancement par excellence—is most evident in its connection with the one true cad in the film, Katia's erstwhile beau, Rodion (who, following the late 1950s fad for all things foreign that the movie also observes, temporarily changes his quintessentially Russian name to Rudolf). Rodion/Rudolf is a television cameraman who seduces Katia by extolling television as the technology of the future ("it's more important than furniture") and, in an apt symmetry, repeats this in the second half of the film, when the roles of the characters have been reversed. Metaphorically apt, too, this cameraman's seduction of Katia, by turning his camera on her while he is filming a national broadcast, is a telling if ambivalent image of TV's seductive power.[16]

Noteworthy too in *Moscow* is the post-Stalin generation's passion for adequate housing. Here the focus is on new construction, and the film itself goes on to repudiate a certain style—that of high-Stalinist "triumphal" architecture, with its "wasteful and atavistic 'excesses' and superficial embellishments" (Reid, "Women in the Home," 177)—in favor of the pale, Khrushchevian *moderne* that increasingly dominated urban skylines in the last thirty years of Soviet power.[17] Boym comments that "the plot develops around various housing displacements, false identities acquired through other people's apartments, envy, love, imposture, and a final resolution of crises, including the housing crisis" (137). These very homes—the workers' dorm and the professor's apartment from the 1950s and Katia's spacious 1970s apartment, each with its own distinctive style that offers an unambiguous commentary on the period and ambitions of its inhabitants—would have resonated with the movie's Soviet viewers. These viewers could—and I would argue *did*—see the transition from the clutter and shoddiness of the first space and the ostentatiousness of the second to Katia's orderly and restrained space as a reflection on her maturation to consciousness as a Soviet woman who is fulfilled in both home and work.

My argument, then, is that these two very different reconstructions of the Khrushchev era share three aspects of womanhood as conceived in the Khrushchev period. The characters of Eugenia and Katia, as constructed in *Whirlwind* and in *Moscow*, are both presented by their authors as exemplary of the synthesis of the "feminine" and the professional. Along her journey from model Communist to Gulag prisoner and deportee, to public witness to the experience of her generation, Eugenia integrated into herself what Holmgren has summarized as the three pillars of the exemplary woman in postwar Soviet society: "the good worker, the good citizen (this can include dissidence), *and* the 'whole woman' (maternal, loving, heterosexual, attentive to home, family and friends, susceptible to romance, and reasonably concerned about her looks" (Holmgren, "Writing" 231, italics in original). The persistence of this tripartite paradigm well into the 1970s and 1980s becomes apparent with *Moscow Doesn't Believe in Tears*. By movie's end, Katia, too, has integrated private and public expectations into her life, and she sits in her modern kitchen with her now complete family—the beautiful daughter and the perfect husband-to-be. Although Katia's was a shorter and easier journey, "normalcy" for both Eugenia and Katia is conceived as rejecting a first, self-absorbed, "false" lover or husband who is symptomatic of the heroine's own early false consciousness. As a more authentic self emerges, its development not only entails the construction of new and more meaningful personal relationships, but also the merging with the dominant discourses articulated by the community with which the author most closely identifies. For Ginzburg, this means coming out into the public sphere with her memoir. For Menshov, it means blending his heroine's public successes with her private life. In both narratives, the emergence of this new heroine is embedded in the details and objects of everyday life, and both heroines successfully negotiate the transition from dislocation and deprivation.

As examples of middlebrow discourse, both Ginzburg's oppositional memoir and Menshov's mainstream soap opera can be seen as an antidote to the dominant discourses of the Russian intelligentsia and its Soviet successors' traditional valorization of the idea over reality, of the ideal over the practical, of the utopian over the ordinary. It is in this light that I would suggest that they create useful lenses through which to examine the 1950s in the Soviet Union.

NATASHA KOLCHEVSKA is professor of Russian and chair of the Department of Foreign Languages and Literatures at the University of New Mexico. In addition to her translation of Sofia Kovalevskaya's nineteenth century novel *Nihilist Girl*, she has published widely on twentieth-century women's writing, especially on writings from the Gulag and the Soviet period.

NOTES

1. Khrushchev's liberalization policies were quite erratic. Historians generally identify three "thaws" during Khrushchev's leadership: 1954–56, 1956–57, and 1961–3, each of which was followed by a "freeze" that paralleled domestic and international policies and crises (the uprisings in Hungary and Poland in 1956, the Cuban missile crisis in 1962). As Helen Segall writes, each thaw "was built on the achievements of one stage and pushed liberalization several steps further in the succeeding stage." It was only during the last thaw that some of the great works of the post-Stalin era (for example, A. Solzhenitsyn's *One Day in the Life of Ivan Denisovich* and Evgeni Evtushenko's long poems *Heirs of Stalin* and *Baby Yar*), were published (469–70).

2. Much of the historical information here has been summarized from three sources: Melanie Ilic, Susan E. Reid, and Lynne Attwood, eds., *Women in the Khrushchev Era* (2004, Barbara Evans Clements, "Later Developments: Trends in Soviet Women's History, 1930 to the Present," in Clements et al. (1991) and Vladimir Shlapentokh, *Public and Private Life of the Soviet People: Changing Values in Post-Stalin Russia* (1989).

3. For more on work and education in this period, see Dodge, "Women in the Professions," 205–24.

4. For a reasoned discussion of earlier models and discussions of gender equality, see Engel, "Transformation vs. Tradition," 135–47.

5. Hixson gives a an excellent overview of what *Time* magazine at the time described as "peacetime diplomacy's most amazing 24 hours" in his *Parting the Curtain*, 178–83. Also see Reid's analysis of the role of the Kitchen Debate in her discussion of the relationship between consumption and *kul'turnost'* in "Cold War in the Kitchen," esp. 223–28.

6. For example, as Reid notes in "Women in the Home," "The withering away of such oppressive bourgeois institutions as the family, along with the absorption of individual interests into those of the collective, was fundamental from the start" (161).

7. In addition to Ilic's excellent overview of the status of women under Khrushchev, in Ilic et al., 5–29, also see Kelly's chapter, "Who Wants to Be a Man? De-Stalinizing Gender, 1954–1992," in her *A History of Russian Women's Writing*, esp. 338–47.

8. Clark, *The Soviet Novel*. For an enlightening discussion of the widely felt need for reimaginings of motherhood in light of the loss of "the great father," see Haynes, "Reconstruction or Reproduction?", 114–30.

9. *Kul'turnost'* has been widely discussed in recent scholarship. Field, in her essay on "Mothers and Fathers and the Problem of Selfishness in the Khrushchev Period," 96–113, captures the highlights of this important concept. For a broader treatment of the topic, see Kelly and Volkov, "Directed Desires," 290–313, esp. 297–304.

10. After first being published in Russian in Italy and Germany, Ginzburg's memoir was translated and published in the United States in two volumes: *Journey into the Whirlwind* (1967) and *Within the Whirlwind* (1981). In the Soviet Union, the complete text was published in Russian as *Krutoi marshrut* (Moscow: Sovetskii pisatel, 1990). Citations refer to the volume and page number of the English translation.

11. As Svetlana Boym perceptively observes, "there is a radical difference between the American dream of private pursuit of happiness in the family home, and the Russian dream, which, at least in the conceptions of Dostoevsky and his great admirer [the philosopher] Berdiaev, consisted of spiritual homelessness and messianic nomadism" (31–2).

12. For more on that compact, see Dunham's groundbreaking study, *In Stalin's Time*. In *The Cultural Front*, Fitzpatrick addresses the major social and power shifts between party and leader that characterized the first decades of the Soviet Union.

13. Gillespie, "Vladimir Men'shov's *Moscow Doesn't Believe in Tears*" (forthcoming). According to Richard Stites, in addition to winning an Academy Award for Best Foreign Film, *Moscow* "sold a record 75 million tickets; in two Moscow cinemas; 1,860,000 people saw it in the two months after its release. . . . Soviet viewers expressed their admiration of the film's closeness to real life and what they saw as honesty and they used the word *dobryi*, kind, to denote what we in the West often call a 'feel-good' movie" (173). Nevertheless, it was dismissed by most Soviet critics and scholars. For example, the father and son émigré academics Dmitry and Vladimir Shlapentokh make no mention of *Moscow* in their 1993 sociological study of Soviet and post-Soviet film.

14. Francoise Navailh discusses several of these "women's films," all directed by men, in "The Image of Women in Contemporary Soviet Cinema." The earliest example of the genre, but with a very different and emancipatory message, is A. Room's 1927 film, *Bed and Sofa*, a film widely known in film circles in the Soviet Union but rarely seen outside of that elite audience.

15. In one of the movie's many small nods to the realities of late-1950s life, soon after this conversation Katia is shown washing her clothes the old-fashioned way—on a washboard. For more on the dissonances between state plans to ease domestic work and actual achievements, see Ilic et al., 10–12.

16. Ironically, the scene in the television studio involves the filming of a routine by two standup comics, a far cry from the hopes raised in "high-culture" reformist discussions of "the potential of television for introducing art to a broader public and rooting out 'vulgar taste.'" See Susan E. Reid's illuminating essay on the discourse of taste during the Khrushchev thaw, "Destalinization and Taste, 1953–1963," 187.

    In the second part of *Moscow*, Menshov again slyly uses a highly desirable object—the automobile—as a narrative device that foreshadows the film's ultimate resolution. As a sign of her professional success, Katia now owns a car, which she drives to a rendezvous with a married lover. Once he appears, he takes over the wheel. In a later scene, Katia limits her driving to trips around town, and she takes the suburban train to Tonia's place in the country. This is necessitated narratologically—she will meet Gosha on the train—but it also says something about women's limitations in the larger world.

17. Reid notes that, "as early as 1957, the *Yearbook* of the *Great Soviet Encyclopedia* included a page of optimistic images of new housing" (189).

WORKS CITED

Boym, Svetlana. *Common Places: Mythologies of Everyday Life in Russia.* Cambridge, MA: Harvard University Press, 1994.

Brown, Bill. *A Sense of Things: The Object Matter of American Literature.* Chicago: University of Chicago Press, 2003.

Clark, Katerina. *The Soviet Novel: History as Ritual.* Chicago: University of Chicago Press, 1983.

Clements, Barbara Evans. "Later Developments: Trends in Soviet Women's History, 1930 to the Present." In B. E. Clements, B. A. Engel, and C. D. Worobec, eds. *Russia's Women: Accommodation, Resistance, Transformation.* Berkeley: University of California Press, 1991, 267–78.

Cooke, Olga M., and Rimma Volynska. "Interview with Vasilii Aksenov." *Canadian-American Slavic Studies* 39.1 (Spring 2005): 9–37.

Dodge, Norton. "Women in the Professions." In D. Atkinson, A. Dallin, and G. W. Lapidus, ed. *Women in Russia.* Stanford: Stanford University Press, 1977, 205–24.

Dunham, Vera. *In Stalin's Time: Middleclass Values in Soviet Fiction.* Cambridge: Cambridge University Press, 1976.

Engel, Barbara A. "Transformation vs. Tradition." In Clements et al., *Russia's Women*: 135–47, 1991.

Field, Deborah. "Mothers and Fathers and the Problem of Selfishness and in the Khrushchev Period." In Ilic et al., *Women in the Khrushchev Era*, 2004, 96–113.

Fitzpatrick, Sheila. *The Cultural Front: Power and Culture in Revolutionary Russia.* Ithaca: Cornell University Press, 1992.

Gillespie, David. "Vladimir Men'shov's *Moscow Doesn't Believe in Tears.*" In ed. Birgit Beumers, ed. *24 Frames: A History of Russian and Soviet Cinema*. Oxford: Berg Publishers, forthcoming.

Ginzburg, Eugenia. *Journey into the Whirlwind*. San Diego: Harcourt Brace Jovanovich, 1967.

———. *Within the Whirlwind*. San Diego: Harcourt Brace Jovanovich, 1981.

Haynes, John. "Reconstruction or Reproduction? Mothers and the Great Soviet Family in Cinema after Stalin." In Ilic et al., eds. *Women in the Khrushchev Era:*, 2004, 114–30.

Hixson, Walter L. *Parting the Curtain: Propaganda, Culture, and the Cold War, 1945–1961*. New York: St. Martin's Griffin, 1997.

Holmgren, B. "For the Good of the Cause: Russian Women's Autobiography in the Twentieth Century." In T. W. Clyman and D. Greene, eds. *Woman Writers in Russian Literature*. Westport: Praeger, 1994, 127–48.

———. "Writing the Female Body Politic (1945–1985)." In A. M. Barker and J. M. Gheith, eds. *A History of Women's Writing in Russia*. Cambridge: Cambridge University Press, 2002, 225–42.

Ilic, Melanie, Susan E. Reid, and Lynne Attwood, eds. *Women in the Khrushchev Era*. New York: Palgrave Macmillan, 2004.

Ilic, Melanie. "Women in the Khrushchev Era: An Overview." In Ilic et al., eds., 2004, 5–28.

Kelly, Catriona. "Who Wants to Be a Man? De-Stalinizing Gender, 1954–1992." In Kelly, *A History of Russian Women's Writing, 1820–1992*. Oxford: Clarendon Press, 1994, 337–96.

Kelly, Catriona, and Vladimir Volkov. "Kul'turnost' and Consumption." In C. Kelly and D. Shepherd, eds. *Constructing Russian Culture in the Age of Revolution, 1881–1940*. Oxford: Oxford University Press, 1998, 290–313.

McReynolds, Louise. "Home Was Never Where the Heart Was." In L. McReynolds and J. Neuberger, eds. *Imitations of Life: Two Centuries of Melodrama in Russia*. Durham: Duke University Press, 2002, 127–51.

McReynolds, Louise, and Joan Neuberger. Introduction to L. McReynolds and Joan Neuberger, eds. *Imitations of Life*, 2002, 1–24.

Navailh, Francoise. "The Image of Women in Contemporary Soviet Cinema." In A. Lawton, ed. *The Red Screen: Politics, Society, Art in Soviet Cinema*. London: Routledge, 2002, 211–30.

Prokhorov, Alexander. "Soviet Family Melodrama of the 1940s and 1950s. From Wait for Me to Cranes are Flying." In L. McReynolds and J. Neuberger, ed. *Imitations of Life*, 2002, 208–31.

Reid, Susan E. "Destalinization and Taste, 1953–1963." *Journal of Design History* 10.2 (1997): 177–201.

———. "Cold War in the Kitchen: Gender and the De-stalinization of Consumer Taste in the Soviet Union under Khrushchev." *Slavic Review* 61.2, (Summer 2002): 211–52.

Schor, Naomi. "Cartes Postales: Representing Paris 1900." *Critical Inquiry* 18 (Winter 1992): 188–241.

Segall, Helen. "The Thaw." In Victor Terras, ed. *Handbook of Russian Literature.* New Haven: Yale University Press, 1985, 469–70.

Shlapentokh, Vladimir. *Public and Private Life of the Soviet People: Changing Values in Post-Stalin Russia.* Oxford: Oxford University Press, 1989.

Shlapentokh, Vladimir, and Dmitry Shlapentokh. *Soviet Cinematography, 1918–1991: Ideological Conflict and Social Reality.* New York: Aldine deGruyter, 1993.

Stites, Richard. *Russian Popular Culture: Entertainment and Society Since 1900.* Cambridge: Cambridge University Press, 1992, 123–47, 173–74.

Thompson, John. *Russia and the Soviet Union: An Historical Introduction.* Boulder: Westview Press, 1990.

Vainshtein, Ol'ga. "Female Fashion, Soviet Style: Bodies of Ideology." In ed. Helena Goscilo and Beth Holmgren, eds. *Russia*Women*Culture.* Bloomington: Indiana University Press, 1996, 64–93.

Woll, Josephine. *Real Images: Soviet Cinema and the Thaw.* London: I. V. Tauris, 2000.

MEXICO IN THE FIFTIES: WOMEN AND CHURCH IN HOLY ALLIANCE

In the 1950s Mexico underwent a powerful process of modernization.
Rapid and sustained economic growth encouraged social mobility, and
the values and attitudes of an urban and industrial society challenged
traditional institutions that still prevailed after more than three decades
of revolutionary struggle and political and economic uncertainty from
1910 to 1940. The impact of internal transformations was compounded
by external influences. By participating in World War II in alliance
with the United States, Mexico became an actor in international
politics and markets, however minor. Thanks to this, during and after
the war Mexican society grew more exposed than ever before to the
outside world. In this context of swift social change and increasing
external influences, internal stabilization was the overriding goal of the
Mexican state. The Catholic Church and the family were called on to
contribute to this end and to the building of postrevolutionary society
within the framework of political authoritarianism. In the ensuing
consolidation of a patriarchal order, women held a key position.

Historically, Mexican women had been excluded from the public
sphere and held in the private realm of home and family life, even if
during the revolution (1910–20) there were a few episodes in which
they had an intense political involvement. At first sight women's
situation in the 1950s was the same as in the past. However, in the Cold
War context the defense of the family became a central political battle
and a common cause for the Church and Mexican women. Traditionally, the continuity of the family had been a private matter, but in the
face of an alleged Communist ideological offensive it became an issue
of public concern around which women were mobilized. In their fight
they created new forms of political participation, and they acquired an
unprecedented sense of political competence. Thus, in spite of the
profoundly conservative nature of their endeavor, this experience

[*WSQ: Women's Studies Quarterly* 33: 3 & 4 (Fall/Winter 2005)]
© 2005 by Soledad Loaeza. All rights reserved.

made women aware of their own potential in the public sphere.

In the fifties the missions of women were to preserve the family against the disintegrating effects of modernization, to restore continuity, and to alleviate the pressures of change. The state, the Catholic Church, the school, and the family all converged in assigning women this role. One of the most significant consequences of this design was the reinforcement of the ties that attached women to the family. Women's identity was residual, the by-product of a relationship: they were mothers, wives, daughters, or sisters. Women were not individuals; they were either part of the mother/child duo or of the family set.

However, the bonds between women and the family were transformed by the features that Cold War ideology took on in the Mexican context. Family depended on women at least as much as women depended on family. The enhancement of the status of the family as a bulwark against Communist influence and as a shield against the disruptive effects of social change brought about a re-evaluation of women's role; this also derived from the need to assure their loyalty to the stabilization of postwar society. Thus, on the one hand, the links between women and the family curtailed women's liberty; but, on the other, the relevance of their social responsibility increased the reach of their influence, even if this did not have a direct political expression.

In *Homeward Bound: American Families in the Cold War Era*, Elaine Tyler May has described the interconnection between post–World War II anti-Communism and the domestic ideology in the United States unmasked by Betty Friedan in *The Feminine Mystique*.[1] A similar interconnection appeared in Mexico. The cooperative relationship that had developed between Mexico and the United States during the war led after 1945 to the appropriation of anti-Communism by Mexican political actors; however, the anti-democratic characteristics of a political system founded on nonparticipation and apathy, and the role of religion and the Catholic Church in the battle against the alleged Communist threat, introduced important variations between the two societies. The ideological and political context of the fifties enabled the Church to restore the moral authority and the social influence it had known in prerevolutionary times. Women were at the center of this pursuit.

Catholic restoration gave the Church control over the definition of feminine identity. By the same token, the notion of the ideal woman prevalent in those years carried a dominant religious component derived from the position the Virgin Mary—or her more vernacular representation, the Virgin of Guadalupe—held as the role model for girls and women, one characterized by passivity, self-denial, abnegation, and chastity. However, it was the Virgin in her maternal role that governed attitudes and symbols sustaining women's status. From the religious component of the feminine ideal disseminated by the Church, women derived moral authority and were attributed a spiritual strength that enhanced their social status in the context of the battle against the forces of moral disintegration[2]—Communism and the great subversive forces of social change. This form of empowerment was the unintended consequence of women's responsibility for the survival of the family in the Cold War context, although as individuals they were practically nonexistent.

This article examines the impact of the Cold War context on Mexico's internal politics and its interconnections with social values and attitudes regarding the position of women, their role within society, and the norms regulating their behavior. It argues that in the postwar years the framework of traditional social conventions was renewed by the appropriation by church and state of Cold War ideology. This strategy had an ambiguous impact on women's status and on their relation to the family; the ties that attached women to the family hardened, but thanks to this development they became protagonists in the vital political battle of the times: the campaign against Communism. The first part of the article describes the reemergence of social conservatism in 1950s Mexico in the context of an accelerated modernizing process that took place under the shadow of U.S. fears of Communist expansion; the second part discusses Catholic restoration in a society that had lived an intense revolutionary experience marked by Jacobinism. (This highlights the significance of the religious component in Mexican anti-Communism.) This is followed by a description of some of the consequences of the role of the Catholic Church in shaping notions and attitudes toward women. Lastly, the article discusses the features of the relationship between women and family and its impact on women's development.

THE COLD WAR, MEXICAN CONSERVATISM, AND PARTIAL MODERNIZATION

Mexican conservatism in the fifties countered some of the effects of the revolution's transforming energies. This regression may be explained by the policies that Mexican governments followed from 1940 on. After almost three decades of upheaval and policy changes, the elite in power opted for moderation and turned its back on the radicalism of the thirties. The international context determined this reorientation. Moderate policies were also in tune with the cooperative relations that developed with the United States, one of the postwar world's two superstars and Mexico's immediate neighbor. The cornerstone of the bilateral relationship after 1946 was anti-Communism. At that time, Washington expected from its allies unequivocal support in the fight against Soviet expansion. Given the actual weakness of Communism in Mexico, a commitment to confront it or to check the growth of related organizations and activities in its territory did not seem to entail meaningful consequences to the country's internal political balances or to its sovereignty.

Despite the fact that Mexico, and the rest of Latin America, was peripheral to the Soviet–American conflict, the country was enveloped by the shadow of the United States' fear of the expansion of Communism. Successive governments adopted the anti-Communist stance as their own and as part of a general strategy of political stabilization that then became a domestic replica of the U.S. international strategy of containment. The Partido Revolucionario Institucional (PRI) was created in 1946, mainly as an instrument to contain protest and opposition and to limit and control independent political participation. From then on, the official party held a virtual monopoly on elective offices and administrative positions. The 1950s were the PRI's golden age.

There were many reasons for the Cold War to be a distant problem for Mexican society. Three of these were geography, the world's strategic equilibrium, and the weakness of Mexican Communists. Nevertheless, the ideological tensions of the Cold War shaped the domestic ideological debate, and the democracy/Communism dichotomy became an ordering structure of alternatives and political identities; this ideological bipolarity was a frame of reference for power struggles in that it also defined the positions and strategies of domestic political actors. By the same token, the period from 1950 to 1960 bears the mark of the Communism/anti-Communism conflict, even when the weakness of the former did not justify the vitality of the latter.

In those years, anti-Communism in Mexico was an undifferentiated mixture of vague concepts involving class conflict, social revolution, atheism, persecution of Catholics, Soviet-American antagonism, military aggression, and political repression. As will be shown, the images of Communism many Mexicans held came from U.S. propaganda, but above all from the Vatican's anti-Communist message. Anti-Communist expressions and demonstrations in Mexico were routine; they were directly present or implicit in presidential addresses, declarations, and speeches, as well as in statements made by union leaders, governors, and members of Congress. The Catholic Church's warnings against the Communist threat helped structure Catholic militancy, but anti-Communism also gave "ideological" substance to business's antistate attitudes. It became a component of the country's nationalism, and as such it contributed to laying the foundations for social cohesion at a time when secularization was eroding traditional values: literacy was on the rise; education was improving; women were entering the labor market; urban life was spreading beyond Mexico City; and migration rates from the country to the city were swelling. In this context, Mexican governments manipulated fears of social revolution to induce political demobilization and to justify their intolerance of almost any form of opposition.

The Mexican experience shows that vigorous anti-Communism could grow even in the absence of a real Communist threat. The influence of Communists in Mexican politics had always been marginal; they were late arrivals to the revolution (the Mexican Communist Party [PCM] was founded in 1919), and they only succeeded in penetrating the unions through alliances with the non-Communist radicals in power. Relations between Mexico and the Soviet Union were relatively friendly but rather vague and concentrated on cultural exchanges, in which, not surprisingly, mostly Mexican Communists took part.

In spite of its limited influence, after 1946 the PCM was a victim of the government's repression when the PRI undertook a profound reorganization of labor unions that included the expulsion and merciless repression of Communists mainly in the railroads' and teachers' unions. In the 1950s the PCM practically disappeared from the map of Mexican politics and became one of the smallest Communist parties in Latin America. In 1946 it numbered 10,000 members; ten years later, only half that.

Hard data, however, did not dispel the fear shared by millions of Mexicans that the Communists were conspiring against their religion, their country, their families, and private property. Many believed that plans to destroy the nation's "true values" were being hatched in the Soviet embassy.

The shapeless shadow of the Communist threat actually served to hide the real sources of apprehension for many Mexicans, which came from two profound social cleavages that could precipitate internal strife and confrontation. These were increasing social inequality and the tensions derived from the opposition between modernity and tradition.

The centralization of power achieved by the PRI after the war added to sustained rates of economic growth and a vigorous process of social mobility, which stimulated the expansion of the middle class. The groups that had benefited from upward mobility were overtaken by optimism and self-confidence and participated enthusiastically in the constructive fever that drove the building of highways, dams, bridges, and power stations, as well as telephone networks, schools, hospitals, and public housing. The elites and the middle class believed that Mexico was on a firm path to the promised land of modernity. However, the benefits of the economic take-off were unequally distributed. The disparities between the poor and the rich were deep and growing. While less than half of the population shared in the advantages of economic growth and modern life, many more lived in misery and desperation. This was a major failure of the Mexican model of development.

This divide was aggravated by a second cleavage that separated Mexican society into two nations: modern and traditional. The first was urban and cosmopolitan; it was mainly built in and around Mexico City, the nation's capital, which had a population of 3 million and was the seat of political power and the industrial, educational, and cultural center of the country. By contrast, the majority of the population (22 million) lived in traditional Mexico, a nation that was predominantly rural and anchored in the past.

These social cleavages were a potential threat to the recently achieved political stability of the country. Therefore, PRI governments sought to prevent the political expression of these differences. In this context, anti-Communism was also instrumental in introducing or imposing political homogeneity and crushing ideological diversity. More generally speaking, anti-Communism was behind the freezing of political participation characteristic of authoritarian Mexico. It was used to slow down social change and to build a new coalition of power with business and the Catholic Church, whose cooperation with succeeding governments was one of the driving forces of social stabilization in the postwar period.

Women's position in these two nations did not reproduce the contradictions between tradition and modernity. Across the country women lived by the codes of a patriarchal order and a paternalist society; in both rural and urban Mexico they were expected to be the center of the family and the keepers of continuity and tradition. In spite of the glaring economic and educational differences that separated the two Mexicos, symbols, values, attitudes, and patterns of behavior concerning women and their role in society were consistent. There were sharp differences between poor and rich women; however, gender was a stronger determinant than class of a person's position in life and of his or her functions within the family and society. Values and attitudes kept women subject to male authority and translated into discriminatory treatment in education and in the labor market, but in the private sphere of the family women held a position of moral authority. The renewed influence of the Church accounts for this uniformity.

MEXICAN ANTI-COMMUNISM: THE MOTOR OF CATHOLIC RESTORATION

The 1950s marked the apogee of Mexican Catholicism. Relations between the state and the Church were harmonious and characterized by close collaboration. Most important, however, was the widespread influence of the Church in Mexican society. Backed by the international context and a domestic political system obsessed with stability and control, the Church was able to recover from the conflicts of the past, to reorganize itself, and to reestablish its position as a stabilizing institution in the midst of social change, exercising a hegemonic influence over religious beliefs as well as over social conventions and values.

This was an unexpected development. In the first half of the twentieth century, the destruction of Church power and influence had been a priority for the revolutionary elite. For them the Catholic Church symbolized the *ancien régime*, and they believed that its social influence was synonymous with obscurantism and ignorance and that from the pulpit, in the classroom, and in confessionals, priests took control of the minds and hearts of children and women. Therefore, revolutionary legislation (1917) sought to destroy the bases of ecclesiastical power, denying juridical status to churches in general and excluding the clergy from educational activities.

The conflict between the Church and the revolutionary state led to a bloody war that lasted three years, la Cristiada (1926–29), in which almost 50,000 people lost their lives. Armed battles were fought in the heart of the country between the regular army and the mostly peasant forces, the Cristeros, who defended the rights of the Church and of Cristo Rey. The Church's whole institutional structure was deeply affected by the closing of churches, monasteries, convents, and schools, as well as by the expulsion of religious orders from the country and the persecution of priests and nuns. During this time, religious ceremonies and the activities of Catholics were clandestine, as was the organization of the entire resistance movement. Finally, in 1929, the Church and the state signed an agreement that ended the conflict. No changes were made to the legislation, but neither was it fully enforced; moreover, constitutional rules regarding the Church were gradually abandoned in practice even if they remained on paper.

The Cristiada was an episode of intense political involvement for many women. During the conflict they were couriers, spies, and uniform and flag seamstresses; they dressed the wounds of Cristero fighters; they played a decisive role in the organization of clandestine networks; they helped priests and nuns who went into hiding; and they arranged secret meetings between bishops and priests and the faithful. In 1928 a nun, Mother Conchita, plotted the murder of President-elect Alvaro Obregón.[3] At times, the engagement of Catholic women in the defense of the Church's rights reached a hysterical pitch. The United States ambassador to Mexico, Dwight S. Morrow (1927–29), who acted as an intermediary in the conflict, complained bitterly of Catholic women who opposed the proposals for resolution and boisterously expressed their antagonism in front of the U.S. embassy in Mexico City.

This experience sustained for years the belief that women were political agents of the Church, and the accusation was used against women's suffrage (which was finally introduced in 1953). These reservations seemed to be well founded: in the 1955 midterm election, in which women voted for the first time, the conservative Partido Accion Nacional (PAN) won more than 30 percent of the vote in Mexico City, doubling the party's share from the previous election.

Thanks to the religious Cold War launched by Pope Pius XII against the Soviet Union in 1945, the *modus vivendi* reached by the state and the Church in Mexico, instead of containing the influence of Catholicism, became a springboard for its restoration in Mexican society.[4] Between 1950 and 1960 many parishes, seminaries, convents, and religious schools were built or rebuilt in Mexico. In the context of rapid population growth (from 1940 to 1960 the Mexican population grew from 16 million to 35 million), the number of Mexicans per priest increased from 3,791 to 5,413.[5] In those same years, the number of priests grew from 4,220 to 6,466 reaching 8,451 in 1968.[6]

The restoration of the Church included an energetic development of lay organizations that remained under tight clerical control and in which women played a leading role. The most powerful of these organizations was Acción Católica Mexicana (ACM), which in 1953 had more than 400,000 members, of whom 80 percent were women. Its membership was comparable only to that of the PRI and the national teachers' union, Sindicato Nacional de Trabajadores de la Educación (SNTE), in which women were also a majority. Private education was, for all practical purposes, in the hands of the Catholic Church; and although these schools educated a minority, mostly the children of the middle classes, they were forming the elites of the future. Catholic organizations provided a solid infrastructure for mobilization that could be activated in times of crisis, as happened in the early 1960s when Catholics organized to oppose the spread of the influence of the Cuban revolution.[7]

The Cristiada had consecrated the Mexican Catholic Church's condition as persecuted and martyred. Hence, in the Cold War context, Mexican Catholics identified themselves almost automatically with the struggle of the Church against the Soviet offensive in central Europe. When Pius XII called for a holy war against Communism, the participation of the Mexican Church on the first line of combat did not come as a surprise, not only because every Catholic was committed to obedience to the Pope, but also because every Mexican Catholic saw that battle as his or her own. Anti-Communism in Mexico was not just driven by U.S. foreign policy, it was dictated from the Vatican, which for many Mexicans was a more legitimate authority than any other.

Following the Vatican's vast anti-Communist call to arms, the Mexican Church engaged in intense propaganda activities. Women were at the forefront of this battle. They held this privileged position because Catholic anti-Communism of the 1950s saw in the family the main bulwark against what it denounced as the moral disintegration brought about by atheism, and women were primarily responsible for the preservation of the family. According to Catholic propaganda,

Communism sought to overthrow the social order, promoting anarchy which in turn would lead to the downfall of moral values—the sanctity of matrimony, of human life, and of paternal authority. The same propaganda accused Communists of attacking the chastity and honesty of women by imposing a social order in which they were "common property" and the state usurped the natural functions of the family, such as the care and education of children.

The increase in the number of nuns may be seen as an indicator of the reinforcement of the bonds among women and religion and church in the Cold War context. It also explains the role women were given in the dissemination of the church's message and in the extension of its social influence. In 1954 there were 8,123 nuns in Mexico; in 1960 their number had grown to 19,400, an increase of almost 139 percent within a period of fifteen years. There were three times as many nuns as priests. The appeal of the convent in these years can also be seen as an alternative for women who, for various reasons, did not marry and for whom, given the fact that a woman's status depended on marriage and motherhood, staying single would have meant social degradation.

The Mexican Catholic Church's involvement in the anti-Communist campaign also strengthened its collaboration with the government and provided a vehicle for its reinsertion into the political system; the secularism of the Mexican state did not hamper the alliance of political and religious authorities. Past disputes were overcome or became secondary. The Church benefited greatly from cooperating with the state, for the PRI did not use it to disseminate values different from Catholic values and images, as happened in Eastern Europe. The prospects for social mobility that were incessantly propagated in the official discourse were consistent with the notions of conformism and resignation preached by the Church. Along with government authorities, the Church also encouraged respect for natural hierarchies and a vertical and centralized vision of the structures of authority. Moreover, given the key presence of Catholic symbols in national mythology, Church collaboration with the government bolstered nationalism. The Mexican clergy strongly promoted devotion to the Virgin of Guadalupe—mother and patron of the Mexican nation—as the religious counterpart of the nationalist ideology propagated by the government.

Numerous and diverse Catholic publications spread the Church's message. The religious press, which had remained active even during the years of conflict, thrived in the postwar period. In the years 1940 to 1942 alone, the number of religious newspapers increased from 45 to 84; by 1960 there were 186. In 1942 the *Obra Nacional de la Buena Prensa* produced close to 11 million copies of low-priced or free magazines, pamphlets, and leaflets that were distributed mainly to women and children, exposing alleged Communist conspiracies against the church and Catholics. The reach of the anti-Communist propaganda throughout Mexican society was ensured by the addition to the Catholic press of 200,000 copies of *Life* magazine and selections from *Reader's Digest*—both giants of anti-Communism—that were produced in Spanish and sold in Mexico at the time.

However, Communism was not the Catholic Church's only opponent in the defense of traditional values. Paradoxically, its main ally in the anti-Communist crusade was also a feared adversary. In the fifties, Mexican Catholicism waged a two-front war—against Communism, on one side and, the other, against the growing influence of liberal U.S. values and social prototypes, which were being disseminated across Mexican society by the popular press, movies, and television. The Church saw in the example of U.S. permissiveness a threat as dangerous to the continuity of the family as Communism.

Historically, the United States had been a hated adversary of the Church for its energetic promotion of Protestantism, which was, to Mexican Catholics, also a frightening threat. Many of them feared and criticized the destructive consequences to the family of various habits or institutions identified with U.S. society, such as divorce, birth control, permissive attitudes toward women, fashion, coeducational schools, rock and roll music, and the precocious sexuality of the young. Thus, even if the church recognized the United States' leading role in the anti-Communist battle, it wanted to protect Mexican society from the cultural influence that inevitably accompanied U.S. presence in foreign societies.

The Mexican Church ignored the similarities between the United States' and Mexico's social values in those years, some of which are noteworthy—such as the notion that domestic life was an alternative for a woman's fulfillment superior to any other.[8] Thus, religion introduced a striking difference in each society's response into the international environment; whereas in the United States the anti-Communist battle was mainly political and strategic, in Mexico it took on a strident religious quality.

To counter the undermining influence of U.S. liberalism, the Church turned to Franco's Spain in search of social values, rules, and prototypes to strengthen *real* Mexican traditions. This strategy led to a deepening of the conservatism of Mexican Catholicism. The Spanish dictatorship and the Mexican political system shared basic characteristics—the concentration of power, the discouragement of political participation, and intolerance toward opposition—but they were also separated by important differences. Whereas Spain was ruled by a dictator who remained in power for thirty-four years, in Mexico electoral processes took place periodically, even if they were rigged. Nevertheless, Mexican society in the 1950s had more in common with Franco's society—rigidly hierarchical and culturally dominated by the Catholic Church—than with U.S. prototypes of modern life. Carmen Martin Gaite's description of middle-class women's attitudes toward love, sex, and marriage in postwar Spain brings to mind the ignorant and guilt-ridden views of Mexican women on the same subjects.[9]

The similarities between the Mexican and Spanish societies during those years are paradoxical. First, unlike the Franco dictatorship—which set about reconstructing the traditional order the Republic (1931–39) had tried to dismantle—the Mexican elites that emerged during the revolution were committed to modernization, and they publicly disavowed Franco's anachronism. Secondly, whereas Mexico was a secular republic, Catholicism was Spain's official religion. Mexico never granted diplomatic recognition to the government of Francisco Franco, which had come to power through a military coup and a civil war. Diplomatic relations between Mexico and Spain were not reestablished until after Franco's death in 1976. Nevertheless, commercial, religious, and cultural ties between the two countries were relatively strong from the beginning of the postwar period until the early sixties.

Since the 1940s, the Spanish government had used religion as an instrument to regain influence in Latin America by leading a sort of crusade of traditionalist and Catholic values against Communism and liberalism.[10] The ties between the Spanish and the Mexican churches were reinforced and steadily increased.[11] Sponsored by the Spanish Jesuits and the Ministry of Foreign Affairs, religious representatives and missionaries were sent to Mexico with the primary goal of checking the growth of Protestant churches.[12] Spanish bishops and prelates became frequent visitors to Mexico, and increasing numbers of members of the

Mexican clergy traveled to Spain. In 1963, 16 percent of all Catholic clergy active in Mexico were foreign, most of them Spanish, and more than 30 percent of these priests and nuns worked in schools and universities, where 17 percent of them held leading positions.

Religious ties were only one aspect of the exchanges that developed between the two countries. The presence of the Spanish model of society in Mexico was also spread through films and in the popular press. From 1945 until the end of the 1950s, exchanges between Mexican and Spanish cinema were significant. A good indicator of the cultural affinities between the two societies is the fact that Mexican films were modified only exceptionally by the Spanish Junta Superior de Orientación Cinematográfica, a censoring body that supervised the political, religious, moral, and sexual content of movies prior to exhibition. Most films were generally well received in Spain for the same reasons that Spanish cinema found Mexico's doors wide open: they were a healthy alternative to the avalanche of Hollywood films that flooded both countries.[12]

Spanish films shown in Mexico promoted religious and patriotic values and exalted the greatness of the Spanish empire and the goodness of the missionaries who had converted Mexican Indians. Mexican film exports were much more numerous than Spanish imports, but the relationship was the reverse in publishing. In the 1950s, Mexican publishers translated academic books and works of high culture into Spanish and exported them throughout the whole Spanish-speaking region. Spain was not among the main buyers. But then, it was second only to the United States as a *provider* of foreign books to Mexico, most of which were religious. (Many of the others were classical novels; but the number of romance novels written and produced in Spain that were exported to Latin America was overwhelming.)

The relative ease with which Mexican society accepted the social and cultural Spanish prototypes might also be explained as an almost instinctive response to the United States' growing influence in Mexico. From a historical point of view, this was neither the first nor the last time that Mexicans looked toward Europe to counterbalance their very powerful northern neighbor.

WOMEN: BETWEEN MORAL SUPERIORITY AND HUMAN INFERIORITY

Julia Tuñón's *Women in Mexico: A Past Unveiled* provides an example of the discomfort feminist history experiences in dealing with episodes in which women did not fight subordination, seemed oblivious to their marginalization, and were quite content in their role as restorers of continuity and keepers of the family.[14] Tuñón describes Mexican women's involvement in revolutionary struggles and the different attempts to organize their political participation or to fight for their emancipation. However, when it comes to women's role in postwar Mexico, Tuñón simply passes over those years and goes directly from the radical thirties to the beginnings of feminism in the seventies. In this perspective, the fifties were the dark ages of women's history in Mexico, a period of regression to prerevolutionary times. Nevertheless, there is a striking continuity throughout most of the twentieth century—until the eighties—in the structure of the family and women's roles and subordinate position in the public sphere. In this respect the experience of Mexican women in the fifties was very different from that of Spanish women, who under the Franco dictatorship lost the freedoms and rights they had enjoyed during the years of the Republic—all this while women in the U.S. seemed to have been "catapulted into the nineteenth century" after the liberating events of previous years.[15]

The confinement of women to the realm of the family had a deep political significance. In spite of the seemingly unchanging exclusion from the public sphere, the status of women was enhanced by the sense of danger and urgency created by the Cold War. If the social status of an individual is defined in terms of society's goals, then women in Mexico in the fifties were far from irrelevant, and their conformity with prevailing values and norms was more significant than during previous years. The importance of a stable social order as an overriding objective of the Mexican state, the centrality of the family in this design, and the role of women in its preservation suggest that even when the family could crush women's development, it was also a source of empowerment.[16] Moreover, if the family was a woman's source of social power and prestige, she had a personal stake in preserving an environment that provided her with security and with the role that was a warrant of her importance.[17] This would explain the missionary zeal most Mexican women showed in the fulfillment of their social duties as dictated by church and state.

The Cold War gave women a sense of mission and made them protagonists in a decisive struggle. This was a new experience for them. They had participated in various ways in the revolution, but in a context of war and turmoil: "For the most part they maintained their traditional role . . . They were cooks, launderers and concubines."[18] Adelita, the emblematic female figure of the Mexican Revolution, was not a leader or an audacious guerrilla fighter, but rather a faithful woman who accompanied her man—almost always with her children— and took care of him, transferring traditional roles to the battlefield. She incarnated the home; she remained in the battle next to her man and helped him, fed him, dressed his wounds, and substituted for him when necessary. Most Adelitas went into battle to keep their family together when they had not been violently taken away by the soldiers and raped, making their return to their families unthinkable. Many of them were heroic, but very few acted alone or for themselves. They risked their lives for their men or children; they did not fight for other Adelitas, but more likely competed with them when it was necessary to find food, a place to sleep, or ammunition for their men's weapons.[19] The essentially domestic role of the Adelitas was emphasized by the Mexican film industry in the fifties, when the revolutionary epic became a central chapter of the official discourse.[20]

Some women distinguished themselves as individuals assuming masculine attitudes, dressing up as soldiers or forming their own battalions, but they have been mostly forgotten as they were more the exception than the rule.[21] The Mexican Revolution has no equivalent to the Pasionaria or Federica Montseny in the Spanish republic. Antonieta Rivas Mercado and Frida Kahlo, iconic figures of the revolution, stand out, but in the world of arts and literature; and although Jean Franco sees in their respective lives a struggle to understand female identity, they "could not envisage any woman's space that was outside the shadow of a man."[22]

The new opportunities for women that were nevertheless created by the revolution, the emergence of female activists and the organization of feminist congresses, were short-lived experiences, either too weak or too narrow to resist the weight of traditional practices. Throughout the 1920s and 1930s, some revolutionary authorities adopted radical positions on free love, sex education, and birth control, but failed to mobilize wide support even among women. They were either uninterested or rejected these issues, expressing the belief that a change in the family structure or in the rules governing its functioning were unnecessary. Further evidence of Mexican women's basic conservatism is found in their commitment to causes such as La Cristiada, as has already been described. In 1938 the Frente Unico Pro Derechos de la Mujer became a national umbrella group for the promotion of women's suffrage; it assembled women from every social class across the country, attaining a peak membership of 50,000.[23] By contrast, 300,000 women were affiliated to Accion Catolica Mexicana in that same year.

However strong the position of women within society may have been in the fifties thanks to Cold War ideology, women bore with strong pressures to conform to the prescriptions of the Church, if only because their status depended on their ability to sustain the moral authority they derived from their loyalty to the Catholic feminine ideal. Even women's exclusion from politics was rationalized in moral terms. In 1947, the president of the conservative PAN, Manuel Gomez Morin, introduced the discussion on women's suffrage, asking his audience whether it was fair to expose a woman's purity to the "filth of politics." Nevertheless, given the centrality of the family in conservative thought, PAN was the first to incorporate women into positions of authority within the party. Also, the first women candidates to Congress and governorships were Panistas.

In addition, a woman could only claim moral authority if she fulfilled the conditions set by the prevalent feminine ideal, among which forming a family or being part of a family were determinant. This notion had serious implications for single women. A "decent" woman did not live by herself; respectability demanded that she remain at home with her family, taking care of her aging parents or ailing relatives or looking after nephews and nieces. Being single was never perceived as a matter of choice; it was seen, rather, as a major failure to accomplish a woman's natural goal and destiny: marriage followed by maternity. In her novels, Rosario Castellanos, the sharp and gifted writer whose work in the sixties and seventies pioneered Mexican feminism, captures the paramount significance of motherhood in the determination of a woman's status.[24]

It is likely that many women entered the convent to avoid the stigma that attached to single women. Moreover, a nun had been *chosen* by God. From a different perspective, life in a convent was an honorable way out for women who were perceived as too unlucky or too incompetent to find a husband. It was also an alternative for young women from poor families who wanted to continue studying or for whom the convent provided stable employment, bed, and board.

The notion that a woman's place was at home was an argument against the education of women. In the fifties women represented just over half of the total population, yet only in primary schools did the proportion between girls and boys reproduce the demographic ratio; the presence of girls in the educational system decreased significantly in high school, where in 1955 the percentage of women was below 20, and naturally they were a minority in the national university. A family that could not afford a college education for all their children would automatically give precedence to the sons over the daughters. Most working middle-class women had a short preprofessional education; they were trained to do clerical work or to become nurses, accountants, or school teachers. They were educated to carry out support activities, not to make executive decisions.[25]

The primacy of women's virtue over any other personal quality justified keeping them in complete ignorance of sexual matters. To prevent "strange ideas" from getting into young women's heads, only rarely were they given sexual information. In 1941 the government suppressed coeducation in public schools because, according to President Manuel Avila Camacho, it was an institution "repulsive to the nation's feelings." Women were expected to remain virgins until they married; a woman's purity was part of her personal value so that at times it was the only capital she brought to a marriage. It was a matter of honor for men to guard their girlfriend's or their sister's virtue.

Matrimony was a promised land for women both rich and poor; but it was also the goal of the life-plan God had designed for each of His daughters. However, while marriage was the more "natural" option for middle-class women, for women of lesser means matrimony was an attractive alternative to low-paid domestic service or factory work. For those who had to make a living, finding a husband was tantamount to having more freedom and a steady income. Ideally marriage meant no longer having to clean other peoples' homes, wait on strangers, or spend entire days in front of a machine. According to the prevalent stereotype, marriage provided protection and respectability. A man in the house was a principle of order because the male figure was by definition a figure of authority.

Maternity was the next stage in God's life-plan for young Mexican women. Between 1950 and 1960, the population's annual rate of growth was 3 percent; an average Mexican family had six children—as many as

God willed. Very few couples used birth control; abortion was a word not spoken out loud, much less in front of young women.

The low level of education of most women kept them perpetual children. Most middle-class women grew up holding puerile notions of love relationships; this was only a facet of the childish world to which they had been condemned by the Church and a political system whose presidents referred to society as the "great Mexican family." This metaphor is a reflection of the patriarchal structure of Mexican society, a hierarchical organization presided over by the authority of a mother and a father (Church and state), within which male children gradually reached adulthood, whereas women remained minors throughout their lives.[26]

Literary criticism of romance novels read in Mexico and Colombia in the fifties and sixties shows that romantic heroines are gentle and self-sacrificing and that a positive feminine identity implied passivity, abnegation, and modesty. Even ineffectuality was perceived as an "endearing feminine quality,"[27] and dependence was a desirable feature in women, though an undesirable one in men. "The plot of the majority of the stories [examined] centered upon the female achieving the proper dependent status either by marrying or manipulating existing dependency relationships to reaffirm the heroine's subordinate position. The male support—monetary, social and psychological—was generally seen as well worth any independence or selfhood given up in the process."[28] However, these novels also reflect the female's moral authority, which imposes itself on the errant male; he is usually reformed by a highly passive feminine character who waits patiently for him to acknowledge and appreciate her moral superiority.[29]

The fact that the reference point for the ideal woman in Mexico was a religious symbol of sanctity explains the severity of a girl's education compared with that of a boy, and the rigid demands on her self-control. It also explains why women were expected to assume the self-denial symbolized by the Virgin of Guadalupe. This entailed boundless generosity, patience, and understanding of the failings of men, who were so weak.

The code of conduct was the same for all women, regardless of class distinctions. Yet some of them were in a better position than others to live by this code and to perform their social duties. In 1961 the U.S. anthropologist Oscar Lewis published *The Children of Sanchez*, a study of urban poverty in Mexico City. The book caused a scandal and sparked a furious reaction on the part of the Mexican government. An attempt was made to ban the import of the book from the United States, and the executive director of the Mexican publishing house that produced it in Spanish was dismissed by the president himself. Lewis's book was a tragic portrait of a lower-class family: violence between brothers and sisters, and between parents and children; stories of promiscuity, physical brutality, incest, abortion, alcoholism, homosexuality, and rape. All of this happened in the bosom of a family, as though God had forgotten to design a life-plan for the women of the Sánchez family.[30]

All the images, values, and prejudices that governed women's behavior constituted more complex realities than those pictured in the romance novel or in the magazines and leaflets distributed in parochial churches every Sunday after Mass. Pope John XXIII chose *Mater et Magistra* as the title of his 1962 progressive encyclical, which set down the guidelines for Christians in the second half of the twentieth century. To be a mother and a teacher was also what was expected of women. But there were many who could not fulfill this exemplary role, and when they didn't they had to learn to live with the shame and guilt of having failed. The punishment for not following the rules was greater subordination and marginality.

CONCLUSIONS

Octavio Paz's classic study on the Mexican character, *The Labyrinth of Solitude*, first published in 1950, portrays the ambivalent perceptions of Mexican women as objects of men's aggression and lust. In men's fantasies they were perceived as passive, inert, and open, and at the same time as threats, as symbols of the strangeness of the universe.[31] Paz critically observes that "woman [was] only a reflection of male will and desire."[32] The Cold War context accentuated the ambiguity of a vision that saw women as being both movingly weak and in need of protection, and at the same time tremendously strong and capable of giving protection. The religiously charged notion of femininity that prevailed in the fifties attributed to women moral superiority while it justified a basic inequality and gender-based discrimination.

The condition of Mexican women has been explained from an anthropological perspective and examined as a cultural phenomenon.

Here, it has been analyzed as one facet in the consolidation of an authoritarian political system, buttressed by the Catholic Church's control of social values, all within the ideological framework of the main international conflict of the fifties. The United States first projected the ghost of anti-Communism over the entire hemisphere. Nevertheless, thanks to the intervention of the Catholic Church, the ghost toured the region day and night. Every country received it with its own fears and fantasies; every country welcomed it into its bosom and allowed it to sit at the head of the table, where it guided conversations, controlled individuals' behavior and their expectations, and protected morality and etiquette.

The empire of anti-Communism in Mexican society throughout this decade clashed with the goals of modernization, and soon many Mexicans translated it into a deep mistrust of change; thus anti-Communism overreached its original intention to become a powerful constraint on the prospects of social transformation. Mexican conservatism of the fifties provides important elements for the explanation of the persistence of long-term social inequalities and authoritarianism.

In contrast with the past, when women's subordination was founded on their seeming irrelevance, in the fifties they were subordinate to male authority though, given the centrality of the family in the Cold War ideological construct of a Catholic-dominated society, they held a position of power. They were pillars of society, the shield against the family's enemies. The very strategic importance of their position in the family empowered them but also curtailed their freedom.

Values and attitudes regarding the position and role of women and the importance of the family give an accurate measure of the oppressive and repressive character of Mexican society in the fifties. The events of the following decade were a vigorous, and in many cases violent, reaction to the asphyxiating atmosphere of the fifties. Throughout the 1960s, which in Latin America were inaugurated by the victory in January 1959 of Fidel Castro and Ernesto Che Guevara in Cuba, Mexico experienced extended student protests, the explosion of the hippie culture among the children of the middle class, the first signs of the emancipation of women, and the upsurge of guerrillera groups in rural and urban areas. This brought a tumultuous, and at times dramatic, end to the stability of the previous decade.

The importance of the Cold War experience for the development of Mexican women is that despite all tensions and contradictions, this was a period when the political discourse acknowledged the significance of women's participation in the accomplishment of society's goals. When in the late sixties the political context changed, women were aware of the potential reach of the challenge they could pose to established values and institutions, and they started acting accordingly. The fifties were a prelude to the very significant changes Mexican women have made in the last forty years toward equality and the building of a secular identity as individuals.

ACKNOWLEDGMENTS

This article was written while the author was a Visiting Fellow at the Kellog Institute, University of Notre Dame.

SOLEDAD LOAEZA is professor of political science at El Colegio de Mexico, where she was director of the International Relations Center (1990–1994). In 1999 she held the Alfred Grosser Chair at the Institut d'Etudes Politiques de Paris. She was a Fellow at the Radcliffe Institute of Advanced Studies in 2003-2004, and Visiting Fellow at the Kellog Institute of Notre Dame University in 2005. Her book *El Partido Acción Nacional, la larga marcha, 1939-1994* (Fondo de Cultura Economica, 1999) traces the institutional development of the longstanding loyal opposition that in 2000 won the presidency from the ruling party. In the past year, Loaeza has undertaken a study of presidential power in Mexico. Her current research focuses on President Gustavo Diaz Ordaz's administration (1964–1970). Her article on the presidential style of Vicente Fox will be published by the journal *Mexican Studies/Estudios Mexicanos* in December 2005.

NOTES

1. Elaine Tyler May, *Homeward Bound: American Families in the Cold War Era* (New York, Basic Books, 1988).
2. Evelyn P. Stevens, "Marianismo: The Other Face of Machismo in Latin America," in *Female and Male in Latin America*, ed. Ann Pescatello (Pittsburgh: Pittsburgh University Press, 1973), 89–102.
3. This event was decisive in the distrust women's political participation inspired in revolutionaries who saw them as hypocritical and dangerous conspirators. For the image of Mexican women as treacherous and unreliable, see Jean Franco,

Plotting Women: Gender and Representation in Mexico (New York: Columbia University Press, 1989).

4. In 1949 the Sacred Office made public an excommunication decree against all Communist party members and sympathizers, as well as all those who published, read, wrote or disseminated documents in support of Communist doctrine and practice. See Peter C. Kent, *The Lonely Cold War of Pope Pius XII: The Roman Catholic Church and the Divisions of Europe, 1943-1950* (Montreal: McGill University Press, 2002).

5. In 1960 Puerto Rico had the same ratio of population per priest as Mexico, more than five thousand to one. Argentina, Costa Rica, Paraguay, Peru, Venezuela and Uruguay had one priest for every four thousand to six thousand inhabitants. Cuba, Guatemala, Honduras, and the Dominican Republic registered a population of nine thousand to twelve thousand per priest. The rate of increase of priests in Mexico between 1945 and 1960 was among the highest in the region. See Rutilio Ramos, Isidoro Alonso, and Domingo Garre, *La Iglesia en América Latina* (Madrid y Friburgo, 1964), 208-209, 214-215.

6. Manuel Gonzalez, *La Iglesia Mexicana en cifras* (México, Centro de Investigación y Acción Social, 1969), 100.

7. See Soledad Loaeza, *Clases Medias y Política en México: La Querella Escolar, 1959-1963* (México: El Colegio de México, 1988).

8. Gail Collins, *America's Women: 400 Years of Dolls, Drudges, Helpmates and Heroines*, (New York: Harper Perennial, 2004), 397-420.

9. Carmen Martin Gaite, *Usos Amorosos de la Post Guerra Española* (Barcelona: Editorial Anagrama, 1984).

10. Ricardo Pérez Montfort, *La Mirada oficiosa de la hispanidad: México en los informes del ministerio de asuntos exteriores franquista, 1940-1950*, in *México y España en el primer franquismo Rupturas formales, relaciones oficiosas*, ed. Clara E. Lida (Mexico: El Colegio de México, 2001), 61-119.

11. Perez Montfort, 94.

12. Perez Montfort, 88

13. See Seth Fein, "La diplomacia del celuloide. Hollywood y la edad de oro del cine mexicano," *Historia y Grafía* 4 (1995), Universidad Iberoamericana. See also Julia Tuñón, "Relaciones de celuloide," in: Lida.

14. Julia Tuñón Pablos, *Women in Mexico: A Past Unveiled* (Austin: University of Texas Press, 1999).

15. Collins, 398.

16. Family would always be a source of empowerment, but in the Cold War context it was more so for Mexican women. Jean Franco cites Julia Kristeva's observations regarding the maternal role as a form of empowerment among Catholic women and its influence on the contrasting attitudes between them and Protestant women who lack this element. Franco, xvi.

17. In the sixties and seventies, anthropologists and sociologists who examined women's status in Latin America found that the family as a source of empowerment was a common phenomenon. Stevens writes: "The prevalence of the

extended family and *compadrazgo*, the relative lack of geographical mobility and the survival of the family as an important instrument of social regulation over a fairly broad range of activities, give women who dominate their families a considerable degree of power and influence. The figure of the matriarch is a common one in Latin America."

18. Tuñón Pablos, *Women in Mexico*, 88.

19. For a discussion of the various functions of women in the revolutionary battle-field, see Elizabeth Salas, "The *Soldadera* in the Mexican Revolution: War and Men's Illusions," in: Tuñón Pablos, *Women in Mexico*, 93–105. See also Eli Bartra, *El género en la Revolución Mexicana* (México Difusión Cultural, Revista UAM, October 1999).

20. See the compelling analysis by Franco of the film *Enamorada* (1947) as a successful resolution of the conflict between militant conservative women and the postrevolutionary regime. Franco, op. cit., 148–52.

21. See Salas.

22. Franco, 128.

23. Julia Tuñón Pablos, *Por fin podemos elegir y ser electas* (México: Plaza y Valdez, 2002).

24. In Castellanos's writings, "Motherhood is to sterility what virility is to impo-tence in the male." Franco, 142.

25. Rosario Castellanos, *Mujer que sabe latín.* (Mexico: Sepsetentas, 1973.)

26. At least three generations of Mexican women—and of Latin American women—of the postwar period were educated by the Spanish romantic novel, exported by the publishing house Bruguera or published by the women's maga-zine *Vanidades*, started in Cuba in 1951, and distributed throughout the entire Latin American market. In 1962, UNESCO declared Corín Tellado—who became the star of the romance novel in Spanish and who in the 1950s published a weekly novel—the most widely read Spanish author, her books outstripped only by the Bible and *Don Quixote*. Tellado began her career as a novelist in 1945, at the age of eighteen. By 2005 she had published more than 2,300 novels.

27. Cornelia Butler Flora, "The Passive Female and Social Change: A Cross-Cultural Comparison of Women's Magazine Fiction," in: Pescatello, 59–85.

28. Ibid, 71.

29. Ibid., 69–70.

30. See Oscar Lewis, *The Children of Sanchéz: Autobiography of a Mexican Family.* (New York: Random House, 1961).

31. Jane S. Jaquette, "Literary Archetypes and Female Role Alternatives: The Woman and the Novel in Latin America," in Pescatello, 89–102.

32. Cited in Franco, 133

A NEW KIND OF MISSIONARY WORK:
CHRISTIANS, CHRISTIAN AMERICANISTS, AND THE
ADOPTION OF KOREAN GI BABIES, 1955–1961

ARISSA OH

In a 1954 article in *Life* magazine, Dr. Howard Rusk, President of the American-Korean Foundation, recollected a scene from war-torn Korea:

> You remember the brass band at the Presbyterian Leprosarium just outside Taegu. You remember there was snow on the ground and more than half the musicians stood barefoot as you went by. These were the untouchables. A little leper boy with his face half-gone held the music for those who played on the battered old brass trumpets and trombones, and as you drew near, you recognized the hymn, What a Friend We Have in Jesus. You remember the eyes of those in your party. They were tough people, long hardened to misery because they had to be: generals, admirals, statesmen. The tears ran down their cheeks. They did not bother to brush them away. But the kids did not cry, for we were Americans and Americans to them meant hope for the future.[1]

With these nine sentences, Rusk captured several of the main elements in the story of how Americans came to adopt more than 4,000 orphaned Korean children between 1955 and 1961.[2] There is the pathos: the vivid, moving details of poverty and hardship that characterized American media portrayals of Korea, both during and after the Korean War (1950–53). There is the military: the men who would father and leave behind hundreds of mixed-race "GI babies."[3] There is Christianity: the common faith that united the two nations and that prompted countless Americans—GIs, missionaries, ordinary churchgoers—to generously

[*WSQ: Women's Studies Quarterly* 33: 3 & 4 (Fall/Winter 2005)]

donate food, clothes, dollars, and time. There is America: as much a symbol of hope as it was a country, a heaven on earth where tears and pain would be washed away. Finally, there are the children—stoic, hopeful, and wise—who knew better than to cry in the presence of those who would deliver them from their suffering.

Basic human compassion was at the root of American relief efforts after the Korean War, but something more complex motivated certain families to take their efforts a step further by adopting orphaned Korean children. The move to adoption was largely propelled by religious and humanitarian beliefs and a desire to "save" children from the effects of war, but it was also a manifestation of a peculiar kind of secular religion that arose in the United States in the 1950s. "There seems to be a wave of enthusiasm for a rather undefined 'religion' in America," noted the *Christian Century* in 1954. That undefined religion—which I call "Christian Americanism"—was a fusion of vaguely Christian principles with values identified as particularly "American"—specifically, a uniquely American sense of responsibility and the importance of family. Never a fully articulated doctrine, it was nevertheless strongly promoted by American churches, the government, and the mainstream media, and it took hold in white, middle-class America—the segment that adopted the majority of Korea's mixed-race GI babies. Christian Americanism encapsulated the prevailing 1950s belief that equated being a good Christian with being a good American.[4]

This article considers the seven-year period beginning in 1955, when Harry and Bertha Holt, a farming couple from Oregon, adopted eight Korean GI babies, established their adoption agency, and triggered what would eventually become a tidal wave of intercountry adoptions. Until 1961, when the U.S. government banned proxy adoptions,[5] evacuation efforts focused on mixed-race GI babies. The 1955–61 period is a distinct moment in the history of Korean adoption, since the composition of the U.S.-bound Korean orphan population shifted in the early 1960s from mostly mixed-race to mostly non-mixed-race children.

Two groups of Americans—Christians and Christian Americanists—took on Korean adoption as a new kind of missionary work. The Christian adoptive families were deeply religious and motivated by faith to adopt; although some of them expressed Christian Americanist beliefs, they were first and foremost Christian. This group was a subset of a second, much larger group, the Christian Americanists, as represented by the mass media and Congress. This second group infused these religiously motivated adoptions with nationalist meaning and celebrated them as an affirmation not only of the adoptive parents' Christian goodness, but also of their Americanness. In addition, Christian Americanists used the apparent color blindness of the Christian adoptive families to support Cold War claims of racial democracy. Through this interplay of religious and nationalistic concerns, what began as an essentially Christian adoption movement became the shared crusade of devout Christians and Christian Americanists alike.

KOREA IN THE AMERICAN IMAGINATION

The post–Korean War orphan population consisted of children of full Korean parentage and mixed-race Korean-white and Korean-black GI babies, who were the product of sex between Korean women and the foreign troops of the United Nations Command.[6] A longstanding emphasis on racial purity led Koreans to openly discriminate against GI babies, who constituted only a small portion of the postwar orphan population—of an estimated 100,000 orphans, approximately 1,500 were mixed-race[7]—but suffered a disproportionate amount of hostility and abuse. These children faced the prospect of having few opportunities as they grew up, and even as young children they suffered physical and verbal abuse from adults and other children alike.[8] Observers of the orphan situation in Korea concurred with the United Presbyterian Mission of Korea's opinion that "Korean society massively rejects the mixed-blood" and that a mixed-race child faced "a radically impossible situation."[9]

Although some mothers tried to keep their mixed-race children disguised and hidden, abandonment seems to have been the more common choice.[10] GI babies were found in every conceivable place—at missions, churches, and orphanages; "in train stations, shops . . . public toilets, the market place, [and] on doorsteps." In the most desperate cases, the babies were left to die in garbage dumps or on mountainsides, or worse: "some little blonde-haired babies were washed up on the seashore."[11] Some observers in Korea reported that up to 90 percent of mixed-race children died. Although this figure was probably substantially overstated, it is significant because it denoted the grim fate that social service and missionary groups believed awaited the GI baby, and it was this vision of the GI baby's future that media and relief organizations showed the American public.[12] Given these conditions, it is unsurprising that Western observers believed that the only solution for GI babies was to find homes for them outside Korea. "In the absence of such placements," said one case worker at International Social Services, "they will not live and if they do, they will have nothing to live for."[13]

Korean orphans captured the American imagination from the moment the Korean War erupted in 1950. Photographs and articles in newspapers and mass-market magazines like *Life*, *Collier's*, and *Look*, as well as on newsreels and radio programs, showed Americans a ruined Korea and painted vivid images of a land of suffering and poverty.[14] Smoke rose from deserted villages, ancient city gates towered over smashed buildings, lines of laden refugees wove their way through driving snow past jeeps full of UN personnel. Juxtaposed on the devastation were the faces of orphaned Korean children. Babies sat in ditches next to the bodies of their dead mothers. Gangs of children roamed the streets, foraging for food and sleeping in the rubble. Little girls with their baby brothers or sisters tied to their backs walked from Seoul to Pusan and back again. In almost every human-interest story about the Korean War, these "waifs," "urchins," and "moppets" figured prominently.

Christian organizations such as World Vision, Save the Children Federation, and Christian Children's Fund established programs through which Americans could "adopt" Korean orphans through financial sponsorship.[15] Their advertisements featured photographs or line drawings of emaciated Korean children and carried ominous headlines like, "*You could have saved this little girl!*" These organizations appealed to Christians' sense of responsibility—describing the thousands of war orphans in Korea as "a challenge to Christians all over the world"—and put the onus directly on Americans: "For these children there is only the hope that kindly Americans will send aid to them."[16] A sponsor took on the financial responsibility of a child for several dollars a month. The child corresponded with his or her sponsor, and the latter received photos and reports on the child from the director of the orphanage.[17]

Child relief efforts in Korea gained a new dimension when Harry and Bertha Holt established the first adoption agency specifically geared to Korean adoption. Rather than virtually adopting a Korean orphan through a sponsorship program, concerned Americans could now actually and legally adopt one. In 1955, Harry Holt had brought twelve GI babies to the United States; he and his wife adopted eight, and the other four went to three other families. The publicity around this undertaking was so great that the Holts were inundated almost immediately with inquiries from Americans who wanted to adopt.[18] Seeing the need of the orphans in Korea and the demand for them in the United States, Harry Holt began shuttling back and forth between the two countries, bringing Korean GI babies to families in the United States while at the same time campaigning for legislative changes to facilitate the adoptions. In 1956, the Holts placed 191 orphans and established the Holt Adoption Program, which placed 2,587 Korean children with American families by 1961. Between 1955 and 1961, Holt placed the majority of Korean orphans in the United States.[19]

There are several explanations for the American media's sympathetic portrayal of Korea and Koreans and for the American public's receptiveness to this portrayal. One is the dawning of the Cold War, which prompted the United States to scramble to correct its racist image. Racial violence, segregation, and other manifestations of American racism threatened to undermine American efforts to gain the allegiance of nonwhite nations around the world and were, in the words of Secretary of State Dean Acheson, "a source of constant embarrassment to this Government" that jeopardized "the effective maintenance of our moral leadership of the free and democratic nations of the world." Acheson called on the media "and other social and cultural institutions" to assist in winning public support for the government's new internationalist stance by creating a "global imaginary" that would make Americans feel linked to "nations and peoples around the world." One way to accomplish this goal was by using and promoting racially democratic rhetoric.[20]

The physical absence of Koreans from the American landscape may also have influenced the fairly positive view of Koreans put forth by the American media. In the 1950s, Korean Americans were a virtual nonentity in the national consciousness. The Immigration Act of 1924 had barred all immigration from Asia, and those Koreans who had entered the United States prior to 1924 were scattered throughout Hawaii and the mainland. Anti-Asian racism was directed at the Chinese and the Japanese and hardly ever recognized Koreans as a distinct group. When they did distinguish Koreans as a separate entity, Americans simply grouped them with the Japanese, especially after Japan colonized Korea in 1905. In the absence of a significant Korean population in the United

States, then, the media had considerable latitude in constructing an image of Korean people for American consumption.[21]

Interestingly, the media made an important distinction between "bad" North Koreans (and their Chinese allies) and "good" South Koreans. While white racism in 1950s America would have normally lumped these people together in one "yellow" mass, political distinctions determined racist stereotyping in the context of the Korean War. Thus, North Korean and Chinese Communists were characterized as barbarians, "Nazis, locusts, primitives, hordes, thieves," while South Koreans were represented in a fairly positive light.[22]

Finally, although a great deal of the positive perception of Koreans sprang from the simple fact that Koreans and Americans had fought together against the Communist foe, a sense that the two peoples shared a similar "character" and a common Christianity also strengthened Americans' affective ties to Korea. In his 1956 article for *Life*, Howard Rusk, President of the American-Korean Foundation, wrote sympathetically about how the "gallant" nation was working to rebuild itself. He used an assortment of vignettes to illustrate qualities that Americans would consider themselves to have in common with Koreans: "the deep personal and spiritual resources of the Korean people: their remarkable mixture of stoic courage, dignity, adaptability and humor; their thirst for education; and their deep traditions of the family as the basic social unit." Perhaps most importantly, Rusk portrayed Koreans as being as committed to freedom and democracy as Americans by recounting the words of one anonymous Korean, who spoke for all Koreans when he pleaded, "Won't you help us off our knees so we can continue to fight for the free world?" Cold War Americans could not help but respond to such a person except as a brother and friend.[23]

Koreans and Americans also shared a common Christian faith. American missionaries in Asia had "encouraged their fellow Christians to feel a bond of sympathy with Asia" since the mid-nineteenth century, and continued to act in this quasi-ambassadorial role during the Korean War. The widely read nondenominational Christian weekly, the *Christian Century*, contained an editorial or feature story on Korea in almost every wartime issue. These pieces documented the persistence and ingenuity of the Korean people and pleaded on their behalf for aid from American churches. The periodical also highlighted the bravery and faithfulness of Korean Christians, noting that they were the special targets of Communist guerillas and describing refugee camps as overflowing with Koreans incessantly reading their Bibles, singing hymns, and holding prayer meetings.[24] Stories about orphans living in institutions—most of which were run by American mission groups—also emphasized their supposed Christianity by describing them singing Christian songs like "Jesus Loves Me."[25] In these ways, the American media positioned the Korean War as a battle between Christian South Korea and Communist North Korea. Against such a backdrop, the adoption of Christian South Korean babies could be construed as a deliberately anti-Communist act that directly supported the Christian Americanist cause.[26]

Antiracist rhetoric may have been the official language of Cold War discourse, but beyond the high-minded media and government spheres, Koreans, like other Asians, were simply "chinks" and "gooks." Thus, the act of adopting a Korean-white or Korean-black child during the 1950s was an extraordinarily progressive act, particularly given the profile of the adoptive families: predominantly white middle-class Protestants who were very religious, fairly conservative, and living in small towns or rural areas.[27] The Holts launched the movement to adopt Korean GI babies in 1955, just a year after the *Brown v. Board of Education* decision and at the very beginning of the civil rights movement. The United States was still intensely racist and deeply segregated. Why were these adoptive families taking the revolutionary step of bringing a foreign, mixed-race child from a third world country into their white homes, schools, churches, and communities?

CHRISTIAN AMERICANISM: AMERICAN RESPONSIBILITY, AMERICAN VALUES

Commenting on the Refugee Relief Act of 1953, which authorized exceptions to existing quota restrictions and increased the number of refugees to be admitted to the United States, President Eisenhower stated, "[T]hese refugees, escapees, and distressed peoples. . . look to traditional American humanitarian concern for the oppressed. . . We should take reasonable steps to help these people to the extent that we share the obligation of the free world."[28] In the 1950s, the now-familiar Cold War rhetoric that positioned the United States as the savior of the world and the standard bearer for democracy and freedom was still very new, and the division of the world into spheres of good and evil, democracy and Communism, United States and Soviet Union, induced profound anxiety in Americans.[29]

The situation in Asia only heightened that anxiety, for between Mao's China, the Korean War, Ho Chi Minh's North Vietnam, and Communist insurgencies throughout Southeast Asia, it seemed that the United States was rapidly losing ground to Moscow: "[W]hen Americans looked East during the 1950s, they saw the majority of the world's population and a wealth of strategic resources teetering on the brink of Soviet control—and they felt the global balance of power in danger of tipping permanently against the United States." Relief efforts became a way that Americans attempted to win "the allegiance of Asia." Ordinary Americans could take part in this project by adopting Korean war orphans and—in yet another iteration of the white man's burden—raising them up; by bringing them into their homes and inculcating them with the values of Christianity and the American way of life.[30]

The belief that Americans had an international Americanizing and Christianizing mission permeated the discourse of popular and Christian media alike. The United States was the standard-bearer not only of democracy but also of Christianity. In *Life* magazine's Christianity issue, published in December 1955, the editors noted that the United States was "the world's largest and most dynamic Christian country," and firmly situated American Christianity at the center of worldwide Christianity by showing "how the rest of world Christendom is related to this country's faith."[31] *Life*'s Christianity issue opened with "The Testimony of a Devout President," a compilation of seven speeches given by President Eisenhower between 1946 and 1955. Eisenhower praised the righteousness of the American people and emphasized the importance of America's mission and its responsibility to the world: "Our forefathers proved that only a people strong in godliness is a people strong enough to overcome tyranny and make themselves and others free. Today it is ours to prove that our own faith, perpetually renewed, is equal to the challenge of today's tyrants." Because America held a special position in the world and in the eyes of God, Eisenhower exhorted Americans to put their trust in Him: "The path we travel is narrow and long—beset with many dangers. Each day we must ask that Almighty God will set and keep his protecting hand over us." That Almighty God would answer the American prayer was surely the underlying message, for in a world divided between good and evil, God was on America's side.[32]

Scholars of the 1950s agree with *Life*'s assertion that "the sights and sounds of an unprecedented revival in religious belief and practice were everywhere in the United States." In 1955, noted *Life*, "nearly 100 million Americans—three of every five—belonged to some Christian church." Elaine Tyler May writes that between 1940 and 1960, "religious affiliation became associated with the 'American Way of Life,'" although she also notes that "many observers have commented upon the superficiality and lack of spiritual depth in much of this religious activity." Whatever the character or depth of American religiosity in the 1950s, there is no question that it was pervasive. The fact that the words "under God" were added to the Pledge of Allegiance in 1954 illustrates neatly the pious mood of the country.[33]

Criticism of the conflation of American values with Christianity came not from popular magazines like *Life*, but from Christian periodicals such as the *Christian Century* and *Christianity and Crisis*. "Religion . . . seems to have become the vogue in America," noted A. Roy Eckardt in the *Christian Century*. In an article criticizing "the new look in American piety," Eckardt expressed concern at the zeitgeist of the times, which seemed to hold that "it is un-American to be unreligious." He called the binaries of the political situation—United States versus the Soviet Union, democracy versus Communism—a "cult of 'we' versus 'they'" and denounced as perverse America's smug conclusion that its cause was God's cause.[34] *Christianity and Crisis*'s resident satirist, Saint Hereticus, took the matter even further, claiming that American Christians had abandoned Christianity altogether in favor of something he called "Americanity." The apostles' creed of this religion, he said, began, "I believe in America the nation almighty, creator of heaven on earth," and its doctrine was "'extra American nulla salus est' (outside America there is no salvation)."[35]

As these writers point out, what many Americans called Christianity in the 1950s was actually a watered-down collection of selected Christian values. This "culture religion" contained little of the practice and belief of true Christianity, retaining instead vague principles about kindness and doing unto others, and it became general enough that Americans of all religious denominations could share a common rhetoric. In fact, it became so emptied of any specific Christian meaning that Oregon Senator Richard Neuberger, a Jew, came to regularly employ the language of Christian Americanism on the Senate floor to appeal to his colleagues' religious and nationalistic sentiments during debates about orphan-friendly immigration legislation. After reminding them of the words of Emma Lazarus that were engraved in the pedestal of the Statue of Liberty, he drew a direct line between Christ and Jefferson: "Somehow, I feel that the author of the Sermon on the Mount and the writer of the Declaration of Independence would approve of granting sanctuary in America to abandoned orphans and other persons who are wracked by sickness and misery."[36]

A sense of American duty was central to Christian Americanism, and it registered on three different levels after the Korean War: responsibility for the world, responsibility for Korea, and responsibility for the GI babies of Korea. In the first instance, the United States had a general responsibility to fulfill its new roles as world power, protector of democracy, and bulwark against Communism. To support their nation in these roles, it was important that patriotic Americans demonstrate their good, responsible citizenship both at home and abroad and take seriously their moral and civic obligations as leaders of the free world. As President Eisenhower asserted, religious faith would be essential to this task: "[R]eligion nurtures men of faith, men of hope, men of love; such men are needed in the building of a new world reflecting the glory of God."[37] The United States, as the most powerful country on earth and the nation most loved by God, had a special charge to build a new, Christian, American world.

Americans had a second responsibility: to Korea, where war had wreaked such havoc and produced such extraordinary numbers of refugees, orphans, and civilian dead. In the absence of a clear-cut victory against Communism in Korea, the United States could salvage an ideological win by caring for Korea's people and helping the nation to rebuild. This attitude was apparent in Howard Rusk's 1956 *Life* magazine article, in which he stated: "Here in a country halfway around the world, where we fought a war we did not win, we have at long last a chance to win the peace. For the first time in history U.S. soldiers who have had to devastate a country are voluntarily helping to reconstruct it."[38] Although the United States had not won the war by clearing the Korean peninsula of Communists, it could still prove that its participation had not been for nothing.

The media were particularly adept at showing that it was Korea's children who were the true victims of Communist aggression, and the "real" reason the United States was involved in the war on that little-

known, faraway peninsula.[39] Their grimy little faces were oddly photogenic, filling article after article about the Korean War. A description of
nine-year-old Tae in *Collier's* is representative of the stories of the time in
showing how orphans teetered on a razor's edge between life and death:

> During [the nearly three years that he'd been orphaned] the
> only food Tae had eaten was what he could steal or beg or buy
> with the few pennies he earned. His only home was the closest
> shelter he could find—a dry corner in some bombed-out build-
> ing, a pile of boards in an alley. . . But then Tae got sick. One
> of the worst things that can happen to a war orphan is to get
> sick. When you're sick, you can't work to get food and there's
> nobody to look after you. You may die for lack of treatment or
> you may starve to death because you can't help yourself.[40]

Implicit in these kinds of stories was the message that Americans
could win the ideological battle with North Korea and its allies by helping these orphans. Even before the war had ended, magazines like *Life*
and *Collier's* featured articles and photographs illustrating how GIs cared
for Korean waifs: cuddling them, sewing handkerchiefs and overcoats
and dolls for them from rags, feeding them, and distributing Christmas
gifts. American military units airlifted children out of harm's way, built
or supported orphanages and hospitals, and gathered contributions of
food, clothing, and money from friends and family back home.[41] American troops also made cash donations out of their own pay; by 1954 they
had contributed more than $25 million to Korean relief.[42]

The story about the sick orphan Tae was representative, not only
because it described a Korean orphan's miserable life, but because it
included the stock character of a good Samaritan American GI: Tae met
an American sergeant, who took him to a hospital for treatment. As in
many other stories of the time, it was the American who brought a ray
of happiness and hope to a wretched orphan's life.

The third form of American responsibility—responsibility for children fathered by American troops—was the most specific and potent.
Extensive and frank media coverage had alerted Americans to the
ostracism and persecution that GI babies suffered, and adoptive families,
agencies, government officials, and the media remarked repeatedly
about the special responsibility that the United States had to these

children. In the midst of discussions about orphan legislation in July 1956, Oregon Senator Wayne Morse entered twenty-five letters into the *Congressional Record*, all of which had been written by supporters of legislation that would allow GI babies to enter the United States. Many were from parents whose children—adopted for them by proxy—could not enter the country because of existing immigration laws. The majority of these letters attested to a profound sense of responsibility toward the GI babies. "There is not only the moral obligation we Americans feel toward all uncared-for children, but the more definite obligation, knowing our Armed Forces were responsible for these little Korean outcasts," wrote one adoptive couple. Another couple expressed a more prescriptive, though equally widespread, sentiment: "[W]e feel it to be the duty of the United States Government to take over the care of these unfortunate children, for the United States Government sent the fathers of these children into the foreign countries and is therefore responsible for their conduct." Private American citizens could act as proxies for their government and demonstrate their patriotism by "taking over care" of these orphans themselves.[43]

While criticism of the irresponsible fathers of these children was limited in the popular media, these letters reveal a sterner attitude.[44] A letter signed by more than thirty people stated: "We feel that since so many American boys have proved themselves delinquent fathers, that other American families who feel so inclined should be given the opportunity of taking these children who so badly need a home." Not only was the United States responsible for the care of these children, but it had a vested interest in addressing the problem of the mixed-race children that many of its GIs had left behind all throughout Asia, for it would hardly do for the leader of the free world "to have half-American children running about as beggars and potential criminals in the streets of Asian cities."[45] Senator Neuberger invoked a theme of atonement on the Senate floor, stating, "[I]n view of the shabby legacy left by American GIs who fathered these infants. . . [Harry] Holt's work stands out like a beacon of light. We may hope that the Korean people judge America just a little bit by his standards."[46]

CHRISTIAN AMERICANISM: HOME AND HEARTH

Historians including Elaine Tyler May and Wendy Kozol have noted that Americans reacted to the new world of the Cold War by turning inward: getting married, having babies, and moving to the suburbs. In an age of profound danger and uncertainty in the public political arena, 1950s Americans embraced private life, seeking safety and reassurance in their homes and families. For such a society, the thousands of dispossessed Korean waifs in the midst of their devastated country were a stark reminder of the tenuousness of the American image of the home and family as a "secure, private nest removed from the dangers of the outside world." Seeing the plight of Korean orphans was like seeing their own nightmares made real. The utter aloneness of these children, the simple fact that they had neither the comforts of home nor the love of their families struck at the very heart of the values that were important to white, middle-class Americans and offended their vision of how the world should be.[47]

Journalists writing about the orphans increased their punch by hooking into Americans' obsession with domesticity. Like many other pieces of the time, a *Time* story contained the standard description of the privations of an orphan's life—"they sleep in doorways, each noon go to the Pyongyang Noodle Shop, where the proprietor fills their pails with slops from the tables. Neither of them has a pair of shoes"—but the story was made all the more poignant because it included one orphan's memories of his vanished home and family: "[A]t first I used to dream of my mother holding out her arms to me. When it rains I still remember how it was on the warm floor at home. But I don't think so much about my mother now."[48]

Similarly, *Life*'s story of five-year-old Kang Koo Ri, whom the magazine dubbed "the little boy who wouldn't smile," was made all the more heartbreaking by the author's description of Kang's homey little village, the few precious toys that his father had lovingly crafted for him, and the rhythm of his family's daily life before the Communist invasion. After painting this idyllic background, the author related how American GIs found Kang in his deserted house, which reeked with the odor of decay: the naked little boy was sitting next to the decomposing body of his mother.[49]

Many adoptive parents took a child virtually sight unseen, relying on only a picture and a brief description. "The extent of their knowledge was usually that the child was homeless, hungry, and very often ill and that he needed food, parents, and love." In fact, after *Life* featured the story of "the little boy who wouldn't smile," he was adopted by a reader who "got down on [her] knees and prayed and was told to adopt him." Although dramatic, this adoption was far from atypical. In many cases, a few pictures, some prayers, and—notwithstanding some red tape—the adoption was complete.[50]

Harry Holt launched his adoption program "with a three-fold purpose: to save lives, to get these children into homes, and to get them into Christian homes." Moreover, he sought out a certain kind of Christian home for his charges, as indicated by the fact that his agency referred not just Jews, but Catholics, elsewhere.[51] The writer Pearl S. Buck, a contemporary of the Holts and a fellow activist for mixed-race children in Asia, commented on Harry Holt's brand of Christianity in her 1964 book, *Children for Adoption*.[52] She was shocked by her first contact with him:

> [It was] in the form of a questionnaire, which, it seems, he sent to all prospective parents. To me it was an astonishing document. Very few of the questions related in a material sense to the adoptive family. They pertained to religion and, to my thinking, rather a primitive kind of religion. I had grown up in a missionary environment and had seen and known all kinds of Christians. The questionnaire was distinctly what is called Fundamentalist . . . The point was that Harry Holt was giving children to couples who believed in Christian dogma, and not to others who might be far more worthy of parenthood but who did not so believe.[53]

In defense of her father, one of Holt's daughters explained to Buck, "It is the quickest way he knows of finding out whether people are good . . . He realizes that it is an inadequate method, but . . . in his experience the people who believe in a simple practical Christianity are usually good people and will be good to the child."[54]

That Harry Holt's paramount concern was to place GI babies in Christian homes is the clearest evidence of how central his Christian faith was to his mission. Harry Holt was not a Christian Americanist; there is no evidence that he ever articulated any connection between his Christian faith and nationalistic beliefs. His work was wholly centered on a single foundation of Christian doctrine, rather than resting on the twin pillars of Christian Americanism. He was serving God alone, not

God and America. Nonetheless, Christian Americanists anointed Harry Holt their figurehead. The American media celebrated his good works as a Christian as an affirmation of his Americanness, using biblical terms like "mission" and "crusade" to describe his work, while in Congress Senator Neuberger declared that Holt "symbolized. . . the Biblical Good Samaritan."[55]

Moreover, the Holts more than fulfilled what Elaine Tyler May describes as postwar America's "utopian vision" of domestic life, which "included 'replenished' families with male providers 'secure in stable careers' and female housewives 'in comfortable homes' who would 'raise perfect children.'"[56] With her old-fashioned braids, unrouged face, plain dresses, and sensible shoes, Bertha Holt embodied the profoundly domestic spirit of Cold War America. World Vision's Bob Pierce described her as "typical of women who have worked hard to make America a sanctuary for family life."[57] She was also an ideal mother, as evidenced by her six biological children, who were all devout, generous, hardworking, and family-oriented—in other words, "perfect children." For his part, Harry Holt had been a successful lumberman and farmer before embarking on his second career as a missionary and crusader. The Holts, in short, were a utopian American family.

Adoptive parents and the public at large responded to the Christian Americanism that became associated with the Holts. Christian Americanist discourse became the language of the adoption movement, and although religious belief remained the prime motivator of the adoptive parents, Christian Americanist logic seems to have penetrated them also. While it is impossible to discover what exactly motivated the thousands of parents who adopted GI babies between 1955 and 1961, their voices can be found in the letters they wrote to Senator Morse in 1956 and in the testimonials they later gave to social workers and psychologists studying intercountry adoptions. These sources indicate that many adoptive parents regarded adopting Korean GI babies as a way to bear witness to their Christian faith and meet their missionary obligation, which was often a Christian Americanist one as much as it was a Christian one. The causes of Christianizing and Americanizing—each with its own unique logic of rescue—were so closely interwoven in Cold War America that Christian and nationalistic purposes were uttered in the same breath and impossible to separate. Both Christianity and Christian Americanism contributed, in varying proportions, to the decision to adopt.[58]

One set of parents explained to a social worker that their Christian faith was a primary motivation in their decision to adopt: "[W]e all had a strong feeling that to live as professing Christians, we had to do something to help relieve the misery of malnutrition and death for at least one person . . . not just sending monies . . . Korea seemed like a logical place at that time." While these parents saw adoption as a way to demonstrate Christian belief, they also indicate that a feeling of responsibility for the GI babies played a role: "[W]e felt these illegitimate children, abandoned by our brother Americans, was our area of service." Christianity was the impetus, but nationalistic considerations also influenced the decision.[59]

Another parent baldly declared both religious and nationalistic reasons for adoption in his letter to Senator Morse, writing: "[T]his is a wonderful missionary opportunity to bring these children into American Christian homes and raise them to be American citizens." This parent styled himself as an evangelist for God, for country, and for the American way. Another couple echoed the same blend of Christian and Christian Americanist sentiment in their letter, which stated: "[W]e would like to urge you to do all you can to pass [this] bill so children of our American soldiers can be brought to the States to be brought up as good citizens in a Christian nation."[60]

COLOR BLINDNESS AND THE KOREAN ADOPTION MOVEMENT

The missionary mindset of adoptive parents seemingly allowed them to transcend questions of race. As one set of parents declared: "Our girls are our mission field, this brings us great pride. We never see a nationality difference." The evidence supports this claim, for all of the written and spoken discourse that surrounded these adoptions virtually ignored the subject of race. Bertha Holt wrote, "[M]ost of the letters indicate the people don't care whether the children look oriental or not," and noted, "[O]ne woman wrote, 'Send me an ugly baby, or a retarded one that nobody wants. I'll transform that little life with love and tender care.'"[61]

It was the Holts' opponents who made the race of the GI babies an issue. First were the people that Bertha Holt called "cranks," who occasionally called or wrote to protest bringing "slant-eyed Orientals" into the United States. In 1956, she reported, "One crank wrote. . . that he was saving his money for a gun and bus fare to come and shoot Harry for 'bringing in those slant-eyed monsters.' Harry replied that he would pay for the gun." Bertha Holt was equally dismissive of these threats, arguing that these babies were simply "returning to their fathers' land." Like their religious activist predecessors in the abolitionist movement, and their contemporaries in the civil rights movement, the Holts demonstrated a progressive attitude toward race that almost seemed incompatible with their media image as a traditional American family.[62]

A more formidable opponent of the Holts' mission was the American social work establishment, most notably the International Social Service (ISS), which had voted against the Holts' adoption of their own eight children, and refused to cooperate with the Holts once they had established their own agency. In fact, the ISS worked for several years to block the Holts' activity in both Korea and the United States.[63] The primary reason for this resistance was the ISS's opposition to proxy adoptions, which it considered heretical and dangerous. The ISS also felt uneasy about the interracial nature of these adoptions. Midcentury social work orthodoxy dictated the use of careful matching—particularly racial matching—to create adoptive families that simulated biological families and thereby concealed adoption. As such, these guidelines proscribed the placement of Asian or even Amerasian children in white homes. Consequently, as Bertha Holt noted, "in three years they had adopted only seven children overseas."[64]

Matching was an important consideration for a social work establishment that continued to ascribe great power to biology in discussions about race. A midwestern Catholic children's agency placed a mixed black-white child in a white home, but "because his features could not be changed by environment [the agency decided that] the best interests of the child were not being served" and returned him to an institution. Distinctions between races remained as arbitrary and fluid as the definition of race itself. At a 1960 symposium on "The Adoption of Oriental Children by American White Families," an ISS caseworker recounted a colleague's attempt to prevent a white family, who already had a Korean-white son, from adopting a Chinese girl, since he thought "it would be hard for the Korean-Caucasian boy to have a sister of a different race." The drawing of a distinction between Korean (or Korean-Caucasian) and Chinese illustrates how scrupulously social workers attempted to draw racial boundaries, even within the "Oriental" category. At the same time, a monolithic view of whiteness prevailed, as indicated in the belief that white couples could raise mixed-race children "as members of the white race."[65]

American social workers classified nonwhite and mixed-race children such as GI babies—along with older children and those with health problems or disabilities—as unadoptable. As Harry Holt explained to Pearl Buck, "Our children could never meet the standards of some of the state agencies, just because they are of a different race from the adoptive parents. I remember that on the back of one of our applications, sent to a state agency, a few words were scrawled: 'We will help bring a child from Europe, but from Asia? Never!'" Racism in the United States deterred social workers, who feared for the well-being of the child: "The feeling that complete desegregation is generations away fosters a strong reluctance. . . to mix the races." It was not until the end of the 1950s that these mainline agencies began to place children across the color line in significant numbers.[66]

Members of the social work establishment also expressed pessimism about how white Americans would respond to nonwhite children and expressed surprise at instances of acceptance: "When the [GI babies] began coming into the communities, we had some question about whether the community would accept the child. We found, however, that the reaction was: 'They're sweet.'. . . This was a bit of a surprise to us." Social workers also worried that a dearth of future marriage prospects might discourage adoptive parents from adopting a nonwhite child: "So many people say, 'I would like to adopt except what is going to happen to them later?'" An anthropologist fretted: "[I]nterracial marriage, though on the increase, is still a real problem in this country. . . even if the child learns to compensate for his foreign background and physical distinction by competitive striving—what about intermarriage?"[67]

Although labeled unadoptable, mixed-race children were considered more adoptable than non-mixed-race Asian children. Whereas one drop of black blood made a person black in the United States, one drop of Asian blood did not seem to render a person Asian. Instead, in a reversal of the "one-drop" rule, Korean-white children were thought to be whitened—redeemed—by the presence of "white" blood. Although still "other," they were tolerably so. An ISS case worker noted that "a certain family and community identification with these children as half-American" made it easier to place mixed-race children. Possibly, the ASA believed that living in his or her father's land would encourage the development of the white "half" of a child, which would then defeat or suppress the alien Korean "half." On the other hand, non-mixed-race Asian children remained difficult to place: "[A]gencies will report that a family would like to be considered for an Oriental-American child, but could not accept a purely Oriental child. The family themselves might accept the latter but doubt that the community would."[68]

For their part, the Holts only raised the issue of race when discussing the Korean-black orphans, as it was difficult to find homes for them almost from the beginning. In keeping with accepted social work practice, the Holts had initially attempted to match Korean-black children with black adoptive parents. Bertha Holt noted, "Some people say they'd be willing to take the babies with oriental and negro blood; but Harry and I are hoping the negro people will open their hearts and homes to those children. It would be so much kinder for the children to grow up in the society of the race their fathers belonged to."[69] The problem of finding black homes for Korean-black children persisted through the first several years of the Holt Adoption Program, although placement was easier in the case of girls. In 1956, the Holts noted a shortage of Korean-black girls, while orphanages were filled with Korean-black boys. In 1959, the Holts listed "homes for little Black-Korean boys" among their prayer requests, and three years later, the program's newsletter indicated that placing Korean-black children was still a problem.[70]

By the mid-1960s, the Holts seem to have solved this problem; they began placing Korean-black children with any available family—that is to say, with white families—just as they did with Korean-white children. This shift was necessitated by the unavailability of black adoptive families, but it also may have reflected a larger shift in Holt adoption policy that was prompted by the changing orphan population. By the beginning of the 1960s, non-mixed-race Korean children comprised the majority of the orphans being placed in the United States. Whereas the Holts had placed GI babies in the community that corresponded with their American "half" (Korean-blacks in black families and Korean-whites in white families), there was no corresponding community for children of full Korean parentage, and the Holts placed these children with any available family. It seems characteristically pragmatic of them to have extended that practice to Korean-black children as well.[71]

One final question looms large on the subject of racelessness and GI babies: Why were white families willing to adopt Korean-black babies?

If the presence of white blood might have diminished the "otherness" of Korean-white children, in a parallel phenomenon, a triangulation of race may have operated to mitigate the blackness of Korean-black babies. Just as the white blood of Korean-white babies whitened them, the Korean blood of Korean-black babies may have served a similar function. Korean-black babies were less white than Korean-white babies, but they were also less black than fully black babies. Thus, if an adoptive parent were to choose between nonwhite babies, a partly Korean one may have been preferable to one that was wholly black.

CONCLUSION

Commenting on the 1958 memoir *White Mother*, written by a black woman who had been raised by a white woman in the American South, Pearl S. Buck praised what she saw as the book's solution to racial conflict: "I am not saying too much when I declare that were we all to follow in the footsteps of this one white mother, we would need not ask how to achieve peace on earth. Peace would be here." For Buck, inter-racial adoption was not only a personal choice, but a profoundly politi-cal act available to any concerned American. By ending racial conflict, these adoptions could ultimately end the problem of Communism, for a United States that showed such love to nonwhite children could be assured of winning Asia's allegiance, as well as the loyalty of the entire free world.[72]

The adoptions of Korean GI babies between 1955 and 1961 offered Christians and Christian Americanists alike a means by which to enact their beliefs. For devout Christians like Harry Holt, adopting a GI baby was missionary work, through which they could bear witness to their faith and serve God. For Christian Americanists like Pearl Buck, these adoptions represented a way for patriotic Cold War Americans to partic-ipate in their country's international Christianizing and Americanizing mission.

The American social work establishment stood conspicuously out-side this arrangement, for whereas both Christians and Christian Americanists claimed to be unconcerned with color, social workers' preoccupation with it was almost paralyzing. Perhaps their difficulty with race reflects a candor about the subject that is absent from the more simplified perspectives espoused by Christians and Christian Americanists, who somewhat naively—or perhaps disingenuously—

believed that "the deliberate nonrecognition of race" would end racial conflict. The hope of ultimately eradicating racism may not have been their primary motivation for adopting, but both groups clearly believed in the power of color blindness.[73]

Yet the idea of color-blind interracial adoption insists on racial difference at the same time it disavows it. On the one hand, the adoptive parents of a GI baby demonstrated a willingness and ability to rise above race; but on the other hand, they acted out a central allegory of imperial discourse, in which the pairing of the white parent and the nonwhite child served to justify and naturalize hierarchical power relations between white and nonwhite races. It may be that mainline social workers were the only ones to acknowledge that conscious color blindness might not make race—or racism—disappear. Race would continue to do work in interracial adoptions, even when the people involved denied its existence.[74]

Interracial adoption from Korea served an important ideological function during the Cold War by providing the American government with the language of love and family to explain what looked like imperialistic activity in Asia. Christians like Harry Holt and the other adoptive parents of GI babies contributed to this trope, by embodying how a family's love could "transcend the boundaries of race and nationality." For their counterparts, the Christian Americanists, the American nation was the family that lovingly transcended boundaries, and spread the Christian and American values that would end racism and Communism everywhere.[75]

ARISSA OH is a Ph.D. candidate in the history department at the University of Chicago. She studies twentieth-century U.S. history with a focus on race and immigration. She is currently working on her dissertation about the history of Korean adoption in the United States.

NOTES

1. Howard A. Rusk, "Voice from Korea: 'Won't You Help Us Off Our Knees?,'" *Life* 36 (7 June 1954): 178–80.
2. In an attempt to reflect the language used during the period I am studying, I use the term *orphan* to describe both mixed-race GI babies and non-mixed-race Korean children who were abandoned, lost, or otherwise left without adults to care for them. However, it is extremely important to remember that not all of

the Korean children who were institutionalized or adopted during and after the Korean War were orphans. Many still had one or both parents but had been relinquished for one reason or another.

3. Although American GIs were not responsible for all of these children, Koreans and Americans alike persisted in calling them "GI babies" and the term stuck. I use the term throughout this essay to reflect the discourse of the period.

4. Roy A. Eckardt, "The New Look in American Piety," the *Christian Century* 71 (17 November 1954): 1396.

5. Adopting by proxy was the method through which Harry Holt completed adoptions from Korea in the early years of his adoption program. In such an adoption, American parents living in the United States gave power of attorney to a proxy in Korea—such as Harry Holt—who completed the adoption in Korean courts recognized by U.S. law. The child then entered the United States as the legal son or daughter of the American couple. Proxy adoptions took up to three months to complete, compared to more than two years. The American social work establishment tried to put a stop to proxy adoptions, which it opposed from the beginning, maintaining that the practice was inconsistent with established methods for matching children and families. Ron Moxness, "Good Samaritan of Korea," *American Mercury*, October 1956: 86; Bertha Holt, *Bring My Sons from Afar* (Eugene, OR: Holt International Children's Services, 1986), 12; Dong Soo Kim, *Intercountry Adoptions* (Ph.D. dissertation, University of Chicago, 1976), 6.

6. Although sixteen countries sent troops to fight as part of the U.N. Command (UNC), American forces constituted the vast majority of the UNC. As of the 1953 Armistice, American troops constituted 32.4 percent of the total UNC and 88.5 percent of the non-Korean UNC. U.S. Forces Korea, Public Affairs Office, "Backgrounder No. 1: United Nations Command," accessed 24 February 2005, http://www.korea.army. mil/pao/backgrounder/BG1.htm.

7. In 1953 UN estimates pegged the total orphan population at between 100,000 and 125,000 children, but 100,000 is the figure most frequently cited. The estimated number of GI babies is an American Embassy estimate. "Amendment of Refugee Relief Act of 1953," *Congressional Record*, 84th Congress, 2nd Session, Vol. 102, Part 6 (30 April 1956): 7247–9.

8. According to Korean law, a child must be listed under his or her father's name in a family registry to be a citizen. While an illegitimate Korean child could be secretly added to the family register, obvious physical differences made this impossible for GI babies. Without a family register, a GI baby could not be accepted socially. He or she would find it nearly impossible to attend school, find work, or get married, and would not even receive proper Korean funeral rites. Louis O'Conner, *The Adjustment of a Group of Korean and Korean-American Children Adopted by Couples in the United States* (M.A. thesis, University of Tennessee, 1964), 18; Margo Okazawa-Rey, "Amerasian Children of GI Town: A Legacy of U.S. Militarism in South Korea," *Asian Journal of Women's Studies* 3 (1997): 71–102.

9. O'Conner, 18.

10. Mothers "made pathetic attempts to disguise the identity of their children by dying their hair and eyelashes black or keeping the hair always covered up." Margaret A. Valk, *Korean-American Children in American Adoptive Homes* (New York: Child Welfare League of America, 1957), 6; O'Conner, 19–21.

11. Bertha Holt and David Wisner, *The Seed from the East* (Los Angeles: Oxford Press, 1956): 2; O'Conner, 11.

12. In 1957, International Social Service estimated that more than 500 orphanages in Korea housed more than 50,000 homeless children of *purely Korean* parentage; that figure excluded countless other homeless Korean children and an unknown number of GI babies. The option of in-country adoption was also unavailable to GI babies. The Korean culture's emphasis on purity meant that Koreans rarely adopted, and adopting mixed-race children was out of the question. Furthermore, the Korean preference for sons meant that girls were almost never adopted. Valk, 4; *Alien Adopted Children: Hearing before the Subcommittee on Immigration, Citizenship, and International Law of the Committee on the Judiciary House of Representatives* (Washington, DC: U.S. Government Printing Office, 1978), 23–5.

13. Valk, 4; O'Conner, 22.

14. With a readership of about 20 million, *Life*—the most widely read general magazine of the 1945–60 period—played a major role in structuring Americans' understanding of the world around them. See Wendy Kozol, "'Good Americans': Nationalism and Domesticity in *Life* Magazine, 1945–1960" in *Bonds of Affection: Americans Define Their Patriotism*, ed. John Bodnar (Princeton: Princeton University Press, 1996), 231–32. Kozol notes that "[a]lthough television was fast becoming the dominant form of visual entertainment. . . *Life* was the main source of visual news for Americans during the 1940s and 1950s." For an in-depth discussion of how *Life* shaped Americans' view of themselves and their world, see Wendy Kozol, *Life's America* (Philadelphia: Temple University Press, 1994).

15. The Christian Children's Fund (CCF) was founded by Dr. J. Calvitt Clarke, a Presbyterian minister, in 1938. It was originally intended to aid Chinese children orphaned by the Sino-Japanese war. American response to its sponsorship program was so great that CCF was able to expand throughout Asia. By 1955, CCF supported children in fifteen Asian countries, with a yearly budget of $1.8 million. Christina Klein, "Family Ties and Political Obligation: The Discourse of Adoption and the Cold War Commitment to Asia," in *Cold War Constructions: The Political Culture of United States Imperialism, 1945–1966*, ed. Christian Appy (Amherst: University of Massachusetts Press, 2000), 45.

16. Advertisements found in various issues of the *Christian Century*, 1953.

17. Christina Klein argues that the American-Asian family created by this sponsorship was an important two-way site of education. Through this education, Americans developed affective ties to Asia, which were critical to the U.S. government's garnering public support for its anti-Communist activity in various Asian countries. Klein, 50.

18. Holt, *Bring My Sons from Afar*, 9, 11.

19. The Holt agency, now called Holt International Children's Services, has operations in more than a dozen countries and continues to be a leader in intercountry
adoptions. Holt placement numbers are from Holt, *The Seed from the East*.

20. Mary L. Dudziak, *Cold War Civil Rights: Race and the Image of American Democracy*
(Princeton: Princeton University Press, 2000); Klein, 39, 54.

21. More than 7,000 Koreans migrated to Hawaii between 1903 and 1905 to work on
sugar plantations. After the Japanese occupation of Korea began in 1905, the
United States stopped recognizing Korean passports. The 1907 "Gentlemen's
Agreement," designed to curtail immigration from Japan, also curtailed Korean
immigration. However, under the provision for family members, more than
1,000 Korean "picture brides" arrived in Hawaii between 1910 and 1924. Insook
Han Park, James T. Fawcett, Fred Arnold, and Robert W. Gardner, *Korean
Immigrants and U.S. Immigration Policy: A Predeparture Perspective* (Honolulu: Papers
of the East-West Population Institute, No. 114, 1989), 6.

22. Bruce Cumings, "Occurrence at Nogun-Ri Bridge: An Inquiry into the History
and Memory of a Civil War," *Critical Asian Studies* 33:4 (December 2001), 521.
On American stereotypes of North Korean and Chinese soldiers, Craig Coleman writes: "One of the most enduring images of fighting in Korea for both the
GIs and the people back home were the images of hordes of Chinese and North
Koreans attacking GI positions in human waves. What the 'Reds' lacked in
modern weapons they often made up in sheer numbers of troops, and an overrun
attack was often very effective tactic to seize ground from UN forces [sic].
Usually only a small percentage of the attacking Chinese troops actually had
weapons with just a few rounds. As their comrades would fall in front of them,
Chinese soldiers would pick-up [sic] their weapons and continue the charge,
drunk or drugged-up, bugles blowing, with loudspeakers in the back blaring
martial music and anti-UN propaganda." Craig S. Coleman, *American Images of
Korea* (Elizabeth, NJ: Hollym International, 1990).

23. Rusk, 184, 187.

24. Klein, 44. See also Harold E. Fey's five-part series on the Korean War, published in the *Christian Century* in January and February 1952.

25. In orphanages run by American missionaries, children often had English lessons
and learned English-language Christian songs. It is unclear whether they actually understood the words to these songs, or if they simply learned them by rote.

26. Michael Rougier, "The Little Boy Who Wouldn't Smile," *Life* 30 (23 July 1951):
93; Holt, *The Seed from the East*, 20; Bill Stapleton, "Little Orphan Island," *Collier's* 128 (14 July 1951), 51; Sydne Didier, *"Just a Drop in the Bucket": An Analysis
of Child Rescue Efforts on Behalf of Korean Children, 1951 to 1964* (M.A. thesis, Port-
land State University, 1998), 13.

27. The parents were generally middle-aged and held high-school diplomas, while a
smaller proportion of them had completed at least some college. They often had
one or two children of their own prior to adopting a Korean child, and most
adopted two or three children. Louis O'Conner and Dong Soo Kim completed

two of the earliest social work studies of how adopted Korean children were adjusting to their American homes in 1964 and 1976, respectively. Their findings fall in line with other similar studies. I have made general statements here based on information available in all these sources.

28. Eisenhower's statements quoted in Didier, 47. The Refugee Relief Act of 1953 increased by 214,000 the number of visas to be made available to immigrants: 186,000 for refugees and escapees from Communist-dominated countries; 19,000 for over-quota Italian, Greek, and Dutch immigrants; and 4,000 for orphans. In addition, the Act provided 5,000 visas for people already in the United States on limited-stay visas. These 214,000 visas were issued in addition to the 550,000 normally issued visas for a total of 764,000. See Frank L. Auerbach, *The Refugee Relief Act of 1953 as Amended*, Department of State Publication 5615, General Foreign Policy Series 94 (Washington, DC: U.S. Government Printing Office, 1954); and U.S. Department of State, Public Services Division, *The Refugee Relief Act of 1953: What It Is—How It Works,* Department of State Publication 5382, General Foreign Policy Series 87 (Washington, DC: U.S. Government Printing Office, 1954).

29. Elaine Tyler May, *Homeward Bound: American Families in the Cold War Era.* (New York: Basic Books, 1988).

30. Klein, 35, 42. Klein argues that the media used the language of family to create affective ties between Americans and Asians in order to create support for the expansion of American influence during the Cold War.

31. Untitled opening editorial, *Life* 38–40 (26 December 1955): 13.

32. "The Testimony of a Devout President," *Life* 39–40 (26 December 1955): 12.

33. "An Unprecedented Wave of Religious Observance Sweeps Over the U.S," *Life* 39–40 (26 December 1955): 46. On Flag Day in June 1954, Congress passed a law that added "under God" to the pledge. Department of Veteran's Affairs, "The Pledge of Allegiance," accessed February 3, 2002 http://www.va.gov/pubaff/ celebam/ pledge.htm.

34. Eckardt, 1395–96. The *Christian Century* and *Christianity and Crisis* are two nondenominational Christian periodicals that were widely read at the time.

35. In 1955, *Life* devoted several special issues to "The World's Great Religions." Saint Hereticus wrote this article in response to that series. In a sly aside, he made a sharp dig at *Life*, which he clearly felt was to blame for spreading this faith: "Strange irony, that *Life* magazine has failed to give due notice to this religion. Sometimes, apparently, it is the better part of journalistic wisdom not to let the left hand know what the right hand is doing." "The World's Important Religions," *Christianity and Crisis* 15 (13 June 1955): 79.

36. "Admission of Refugee Orphans to Citizenship in United States," *Congressional Record,* 85th Cong., 2nd Sess., Vol. 104, P. 2 (19 February 1958): 2398.

37. "The Testimony of a Devout President," 13.

38. Rusk, 187.

39. In case readers missed this message, editors were conscientious about spelling it out in photo captions that dubbed them "innocent victims of war." William J.

Lederer and Nelle Keys Perry, "Operation Kid-Lift," *Ladies Home Journal* 69 (12 December 1952): 49.

40. Marvin Koner, "Korea's Children: The Old in Heart," *Collier's* 132 (25 July 1953): 24–25.

41. "Operation Kiddy Car," "Operation Mascot," "Operation Kid-Lift," and "Operation Orphan Annie" were just four of the special evacuation and relief operations undertaken by American soldiers on behalf of the orphans. U.S. military newssheets in Korea abounded with news of GI efforts undertaken on behalf of Korean children. Many articles describing the good deeds of the American military were written by military personnel, who had a significant stake in shaping how the American public perceived them and their presence in Korea. Mosier, 652; Didier 13, 18, 25; Coleman, 149–50; Rougier, 92; Lederer and Perry, 48–49 passim.

42. Rusk, 184.

43. "Increase in Number of Visas to be Issued to Orphans Under the Refugee Relief Act of 1953." *Congressional Record* 84th Cong., 2nd Sess., Vol. 102, P. 11 (26 July 1956): 14741–3.

44. Popular magazines like *Life* muted their criticism of the American fathers of these babies, but Christian periodicals were more disapproving. The *Christian Century*, for example, called for preinduction education, which it hoped would better prepare naive young American men for the dangerous temptations of overseas Army life.

45. "Increase in Number of Visas," *Cong. Rec.*, 14742; Pearl S. Buck, *Children for Adoption* (New York: Random House, 1964), 167.

46. "Mr. Holt 'Moves the World,'" *Oregonian,* 9 April 1956, as quoted in "Amendment of Refugee Relief Act of 1953," *Cong. Rec.* 7247; "Admission of Refugee Orphans," *Cong. Rec.* 2397.

47. Elaine Tyler May, "Cold War—Warm Hearth: Politics and the Family in Postwar America," in *The Rise and Fall of the New Deal Order, 1930–1980,* ed. Steve Fraser and Gary Gerstle (Princeton: Princeton University Press, 1989), 153–81. In *Homeward Bound* and *Life's America*, respectively, Elaine Tyler May and Wendy Kozol explore what Alan Brinkley calls "the enormous cultural emphasis on family life in the 1950s." Alan Brinkley, *The Unfinished Nation: A Concise History of the American People,* 2nd ed. (Boston: McGraw Hill, 1997), 809.

48. "The Forgotten People," *Time* 58 (15 July 1951): 23.

49. Rougier, 92.

50. O'Conner, 129.

51. Bertha Holt, *Outstretched Arms* (Eugene, OR: Holt International Children's Services, 1972), 283; "New Faces," *Time* 70 (23 December 1957): 16.

52. Pearl S. Buck established Welcome House, an adoption agency, in 1949. Unlike the Holts, Buck set out to help Amerasian children who were compelled to remain in Asia. Her focus later changed to placing Amerasians for intercountry adoption.

53. Buck, 152–53.

54. Buck,154–55.
55. "Amendment of Refugee Relief Act of 1953," *Cong. Rec.* 7247. Indeed, *American Mercury* published a piece about Harry Holt: Ron Moxness, "Good Samaritan of Korea," *American Mercury* (October 1956): 84–88.
56. May, *Homeward Bound*, 51.
57. Holt, *The Seed from the East*, Notes about the authors [no page number].
58. In his 1976 study of self-concept among Holt adoptees, Dong Soo Kim analyzed questionnaires completed by 406 adoptive families. One of the questions asked was, "What do you believe was your *primary motivation* to seek the adoption of this child?" Kim discovered that the leading reasons behind the adoptions—as reported by these 406 families—were (1) love of children and parenting (32.7 percent of respondents); (2) humanitarian/religious concern (30.9 percent); and (3) responsibility for and interest in Korea (10.3 percent). These findings suggest that Christian Americanist concerns—as represented by the third-most popular reason—did play a small, but significant, role in the adoption decisions. Other less popular reasons were (4) sterility (9.9 percent); (5) compensation or completion for family (8.8 percent); (6) others (6.3 percent); and (7) population explosion (1.1 percent). Approximately half of the 406 respondents had adopted between 1956 and 1962, while the other half adopted between 1962 and 1972. Kim, 87, 90–91.
59. O'Conner, 29.
60. "Increase in Number of Visas," *Cong. Rec.* 14743.
61. Kim, 107; Holt, *The Seed from the East*, 236.
62. Holt, *The Seed from the East*, 200–05; Holt, *Bring My Sons from Afar*, 13, 29; Didier, 115. The Holts did not seem to recognize a relationship between their efforts and the civil rights movement. In fact, Bertha Holt grew frustrated at Congress's inability to consider an orphan bill because of the volume of civil rights legislation before it: "Congress wouldn't quit squabbling about civil rights long enough to save orphans' lives." Holt, *Bring My Sons from Afar*, 44.
63. The ISS attempted to block the adoptions through a number of means: by deliberately misinforming parents about their legal options, by influencing the American embassy to stop issuing orphan visas, and by speaking out in the media against the Holts' practices. See Holt, *Bring My Sons from Afar*. Bertha Holt mentions the American Social Agency (ASA) but I have not found evidence of any such agency, and research suggests she was actually referring to the ISS.
64. Buck, 157; Holt, *Bring My Sons from Afar*, 9.
65. Joseph A. Owens, "Adopting Negro Children," *America* 97 (15 September 1957): 623; *Adoption of Oriental Children by American White Families: An Interdisciplinary Symposium* (New York: Child Welfare League of America, 1960), 12.
66. Buck, 157; Owens, 623. "The introduction of birth control pills in 1960, changing cultural patterns of white teen-age sexuality in the 1960s and 1970s, changing social attitudes regarding single parenting, and the legalization of abortion in 1973, all contributed to an increase in transracial placements in the late 1960s

and early 1970s." Sandra Patton, *BirthMarks: Transracial Adoption in Contemporary America* (New York: New York University Press, 2000), 46.

67. *Adoption of Oriental Children by American White Families*, 26, 32, 34. In contrast to the worried anthropologist, one Holt agency adoptive parent told *Oregonian* reporter William Hilliard that he wasn't worried about intermarriage. Hilliard wrote, "He has confidence in America's free society and feels that by the time his daughters near the courting stage, 'they will take care of themselves.'" Didier, 99.

68. *Adoption of Oriental Children by American White Families*, 11.

69. Holt, *The Seed from the East*, 236.

70. Holt, *Bring My Sons from Afar*, 27, 103, 167; "New Faces," 16.

71. Holt, *Outstretched Arms*, 283–4; Kim, 69.

72. Jessie Bennett Sams won the *Saturday Review*'s Anisfield-Wolf Award in Race Relations for her memoir, *White Mother*, in 1958. Buck was on the judging committee. Klein, 62–63.

73. Peggy Pascoe, "Miscegenation Law, Court Cases, and Ideologies of 'Race' in Twentieth-Century America," *Journal of American History* 83 (June 1996): 48.

74. Klein, 63–4.

75. Holt, *The Seed from the East*, preface; Klein, 60.

STRONGER, SMARTER, AND LESS QUEER: "THE WHITE NEGRO" AND MAILER'S THIRD MAN

FREDERICK WHITING

> *The relationship of a black boy, therefore, to a white boy is a very complex thing.*
> —James Baldwin, "The Black Boy Looks at the White Boy"

The last few years have seen the beginning of a salutary attempt among U.S. cultural historians to complicate the organizing rubrics under which we approach the postwar period in general and the 1950s in particular. Work such as Morris Dickstein's *Leopards in the Temple* and the recent "'50s Culture" edition of *the minnesota review* edited by Andrew Hoberek, to cite just two prominent examples, index in their different ways a developing tendency not so much to abandon keywords such as "Cold War" and "containment" that have presided over postwar studies for the last twenty years as to contextualize and complicate the ideological impulses these terms denote within the broader cultural phenomenology of the postwar period. This reframing of concerns has been geared toward developing new analytic categories for U.S. postwar geopolitical operations (diplomatic, military, and commercial) as well as for the domestic issues and anxieties whose connection to such operations rubrics as "containment" have so persuasively demonstrated. The shift holds great promise not only for reshaping our picture of U.S. international relations but for reworking our understanding of the pressing domestic issues of the postwar period.

In a provocative contribution to this reframing, Christina Klein offers "integration" as an analytic alternative to "containment" as a tool for understanding racial, sexual, and individual identity in the postwar period. Drawing on the insights of revisionist economic and diplomatic historians, Klein argues that the U.S. foreign policy imperative to integrate third world nations into a global free-market economy after World War II helped to produce "a global imaginary, a structure of

[*WSQ: Women's Studies Quarterly* 33: 3 & 4 (Fall/Winter 2005)]

feeling, and a cultural logic" that extended beyond the diplomatic sphere (Klein, 156). Both internationally and domestically, the cultural logic of integration generated images of racial identity that outlined difference principally in order to assimilate it through figures of commonality and pluralistic inclusion. According to Klein, the discourse of sentimentalism constituted a generic cornerstone of this integrationist refiguration of race relations. Understood as a complex of representational conventions, sentimentalism recast race in terms of extended kinship and the bonds of filial affection rather than the often bellicose atomic individualism that informed containment ideology. In so doing, the integrationist imaginary produced an alternative formulation of the connections between race and sexuality. According to Klein, in place of the individualistic erotic desire of the romantic couple, sentimentalism substituted the horizontal and noncoercive relations of the family to characterize race relations. This recasting of race "allows us to see the ways in which postwar culture often decentered masculinity and violence in its construction of a global-ized American national identity and gave pride of place to feminized narratives of international love, friendship, domesticity, and peaceful exchange" (Klein, 156). Through sentimental discourse, the integra-tionist imaginary provided not only an alternative model of collective racial affiliation, but also a model of self-in-relation and a de-emphasiz-ing of erotic desire as an issue in race relations.

In order to gauge the interaction of these competing cultural logics, I want to examine their intersection in one of the postwar period's most incendiary treatments of race and sexuality—Norman Mailer's "The White Negro." Begun as a charged plea for integration in Southern schools, on its publication the essay was alternately applauded and assailed as a radical revision of narratives of race and sexuality. More recently, it has been identified as reactionary—a reiteration of stereo-types of black male hypersexuality and criminality and a strikingly pure endorsement of the freestanding individualism that underwrote contain-ment ideology. Though articulated with varying degrees of approval, critical responses have uniformly characterized the essay as a flight from the sentimental domestication of masculinity to the free-standing masculine individualism associated with containment.

What I want to suggest is that this reception tendency has persis-tently ignored the complexity of the text's configuration of sexuality and race. More particularly, it seems to me that critics have given scant attention to Mailer's quite explicit interest in homosexual and bisexual desire in "The White Negro," as well as in his fictional embodiments of the essay's theoretical centerpiece, the hipster. In my account, the essay neither fully adopts the freestanding phallic individualism of containment ideology nor embraces the domesticated masculinity to which it has, correctly, been taken to be in reaction. Rather, it attempts to construct another position—a third man rather than simply a *tertium quid*—in order to explore the normative exclusions that structure *both* sentimental and containment narratives, namely, same-sex erotic identifications. At the heart of this attempt to formulate an alternative position is an exploration of male passivity—a dimension of masculine experience that containment logic actively repudiated and sentimental-integrationist logic effectively ignored. I intend this reading to be a complement to, rather than a replacement of, those that concentrate on the homophobic, racist, and misogynistic reverberations of Mailer's texts, which seem to me real enough, though only one part of the story. Placed alongside these readings, my own will help make visible the tensions and incoherences *within* the agentive, heteronormative ideal Mailer simultaneously adopts and contests as a solution to problems of postwar life. Mailer's fascination with male passivity points up the interrelation, indeed the utter inextricability, of homo-, bi-, and heterosexual orientations in the period's formulation of masculine desire as well as the scarcity of legitimate outlets for the exploration of that interrelation. Viewed in these terms, the essay helps to illuminate an exclusion shared by ostensibly oppositional cultural logics and should prompt us to more closely examine the continuities as well as the discontinuities between those logics. It should also prompt us to wonder how to account for the critical repression of Mailer's interest in homoerotic identifications and masculine passivity.

First published in *Dissent* in 1957, but more widely disseminated as the centerpiece of Mailer's literary anthology-cum-autobiography, *Advertisements for Myself* (1959), "The White Negro" described the emergence of a new figure, the hipster, on the postwar American landscape as a response to the dilemma of political agency experienced by the postwar subject. According to Mailer, the "psychic havoc" of the war—the image of "a death which could not follow with dignity as a possible consequence to serious actions we had chosen, but rather a death by *deus ex machina* in a gas chamber or radioactive city"—produced the birth of a new form of subjectivity:

In such places as Greenwich Village, a ménage-à-trois was completed—the bohemian and the juvenile delinquent came face-to-face with the Negro, and the hipster was a fact in American life. If marijuana was the wedding ring, the child was the language of Hip for its argot gave expression to abstract states of feeling which all could share, at least all who were Hip. And in this wedding of the white and the black it was the Negro who brought the cultural dowry. Any Negro who wishes to live must live with danger from his first day, and no experience can ever be casual to him, no Negro can saunter down a street with any real certainty that violence will not visit him on his walk. The cameos of security for the average white: mother and the home, job and the family, are not even a mockery to millions of Negroes; they are impossible. The Negro has the simplest of alternatives: live a life of constant humility or ever-threatening danger. In such a pass where paranoia is as vital to survival as blood, the Negro has stayed alive and begun to grow by following the need of his body where he could (Mailer, 314).

Faced with the political and existential crises of Hiroshima and the Holocaust, the hipster is driven to emulate the sexually predatory black male, who by virtue of his economic and psychological marginalization in U.S. society was, according to Mailer, best adapted to resist the loss of individual agency accompanying the increasingly totalitarian political tendencies of the Cold War. In this, Mailer advocates a retreat to what he holds to be the more circumscribed and maneuverable sphere of sexual agency. Through this retreat to the sexual, the hipster departs from the integrationist logic Klein identifies by imitating a figure for whom the mainstays of sentimental domesticity—mother, home, and family—are "impossible." By abandoning domestic ideals, he instead embodies the desire of the romantic couple, which Klein opposes to sentimental forms of affiliation.[1] For the hipster, the black man becomes both model and rival in a competition for "the sweet," Mailer's slang for life-renewing sexual conquest: "Unstated but obvious is the social sense that there is not nearly enough sweet for everyone. And so the sweet goes only to the victor, the best, the most, the man who knows the most about how to find his energy and how not to lose it" (322). This dynamic is ostensibly set against an excluded homoerotic desire. The loser in this competition for the sweet suffers emasculation at the hands of his rival—experiences, in Mailer's words, "the demeaning flip of becoming a queer" (325–26).

The structural dynamic through which this reiteration of normative desire purportedly occurs—the triangle comprising the White Negro, his model/rival (the Negro), and the "sweet" for which they compete (the female object of desire)—anticipates with uncanny precision the coordinates of one of the period's landmark studies of literary representations of erotic attraction, René Girard's *Deceit, Desire, and the Novel* (1965). In Girard's schematization of desire, relations between a desiring subject and a desired object are always part of a larger triangular dynamic. The subject's desire for the object is structured less by qualities intrinsic to the object itself than by the fact that the object is already desired by another. Girard's examination, which concentrates on highbrow European novels, focuses on instances in which the active principle of the triangle is indicatively male, usually two males vying for a female embodying the principle of passivity. And even when no third party explicitly figures in the story, a triangle is established by the woman herself becoming both rival and object through her resistance to the male subject's desire. In this permutation, through her resistance to surrender, the woman's body becomes the object over which subject and rival (the woman herself) struggle. Thus, the subject's desire is always fundamentally imitative, mediated as it is by the desire of the Other.[2]

It is little wonder that recent criticism has seen in Mailer's essay a reassertion of compulsory heterosexuality at the heart of containment individualism. A certain strain of his rhetoric fits perfectly with Girard's universalizing triangle of heterosexual desire—perhaps a little too perfectly. We do well to notice that the triangle in Mailer's myth of the hipster's origins has only male coordinates. Although the Negro is the embodiment of absolute activity and a model for the White Negro's transcendence, he is simultaneously cast in the passive position as bearer of the cultural dowry. And if the ideal of heterosexual virility embodied in the hipster had as its unspoken exclusion same-sex relations between men, Mailer is everywhere unusually willing to speak the exclusion, to formulate its dynamic principle—a willingness that critics have been reluctant to acknowledge.[3]

The much-remarked-on exchange over "The White Negro" between James Baldwin and Eldridge Cleaver, and its more recent deployment by Robert Corber, illustrate the odd blend of acumen and avoidance with which critics have received the text. In his 1961 *Esquire* article "The Black Boy Looks at the White Boy," Baldwin was one of the earliest readers to question Mailer's appropriation of black male sexuality to further his project of describing a new subjectivity for the postwar era. Noting the persistence of the stereotype of the hypersexual African American male, Baldwin describes his fury and perplexity at Mailer's essay and asks, "Why malign the sorely menaced sexuality of Negroes in order to justify the white man's sexual panic?"[4] Robert Corber aligns himself with Baldwin, describing "The White Negro" as "[T]he *locus classicus* of left-wing racist constructions of black male identity" (Corber, 44).[5] On Corber's account, Baldwin's reservations are identical to his own charge that the essay legitimated the criminalization of black male identity in order to critique the domestication of masculinity that accompanied the reorganization of postwar life. To clarify Baldwin's objections and underscore the dangers of Mailer's political position, Corber cites Eldridge Cleaver's homophobic discussion of Baldwin in *Soul on Ice* as the logical extension of Mailer's position in "The White Negro." In *Soul on Ice*, Cleaver hails "The White Negro" as the prelude to a liberatory political platform for black Americans and attacks Baldwin's objections as an anathema to black liberation. He reads Baldwin's reservations about "The White Negro" as symptomatic of the larger problem of black sexual and political emasculation. In this reading, both Baldwin's own homosexuality and that of his literary characters represent the perpetually frustrated desire to have a baby by a white man, a desire tantamount to collusion with whites who would keep blacks politically passive (feminized). Thus, according to Corber, Cleaver's response embodies the linkage of a violent heterosexual regime (underscored by Cleaver's own history of rape) and the homophobia that he alleges Baldwin feared: "Baldwin worried that Mailer's legitimation of racist stereotypes would be used to deny gay African American men their claims to blackness" (Corber, 47–48).

Although the hipster indisputably participates in the life of the stereotype to which Baldwin and Corber object, this particular characterization of Mailer's position operates at the expense of recognizing other equally striking features of "The White Negro" and *Advertisements for Myself* as a whole. In the first place, the many shortcomings of Mailer's appropriated fantasy of the sensual superiority of African Americans may blind us to his acumen in articulating an important linkage between race and sexuality during the period: "Can't we have some honesty about what's going on now in the South? Everybody who knows the South knows that the white man fears the sexual potency of the Negro."[6] Such a social diagnosis, by now a critical commonplace, was certainly radical for the period, particularly when it was articulated so baldly and by a white intellectual. If Mailer's attempt to subvert the situation entailed *embracing* the stereotype in order to promulgate an ethics of the body, it was no less subversive of the status quo for that. Likewise, if the allegations of Negro primitivism are clearly the clumsy and clichéd revamping of a long tradition of racist representations of black sexuality, the revamping nonetheless represents a departure from traditional accounts by locating the source of Negro sensualism in historically specific social injustices rather than a biological essentialism. It is precisely this revision, one presumes, that made Mailer's critique so attractive to Cleaver.[7]

Mailer is quite explicit in his assertion that it is a corrupt system that transforms the human into a sexual outlaw. What had traditionally been recognized as a function of natural law becomes in Mailer's redescription behavior rooted in cultural exclusion and social injustice. Indeed, at several points Mailer questions the immutability of the order of biology commonly used to anchor modern conceptions of the natural:

> What characterizes every psychopath and part-psychopath is that they are trying to create a new nervous system for themselves. Generally, we are obliged to act with a nervous system which has been formed from infancy, and which carries in the style of its circuits the very contradictions of our parents and of our early milieu. Therefore we are obliged, most of us, to meet the tempo of the present and the future with reflexes and rhythms which come from the past. It is not only the "dead weight of the institutions of the past" but indeed the inefficient and often antiquated nervous circuits of the past which strangle our potentiality for responding to new possibilities which might be exciting for our individual growth. (Mailer, 318–19)

This sounds about as close to a constructivist argument as one can find during the Cold War. The split between environment and nature is contested, and biologic processes are envisioned as being susceptible to and modifiable through environmental influence. In this context, the hipster is envisioned as a social mutation that possesses survival value.

Of course, one way to accommodate the kind of qualifications I've been making would be simply to say that Mailer articulates a progressive position on integration at the expense of putting forth a reactionary sexual politics. Certainly his rhetoric frequently supports this split: "And in turn the Negro has been storing his hatred and yet growing stronger, carrying with him the painful wound that he was usually powerless to keep from being cuckolded" (307). Here he speaks as if the chief sin of slavery were to deprive black men of their exclusive sexual prerogative over black women. And as Corber notes, this tendency is picked up and intensified by Cleaver, who, in doing so, exposes the connection between homophobia and women's sexual subordination in a heterosexual regime. Sharing the feminine sexual passivity (the desire to take in the man's sperm), that characterizes all homosexuals, Cleaver asserts, black homosexuals are a particular political liability. Because his political program depends on a conflation of sexual and political agency, black homosexuals for him represent a threat to the political advancement of the race. In this, he adheres to stock representations of homosexuality during the Cold War, which depicted homosexuals as a national security threat on the grounds that they were uniquely vulnerable to the blandishments and blackmail of Communist agents. Thus, what Cleaver describes as the collusion between whites and gay black men to emasculate African Americans is in fact a collusion (via the conflation of political and sexual agency) between white and black heterosexual men to exclude homosexuals.

But though Cleaver's own politics reflect the period's mutually reinforcing constructions of heterosexuality and homophobia, his appropriation of "The White Negro" rests on a distortingly selective reading of the text. Likewise, Corber's reading of Baldwin glosses over much of the nuance in Baldwin's response to Mailer's text. It trades on Baldwin's homosexuality far more than anything explicit that he says concerning Mailer's essay, as though the fact of his sexual orientation automatically entailed a particular position toward Mailer's essay. Throughout his article, however, Baldwin evinces an interest in Mailer's project despite disagreement with his conclusions:

"Man," said a Negro musician to me once, talking about Norman, "the only trouble with that cat is that he's white." This does not mean exactly what it says—or, rather, it *does* mean exactly what it says, and not what it might be taken to mean— and it is a very shrewd observation. What my friend meant was that to become a Negro man, let alone a Negro artist, one had to make oneself up as one went along. This had to be done in the not-at-all metaphorical teeth of the world's determination to destroy you. The world had prepared no place for you, and if the world had its way, no place would ever exist. Now, this is true for everyone, but, in the case of a Negro, this truth is absolutely naked: if he deludes himself about it, he will die. This is not the way this truth presents itself to white men, who believe the world is theirs and who, albeit unconsciously, expect the world to help them in the achievement of their identity. But the world does not do this—for anyone; the world is not interested in anyone's identity. And therefore, the anguish which can overtake a white man comes in the middle of his life, when he must make the almost inconceivable effort to divest himself of everything he has ever expected or believed, when he must take himself apart and put himself together again, walking out of the world, into limbo, or into what certainly looks like limbo. This cannot yet happen to any Negro of Norman's age, for the reason that his delusions and defenses are either absolutely impenetrable by this time, or he has failed to survive them. (231–32)

This paragraph is instructive as much for what it says about Mailer as about Baldwin. In describing a difference between himself and Mailer accruing to race, Baldwin establishes an important correspondence between them concerning sexuality. The truth that Baldwin, as a black man, has long recognized—a truth that, it bears noting, is strikingly similar to Mailer's description of the daily threat of violence under which the hipster lives—Mailer has only recently arrived at, to wit, that "one ha[s] to make oneself up as one goes along" and must "divest himself of everything he has ever expected or believed, when he must take himself apart and put himself together again." At the same time that it acknowledges Mailer's middle-aged panic at the revision of identity to which his project has led him, the passage registers Mailer's recognition of the fundamental fluidity of that identity, a fluidity that, although Baldwin does not say so directly, quite clearly extends to sexual orientation. As he puts it earlier in his essay, "the sexual battleground, if I may call it that, is really the same for everyone" (220). Baldwin's blend of criticism and constructive concern, a kind of critical tolerance that permeates the essay, seems to me to arise less from charity than from a recognition that there's more to Mailer's program than either Corber or Cleaver is willing to acknowledge.

One index of this refusal of acknowledgment is the critical silence regarding structural importance of same-sex erotics both in "The White Negro" and elsewhere in *Advertisements*. Consider Mailer's attribution of a homoerotic dimension to the hipster in "The White Negro" itself. His figuration of homosexuality in the hipster's provenance—the all-male ménage-à-trois that constituted the White Negro's myth of origin—is insistently literalized in the rest of the essay. Mailer is quite pointed, if provocatively unexpansive, in his assertion in the piece that the hipster is frequently bisexual: "What he [the hipster] must do before that is find his courage at the moment of violence, or equally make it in the act of love, find a little more between his woman and himself, or indeed between his mate and himself (since many hipsters are bisexual)" (324). Though parenthetical, the characterization was apparently germane to Mailer's concept of the hipster, because he is at pains to insist on it in subsequent remarks about the essay. In his reply to Ned Polsky's *Dissent* article on "The White Negro" (also included in *Advertisements*), for example, Mailer draws on this aspect of the hipster yet again: "'Uncle,' said a bisexual Negro to me once, "I couldn't have more charge for that chick if I'd gone down on a platoon of Marines'" (342).

Importantly, Mailer insistently distinguishes between bisexuality and homosexuality when discussing the hipster. If he explicitly accords same-sex sexual experiences a place in the hipster's profile, he is just as explicit that they are part of a bisexual rather than a homosexual orientation. The hipster's liberatory bisexuality is set against the negatively charged notion of homosexuality, the "demeaning flip of being queer," that he describes in terms of passivity and femininity. The distinction effectively splits the active and passive dimensions of sexual experience and parses them out into bisexuals and homosexuals, respectively. The sexual agency of the hipster is indiscriminate and all-encompassing, indifferent to the sex of its object, whereas the pure passivity of the homosexual requires submission to another male. Thus Mailer's characterization might seem to be a partial and complicated qualification of the idea that his sexual politics are reactionary. By admitting bisexuality, he extends legitimacy to select forms of same-sex behavior. At the same time, however, he preserves the negative valence of so-called passive homosexuality as well as female sexuality in general and, ultimately, he reinforces the active/passive binary that underwrites thinking about sexuality in general. Significantly, however, both his theory and fiction seem unable or unwilling to sustain the separation of activity and passivity that Mailer labors to establish. As the example of his hipster acquaintance's fantasy about fellating the marines makes clear, the two are not always separable and, even when they are, passivity is not always aversively charged.

The theoretical tension in his third-person account—the valorization of bisexuality and simultaneous use of homosexuality as an all-purpose pejorative—is accompanied by kindred textual repressions when Mailer's voice is more autobiographical. In the prefatory advertisement that precedes "The White Negro" in *Advertisements for Myself*, Mailer reproduces William Faulkner's response to his (Mailer's) description of white fear and fascination concerning the superior sexuality of African Americans: "I have heard this idea expressed several times during the last twenty years, though not before by a man. The others were ladies, northern or middle western ladies, usually around 40 or 45 years of age. I don't know what a psychiatrist would find in this" (Mailer, 308). To this, Mailer responds that Faulkner has led a sheltered life and so it's not surprising that his most interesting conversations have been with middle-aged ladies. A few paragraphs later, Mailer acknowledges his debt to Faulkner for this act of literary banishment, which goaded him to expand the essay: "Like a latent image in the mirror of my ego was the other character Faulkner must have seen: a noisy pushy middling ape who had been tolerated too long by his literary betters" (310). What interests me in this little exchange is both Mailer's need to rehearse Faulkner's icy remark and his refusal to confront its content. Although he is pleased to recount his humiliation at Faulkner's hands, he is unwilling to examine its lines of attack. What Faulkner meant was that he knew exactly what a psychiatrist would find in this: his image of the corseted desire of middle-aged ladies is intended to suggest, none too subtly, a homosexual attraction on Mailer's part toward the image of the hypersexual black male at the center of "The White Negro." Content to showcase Faulkner's allegation, Mailer nevertheless displaces it into the realm of literary ambition, the (in this case) desexualized image of the "pushy middling ape."

Mailer's efforts elsewhere in *Advertisements* to effect the separation I've described are likewise highly ambivalent. "The Homosexual Villain," an essay originally published three years before "The White Negro," professes a conversion to the cause of homosexual equality that his rhetoric consistently compromises. He describes the essay in retrospect, in the piece's "advertisement," as both "honorable as a piece of work" and "without a doubt the worst article I have ever written, conventional, empty, pious, the quintessence of the Square" (205). To the article itself he appends, in closing, an entirely gratuitous and absurd cautionary remark to homosexuals, likening what he imagines to be their antihetero prejudices to the homophobia he himself has supposedly overcome. More interesting, though, is the gamut of rhetorical maneuvers he rehearses in an attempt to displace any possibility of personal homosexual identification:

> There is probably no sensitive heterosexual alive who is not preoccupied at one time or another with his latent homosexuality, and while I had no conscious homosexual desires, I had wondered more than once if really there were not something suspicious in my intense dislike of homosexuals. How pleasant to discover that once one can accept homosexuals as real friends, the tension is gone with the acceptance. I found that I was no longer concerned with latent homosexuality. It seemed vastly less important, and paradoxically enabled me to realize that I am actually quite heterosexual. (209–10)

His assertion seems facile in its summary dismissal of previous anxieties, as though his former prejudice that homosexuals were somehow less than human (an evasive description in the first place) were itself sufficient to explain his dangerous flirtation with identification. Moreover, such a position in turn leaves the original prejudice unexplained, creating a vacuum that he attempts to fill with flatly contradictory explanations. On the one hand, for example, he attributes his prejudice to artistic expedience: describing the ready-made convenience of homosexual villains, he remarks, "What I have come to realize is that much of my homosexual prejudice was a servant to my aesthetic needs. In the variety and contradiction of American life, the difficulty of finding a character who can serve as one's protagonist is matched only by the difficulty of finding one's villain, and so long as I was able to preserve my prejudices, my literary villains were at hand" (211). On the other hand, he describes the prejudice as destructive of those same artistic needs: "Now, it is easier to understand why I did this piece ["The Homosexual Villain"]. *The Deer Park* was then in galleys at Rinehart, and I was depressed about it. Apart from its subject, I thought it a timid inhibited book. I must have known that my fear of homosexuality as a subject was stifling my creative reflexes" (205). Significantly, both poles of this contradiction preserve a clearly concerned disavowal of any more personal interest in same-sex erotics—and, as the rest of the sentence just quoted suggests, a vexed disavowal at that: " . . . and given the brutal rhythms of my nature, I could kill this inhibition only by jumping into the middle of the problem without any clothes" (205–6). Mailer's fantasy of his own nudity in this passage transcends metaphorical caprice. Here, as in so much of his other work, there emerges obliquely a fascination with the spectacle of male passivity—a wedding of exposure, helplessness, and passivity before a spectator's gaze with brutality, violence, and death.

Predictably, Mailer's attempt to fictionally embody the hipster in his subsequent fiction displays the same perplexing blend of heterosexual triumphalism and direct homoerotic interest as his theoretical work. "The Time of Her Time" offers an illuminating artistic resolution to his complicated and contradictory formulations of race and sexuality elsewhere in *Advertisements*. Written after his conversion to Hip, "The Time of Her Time" is Mailer's preliminary attempt to put the theoretical agenda of "The White Negro" into practice. The triangles that he sets up in the story support the Girardian notion that interrival relations are as important as those between either the subject or the mediator and the object. At the same time, they point up the costs of ignoring the erotic dimension of interrival relations.

Considering that it was written in the wake of Mailer's conversion to Hip, "The Time of Her Time" may at first seem an oddly unpromising prospect for examining Mailer's engagement with the topics of masculine sexual passivity and race. The interest in black masculinity and homoerotic desire that receives so much attention in "The White Negro" is far less pronounced in this story. Instead, "The Time of Her Time" seems to concentrate on the unabashed heterosexual misogyny for which Mailer is renowned. Nevertheless, race and homosexuality are, in fact, central to the story, although the text presents them through a series of displacements.

The story itself is a first-person recounting of two episodes in a hipster's life: his arrival in New York City, and a minute anatomy of a particular sexual encounter. The narrator, Sergius O'Shaugnesey, is the proprietor of a bullfighting school, which he runs out of his Greenwich Village loft. After describing the first episode, his acquisition and renovation of the loft, he moves (via a peculiarly abrupt transition) to the second, an in-depth recollection of his efforts to be the first to bring a young Jewish college student named Denise to a sexual climax—an eventuality that, though the intercourse itself is consensual, she resists. The description is cast in Mailer's usual oppositional terms war, athletics, competition. After a close description of the ups and downs of his attempts, Sergius ultimately succeeds, thereby eliciting a mixed response from Denise: immediately, gratitude; in the morning, a sullen hatred. Denise's parting shot before leaving, that her analyst has conjectured that Sergius is a latent homosexual, seems less to proffer this explanation for serious consideration than to disarm it as a possible reading. The remark is at once an index of her bitterness in defeat and a proleptic dismissal of the all-too-familiar narrative of homosexuality-as-arrested-development that was a mainstay of postwar pop psychology. Against this, the terms of the "conquest" suggest that Sergius, in his competition with Denise (figured as a masculine mediator struggling with Sergius for control of her own body), has, in fact, avoided the "demeaning flip of being queer." The image of the hipster as unbounded sexual agency that characterizes one strain of the "The White Negro" seems here reaffirmed.

But the lines of sexual agency and passivity and the purity of the valuations assigned to them are blurred from the outset. Likening his sexual escapades to the art of bullfighting that he teaches, Sergius allots himself no fixed position in the interaction: "Over and over in those days I used to compare the bed to the bullfight, sometimes seeing myself as the matador and sometimes as the bull" (457). In his description of Denise, this instability is translated into terms of sexual difference by her resemblance to a male. Her "flat breasts" and the "flat thin muscles of a wiry boy" as well as the short cropped haircut that she acquires on the evening of Sergius's triumph give outward form to a masculine character. And this masculinity is manifest in her resistance to Sergius's domination, her willful refusal (as against mere inability) to give herself over to the climax he assiduously works to bring her to. On their first encounter, Sergius recounts his failure this way: "As I ebbed into what should have been the contentments of a fine after-pleasure, warm and fine, there was one little part of me remaining cold and murderous because she had deprived me, she had fled the domination which was liberty for her, and the rest of the night was bound to be hell" (452). Although he has achieved climax, he has failed in the attempt to force her to one. After confronting him with his inadequacy, she penetrates him anally with her finger, a gesture that simultaneously registers his passivity and her agency, thereby fueling his resentment and goading him to another, equally unsuccessful attempt. This second bout is likewise coded as an affair between men: "I was weary of her, and the smell which rose from her had so little of the sea and so much of the armpit, that I breathed the stubborn wills of the gymnasium where the tight-muscled search for grace, and it was like that, a hard punishing session with pulley weights, stationary bicycle sprints, and ten breath-seared laps around the track" (453-54). The eroticized and, in the postwar era, indicatively male space of the gymnasium reinforces her masculine identification. And as his initial failure on their final evening together makes explicit, the necessary implication of her masculinization is his own feminization. After ejaculating prematurely during his preliminary attempt, he says with resignation: "She it was who proved stronger than me, she the he to my silly she" (461).

Of course, nothing in this reading is necessarily at odds with the theoretical apparatus by which Mailer explains the hipster in "The White Negro." The same-sex element in Sergius's interaction with Denise is amply provided for by Mailer's inclusion of bisexuality in the hipster's sexual profile. According to the profile, Sergius's problem is not the same-sex overtones of his relationship as much as his own failure to gain the upper hand. The difficulty is that Denise has successfully usurped the hipster's prerogative, leaving Sergius a passive vehicle for her pleasure—in this case, the pleasure of withholding. However, the details of Sergius's identifications during their interaction are not so easily assimilated into the picture of the hipster's unalloyed desire for absolute sexual agency. Or perhaps more accurately, aspects of Sergius's erotic life point up a necessary dimension of the hipster's ontology that "The White Negro" is reluctant to fully confront. Sergius's descriptions of their final sexual encounter repeatedly indicate that his need to dominate is mixed with—in fact is in service to—other desires. When Denise informs him that she has just come from sex with her boyfriend, Arthur, Sergius notes that, rather than dampening his desire, this only contributes to his arousal:

> The worst of it was that it quickened me more. I had the selfish wisdom to throw such evidence upon the mercy of my own court. For the smell of Arthur was the smell of love, at least for me, and so from man or woman, it did not matter—the smell of love was always feminine—and if the man in Denise was melted by the woman in Arthur, so Arthur might have flowered that woman in himself from the arts of a real woman, his mother?—it did not matter—that voiceless message which passed from the sword of the man into the cavern of the woman was carried along from body to body, and if it was not the woman in Denise I was going to find tonight, at least I would be warmed by the previous trace of another. (460–61)

Opaque as the rhetoric of his self-analysis is here, it indicates that the homosexual dimension of Sergius's attraction extends beyond Denise's boylike sexual agency. The observation is important less because it introduces an actual male into Sergius's erotic imaginings than because it highlights a crucial structural feature of Sergius's desire: the identification on which his project is built entails the adoption of Denise's desire—or more accurately, the substitution of his own. Denise is in effect a position through which Sergius enters into *erotic* relation with her lovers. Sergius's explanation of his desire to force Denise to a climax despite her resistance clarifies this dynamic:

> There was a quality about her I could not locate, something independent—abruptly, right there I knew what it was. In a year she would have no memory of me, I would not exist for her unless . . . and then it was clear . . . unless I could be the first to carry her stone of no-orgasm up the cliff, all the way,

over and out into the sea. That was the kick I could find, that a year from now, five years from now, down all the seasons to the hours of her old age, I would be the one she would be forced to remember, and it would nourish me a little over the years, thinking of that grudged souvenir which could not die in her, my blond hair, my blue eyes, my small broken nose, my clean mouth and chin, my height, my boxer's body, my parts— yes, I was getting excited at the naked image of me in the young-old mind of that sour sexed-up dynamo of black pussied frustration. (Mailer 457–58)

The full implications of Sergius's moment of expanded consciousness here emerge only in his feverish final image. There is more to his anxiety than the fear that he won't be remembered. His wish is not for her recollections (fond or otherwise) of him to occupy her old age. Rather, the desire to be the object of her remembrance takes its force from imaginatively occupying her fear and submission before him. His arousal at his own naked and aroused image as seen from Denise's perspective points up the crucial aspect of his need to force her to this climax: by identifying with her he can indulge the fantasy of being dominated himself—*by* himself. This desire to experience domination at his own hands, which is to say, by a male, importantly revises his description of forcibly sodomizing her during his final attempt to bring her to climax. He couches it as "the last of the liberties"—an attempt to break her spirit of resistance. What he neglects to add is that, to someone without a vagina, penetrating her anally has the significant effect of making her domination anatomically intelligible, a position he can inhabit imaginatively. Thus his earlier paradoxical explanation of his animosity toward Denise—"there was one little part of me remaining cold and murderous because she had deprived me, she had fled the domination which was liberty for her" (452)—doesn't quite mean what it says. Or rather, it means exactly what it says: her refusal to be dominated deprives Sergius not of dominating her but of the imaginative experience of being dominated *through* her.

The story's simultaneous repression and mobilization of homosexual interests is sutured onto a kindred and connected racial dynamic. Although the plot doesn't seem to accord African American sexuality the priority that it occupies in "The White Negro," both the narrator's associative transitions and his deployment of Jewish racial markers illuminate the sexual function of race in Mailer's theorization of the hipster. The initial section of Sergius's narrative is largely devoted to an incident that occurs when Sergius accompanies a black painter he has hired to whitewash his loft to a "Negro hashhouse" in the neighborhood. He describes the anxiety of being the only white man in the restaurant: "I felt the clear bell-like adrenalines of clean anxiety, untainted by weakness, self-interest, neurotic habit, or the pure yellows of the liver. For I had put my poker money on the table, I was the new gun in a frontier saloon, and so I was asking for it, not today, not tomorrow, but come sooner, come later, something was likely to follow from this" (443). The terms of the interaction—economic competition between cowboys—constitutes an implicit disavowal of any sexual dimension to the interaction. This is a disavowal, it's worth noting, whose underlying sexual significance Mailer himself makes explicit in a similar remark about the competition between writers: "You are considered important by some and put down by others, and every time you meet a new man, the battle is on: the latest guest has to decide if you are a) stronger than he, and b) smarter than he, and c) less queer" (17–18). Moreover, the sexually charged, racist stereotypes Sergius uses to describe the hashhouse clientele ("the bucks bridled a little when I came in") indicate that the anxiety he feels is not merely his uncertainty in unfamiliar cultural or socioeconomic terrain but includes an erotic component. And the observation with which he closes this episode suggests his reaction is not entirely aversive:

> As we got up to go, I managed to turn around and get another look at the three spades in the next booth. Two of them were facing me. Their eyes were flat, the whites were yellow and flogged with red—they stared back with no love. The anxiety came over me again, almost nice—I had been so aware of them, and they had been so aware of me. (446)

He feels an element of pleasure in the threat that he imagines the "bucks" posing and in his passivity before their silent gaze.

The importance of this episode for the story's sexual politics becomes clearer when one considers the abrupt and seemingly offhand transition that prompts its recounting. The narrator's shift between this vignette and the story about Denise reinforces the connection between his racial and sexual anxieties by drawing an associative connection between them: "That [the hashhouse episode] was in October, and for no reason I could easily discover, I found myself thinking of that day as I awoke on a spring morning [the morning after his conquest] more than half a year later." (446). The reason resists easy discovery because it exposes a similarity between his own experiential domains that Sergius's account of himself strictly separates. His recollection of the hashhouse episode occurs on the morning after he has brought Denise to climax; in fact, the recollection is precipitated by her resentful stare (akin to the stare of the hashhouse "bucks") at having lost the battle to withhold her climax from him. It is, for him, at once a mark of his triumph and of his imaginative domination.

Although the axis of racial interaction changes from black/white to white/Jewish in his relationship with Denise, the details illuminate important relays between race and sexuality in both this story and "The White Negro." After sodomizing Denise, an act that Sergius tells us sends her on her way to a true climax, he feels her making a final gesture of resistance:

> but she was away, following the wake of her own waves which mounted fell back, and in new momentum mounted higher and should have gone over, and then she was about to hang again, I could feel it, that moment of hesitation between the past and the present, the habit and the adventure, and I said into her ear, "You dirty little Jew." (464)

Sergius finds the extra bit of sexual energy he requires to overcome Denise's resistance in the invocation of race. His remark condenses the differential between positions in a social hierarchy into a point of sexual leverage, converting racial inferiority into the basis for sexual submission. The relation between African American racial identity and sexuality both here and in "The White Negro" relies on this same dynamic, only with the terms reversed. Although blacks are, like Jews, an oppressed minority, unlike Jews, owing to different representational histories, they occupy the dominant position in sexual relations. As the product of an Irish father and a Jewish mother,[8] Sergius occupies a position in a racial/sexual hierarchy midway between the "sensual superiority" of Negroes and the sexual inferiority of Jews. Thus he insists on the distinctions between racial identities with Denise because her position of racial inferiority enables him to vicariously experience domination by a sexually superior white man. Likewise, Sergius's hypersexualized fantasy of black men ensures that whoever occupies the object position in his sexual relationships, he will, through those objects, be able to experience domination by a superior black sexuality. Sergius's anxiety about being the first to make Denise climax supports the terms of this racial/sexual economy: "[S]he was ready, she was entering the time of her Time, and if not me, it would be another—I was sick in advance at the picture of some bearded Negro cat who would score where I had missed and thus cuckold me in spirit" (458). I take the substitution of nausea here for the titillation that characterizes so many of his imaginings elsewhere as an index not of jealousy (at least as standardly understood), but of the threat of a scenario that leaves him no position in the racial/sexual hierarchy *from* which to identify. In this fantasy of the "bearded Negro cat," the white middle term falls out leaving Sergius no position from which to participate, much less to imagine his own domination. The only thing more potent than a White Negro is a black one.

I understand the foregoing readings to have a number of implications for approaching Mailer, the postwar imaginary, and sexuality and critical practice more generally. Most immediately, they qualify and complicate, rather than simply dismiss, a commonly held picture of the sexual and racial politics of Mailer's advocacy of Hip. In so doing, they constitute neither a straightforward endorsement of the liberatory possibilities of Mailer's program nor a denial of its antihomosexual, sexist, and racist effects. They do suggest, however, that the effects are not confined to these, nor do they form an internally self-coherent set. If the hipster's flight from the postwar domestication of masculinity is clear enough, the notion of his uncomplicated embodiment of the competitive, heteronormative, masculine individualism associated with containment is considerably less certain. Rather, as the complexities of these texts suggest, the hipster might be better understood as an inchoate bid to articulate a third man, one who departed from both sentimental-integrationist and containment models of masculinity in his vexed interest in homoerotic relations and masculine passivity.

In turn, this more complicated picture of Mailer's attempts to think sexuality and race through the figure of the hipster has implications for our efforts to generate the analytic categories through which we understand the postwar period. It reminds us that, in our efforts to formulate a cultural imaginary, what may appear to be contradictory ideological impulses according to one set of concerns, when viewed in connection with other concerns, may share fundamental continuities—and vice versa. In the case of the sentimental-integrationist and containment narratives in question here, it underscores the fact that, despite providing different representational possibilities for figuring race, both of these narratives were predicated on the systematic exclusion of homosexual relations. Though this exclusion has long been recognized as a structuring feature of containment ideology, in the context of integrationist discourse it should lead us to rethink the opposition between the noncoercive filial bonds supposed to characterize sentimental relations and the self-interested love of the romantic couple with which those relations have been contrasted. However deemphasized or suppressed romantic desire may have been in particular representations of sentimental discourse, the postwar domestic narrative was, in fact, predicated on a notion of erotic desire conceived as a self-authenticating phenomenon institutionalized through the standard mechanism for enacting liberal rational self-interest—the contract. At the same time that they figure horizontal exchange and reciprocity, contract relations also mark the competition among individual interests and the ideal of autonomous agency at the heart of containment individualism. Thus, if sentimental discourse seemed to offer an alternative to the freestanding individualism at the core of containment, its conventions nevertheless depended on a notion of erotic desire that was identical with that of the containment subject. Recognizing this internal tension helps make visible the determining parameters of the sentimental narrative's inclusivity. If the family often provided a politically salubrious alternative to containment figurations of race relations after the war,[9] it did so at the expense of excluding homoerotic relations foundational to its heteronormative structure.

In a still broader context, the critical evasion of Mailer's homoerotic engagements has implications for our ongoing efforts to think about sexuality and critical practice. I want to suggest that critical refusal to take up Mailer's interest in passivity and homoerotic desire reflects our standing difficulties—during the 1950s and, in different form, in our own moment—with the complexities of the premier discourse for thinking about both sexuality and critical interpretation in the last century, namely, psychoanalysis. As Paul Ricoeur so penetratingly observed, psychoanalysis at once informed and reflected a central tendency in twentieth-century reading practice through the interpretive habits that he designated the "hermeneutics of suspicion." Exemplifying the "hidden-shown" relation that Ricoeur identified as the principal category of consciousness for Freud (and much of modern philosophy generally), psychoanalytically inflected literary criticism during the 1950s and 1960s framed homoerotic desire in terms of latent and manifest content.[10] Depth psychology required depth narratives, and reading them required a species of psychic cryptography. Under such interpretive imperatives, the very obviousness and visibility of Mailer's direct invocations of homosexuality, to say nothing of their often proleptic content, rendered reading them as Mailer's own or his characters' repressed desire impossible. The fact that Mailer's homoerotic interest was not sufficiently buried paradoxically produced a critical repression—one indexed by the tendency on the one hand to characterize the interest in terms of fantasy and fascination and on the other to refuse to fully read it in those terms.

More recently, "suspicious" readings have presented a somewhat different problem for approaching the issue. In our present critical moment, as Eve Sedgwick has observed, the hermeneutics of suspicion are still prevalent enough to seem "nearly synonymous with criticism itself."[11] Hence the more recent devotion to rooting out the reactionary tendencies in Mailer's ostensibly radical sexual and racial politics. At the same time, however, psychoanalysis itself has increasingly become an object, rather than the method, of scrutiny—particularly for criticism concerned with gender and sexual orientation. Our recognition of psychoanalysis's historical complicity in designating homosexuality a form of pathology makes reading Mailer's homoerotic engagements as a type of repression difficult. More generally, our sense of the inadequacies of naïvely empirical or strictly normative accounts of Freud have prompted a search for new alternatives.

Thus far, I have resisted belaboring the parallels between the erotic and critical ménages à trois I have been discussing, but I want to briefly suggest that the interest in passivity that I see complicating Mailer's texts might serve as the figure for a revised approach to psychoanalysis, sexuality, and critical interpretation. This would entail viewing Freud's work in much the same way that Leo Bersani does in *The Freudian Body*: as driven, in the course of outlining particular theoretical tenets, to an inevitable demonstration of their unsustainability—a project of theoretical collapse figured as a masochistic, and in this sense passive, shattering. Such an approach requires a denial of neither psychoanalysis's normative impulses nor of their pernicious historical effects. It does, however, contextualize such impulses within the far more varied landscape of interests, engagements, and uncertainties alive in Freud's work. This contextualization effectively underscores the instability, which is to say the fundamental fluidity, of identificatory positions within Freud's texts, and the manifold possibilities such motility opens up for thinking about sexuality—queer, straight, what-have-you. Rather than functioning as simply a negativity or the index of a failure, passivity in this sense would operate as a position of receptivity, a preparedness to recognize the rich combinatorics of individual sexual experience as well as the proximity of kinds of experience that we have perhaps too rigidly segregated. Such a characterization would almost certainly blur the lines between queer and nonqueer interests, texts, and authors.

In terms of critical reading, a productive passivity would amount to bringing a similar sense of receptivity and variability to interpretation itself. It would not constitute an abandonment of the agency and vigilance associated with the hermeneutics of suspicion. Those very valuable critical practices would certainly continue to inform our readings, but as only one possible critical stance among many that might be brought—simultaneously—to bear on a text. Rather, passivity in this connection would entail an attentiveness to the coexistence of contradictory and sometimes noncoherent, or not-yet-coherent, ideological impulses within texts. Practically speaking, it would require, among other things, a renewed commitment to close, and slow, reading. It would also entail the recuperation of a notion of readerly disinterest, understood neither as a fantasy of absolute and objective neutrality nor as a denial of the ideological circumstances of our acts of reading, but instead as a posture of relaxation—a willingness in our readings to try to suspend what we care about in order to see what we might come to care about and how the two might be related.

ACKNOWLEDGMENTS

This article has profited from the criticism and suggestions of Bill Brown, Deborah Nelson, Jay Schleusener, William Veeder, and Deborah Weiss. I am extremely grateful to them for their help. I would also like to thank Jen Gieseking, Shari Chappell, and the *WSQ* editorial staff for their help in preparing this manuscript for the press.

FREDERICK WHITING is an assistant professor of English at the University of Alabama. He has published articles on sexuality, subjectivity, and American literature and is currently at work on a book entitled *The Inner Limits: Persons, Novels, and the Search for Form in Modern American Literature*, which examines mid-twentieth-century transformations in concepts of human and novelistic form under the sign of monstrosity.

NOTES

1. "Within sentimental discourse, the family has traditionally stood as the most prized form of community and the highest achievement of the self-in-relation. In contrast to the romantic couple, whose formation is motivated by individual sexual desire, the family, whose members are knit together by a selfless concern for each other, institutionalizes the sentimental values of compassion and sympathy." Klein, 162. As will become clear, though I find her account of integrationism a productive complication of the postwar imaginary, I disagree with Klein's separation of romantic desire from sentimental narrative.

2. See René Girard, *Deceit, Desire, and the Novel*. As Eve Sedgwick has pointed out, a structural account of desire such as Girard's offers a certain synchronic clarity at the expense of a sense of the historical variability of erotic configurations and dynamics. Girard's approach suggests that the gender of the participants, indeed all social positioning, is incidental and that the erotic dynamic it outlines will hold for any combination of individuals. The neat ascription of agency and passivity to masculine and feminine positions, respectively, for example, must, on this model, be taken as an unexamined and invariable given. Thus, such an account makes little provision for the asymmetries arising from the uneven distribution of power across social positions, where power is understood not only as sexual power but also includes "control over the means of production and reproduction of goods, persons, and meanings." Sedgwick, *Between Men*, 22. What I want to further suggest is that historicizing erotic triangles involves not only attending to the differing positions of power that different subjects occupy by virtue of historically scripted social categories and rules of erotic engagement, but also recognizing that these subject positions will not always be of a piece or unconflicted. Rather, they will likely contain tensions and incoherences that arise owing to asymmetries in the configurations of power of their moment.

3. This is not to say that critics make no mention whatsoever of homoerotic relations; indeed the salience of Mailer's engagement effectively prevents that. Rather, the homoerotic interests of Mailer's texts typically receive passing reference, usually as the object of phobia or the spectral index of closeted homosexual desire, which is never taken up or examined. See, for example, Robert J. Corber, *Homosexuality in Cold War America*; Shelly Eversley, "The Source of Hip"; Eric Lott, *Love and Theft*.

4. Baldwin's essay appears in his 1961 collection, *Nobody Knows My Name*, 216–39.

5. To be sure, Corber's concern is first and foremost with Baldwin, less with Cleaver and Mailer. He does not undertake a full-fledged reading of "The White Negro." Nevertheless, his characterization of Mailer and his essay elides interesting and important features of the sexual issues at stake, for Baldwin as well as for Cleaver and Mailer.

6. From Mailer's preliminary version of "The White Negro" in the *Independent*, March 1957, quoted in Mailer, 307.

7. Despite Mailer's often-aired antipathy to the timidities of psychoanalysis, his description here tracks the metapsychological concerns of Freud's later writings. Excluded by centuries of white imperialism from the trade-off described in *Civilization and Its Discontents*, the black man, reaping none of the advantages of civilization, had, in Mailer's view, no incentive to undergo the repression on which it is predicated:

   . . . when one lives in a civilized world, and still can enjoy none of the cultural nectar of such a world because the paradoxes on which civilization is built demand that there remain a cultureless and alienated bottom of exploitable human material, then the logic of becoming a sexual outlaw (if one's psychological roots are bedded in the bottom) is that one has at least a running competitive chance to be healthy so long as one stays alive. (321)

8. Though he is half-Jewish, Sergius's identifications are all with the Irish half of his lineage.

9. It's likewise important to distinguish, as Klein (in her focus on Asian ethnicity) and Levine (in her attention to Jewish identity) both persuasively do, that distinctions in this connection very much depend on the differences in historical constructions of racial categories.

10. Paul Ricoeur, *Freud and Philosophy*.

11. Eve Kosofsky Sedgwick, *Novel Gazing*, 4. My interest in passivity here has obvious connections with Sedgwick's notion of reparative reading, though she expresses rather less interest in a philosophical recuperation of Freud.

WORKS CITED

Baldwin, James. *Nobody Knows My Name*. New York: The Dial Press, 1961.

Bersani, Leo. *The Freudian Body: Psychoanalysis and Art*. New York: Columbia University Press, 1986.

Corber, Robert J. *Homosexuality in Cold War America: Resistance and the Crisis of Masculinity*. Durham: Duke University Press, 1997.

Eversley, Shelly. "The Source of Hip." *the minnesota review* 55–7 (2002): 257–70.

Girard, René. *Deceit, Desire, and the Novel: Self and Other in Literary Structure*. Trans. Yvonne Freccero. Baltimore: Johns Hopkins University Press, 1965.

Hoberek, Andrew, ed. "Fifties Culture," special section in *the minnesota review* 55–7 (2002), 143–288.

Klein, Christina. "The Sentimental Culture of Global Integration." *the minnesota review* 55–7 (2002): 153–66.

Levine, Andrea. "The (Jewish) White Negro: Norman Mailer's Racial Bodies." *MELUS: The Journal of the Society for the Study of the Multi-Ethnic Literature of the United States* 28.2 (2003): 59-81.

Lott, Eric. *Love and Theft: Blackface Minstrelsy and the American Working Class*. Race and American Culture. New York: Oxford University Press, 1993.

Mailer, Norman. *Advertisements for Myself*. New York: G.P. Putnam's Sons, 1959.

Ricoeur, Paul. *Freud and Philosophy; an Essay on Interpretation*. New Haven: Yale University Press, 1970.

Sedgwick, Eve Kosofsky. *Between Men: English Literature and Male Homosocial Desire*. New York: Columbia University Press, 1985.

———. *Novel Gazing: Queer Readings in Fiction*. Durham, N.C., and London: Duke University Press, 1997.

PATRIOTIC PERVERSIONS: PATRICIA HIGHSMITH'S QUEER VISION OF COLD WAR AMERICA IN *THE PRICE OF SALT, THE BLUNDERER,* AND *DEEP WATER*

VICTORIA HESFORD

For many commentators in today's fraught, shrill (might one say hysterical?) political public sphere, the United States is at a crossroads: Is the world's lone superpower ready to take on the burden of empire, or is it going to remake its commitment to internationalism through a "return" to a (two-faced) liberalism? For critics like Michael Hardt and Antonio Negri, the screech-infested cable-television world of political commentary is almost beside the point. According to Hardt and Negri, we are already in the age of empire in which war is a permanent practice of the political. In a world governed by the processes of global capitalism that secure the wealth and privileges of a few "aristocratic" states at the expense of the many, war has become a means to secure those processes and the wealth they bestow on the few (Hardt and Negri 2001, 179-82). The wars in Iraq and Afghanistan are to be read, therefore, as battles fought to secure the economic, military, and political advantages of the United States and her coalition allies. "Freedom and democracy," as sound bite and as rhetoric, becomes a phrase that performs the epistemic violence necessary to secure an empire in the name of a nation-state that has claimed for itself the mantle of the good society.

Perhaps the shrillness of what passes for political debate in today's media is a symptom of the effort, the cultural work needed to enact precisely this kind of epistemic violence. Within the context of the 2004 American presidential election campaign, conservative appeals to the home, family, heterosexual marriage, and the rights of the unborn child became the organizing rhetoric of patriotism, and, as I will show in this essay, need to be read not just as an echo of the Reagan era, but also of the domestic ideology of the 1950s. The cultural work enacted by these rhetorics is an attempt to conjoin the wars of empire with the ideology of the good society—the privatized society of home and family. In the

[*WSQ: Women's Studies Quarterly* 33: 3 & 4 (Fall/Winter 2005)]

age of "permanent war," as in the age of the Communist atomic threat, the myths of certainty—the naturalness and rightness of heterosexual coupledom, for example—become the necessary counterpoint to the uncertainty of war.

Indeed, in the 1950s a comparable shrillness, even hysteria, dominated the political public sphere. The McCarthy witch-hunts of the early 1950s and the "lavender scare" that, as David K. Johnson makes clear, both preceded and outlasted McCarthy's particular brand of demagoguery, created a "moral panic" that was also the *mise en scène* for postwar anxieties about economic reorganization and the worldwide military and political expansion of American power (Johnson 2004, 4). As many scholars have argued, the Cold War culture of "containment," in which national security was predicated not just on the official foreign policy of containing the expansion of the Soviet Union, but also on containing the internal threat—the possible infiltration of the domestic, interior space of America by various "enemies within"—tended to destabilize, rather than stabilize, conceptions of American citizenship, home, and nation.[1] The rhetorics of patriotism through which McCarthy made his base appeal to paranoia and through which Congress demanded the expulsion of homosexuals from government cast the Communist, and the equally morally degenerate homosexual, as threats to national security. Yet these projections of an enemy within paradoxically provoked a corresponding sense of fragile borders—between nation-states, but also between social groups and spaces, and between individuals, both strangers and neighbors. Such a threat was conjured through images of the privatized space of an idealized domesticity—the white middle-class world of suburbia. The stereotype of the Communist as suspicious next-door neighbor, or the homosexual as the unmarried office colleague with a penchant for hard liquor, situated fears of their "un-Americanness" in "their" proximity to "our" domestic life. That "they" might have participated in the neighborhood softball game or come over for the Fourth of July barbecue not only located the site of invasion in the spaces of private life, but also made those spaces the first line of resistance. The home, marriage, and family life, as Elaine Tyler May has most notably argued, became both the sites of a domestic ideology focused on the production of wholesome and healthy citizens and also the locus around which fears of an "inside" threat were situated and articulated.

The central concern of this essay is to address the ambivalence intrinsic to cultural conceptions of the home and domestic life in 1950s America. In particular I want to explore the construction of a proximate "un-Americanness" as a sign of an unease with, or fear of, Americanness, especially an Americanness in the process of being reorganized through the international realpolitik of U.S. economic and military expansion in the postwar years.[2] I want to explore this ambivalence, and the unease with a changing conception of Americanness it suggests, through a reading of Patricia Highsmith's novels of suburban life in the 1950s. Although Highsmith has recently experienced a (limited) critical and popular renaissance, her work remains relatively unknown, at least in the United States.[3] Highsmith's reputation as a writer of dark, suspenseful novels full of a cynicism about human relationships and pessimism about world affairs meant that she never found a niche in the classification-obsessed American culture industry. Neither simply a "mystery writer" nor a "woman writer," Highsmith and her work evaded categorization, in both form and content.[4] While her protagonists are usually sociopathic or psychotic men, there is rarely any mystery about their crimes. Similarly, her portrayals of heterosexual coupledom make the scenes of a marriage seem strange and even threatening.

The novels I discuss in this essay—*The Price of Salt* (1952), *The Blunderer* (1954), and *Deep Water* (1957)—all have protagonists, who, in their wandering desires and contradictory compulsions, destabilize the borders between inside and outside, heterosexuality and homosexuality, Americanness and un-Americanness. I argue that Highsmith's vision of 1950s America turns the Cold War domestic ideology of the middle-class home as a source of national strength and normality inside out, revealing the undertow of violence and sexual unconventionality that both prop up the public function of the middle-class home and constantly threaten to tear it apart. Murderous violence (both at home and abroad) and perverse sexuality function in Highsmith's work not as some outside threat to the idea of America as middle-class heteronormativity (a threat figured through "the Communist" or "the pervert"), but as internal to it, what the picket fence and the lions on either side of the front door try to negate or repress.[5]

As Therese in *The Price of Salt* suggests, there is a connection between "war and big business and Congressional witch-hunts" (125). That connection can be understood as the process of American empire-building in the era of late capitalism. For Highsmith, writing at the height of the Cold War, that connection also produces the web that prevents people from being able to love each other (Carol, the older woman Therese is in love with, says in the same passage: "[I]t's getting to be a disease, isn't it, not being able to love?" [125]) and traps them in alienating, inhumane, and even violent relationships with each other. The home, domesticity, and the heterosexual couple, far from being an escape from the larger-than-human worlds of war and big business, are at its center; they are the forms of social space and interaction that produce the subjects, the proper citizens of American empire-building. In Highsmith's Cold War novels, then, the space of heteronormative domesticity is often a space of dehumanization in which people are made into effigies of a controlled and functional masculinity and femininity. The unique, the illogical, art, and creativity, like human desire and inexplicable wanting, are what have to be expelled, sometimes violently, from the carefully ordered homes of middle-class life. As such, it is the seemingly unproductive and illogical desire of queers and homosexuals, along with the potentially explosive and uncontrollable mixing of peoples in cities, that symbolize, for Highsmith, an outside to the systematization and alienation of Cold War heteronormative domesticity.

THE "OTHER-DIRECTED" MAN

In his study of the cultural politics of the Cold War, Robert J. Corber argues that the reorganization of the economy in terms of an increasing corporatization of American life and the expansion of Fordism into white-collar jobs and the professions "required the production of new forms of male subjectivity" in the postwar years (Corber, 11). The traditional figures of American masculinity—the frontiersman, or the independent entrepreneur—were no longer credible as forms of masculine identity (even if they remained viable as affective repositories for national feelings about masculinity). Instead, as the "organization man" became the hegemonic figure, the location of the production of masculinity shifted from the workplace to the home. The roles of breadwinner and provider (through the consumption of goods and services) became the forms through which the ideology of masculinity was reorganized in domestic terms. As Corber notes, TV shows like *Father Knows Best* (1954–62) and *Leave It to Beaver* (1957–63), in conjunction with the Servicemen's Readjustment Bill of 1944 and the Housing Act of 1949, "enacted the domestication of masculinity" in both cultural and legislative terms (6–7). In an ironic twist, men who refused to settle down and have a family became the focus of social and political anxiety. If the frontiersman and independent entrepreneur were ideal figures at least in part because of their lack of domestic and communal ties, in the Cold War period those same freedoms became signs of a potentially perverse or subversive masculinity. The meaningfulness of the homosexual and the Communist as "un-American" figures was constructed precisely through their seeming lack of domestic and communal ties.

While the domestication of masculinity in the postwar years was actively promoted and idealized, paradoxically it was also often depicted as a threat to American men (Corber, 14). This ambivalence is made manifest in *The Blunderer* and *Deep Water*, two novels by Patricia Highsmith in which the protagonists—the hapless Walter Stackhouse and the creepy Victor Van Allen—while ostensibly perfect examples of the new ideal of domestic masculinity, are in fact deeply compromised by their conflicted attachment to unruly wives and middle-class norms of respectability. As their weakness in the face of both increasingly immobilizes them, they begin to fantasize an escape through murder: the murder of his wife in Walter's case, and the murder of his wife's lovers in Victor's. In both stories, the transformation of a dominated husband into a murderer suggests that the domestication of postwar American men is a process of emasculation. As a fantasy of escape, the murder of a wife or her lover can function as a triumphant reenactment of masculine power over the feminine and the domestic. Yet, the murder of a spouse or a lover also returns the crisis of masculinity to the home. It is Highsmith's articulation of this ambivalence—between domesticity as the source of masculine power as well as the threat to that power—and the possibility it suggests of a profound incoherency in the binaristic construction of masculinity itself, an incoherency that can lead to a violent disassemblement of gender and sexual identity, that I want to explore in this section of the essay.

In the opening scene of the second chapter of *The Blunderer*, Walter Stackhouse, the novel's protagonist, is sitting in a car in the rain waiting for his wife, Clara. As he looks up from his newspaper, Walter sees "the trim New England houses" that looked "whiter than ever in the graying light" while the "low white fences around the lawns stood out sharply as the stitching on a sampler" (15). As Walter reflects on the scene approvingly—this was "the kind of village where you marry a healthy, good-natured girl . . . go fishing on Saturdays, and raise your sons to do the same things"—he remembers his wife's reaction to a similar New England view: "*sickmaking*," she called it (15). Written in italics, the word punctures the scene with a violence that simultaneously condemns it as clichéd and quaint and makes Walter look pathetic and sentimental, a portrait that is confirmed with the arrival of Clara, whose bossy contempt for her husband is responded to with a pacifying servility. In contrast, in the scene that opens the novel, the reader follows Melchior Kimmel, the immigrant from blue-collar New Jersey and the novel's antihero, as he first carefully sets up his alibi, then follows his wife's Greyhound bus before brutally killing her at a rest stop. The scene of the murder—a piece of wasteland next to a highway somewhere between New York City and Albany—in conjunction with Kimmel's relish in his physical power and dynamism as he first repeatedly hits and then stabs his wife to death, operates as a vivid counterimage to the one that follows.

The contrast between the two scenes sets up competing visions of masculinity, "America," and the relation between them. While Walter Stackhouse's identification with an idealized America full of "trim New England houses" and white picket fences situates him within the context of White Anglo-Saxon Protestant America, his classed and raced position of privilege and power is undercut by his sentimental attachment to the feminine and the domestic (after all, it is Walter who sees the "low white fences" as being like "stitching on a sampler"). Similarly, in his passive and dominated relationship to his wife, Walter's class privilege becomes less a sign of social and economic power and more a sign of his questionable masculinity. As David K. Johnson notes in *The Lavender Scare*, upper-classness was often read in the Cold War period as a sign of effeteness and weakness.[6] Here the portrait of America so admired by Walter becomes the scene of his undoing: the quaintness of a New England village the signifier of effeminacy and weakness. In contrast, Kimmel's immigrant "foreignness" situates his masculinity in an overwhelming physicality. He is described as an "elephant" of a man with a "large pinkish mouth with oversized lips that looked painfully swollen" (234, 71). The America in which Kimmel lives is a working-class, immigrant neighborhood in Newark, New Jersey—a striving, wanting world of social and economic ambition. Kimmel's murdering of his wife by the side of a highway—an undomesticated space in between recognized places—adds to the portrait of Kimmel's foreignness and of his masculinity as foreign. The savagery of the attack, in combination with its location, suggests an underlying lack of control. Kimmel's intelligence and "civilized voice" cannot quite cover over his appetites and desires, nor can they quite hide his strangeness, as evidenced by the fact that his East European "accent" returns when he is under severe physical and mental stress (71).

However, rather than making a clear demarcation between "American" and "un-American" masculinity, Highsmith uses the contrast/comparison between the two men to suggest an internal instability in the production of masculinity. Walter's fascination with Kimmel—after reading about the murder of Kimmel's wife, he visits Kimmel in his bookshop and eventually follows his own wife in a mimicry of Kimmel's actions—suggests a collapsing of the borders between a "foreign" masculinity and an "American" one. What marks that collapse is a transgressive femininity. Walter's passivity in the face of his wife's neurotic vindictiveness and his guilt at her death, which was caused by a lack of action on Walter's part (she kills herself at a bus stop while he is trying to find her, possibly to murder her), feminize him, especially when seen in relation to Kimmel's decisive, and deadly, action. But Kimmel's murderousness isn't so much a sign of a vigorous masculinity as a sign of his lack of sexual prowess. He kills his wife because she has humiliated him by having an affair. Similarly, Kimmel's elephantine body and vulva-like swollen lips suggest an overwhelmingly feminine physicality.[7] In his most private moments Kimmel stares at his naked body, admiring its "sensuous curves" and enjoying the "intensely feminine" feeling it gives him, a feeling that returns as he is being beaten by a zealous police officer (197). Here, the contrast/comparison between Stackhouse and Kimmel dissolves, rather than secures, the borders between foreign and domestic, feminine and masculine. As Stackhouse becomes feminine in gender, Kimmel becomes feminine in body and the (comforting) markers of masculinity disappear altogether. Corber has argued that "the politicization of homosexuality was crucial to the economic restructuring of the postwar period," in that the homosexual male became a figure of containment and projection for feelings of anxiety and frustration at the domestication of masculinity (10). In her portrayal of the shadow relationship between Walter Stackhouse and Melchior

Kimmel, Highsmith makes those feelings less about a separate homosexuality "out there," and more about the internal lack or incoherency of national and class constructions of masculinity. That is, Highsmith returns the feelings of anxiety about changing conceptions of masculinity in the postwar period back to the site of their production: not just the home, but also "America."

RANCH HOUSES AND PICKET FENCES

The suffocating emptiness of Walter Stackhouse's marriage to his wife is illustrated, at least in part, through their deadeningly conventional house on Long Island. Kimmel, in an outburst of class envy, describes it as "just the kind of place he had expected Stackhouse to live in, ample and solidly expensive as a book bound in white vellum, yet without being ostentatious" (255). In *The Price of Salt*, the New Jersey home of Carol, the older married lover of Therese, is a show house of middle-class respectability built for the world outside, not the people within. The two "projecting" wings of the house, "like the paws of a resting lion," suggest a display of power and pride, as if the house were showing off its status as a symbol of social and economic success (55). And, in *Deep Water*, the Van Allens' house, with its garage "big enough for five cars," sweeping lawns, and a brook running behind it, is situated on an estate in the small, exclusive village of Little Wesley, Connecticut, isolated from its neighbors and far from the city (25).

If the economic restructuring of the postwar years produced a corresponding reorganization of masculinity, Cold War discourses of national security incited a cultural reworking of the home and family as the site of the production of a patriotic heterosexuality. In *Homeward Bound*, Elaine Tyler May argues that Cold War discourses of national security constructed the nation as a privatized space of isolated and contained families sealed off from outside dangers.[8] Ranch-style houses, with their low-pitched roofs, attached carports, and fences, became popular in the 1950s because they "exuded this sense of isolation, privacy, and containment" (May, 108). In this section of the essay, I want to explore how Highsmith inverts the Cold War rhetoric of the (middle-class) home as both site and source of national strength. Highsmith's middle-class families may live in idyllic suburban neighborhoods and enjoy the fruits of economic and social privilege, but a deep undercurrent of inarticulate compulsions and desires always threatens to tear them apart. The ways in which people feel and act in Highsmith's novels often undo the ostensibly discrete domains of social life and identity they have to operate in and through. Highsmith's characters often act and feel against the heteronormativity of the middle-class home, making the boundaries between the home and "outside" seem permeable, fragile, and arbitrary.

In *Deep Water*, Victor Van Allen is a man of independent means who can afford to view his job (he owns and runs a small press) as a hobby. He lives with his wife, Melinda, and young daughter, Trixie, in the upper-middle-class hamlet of Little Wesley. Described as "thirty-six years old, of a little less than medium height, inclined to a general firm rotundity rather than fat," Van Allen's bland everyman appearance is undercut by his lopsided mouth, which made his face "ambiguous" and unreadable (13). Van Allen's relationship with his wife, like Walter Stackhouse's relationship with Clara, is an ambivalent combination of "loathing and devotion" (30). From the very beginning of the novel Highsmith sets the scene for a potentially disastrous breakdown in marital relations. The book opens with the Van Allens at a neighborhood party. As Vic stands alone in the corner watching, the narrator declares that "Vic didn't dance. . . . simply because his wife liked to dance" (13).

The combatativeness between Van Allen and his wife revolves around her serial infidelity, a portrait of a marriage that mimics Cold War fears of uncontrolled female sexuality tearing the home apart, leaving it vulnerable to outside attack (May, 109–10). Yet, Melinda's sexual voraciousness contrasts with Vic's asexuality, a comparison that adds to the anxiety provoked by her being "out of control." Highsmith undermines the image of the happy "normal" home not only through the figure of uncontrolled female sexuality, but also, relatedly, through the instability of gendered domestic roles. This instability is reflected in the role reversal between husband and wife, and through the way the Van Allens occupy their house. Melinda lives most of her life away from home, in public bars and the rented spaces of her lovers. In contrast, it is Vic who takes primary care of Trixie, who cooks the evening meals and cleans the house. While Melinda has the master bedroom, Victor sleeps in "a room on the opposite side of the garage," like a maid (26). Vic's domain is the garage and the kitchen, where he fixes things and maintains the household, while Melinda's domain is the living room, where she entertains her lovers.

The house is described as messy, but the scenes of disorder that really "mess" the house up are the moments of illicit love-making that Vic is forced, or determined, to witness:

> In retaliation for the slight to her friend, or perhaps just on a wild whim, Melinda turned the volume up so suddenly that Vic jumped. Then he deliberately relaxed and languidly turned the page of his newspaper as if oblivious of the din. Ralph started to turn the volume down, and Melinda stopped him, violently grabbing his wrist. Then she lifted his wrist and kissed it. They began to dance. Ralph succumbed to Melinda's mood now and was dipping his steps with swishing movements of his hips, laughing his braying laugh that was lost in the booming chaos of sound. (34)

The "din" that jolts Vic out of his chair becomes the disruption of lovers dancing, of "friends" sleeping over on the sofa, and of Trixie being awakened at four in the morning. Here, the private space of the home and family, with its structuring gender asymmetry, has been turned inside out. The patterns of domestic orderliness are threatened by the "chaos of sound" that comes from "outside" the home—Melinda's lover, the third person who represents the world of singles, partying, and sexual desire without a goal. But the chaos also comes from inside: from the desiring of Melinda, and the struggle between Vic and Melinda for control of the house.

Vic's desire, rather than being directed toward his wife or other women, is directed toward domestic order and control. When he begins to kill Melinda's lovers—the first, appropriately enough, in a neighbor's swimming pool—he does so to keep them out of his home in an attempt to gain control over his wife. Rather than feeling sexual jealousy, Vic is resentful of being humiliated and not seen as the kind of powerful, intelligent, superior man he thinks he is. An orderly house without the messy weaknesses of sexual desire threatening to tear it apart suggests a man in control of himself and his world. After the first murder, Vic feels "secure and self-sufficient"; his body full of a "steely hardness" (124–25). Yet any sense of a renewed virility is subverted by the fact that his superman thoughts inspire him not to have sex with his wife, but to clean the house:

> [H]e got the vacuum from the hall closet and plugged it into
> the wall . . . He whistled as he worked, enjoying the swift dis-
> appearance of the dust rolls under the sofa, of the square of fine
> dust he found when he moved the armchair. He enjoyed, too,
> the strain of his muscles as he performed the humble, domestic
> chore of vacuuming his living room. (125)

The ease with which Vic can vacuum away the "square of fine dust," and
the physical pleasure he gains from doing it, can be read as a metaphor
for Cold War policies of social purity, control, and order. But the image
(of a grown man enthusiastically cleaning and finding physical pleasure
in that activity) also betrays the anxiety implicit in those policies: the
fear that the enemy is "us," or that what threatens us is "our" weaknesses. In Vic's psychotic mind, the neatness and order he craves can only be
maintained through threats and violence. However, we can read Vic's
actual physical violence (and his psychosis) as symbolic of the more
subtle structural violences needed to maintain the illusion of the middle-
class home as the site of a masculine autonomy completely in control of
itself and the world around it. If the ranch-style house was popular in
the 1950s because it exuded a sense of containment and isolation, then
Highsmith shows, through her dissection of the dissolution of Vic and
Melinda's marriage, the suffocating claustrophobia that sense of isolation can produce. And while Vic's need for control and orderliness is
extreme, his will-to-power is also indicative of a Cold War discourse of
a privatized, patriarchal, heteronormative intimacy that refused the
possibility of other kinds of affective and social relationships. In his (violent) need to control his household, Vic mimics, in a perverse way, the
discourse of national security that demanded a return to, and a defense
of, the home as the site of a national power that was also masculine.

After being caught in the act of murdering his wife, Vic must finally
surrender control of his home. As Vic is led away from the house by the
police, he feels an emptiness "because he had left his life in the house
behind him, his guilt and his shame, his achievements and failures, the
failure of his experiment, and his final, brutal gesture of revenge" (271).
The Cold War idealization of a comfortable, safe, and routine way of life
lay in a kind of disconnected symbiotic relationship with America's
world ambitions in the postwar years. The self-destructive and conflicted

combination of Vic's superman ego, in combination with his fierce attachment to all things domestic, suggests both the dichotomy of a powerful nation built in the image of a comfortable, risk-free life, but also the violences, big and small, needed to maintain that image, as well as the blindnesses and limits (of community, of social and sexual relations) on which it depended.

If the Van Allens' home is torn apart through an internal struggle between the desire for domestic order and control and the desire for an outside to the home and family life, Carol's house, in *The Price of Salt*, becomes a hollow monument to middle-class heteronormativity. The size and impressiveness of the house is remarked on by Therese, the younger woman Carol meets in the city when she first comes to visit. The interior of the house is similarly impressive in its carefully produced conventionality. The game room has matching green wall-to-wall carpet and walls with a hidden refrigerator, and Carol's bedroom has "flowered cotton upholstery and plain blond woodwork" (56). The house is an extension of the stultifying mechanisms of exchange and production that structure Frankenberg's, the department store where Therese worked. Therese describes the store as being "like a prison," with its "Welcome to Frankenberg" booklet that boasts of vacation awards for "Twenty-five Yearers" and asks, "Are you Frankenberg material?" While the department store is designed to produce the right kind of worker in the endless pursuit of profit, Carol's home is both advertisement and factory for the production of ideal consumer-citizens. Each room complements the others, while each object and person knows its place, from the rug, to the piano, to the maid and the wife. Carol suggests to Therese that her husband married her because of his "acquisitiveness." He didn't so much fall in love as pick her "out like a rug for his living room" (125).

When Therese first comes to the house, she wanders around, following Carol, as if they were both in search of a room they could safely occupy. When Carol turns to look at Therese, the "same puzzled dissatisfaction came back to her face," as if she couldn't quite figure out what Therese was doing there, or where they should go (55). The soon-to-be-lovers seem lost, as if they do not fit into the landscape of the house. Therese's presence jars the picture the house is built to provide, a picture reflected in the family photographs scattered around the house. She is an imposter, someone who has to hide her things when Carol's husband drops by for a visit. Like the love letter Therese slips between the pages of the *Oxford Book of Love Poetry*, the love between Carol and Therese cannot be expressed openly within the house, and indeed, the affair between the two women is consummated on the road, in the rented anonymous space of a hotel room.

The women embark on a road trip to escape from the claims of family and heterosexual union embodied in the figure of Harge, Carol's controlling husband. The now empty house, in its impressiveness and size, becomes a sign of both Harge's power and influence—he is a successful banker from a good family who thought he had married "well"—but also of the hollowness of that power. Harge's pursuit of Carol, in the form of a private detective sent to follow the women and record evidence of their possible perversion, serves as a reminder of his power, but also of his failure as a man. The detective pursues Carol, after all, to collect evidence of her disloyalty—with another woman. Here, the emptiness of the house also stands as a symbol of Harge's impotence—his inability to satisfy his wife sexually. The only (penetrative) action Harge takes against his wife is actually performed through a surrogate—the detective—and comes in the form of a phallic "spike" driven into the wall of the lovers' hotel room to hear their conversations and lovemaking. The spike, as well as the dictaphone Carol finds hidden under the bedside table of the hotel room, are, as Carol remarks, "a portrait of Harge," but it is a portrait that, in suggesting impotence, also makes the artificiality, manufacturedness, and precariousness of Harge's claim to power explicit (209).

When Carol and Therese "escape" from the New Jersey house, they reveal in the process the threat posed by its normative claims. By the end of the novel Carol has lost all custody rights to her child. The "evidence" against her comes not only from the tapes recorded by the private detective but also from the maid, who finds traces of Therese's presence in the house and sells them to Harge. Like Frankenberg's regulatory regimes of employment, which offer the "scripts" of a successful career as a department store worker, the regimes of gender and sexual norms that structure the middle-class home operate as a kind of prison, locking people into roles that limit the possibilities of other relationships and affectional ties. Highsmith links the regulatory role of the home quite explicitly to the Cold War rhetoric of patriotism, but in a way that inverts the ideology of "homeward-bound" nationness. Carol's portrayal of her marriage to Harge as a loveless form of "acquisitiveness" in which social ambition and the desire for control—over people, things, and places—are what make it attractive to Harge, causes Therese to remember conversations about "war and big business and Congressional witch-hunts" (125). What relates the two, according to Therese, is lovelessness and a desire by "Man" to "catch up with his own destructive machines" (125). The oppressive threat facing Therese and Carol is not Communism or sexual perversion, but the interrelated domains of big business, war, and heterosexuality, a matrix of intersecting forces that threaten people's ability to love one other. Here, the ability to love, and the possibilities for social expansion and human interaction it signifies, is located not in the family unit organized through heterosexual union, but in the possibilities, however threatened, of homosexual relations.

"IN A THOUSAND CITIES"⁹

In their essay "Sex in Public," Lauren Berlant and Michael Warner contend that "national heterosexuality is the mechanism by which a core national culture can be imagined as a sanitized space of sentimental feeling and immaculate behavior, a space of pure citizenship" (189). And Berlant has written elsewhere that the American citizen gets to "appear" at his "most national" when "at leisure, with his family or in semipublic worlds" like sports ("The Subject of True Feeling," 12). The story of national belonging, in other words, has a consumer-driven romantic plot; it's a story about love, families, home, and leisure. According to Berlant and Warner, this construction of citizenship tends to separate "the aspirations of national belonging from the critical culture of the public sphere and from political citizenship" (189). To be a "good" American means being a good husband, a good father, and a good consumer of goods. It also demands an absence of other identificatory marks like race, or class, or (perverse) sexuality that might bring into the "space of pure citizenship" the spoiling evidence of political movements, battles, and struggles. For Berlant, imagining national belonging as a privatized space of heterosexual union enables a projection of American citizenship as "innocent," and of "America" as a nation full of people "not yet bruised by history" (130).

In the 1950s a similar attempt to wed the notion of an innocent, essentially good citizenship with the projection of the home and heterosexual union as the space of nationness, was intrinsic to the Cold War rhetoric of patriotism. The family home and the married couple became the site and the form of imagining a national resistance to the "outside" threats of Communism and sexual perversion. The dangerous, potentially "un-American" territory in this national dreamscape was the public sphere, not just the "critical culture" of the mass media, politics, and the government (especially the State Department and other civil service branches of the federal government),[10] but also the public spaces of cities. Cities were places of (potentially) unregulated social and sexual interaction, places in which different classes, races, and sexes could mingle and congregate outside the spectacularized glare of the idealized private home. The city offered the possibility of a life lived outside the romantic plot line of heterosexuality, as well as outside the realm of the middle-class home. Yet the city, with its potential for dangerous encounters, was also the place where Americans could lose their innocence and become "bruised" by history. In both *The Blunderer* and *The Price of Salt*, New York City functions as the space in which the protagonists lose their innocence and discover other worlds—worlds outside of the "national" home of middle-class, heterosexual, white suburbia.[11]

In *The Blunderer*, the city functions as an imaginary, rather than actual, alternative space to the life Walter Stackhouse lives on Long Island. Sometimes, when Walter was "standing with a second highball in his hand on somebody's lawn in Benedict" he would wonder "what he was doing there among those pleasant, smugly well-to-do and essentially boring people, what he was doing with his whole life" (26). Walter's dream is to move to the city and open up his own small-claims law office (that is, become the small independent entrepreneur rather than the corporate "other-directed" man he is on Long Island). After Clara dies, the city becomes the place in which Walter also imagines a life lived among friends. The most important relationship Walter has is with his friend Jon, a man who lives alone in the city, and with whom Walter re-creates a domestic comradeship in the wake of Clara's death. It is with Jon that Walter breaks down and cries over Clara's death, and with whom he speaks about his fears of being accused of her murder. The city is also the place Walter imagines having a relationship (though not marriage) with Ellie, a young musician who, unlike Clara, likes a bit of "disorder" (80).

The plurality of possibilities that the city offers—his friendship with Jon as well as a relationship with Ellie—is precisely what appeals to Walter. Yet the city is also the place in which Walter has his final, deadly encounter with Kimmel. As he walks through Central Park one night—a place that signifies the possibility of undomesticated sexuality—he is followed by Kimmel, and after a scuffle in which Walter mistakenly kills a stranger, is murdered by him. In the moment of death, Walter sees "the little blue window he had seen with Ellie, bright and sun-filled, and just too far away to escape through" (263–64). A future with Ellie is now seen, simply, as a form of "escape." In contrast, the final murderous meeting with Kimmel is the moment when the real effects of Walter's attachment to the script of a national heteromasculinity come crashing through. The violence underpinning the construction of an idealized masculinity (the structural racism and classism that project white Anglo masculinity as the national norm) is made explicit in the city—a transgressive space in which the discrete domains of social, gender, and sexual identities are undone by the mingling and interaction of thousands and thousands of strangers.

While the road trip the two lovers take in *The Price of Salt* is an escape from the claims of Harge and the New Jersey house, it is also an opportunity, as Carol remarks to Therese, to see America (168). The America they see, however, is the America of the private detective, the regulatory space of heterosexual norms and middle-class hegemony. When Therese feels a "fervent burst" of patriotism at the sight of a red barn by the side of a road, it is exposed as sentimental misrecognition by the fact that the discovery that the lovers are being followed comes immediately afterward (191). The only place for the lovers to go is the city, a place where they can escape the glare of a heteronormative national culture by mingling with others and becoming two in a crowd. The city is also the place in which they can imagine a future for themselves; it offers the possibility of living together. But the city is also the place where the lovers are forced to confront the loss of their innocence. Although the lovers are faced with the threat of "America" while on the road trip, and are forced apart by that threat, it is only when they return to the city that they understand themselves to be, not simply "flung out of space" (181), but two of many "like them" who must live with and against the claims of a national heterosexuality. When Therese returns to the city she feels older and wiser; she feels different, and her love for Carol is different. The future offered by the city is also, then, a future in which history has made its mark. For Highsmith, writing in the 1950s, history was making its mark on queers, on women, and on others defined as "un-American." In her excavation of suburban life, she returns the hurts of that history to the site of their production, that is, to the (idealized) homes of a "national heterosexuality."

ACKNOWLEDGMENTS

I would like to thank Deborah Nelson for her insightful comments on an earlier draft of this essay, and also Lisa Diedrich, who was the first to read it and who suggested ways to make it better.

VICTORIA HESFORD is a lecturer in women's studies at the State University of New York at Stony Brook. Her fields of interest include cultural memories of the second wave women's movement, queer and feminist literature and history in the postwar era, and media studies. She is co-editor of the forthcoming *Feminist Time Against Nation Time*, a collection of essays that explores the tensions between feminism and nationalism in historical as well as contemporary times of war.

NOTES

1. "Containment" has been a compelling and fruitful metaphor in studies of the Cold War period. It was George Kennan, the director of Secretary of State George Marshall's policy-planning staff in the late 1940s, who first used the metaphor as a foreign policy initiative in his famous 1947 paper, "The Sources of Soviet Conduct," published in *Foreign Affairs*. For a discussion of Kennan's paper and its influence on 1950s domestic ideology, see Ross, 45–47, and Nadel, 5–6. Cold War scholars like Nadel, Ross, Rogin, May, Corber, and Nelson have expanded the explanatory range of the containment metaphor by exploring the ways in which it has framed, for example, the "hegemonic process" more generally in postwar American culture (Ross, 56) and the debates over the shifting spaces and meanings of privacy in the United States in the late twentieth century (Nelson).

2. See Nelson for a related argument about the un-Americanness of private domestic space in postwar American culture.

3. The 1999 film *The Talented Mr Ripley*, directed by Anthony Minghella, and the more recent (and even better) *Ripley's Game*, directed by Liliana Cavani and starring John Malkovich (2002), have reintroduced movie audiences to Highsmith's amoral, psychotic antihero, Tom Ripley. A biography and memoir of Highsmith also appeared in 2003, and Norton has reissued her novels and short stories in a handsome paperback series. See Meaker and Wilson. In his biography of her, Andrew Wilson notes that while Highsmith enjoyed both popular

and critical success in Europe, her reputation in the United States was mainly as a writer of mysteries, and although she was reviewed occasionally in such "highbrow" venues as the *New Yorker*, by the end of her life she had no regular American publisher.

4. Andrew Wilson interviewed Highsmith's American editor at the Atlantic Monthly Press and Knopf, Gary Fisketjon, who is quoted as saying that while the inability to categorize Highsmith's work made it impossible for the U.S. market to get a "fix" on her, the "cynicism" about human relationships in her work was equally problematic (Wilson, 319).

5. I take the term "heteronormative" from Lauren Berlant and Michael Warner's essay "Sex in Public." They define heteronormativity as "the institutions, structures of understanding, and practical orientations that make heterosexuality not only coherent—that is, organized as a sexuality—but also privileged" (187). Here, then, I understand architecture, and the design of suburbs and types of houses in particular, as part of the production of heteronormativity.

6. Johnson's study is primarily concerned with the prolonged attempt during the Cold War years to purge the federal government, especially the State Department, of homosexuals. He notes that the governing stereotype of a civil servant, including the diplomatic corps, during the Cold War era was of an effete upper-class man who could easily morph into a "nance" or "pansy." See Johnson, 69–71.

7. Thanks to Deborah Nelson for pointing out the genital features of Highsmith's portrait of Kimmel's mouth.

8. Organizations like the Federal Civil Defense Administration and the Massachusetts Society for Social Health issued pamphlets and posters promoting the idea that safety from a possible attack was to be found in the family and the home. Wives and mothers were encouraged to stock their pantries and learn first aid, while their husbands were encouraged to construct the "home bomb shelter" in the basement. Similarly, a "return" to domestic femininity was promoted under the guise of national security: "unsupervised homes" put the nation at risk. See May, 104, 99.

9. At the end of *The Price of Salt*, after the lovers have been separated, Therese returns to New York and to Carol, realizing she is still in love with her: "[I]t was like meeting Carol all over again, but it was still Carol and no one else. It would be Carol in a thousand cities" (276).

10. See Johnson, *The Lavender Scare*, for an account of antigovernment feeling in the Cold War period. For many conservative politicians in the 1950s, an antipathy toward the New Deal also meant an antipathy toward the many new government departments that opened in order to implement it. These departments were often regarded as quasi-Socialist entities staffed by Communist sympathizers and liberal bleeding hearts.

11. For a more expansive discussion of the queer space of the city in *The Price of Salt* see my "A Love 'Flung Out of Space': Lesbians in the City in Patricia Highsmith's *The Price of Salt*."

WORKS CITED

Berlant, Lauren. "The Subject of True Feeling: Pain, Privacy, and Politics." In *Feminist Consequences: Theory for the New Century*, ed. Elizabeth Bronfen and Misha Kavka. New York: Columbia University Press, 2001.

Berlant, Lauren, and Michael Warner. "Sex in Public." In *Publics and Counterpublics*, ed. Michael Warner. New York: Zone Books, 2002.

Corber, Robert J. *Homosexuality in Cold War America: Resistance and the Crisis of Masculinity*. Durham: Duke University Press, 1997.

Hardt, Michael, and Antonio Negri. *Empire*. Cambridge: Harvard University Press, 2001.

Hesford, Victoria. "A Love 'Flung Out of Space': Lesbians in the City in Patricia Highsmith's *The Price of Salt*." In "Fifties Fictions," *Paradoxa* 18 (Summer 2003): 117-135.

Highsmith, Patricia. *Deep Water*. 1957; New York: W.W. Norton, 2001.

———. *The Price of Salt*. 1952; New York: W. W. Norton, 2001.

———. *The Blunderer*. 1954; New York: W.W. Norton, 2003.

Johnson, David K. *The Lavender Scare: The Cold War Persecution of Gays and Lesbians in the Federal Government*. Chicago: University of Chicago Press, 2004.

May, Elaine Tyler. *Homeward Bound: American Families in the Cold War Era*. New York: Basic Books, 1988.

Meaker, Marijane. *Highsmith: A Romance of the 1950s*. New York: Cleis Press, 2003.

Nadel, Alan. *Containment Culture: American Narratives, Postmodernism, and the Atomic Age*. Durham and London: Duke University Press, 1995.

Nelson, Deborah. *Pursuing Privacy in Cold War America*. New York: Columbia University Press, 2002.

Rogin, Michael. *Ronald Reagan, the Movie: And Other Episodes in Political Demonology*. Berkeley: University of California Press, 1987.

Ross, Andrew. *No Respect: Intellectuals and Popular Culture*. New York and London: Routledge, 1989.

Wilson, Andrew. *Beautiful Shadow: A Life of Patricia Highsmith*. New York: Bloomsbury, 2003.

AMERICAN ICONOCLAST: *CARMEN JONES* AND THE REVOLUTIONARY DIVADOM OF DOROTHY DANDRIDGE

TIFFANY GILBERT

"There was a time when this business had the eyes of the whole wide world. But that wasn't good enough. Oh, no! They wanted the ears of the world, too. So they opened their big mouths, and out came talk, talk, talk," rants *Sunset Boulevard*'s Norma Desmond about the introduction of sound to film, a phenomenon that precipitated the end of her career.[1] Later, when she arrives at Paramount Studios for an appointment with her former director, Cecil B. DeMille, Norma confronts for the first time her nemesis, sound. As she impatiently waits for DeMille to complete a scene, a microphone passes overhead and ruffles the feathers of her hat. Dismissively batting away the swinging boom, Norma Desmond simultaneously rejects modern technology and reaffirms her own visually centered iconicity. Indeed, *Sunset Boulevard* privileges Gloria Swanson's/Norma Desmond's visibility in the film's final moments when Norma, walking down the staircase toward the photographers and cameramen, informs "DeMille" that she is "ready for [her] closeup." The image/sound struggle animating *Sunset Boulevard* at last appears resolved.

By the time *Sunset Boulevard* debuted in 1950, silent film and its divas were little more than relics of a forgotten era, but the challenges of integrating sound and image nevertheless remained for filmmakers of this decade. Otto Preminger's film *Carmen Jones* filters these opposing logics of image and sound through the politics of American racism and the pervasive prejudice of the Hollywood studio system in the fifties. Released in American theaters in 1954, the same year as the landmark *Brown v. Board of Education* decision that prohibited segregation in public schools, *Carmen Jones* functions as a cinematic analogue, as it were, of the groundbreaking verdict. Yet, as I will demonstrate, because *Carmen Jones* is explicitly routed through the aesthetics and often transgressive politics of opera, Dorothy Dandridge, unlike other black film stars

[*WSQ: Women's Studies Quarterly* 33: 3 & 4 (Fall/Winter 2005)]

before her, penetrates Hollywood's glass ceiling and emerges as a new kind of black female star.

Because of the obvious mismatch between Dandridge and her vocal double Marilyn Horne, the issue of race and voice in *Carmen Jones* continues to intrigue critics of the film. Published in *Velvet Light Trap* in spring 2003, Jeff Smith's article "Black Faces, White Voices: The Politics of Dubbing in *Carmen Jones*" deals extensively with the thorny issues surrounding executive decisions to replace star Dorothy Dandridge's voice with the operatic voice of then-unknown singer Marilyn Horne, while at the same time extending to costar Pearl Bailey, a popular singer in her own right like Dandridge, the privilege of using her own voice in her musical numbers by transposing Bizet's score down to a lower, more suitable octave.[2] In so doing, Smith suggests, *Carmen Jones* invites critical analysis because it erects a system of cultural and musical hierarchies that impinge on the broader complexities of race in opera and cinema and that also reverberate beyond the movie screen itself. To the degree that Horne's vernacularized singing risks putting a minstrel spin on Preminger's adaptation, vocal mixing in *Carmen Jones* potentially serves, at least on an imaginative, more optimistic level, an inspired social purpose. Smith writes: "Although *Carmen Jones* depicts a space of racial segregation on its image track, its soundtrack reflects the prospects of desegregation as an issue associated with the civil rights movements of the fifties and sixties. Blacks and whites could not intermingle in the diegetic world of *Carmen Jones*, but their voices could in nondiegetic and extradiegetic spaces on the soundtrack."[3]

In many ways, Smith supports my own fascinations with the vocal conduit stretching between Dorothy Dandridge and Marilyn Horne and underscores some of the conclusions I arrived at in my own contemplations of the film's complicated vocal politics. Smith's preference to examine image and sound—the cinematic and operatic—as separate registers preempts a discussion of how these two opposing regimes are united in the film to create a space in the cinematic and cultural imagination that could accommodate Dorothy Dandridge's contradictory status as a black woman and as a movie star. Yet, before I examine the complex ways in which the cinematic and operatic schism in *Carmen Jones* actually coheres and works in tandem to construct Dandridge's diva persona, I will detour briefly through the career of Lena Horne, whose own rising cinematic divadom was eclipsed by the casting of Ava Gardner, a white actress, in the 1951 MGM remake of *Showboat*.[4] The Hollywood experience of Lena Horne serves a useful function as a prelude to my discussion on *Carmen Jones* and as a logical counterexample to Dorothy Dandridge's luminous but short film career. For, in spite of her own obvious physical allure and musical abilities, Horne, unlike Dandridge, never quite achieved on screen the diva status she eventually enjoyed on stage and on vinyl. Indeed, as her musical performances were largely secondary to the narrative elements, Horne herself was never fully integrated into the cinematic logic of the films in which she appeared.

Having established herself in the all-black movie musical productions *Cabin in the Sky* and *Stormy Weather*, both released in 1943, Lena Horne was already a known quantity in Hollywood when MGM began casting for an up-to-date version of Edna Ferber's classic tale of music and miscegenation, *Showboat*. An experienced musical performer and a woman of color, Horne, who understood the rigors of singing on screen and the difficulties of mastering choreography, would have been a likely choice for the role of the tragic mulatto character, Julie. But in an ironic twist, the actress, whose complexion could easily have suggested "mulatto" to an audience, was not cast in the part because of her color. In an effort to exoticize Horne's looks and to cash in on all the possible ethnicities her color evoked, studio executives consulted cosmetics maven Max Factor to create a foundation that would sufficiently mask or, at the very least, obscure her blackness in her performances. Marketed as "Light Egyptian," the finished product, unfortunately for Horne, was a better coverup than anticipated, and it essentially eliminated the need for her altogether. In fact, "Light Egyptian" provided an instant loophole for the studio to avoid hiring black actresses for certain roles—white actresses, including Ava Gardner, who was eventually tapped to play the coveted role of Julie, could be made to look more ethnic with the help of Factor's creation. Most important, perhaps, "Light Egyptian" preempted any political fallout that was sure to follow in casting Horne to perform alongside white men in *Showboat* and to have a romance with one of them on screen.

Nevertheless, the noncasting of Lena Horne is relevant to Dorothy Dandridge's star status for other reasons. In the case of *Showboat*, in spite of Horne's vocal and physical suitability for the role, the musical medium alone proved to be insufficient in compensating for her status as a black woman; manipulating her on-screen persona by literally "blacking" out her color turned out to be a less-than-viable cinematic solution, as "Light Egyptian" only made it easier for studio execs not to cast her for certain parts. As an actress and as a black woman, Horne unfortunately was caught within the tight interweave of Hollywood's complicated racial, sexual, and diva politics. To accommodate strict segregation laws in the South, even Horne's musical appearances in certain films were excised. Ironically, though relegated to singing roles that would show off her diva potential, Horne was, more often than not, the most dramatically expendable actor in the cast.[5]

That Lena Horne, equipped with such beauty and talent, failed to attain real superstar status as a Hollywood actress makes, by comparison, Dorothy Dandridge's rise all the more impressive and perplexing. Given the persisting racism and bias in Hollywood, how does Dandridge pass through certain cultural and cinematic prohibitions in *Carmen Jones*, released in 1954 only three years after the remake of *Showboat*? How does she, as the titular siren, achieve cinematic divadom under generic conditions similar to those that virtually prohibited Horne from doing the same? In what ways does *Carmen Jones*'s generically hybrid status foster a cinematic environment that makes it possible for Dandridge's divadom to prosper?

The key to understanding Dandridge's extraordinary rise to superstar status lies in the film's precinematic incarnations. As Wayne Koestenbaum has argued in *The Queen's Throat*, opera, as a form of cultural and artistic discourse, has always been preoccupied with color. He writes, "Color is one of the primary metaphors for the qualities of vocal tone. Singers are taught to avoid the 'white' sound and to cover the tones, to make them darker. . . . The voice of the black operatic or concert diva was imagined to emanate directly from her ethnicity: commentators referred to Marian Anderson's 'Negroid sound.' And listeners have used metaphors of darkness and of racial essence to describe the appeal of certain female operatic voices even when the singer was white."[6] Certainly, the operatic fascinations with color Koestenbaum describes are very much in play in the racial politics that underwrite Georges Bizet's *Carmen*, a musically and culturally diverse composition. Based on Prosper Mérimée's novella, the opera largely works as a result of the ethnic uncertainties embedded in the heroine. Thus, as a racially ambiguous character, Carmen functions as an effective masquerade through which both black and white singers can "pass."

But *Carmen Jones* the movie is a different matter altogether. It challenges the limits of Hollywood's glass ceiling by linking the image politics of the film to the politics of another discourse, opera, to shake industry and audience perceptions of cinematic divadom. Under the cover of Bizet's opera and Hammerstein's musical adaptation, the film circumvents cinematic racism and presents a gorgeous, sexy black woman who appears in iconic fashion, conceivably a disarming image for white audiences at the time to accept and a controversial one for black audiences to embrace. *Carmen Jones*'s generically diverse pedigree stages an end run around Hollywood's racist objections to a black female star. By uniting cinematic and operatic discourses, moreover, the film creates a loophole through which Dorothy Dandridge's vampy performance eventually passes.

In *Carmen Jones*, Dandridge embodies what musicologist Susan McClary has described as "[multiple] categories of alterity" that coalesce into an acceptable example of what I term Hollywood divadom, a mode of iconoclastic being that daringly violates and transcends categorization.[7] As Carmen Jones, Dandridge's exhibition of brazen, resistant sexuality reverberates within and without the diegesis. Carmen's introductory aria "Dat's Love," a vernacularized riff on Bizet's *Habañera*, claims the twin pleasures of sexual license and refusal: "You go for me an' I'm taboo / but if yo're hard to get, I go for you."[8] Carmen Jones, in spite of her alleged sexual excesses, asserts her elective powers, and, as a model of behavior, refutes a history of institutionalized passivity that essentially made it incumbent on black women to submit to advances of both white and black men. Moreover, her foregrounded positioning cuts through the racially inflected caricatures of black femininity Preminger presents through the secondary female leads. In the divide separating Olga James's prim persona as Joe's motherly girlfriend and Pearl Bailey as Carmen's mammified, gold-digging sidekick, Frankie, the film spectacularizes Dandridge's difference, visually isolating her alterities amid these stock characterizations. For example, Carmen's totemic red skirt and black peasant blouse, a nod to the heroine's antecedents in Mérimée's novella and Bizet's opera, clearly operate to augment Dandridge's sex-symbol status as well as to buttress her diva status, which, as I argue, is something related but altogether different. For as *Carmen Jones* and its precursors have demonstrated, female sexuality on screen does not easily—nor does it have to—translate into a kind of "pin-up" passivity.

Prior to the commercial and critical acclaim of *Carmen Jones*, Dandridge's sexual image was cemented on the nightclub circuit, where she beguiled audiences at such landmark lounges as the Mocambo, the Trocadero, and the Cocoanut Grove with the suggestive swivel of her hips and her tight satin designer dresses. Such was the appeal of her erotic stage persona that one impresario even sold copies of the recently published *Sexual Behavior of the Human Female*, Alfred Kinsey's jaw-dropping report on the secret sexual proclivities of American women, to promote Dandridge's cabaret act at his club. That she was even recognized for her physical attractiveness, claims Dandridge biographer Donald Bogle, reflects a subtle cultural shift in the racial and sexual politics in fifties America:

> In past eras, Black women like Josephine Baker, Billie Holiday, Lena Horne, and even dancer/choreographer Katherine Dunham were seen as powerfully sexy and desirable women. Yet they were rarely openly acknowledged as such by the American press. Patrons didn't see them as female ideals or above-the-table goddesses, to be fawned over like Rita Hayworth, Hedy Lamarr, or Betty Grable. Rather, in the dominant cultural and market mainstream, the Negro goddess was only to be appreciated and desired on the sly. . . . Things began to change in the fifties, though, as the Black women making an impact in show business [like Dandridge and Eartha Kitt] found themselves openly saluted as sex goddesses.[9]

Despite the smashing success of her cabaret career, Dandridge nonetheless had misgivings about the cinematic image she projected and misapprehended the iconoclastic potential and importance of her most famous role. Responding in 1957, three years after her performance in *Carmen Jones*, to *Sepia*'s teasing inquiry, "Why Dorothy Dandridge is Afraid of Marriage," she wrote, "in defense of myself":

> Why did I guard myself when I might have met the man I could have found happiness with? I've examined myself over and over on that question, and I think it's been largely a matter of a sense of responsibility to my own people. . . . No, I would rather be lonely, I would rather look at the walls of my hotel room than risk mingling with individuals who turn out to be

unsavory characters. Above all, I wanted to keep an unblemished reputation for the sake of members of my race.[10]

Dandridge's letter appreciates the political force of her sexual image. But even as she acknowledges the volatility of her sexual persona within the black community, she denies the existence of a cinematic culture gradually opening itself to different kinds of stars. In recontextualizing sex outside of its privatized frameworks, she transforms her physical body into a civic, public body. Dandridge vows a life of social and sexual propriety to protect her claim and the image of her race. Lauren Berlant has written quite cogently on this defensive strategy, a phenomenon she terms "diva citizenship." For Berlant, diva citizenship is a "spectacle of subjectivity,"

> a moment of emergence that marks unrealized potentials for subaltern political activity. Diva Citizenship occurs when a person stages a dramatic coup in a public sphere in which she does not have privilege. Flashing up and startling the public, she puts the dominant story into suspended animation; as though recording an estranging voice-over to a film we have already seen, she renarrates the dominant history as one that the abjected people have once lived sotto voce, but no more; and she challenges her audience to identify with the enormity of her suffering she has narrated and the courage she has had to produce, calling on people to change the social and institutional practices of citizenship to which they currently consent.[11]

But Dandridge also departs from the parameters Berlant describes. In writing to *Sepia*, Dandridge addresses an already subaltern audience that, while it may not enjoy significant political power, nonetheless has dynamic cultural force. Appealing to an audience in the same racialized position as herself, and ostensibly one that should have sympathized with her yearning for visible subjectivity, Dandridge nevertheless does not mount an articulated frontal defense of her individual prerogatives or private sexual will. Her tactic is much more oblique. Choosing not to marry, she politicizes her sexuality: Dandridge in fact subordinates her elective power and sexual autonomy to the greater—if not oppressive—cultural legitimacy of the African American community.

Significantly, if Dandridge's quest for acceptance and approval is tempered by her recognition of the pressures and responsibilities on her as a "civic body," Carmen Jones then remains an even more radical example of an independent woman. Living on the fringes of traditional femininity, Carmen rejects conventional marriage or romance to protect her individual autonomy, and does so quite emphatically—to the death, in fact. Following Berlant, we could say that Carmen Jones's operatic and cinematic modes of unapologetic effrontery surpass Dandridge's textual gesture, as if the conventions of public writing somehow inhibit the power (or threat) of her sexuality: "[Diva citizenship] tends to emerge in moments of such extraordinary political paralysis that acts of language can feel like explosives that shake the ground of collective existence. Yet in remaking the scene of public life into a spectacle of subjectivity, it can lead to a confusion of willful and memorable rhetorical performance with sustained social change itself."[12]

Dandridge's quiet protests against scandal sheets' (e.g., Confidential's and Sepia's) subtle censure of her dating preferences (Dandridge was often seen in the company of white men, including Otto Preminger himself) actually manifests itself in the aggressive image and actions of Carmen Jones herself.[13] For Dandridge, the Carmen archetype opens a zone in which her erotic presence and difference can be liberated, a place where racist restrictions on her identity are lifted. In this incarnation, Dandridge enjoys a quotient of liberty that is, in substance, unavailable to her in real life. On screen, as Carmen, she razes the specter of lasciviousness and moral laxity stereotypically ascribed to black women, and in its place she raises the spectacle of empowered sexuality. Her physical spectacularization in the film, consequently, elevates Dandridge from a position of generalized anonymity and acquiescence. Carmen's nonconformist, noncompliant agency spills out onto Dandridge's image and vaults her to a cinematic status associated with other screen queens like Elizabeth Taylor, Ava Gardner, and Marilyn Monroe. Dandridge's own assertion that "America was not geared to make me into a Liz Taylor, Monroe, or a Gardner. My sex symbolism was as a wanton, a prostitute, not as a woman seeking love and a husband, like other women," however truthful, underestimates the cultural impact of her performance.[14] Her star performance as Carmen Jones thus normalizes a sexuality that heretofore may have disturbed both black and white audiences and places her on equal standing with glamourous white actresses of the time. Recalibrating the metrics by which images of female sexuality are measured, *Carmen Jones* validates her sexiness. Thus, Dandridge's arresting pose in the film's promotional stills—in Carmen's famous red skirt, her head thrown back, arms akimbo, legs set apart—can be viewed alongside Elizabeth Taylor's iconic appearance in a wet bathing suit in *Suddenly, Last Summer* (1959) or Marilyn Monroe's in an aerodynamic white halter dress in *The Seven Year Itch* (1955).

More precisely, cinematic divadom for Dandridge fosters an iconoclasm and transcendence beyond narrow definitions of black female sexuality. *Carmen Jones* reorients the visuals of American sexuality, and if we are overly attuned to Dandridge's physical presence, it is not a sign of her diminishment or devaluation. Rather it is evidence that the racial Catch-22 Jane Gaines describes as identifying black women as "all woman and tinted black, or mostly black and scarcely woman" is beginning to short-circuit, at least in part.[15] The operatic dimension of *Carmen Jones* works not so much to negate or obscure Dandridge's race as it does to negotiate her status as an exceptionally beautiful woman, who happens to be black, into the cinematic context of a screen goddess by bridging the distance between Dandridge's blackness and femaleness. Furthermore, because there is no white or black controlling male gaze—the look of the black male characters is summarily denied, returned, or trumped by Dandridge's gaze—neither her race nor her gender is fetishized.

What becomes increasingly apparent as *Carmen Jones* progresses is the extent to which costars Harry Belafonte's and Pearl Bailey's respective star personas either are contained or caricatured in relation to Dandridge's. To start, Belafonte's first musical moment, a duet with Olga James entitled "You talks jus' like my ma," more or less labels him a chaste, unthreatening mama's boy, as if to defuse the threat and dilute the potency of Belafonte's sexual presence. Evident in this and in subsequent scenes in the film in which Belafonte appears, the film's presentation of the actor conforms musically and visually to an image of a black man that is, by turns, aggressively paternalized and aggressively violent. For instance, when he is reprimanded and sentenced to a brief stint in jail for aiding Carmen's flight from justice for fighting with a coworker at the parachute factory, he sings this time an ardent, lovestruck aria for Carmen, not Cindy Lou, his hometown, homegrown girlfriend. But Belafonte's singing, which is dubbed by operatically trained singer Le Vern Hutcherson, is not so much the focus of the scene as is the sight of his bare-chested body. While his performance of the "Flower Song" musically records his physical and emotional incarceration, the dramatic presentation of his imprisonment creates a special tension between *Carmen Jones*'s operatic and cinematic registers. What would perhaps otherwise mark a cinematically iconoclastic gesture in the film, Belafonte's naked body is literally and figuratively stripped of its power. To be blunt, there is something discreetly slavish about this depiction. A member of a prison gang assigned to cut brush in the hot Florida sun, he looks more like a work-weary slave than the dashing, rule-abiding soldier he was trained to be. Moreover, recollecting his desire for Carmen, he seems to sing himself to exhaustion, straining, as the sight of Belafonte's pulsating vocal cords attests, to convey the intensity of his passion over Bizet's score.

Unfortunately, the operatic and cinematic forces do not attach to Belafonte's star persona as they do to Dandridge's. On both levels, he suffers from a lack of agency. And on the few occasions when he dares to assert himself, he is punished by the military brass, by his rival for Carmen's love (Husky Miller), or by Carmen herself. He is either locked up by the military police or hiding from them; his movements are confined, for the most part, to prison cells, rooming houses, or janitor's closets. When he confronts Carmen for the last time at Husky Miller's prizefight, vocally and visually he is desperate, out of control, manic. But even if we can account for the operatic and cinematic differences between Belafonte's performance and Dandridge's, it is doubtful that the outer culture at the time of *Carmen Jones*'s production would have allowed more than one star-powered performance by a black actor, much less one by an attractive black man in a sometimes sexually aggressive role.[16] Moreover, it would seem that the film in effect maneuvers around this impediment by subsuming stereotypical images of blackness and specifically black sexuality into the secondary character roles.

The cinematic and cultural tensions latent in Belafonte's performance are largely absent in Pearl Bailey's, as the film confines her performance to an ethnicized caricature that is repeated in the music as well as in the dramatic idiom. As Smith has observed and explained at length in his own capable discussion of Bailey's participation in the film, there is hardly anything operatic about her character or her performance of the song "Beat out Dat Rhythm." Bailey sings and dances in a highly idiosyncratic manner that curiously deviates from the other vocal performances, which are much more in tune with Bizet's operatic orchestrations. Again, as he asserts, compared to the other major performers in the film, she is the most musically anomalous. Her performance, more than any other, retains the ethnic flavor of such all-black musicals as *Cabin in the Sky* and *Stormy Weather*, which she specifically references in her singing, and interrupts the otherwise musically cohesive structure of *Carmen Jones*.[17]

Pearl Bailey functions as a unique test case against which to evaluate how Dandridge's divadom is achieved in the film. In a strangely counterintuitive way, by allowing Bailey to sing without the assistance of a vocal "ghost," the film confines her to an explicitly racialized context and musical idiom. True, Dandridge "sings" and acts under similar circumstances, but, unlike Bailey, she ironically is granted more "cinematic" freedom via the soundtrack featuring the young, pre–opera star voice of Marilyn Horne. That Bailey's actual singing undercuts her diva presence in the film suggests that vocal authenticity is not essential to Dandridge's cinematic divadom. Thus, it would appear that the insertion of Marilyn Horne's "black" dialect does, in fact, clear a path for Dandridge's image through certain racist prohibitions found in the culture outside the film that would ordinarily impede her claims to cinematic divadom.

Moreover, I would like to suggest that Bailey herself, apart from her idiomatic vocal performance, operates visually as a more "colored" foil to Dorothy Dandridge. Because the film clearly positions Bailey to represent and enact a quasi-African aesthetic, Dandridge, in contrast, does not look "as black" and, as a consequence, would theoretically be more appealing to a broad audience, despite her obvious nonwhiteness. In this vein, it seems, the film cashes in on black America's color-coded intraracial politics that placed a premium on lighter-hued complexions.

In *Carmen Jones*, much of Dandridge's cinematic divadom depends on the multiple generic adaptations through which her difference is filtered. While these alterities of Carmen visually compensate for those Dandridge represents, another class of alterity through which she must pass remains: the operatic "voice" of Carmen Jones, Marilyn Horne. According to Horne, who was only twenty years old at the time of the film and by no means the star mezzo-soprano she would eventually become in the sixties and seventies, dubbing for Dandridge was "fun":

> I had to listen carefully to her speaking voice and try to match the timbre and the accent, so that when it came time for me to record the songs, there would be a little bit of Dandridge in my throat. She sang in a register comfortable for her, then I mimicked her voice in the proper keys. Later, she filmed her scenes with my recorded voice blasting from huge loudspeakers. The tendency in dubbing is to overdo your mouth movements. Dandridge didn't and was sensational. The sound technicians pieced music and film together and the result is a seamless performance by Dorothy Dandridge and Marilyn Horne.[18]

Unlike the opera stage on which the singer's visibility certifies the voice heard, film permits an auditory "bait-and-switch" in which the actor's visibility actually masks the identity of the singer's voice. By reviving the ghost of white culture's ambivalent attraction to black culture in depositing Marilyn Horne's voice in Dorothy Dandridge's mouth, *Carmen Jones* creates an effect that potentially smacks of blackface minstrelsy. If, for the sake of authenticity, Marilyn Horne was cast to preserve the operatic integrity of Bizet's music, her interpretation of faux "blackness" in her enunciation of Hammerstein's lyrics, at least on the face of it, compromises this effort. Nevertheless, however dubious her interpretation of Southern black diction, what her *vocal* performance offers in return is the means by which Dandridge can break through the intricate matrix of Hollywood racism with her image intact. Horne's minstrel performance here is just "bad" enough to prick up the viewers' ears and keep them attuned to Dandridge's presence. And, just as the over-the-top personas of the film's minor characters allow Dandridge to be sexy in an unstereotypical fashion, Horne's vocal excesses show off Dandridge's blackness in a powerful, positive light.

While Susan McClary argues that the film uses a white singer's voice for Carmen instead of Dandridge or another black singer's to preserve the music's European identity, something else, I believe, motivated this decision. A more plausible reason perhaps can be located in Dandridge's controversially positioned sensuality, her enormous erotic appeal in *Carmen Jones*. Consider, by contrast, opera singer Leontyne Price's acts of cultural iconoclasm that took place on television at nearly the same time as Dandridge's rise as a Hollywood player.

Price's portrayal of the eponymous heroine in Puccini's *Tosca* in a 1955 *NBC Opera Theatre* production challenged the televisual racial status quo. Casting Leontyne Price in the role, NBC upset the assumptions of opera as a primarily white genre and of this character's being a white woman. A critic of Price's contributions to and place in television history is Dianne Brooks, who cites one viewer's displeasure over the broadcast company's decision: "I had looked forward to hearing your presentation of *Tosca* this afternoon but was shocked and dismayed by your casting of a negress vis-à-vis white men in such necessarily romantic scenes. Since there is no dramatic excuse for this casting, as there would be in *Aida*, for example. I find this deliberate interracial propaganda extremely offensive and believe it to be both premature and misguided."[19] Conveniently making no allowances for the casting of white women as Verdi's Ethiopian princess Aida, this respondent yokes together racial and sexual politics (and paranoias) in her complaint against Price's appearance.

These objections notwithstanding, Price's high-cultural image immunized her from the type of scrutiny and controversy surrounding Dandridge's persona. Following Wahneema Lubiano, Brooks classifies Price as a "black lady" who "walks a fine line between heroism and cultural betrayal."[20] Singing opera and earning worldwide acceptance and fame, Price risked becoming, in Brooks's words, a "bourgeois assimilationist."[21] Even so, Price's sociosexual image was unblemished, policed to such an extent that in a 1982 interview she explained how she "consciously avoided a public romantic attachment with a white man."[22] This perception of Price's muted or absent sexuality neutralized any scandal or real outrage over her vocal iconoclasm on television.

However iconoclastic Leontyne Price's televisual divadom may have been for the era, her image never was allowed to transgress or transcend the sexual limitations white culture placed on it because of her race. Despite the temporary refuge from racism the music of opera may have offered her, Price nevertheless was recognized primarily as a black woman first and an opera singer second. Meanwhile, for Dorothy Dandridge, the crisscross of operatic and cinematic aesthetics in *Carmen Jones* not only mainstreams her sex symbolism; it ascribes to Dandridge the imprimatur of high culture and further endows her sexuality with a subversive agency that breaks—and then rewrites—the "on-screen" rules of race and gender. Two related scenes in the Chicago rooming house where Joe is forced to hide from the military police illustrate the simultaneous temptation and threat of Dandridge's sexuality. Wearing a black satin robe, Carmen thrusts a bare leg against Joe's chest so he can blow-dry her freshly painted toes; here, she is, as she has been in the entire course of their relationship, the sexual aggressor. Their foreplay is fleeting, for when Carmen returns later that same day after reuniting with Husky Miller, she strips down to her animal-print lingerie to slip into the clinging, mauve dress she wore when she first spotted Husky at Billy Pastor's juke joint. Risking a gratuitous peek at Dandridge's body, this sequence ironically "strips" Dandridge of the passive erotic persona she exhibited—and resented—on the cabaret stage. In this performance, an undressed Dandridge "unmans" Belafonte not only by gaining sexual mastery over him, but also by flaunting her physical freedom in his face; she can come and go as she pleases, while he is confined to the dingy, charmless room. His desperate appeals for her to stay go unheeded, as she is more concerned with the seams of her nylons than with his comfort or his love.

As visually tantalizing as the spectacle of Dandridge's near-naked body may be, this cinematic transgression is, of course, allowed and sustained by the powerful "vocal" performances she gives, especially in the final duet with Belafonte at the close of *Carmen Jones*. That Dandridge's throat subsequently becomes the literal and symbolic target of Belafonte's rage only shows the extent to which her "voice" matters to the radicalization of her star persona. When Joe accosts Carmen at Husky Miller's prizefight and drags her into a storage closet, he once again pleads with her to run away with him. In disgust, Carmen laughs at his naïveté and throws his dime-store engagement ring onto the dirty floor. Her callousness provokes Joe to violence. Seizing Carmen by the throat he strangles her to death amid cheers coming from the boxing arena.

This violent encounter between Dandridge and Belafonte fascinates not only because it is a moving piece of cinema, but also because it deviates substantially from the opera in which Bizet's Don Jose brutally stabs Carmen. In this retelling, when Joe strangles Carmen, he attacks the source of her agency—her throat—and chokes off her dangerous sexuality and subjectivity, her vice and her voice.

Much more than a dramatic stunt to shock the audience or a cinematic gesture to distinguish the movie from its predecessors, Dandridge's celluloid death caps an unabashedly open declaration of independence that she herself could not have articulated with the same gusto in real life, despite her attempts at self-defense in *Sepia* magazine. When she sings, with such brio and conviction, "Ain't gonna lie, ain't gonna lie! / I look at life straight in de eye!", Dandridge not only expresses her character's credo, but can now freely voice a personal philosophy to which she was not otherwise entitled as a black woman living in America nor, before *Carmen Jones*, as a black actress working in Hollywood.

TIFFANY N. GILBERT is a recent Ph.D. graduate from the University of Virginia. Her essay is drawn from a larger project entitled "Nuclear Diva: Constructing Cinematic Divadom in American Film, 1950–1959," which she is currently revising into a book. Working at the intersections of race and gender, she looks behind the veil of what otherwise appear to be rigid categories in order to discover fresh ways of reconceptualizing ideas about representation and identity.

NOTES

1. *Sunset Boulevard*, directed by Billy Wilder, starring Gloria Swanson, William Holden, Nancy Olson, and Erich von Stroheim, Paramount, 1950.
2. In addition to Jeff Smith, "Black Faces, White Voices: The Politics of Vocal Dubbing in *Carmen Jones*," *Velvet Light Trap* 51 (2003): 29–42, see also Marguerite H. Rippy, "Commodity, Tragedy, Desire: Female Sexuality and Blackness in the Iconography of Dorothy Dandridge," in *Classic Hollywood, Classic Whiteness*, ed. Daniel Bernardi (Minneapolis: University of Minnesota Press, 2001), 189–90; and Robert K. Lightning, "Dorothy Dandridge: Ruminations on Black Stardom," *Cineaction!* 44 (1997): 32–9.
3. Smith, 40.
4. Donald Bogle, *Toms, Coons, Mulattoes, Mammies, and Bucks: An Interpretive History of Blacks in American Films* (New York: Viking, 1973), 125–28.
5. Donald Bogle, *Dorothy Dandridge: A Biography* (New York: Amistad, 1997), 96.
6. Wayne Koestenbaum, *The Queen's Throat: Opera, Homosexuality, and the Mystery of Desire* (New York: Poseidon, 1993), 105–06.
7. For extensive and sophisticated historical, cultural, and musical analysis of Bizet's masterpiece, see Susan McClary, *George Bizet: Carmen* (Cambridge: Cambridge University Press, 1992).
8. Oscar Hammerstein II, *Carmen Jones* (New York: Williamson Music, 1943).
9. Bogle, *Dorothy Dandridge*, 254.

10. Ibid., 373.

11 Lauren Berlant, *The Queen of America Goes to Washington City: Essays on Sex and Citizenship* (Durham: Duke University Press, 1997), 223.

12. Ibid., 223.

13. In his biography of Dorothy Dandridge, Donald Bogle chronicles the star's tempestuous affair with Otto Preminger during the filming of *Carmen Jones* and their stormy reunion for *Porgy and Bess* in 1959. While Preminger was perhaps the most controversial white man with whom Dandridge had an affair, he was not the only one. *Confidential* magazine at one point also claimed Dandridge had been romantically involved with white actors Tyrone Power and Farley Granger.

14. Bogle, *Dorothy Dandridge*, 400.

15. Jane Gaines, "White Privilege and Looking Relations: Race and Gender in Feminist Theory," in *Multiple Voices in Feminist Film*, ed. Diane Carson, Linda Dittmar, and Janice R. Welsch (Minneapolis: University of Minnesota Press, 1994), 177–90.

16. Bogle has suggested in his biography of Dandridge that a similar cultural intolerance for multiple black sex symbols characterized the reportage about the simultaneous careers of Lena Horne and the *Carmen Jones* star: "This media-created rivalry between Horne and Dandridge was carried out for the next two years in publications as diverse as *Ebony*, *Life*, *Time*, *Jet*, and *Look*. It was not a new phenomenon. Black female stars of the past had been known for feuds. Josephine Baker drew the ire of Ethel Waters in the 1920s. Later Ethel Waters became angry with Lena Horne during the filming of *Cabin in the Sky*. The stories of Baker and Waters and of Waters and Horne, however, were not covered by the press and became known mainly in show business circles. But now, as never before in mainstream American popular culture, two glamorous and desirable black goddesses were pitted against each other. The media coverage of the Dandridge/Horne rivalry suggested that only one African American goddess at a time could reign" (202).

17. Smith, 33–35.

18. Marilyn Horne, *Marilyn Horne: My Life* (New York: Atheneum, 1983), 75.

19. Dianne Brooks, "'They Dig Her Message': Opera, Television, and the Black Diva," in *Hop on Pop: The Politics and Pleasures of Popular Culture*, ed. Henry Jenkins, Tara McPherson, and Jane Shattuc (Durham: Duke University Press, 2002), 308.

20. Brooks, 304.

21. Ibid., 310.

22. Ibid., 302.

LORIE NOVAK

This is my favorite photograph from my childhood. It is 1956; I am about
two and a half years old. I am sitting on the mantle above the fireplace in
our living room. In between my mother (who is pregnant with my sister
Karen) and me is "the portrait." This framed painting is of me, the first-
born child, the first-born grandchild. My father's uncle had this portrait
painted from a photograph that my parents had sent him. I have no memory
of it being taken; I only remember the story. Until now, I have never even
thought about who took it. In the original snapshot sent to my Uncle Sam, I
was wearing Mickey Mouse ears and a Mickey Mouse T-shirt, my favorite
attire at that age. The painter took the artistic liberty, probably on my
uncle's instructions, of dressing me in a pink dress with puffy sleeves. Mickey was replaced by the number one symbol of the feminine little girl. To
show my uncle how much I looked like the portrait, my parents dressed me
up to match the painting so that the photograph would show the painting to

[*WSQ: Women's Studies Quarterly* 33: 3 & 4 (Fall/Winter 2005)]

be an accurate representation. It is a sign of the times that I did, in fact, have a dress very similar to the one in the painting. And so I looked like the painting that was painted from the photograph, and the photograph proved it.

The mantle snapshot is just one of many hundreds of evocative and classically American photographs that my parents took of our family. I have returned to these snapshots from the 1950s over and over again. I grew up in the San Fernando Valley suburbs of Los Angeles. Until I was twelve, we lived in Van Nuys, in a white middle-class neighborhood of tract houses with front porches and lawns: a perfect backdrop for my handsome father, glamorous mother (neither of whom looked too Jewish), and their three adorable girls. My father lived out the American dream: a child of Russian-Jewish immigrants, he started a successful business and, as his career advanced, we moved to increasingly larger houses. Our family snapshots fit right in with the image of the American family that was being presented at that time in mainstream print media and on TV. In them, our lives appear to be easy and we always look happy. My family's photogenic life was being played out for the camera while the McCarthy hearings were in full swing, Rosa Parks wouldn't give up her seat on a bus, schools were desegregated, the labor force was 5:2 men to women, the United States secretly helped to overthrow governments in Iran and Guatemala, and the fear associated with the Cold War was rampant.

In my late twenties, I searched through boxes and drawers for family photographs that hinted at the true complexity of our lives, hoping I would discover ones that broke away from photographic convention and stereotypes. I came across several groups of photos of me taken between 1954 and 1956 by a professional photographer who came to our house. (At that time, it was common for photographers to go door-to-door seeking jobs.) I have gone through the stacks of proofs from these at-home sessions throughout my adult life, and it is these three to which I return again and again.

I had assumed that the order in which the photos were taken went from smiling to crying, but recently I realized that most likely the opposite was true. I must have been put in the chair, become scared of the camera and/or photographer, started crying, reached for my mother, and, when she held me, stopped crying and then smiled. Am I seeing my struggle to separate? Reading the order either way, it is the center image that haunts me. I am staring at the camera, clutching my mother, and am just on the point of losing—or regaining—my composure. I look at the camera with fear: a moment that is rarely caught on film.

In 1987, my snapshots from the 1950s were the centerpieces of my photographic installations. Since the early 1980s I have engaged in an artistic practice where I project slides (often my family snapshots) into empty rooms to create installations specifically for the vantage point of the camera. Why the 1950s in 1987? Reagan was president and preaching "family values." The Iran-Contra Scandal was unraveling. I turned thirty-three, and Andy Warhol died on my birthday. Klaus Barbie was on trial in France for his Nazi war crimes. Photographs in the newspapers were still black and white, and images of torture and dead bodies were not shown on the front page. But as we know now (and knew then), nothing was as picture-perfect as it seemed.

In early 1987, I created *Fragments* with my beloved mantle photograph. I rephotographed the snapshot as I most remembered it—an object to be looked at. I projected the slide of the snapshot with its push-pins so that it took on the proportions of an image living in my mind. The three of us look so young and hopeful. The woman in pieces on the floor, actually my sister Patricia, might be the little girl grown up. The contemporary image is shattered, but into pieces that look like they can be put back together. The woman's eyes are closed, as if dreaming, and the borders of the snapshot wash over her like a wave.

Fragments, color photograph, 1987, 30″ x 38″

In the summer of 1987, I attended The MacDowell Colony in Peterborough, New Hampshire, for the first time. I brought slides with me of many of the photos in my family's archive, as well as many rephotographed media images of historic events from the mid-1940s on. I wanted to expand my investigation of the relationship between personal and collective memory by looking at my own documented history against the backdrop of public images. I was interested (and still am) in how we come to know the world and ourselves through photographs. That summer I created several photographs that incorporated the image of me fearfully clutching my mother.

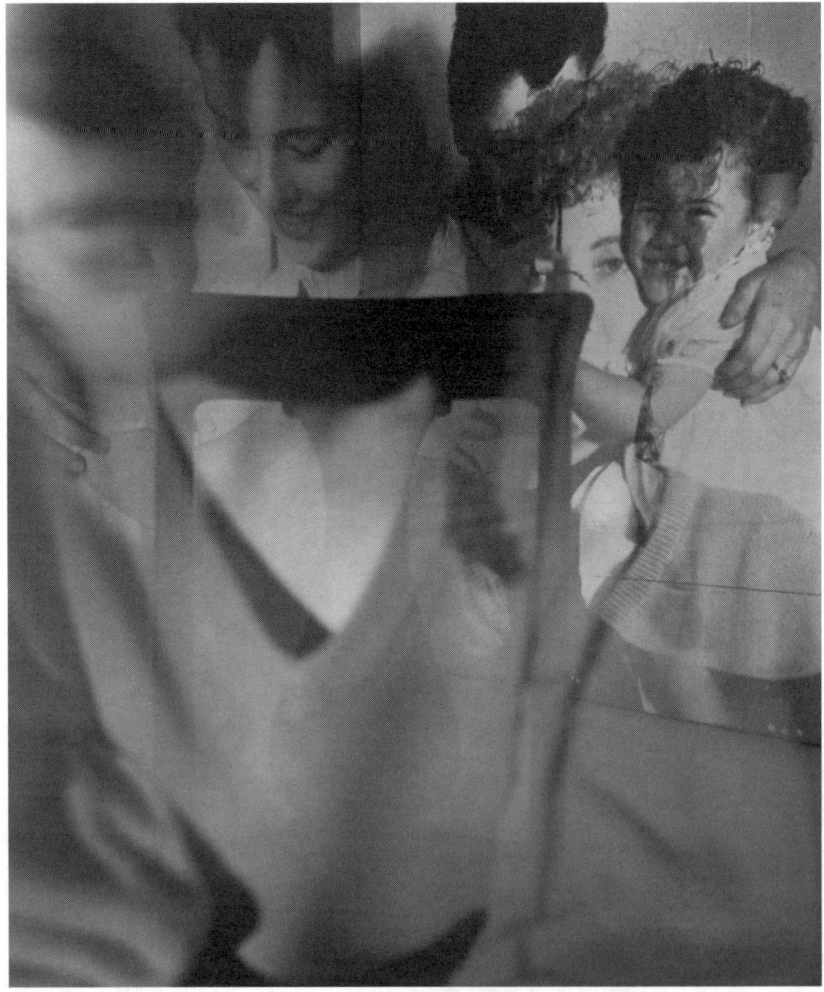

Self Portraits, color photograph, 1987, 36″ x 30″

Past Lives (for the children of Izieu), color photograph, 1987, 36″ x 30″

It was also the time of the trial of Nazi war criminal Klaus Barbie. The floating projected image in *Past Lives* is of a group of children hidden in a boarding school in Izieu, France, who were then deported by Barbie and sent to their deaths in a concentration camp.[1] The photo was widely published and became a symbol of Barbie's crimes against humanity. I was haunted by this smiling image of the children; *Past Lives* is dedicated to their memory. In my projected collage, images of Ethel Rosenberg, the children from Izieu, and me clutching my mother merge. I become the recipient of the weight of my cultural past.

Since the late 1980s, I have cut out of newspapers photographs of people holding photos of their loved ones, a universal sign that they have died or are missing. Seeing the photograph as a symbol of loss was a central theme of *Playback*, my slide installation from 1992. The fifteen-minute floor-to-ceiling projection opens with images of my hand picking up photographs of myself and of my family in the 1950s. These dissolve in and out of newspaper images of people holding photographs. A chronological sequence follows, alternating among my family images more contemporary self-portraits and historic images from World War II to the present. A continuously playing live radio scan is the audio background. Preprogrammed stations are scanned, alternating music, news, and talk shows—the audio equivalents of the types of imagery used.

The image I hold in the beginning of *Playback* is a color photograph of the five of us in the backyard of our Van Nuys house in 1959 (top image in collage on previous page). My father has his arm around my mother and me. I have always noticed my watch in this photo. I am sure that at age five, I was very proud to be wearing it. We all look happy. I begin the piece both looking at this image of my past and presenting it to the viewer.

Playback (mid-dissolve excerpt), slide installation with live radio scan, 1992

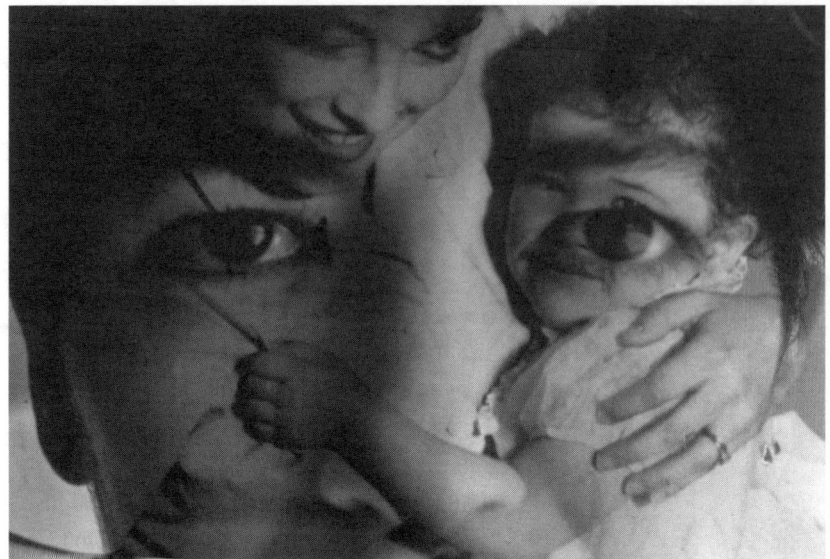

Clutching, final image of *Playback*

Playback ends with a self-portrait superimposed over the photo of me clutching my mother. I can still remember the moment at which, when working at my light table in my studio, I discovered this magical combination of the two slides on top of each other. I gaze directly at the camera, appearing to be holding my past self, who appears to pull at my adult skin. My present and past selves linger on the screen, confronting the camera with resistance, and then they slowly fade away.

My most recent installation, *Reverb*, is a sequel to *Playback*. In the latter part of the 1990s, I noticed that photos of displaced families forced from their homes were regularly printed in newspapers to show the horror of the situation in Kosovo. Both sides in the Elian Gonzalez case used the family photo to show how close they were to Elian. Holding photos of the missing and dead became more commonplace and more of a political act. This was poignantly clear in the United States in the aftermath of September 11. In 2003, the Abu Ghraib prison photos made it seem for a time that amateur photographs could actually change the course of a war and an election.

In *Reverb*, selected audio fragments, taken from online audio archives, play randomly alongside the projected images and are complemented each day by a live news feed taken directly from the Internet.[2] Direct broadcasts of past historical events, political speeches, and

Reverb, (installation view of dissolve between first and second images at ArtSway, Hampshire, England), computer-based projection with Internet audio fragments, 2004

personal testimonies make different sound and image permutations each time the piece is played. The juxtaposition between the visual and the audio changes with each viewing, changing the viewers' perspective on what they see and hear.

In developing *Reverb*, I returned to my boxes of family snapshots once again. The projected sequence begins with an image of my family taken in 1960 or 1961, a time that was still essentially the 1950s. The five of us pose at the entrance to Disneyland in a configuration similar to the backyard snapshot that begins *Playback*. Construction of Disneyland began the year I was born, and it opened in 1955. Starting in 1956, my family visited once a year. Mickey and the Mouseketeers were a big part of my childhood. The second image in *Reverb* shows my hands holding a snapshot of me with Mickey Mouse ears at age two. Maybe this is the image that was sent to my Uncle Sam.

LORIE NOVAK is professor and chair of photography and imaging at the, Tisch School of the Arts, New York University. Her photographs, installations, and Internet projects have been exhibited widely. More information can be found at www.lorienovak.com and in "Collected Memories: Lorie Novak's Virtual Family Album," by Marianne Hirsch in *Inter/Faces: Women's Visual and Performance Art*, ed. Sidonie Smith and Julia Watson (Ann Arbor: University of Michigan Press, 2003).

NOTES

1. See Serge Klarsfeld, *The Children of Izieu: A Human Tragedy*, (Harry N. Abrams, 1985; reprint Holocaust Library, 1995).
2. *Reverb* debuted at ArtSway, Hampshire, England, in 2004. The installation uses software designed by Jonathan Meyer to generate the image dissolves and to stream audio content. For more information and to to hear or view an excerpt from *Reverb*, see www.lorienovak.com/reverb.

"THE GAME SHOW": AN EXCERPT FROM
BOOMING: A MILLENNIAL MEMOIR

ALICE JARDINE

What follows is excerpted from Chapter 6 of Alice Jardine's unpublished novel, *BOOMING: A Millennial Memoir.* (A synopsis of the entire
novel appears below.) In this chapter, entitled "The Game Show," the
main character, Baby, meets up with a gang of notorious "honorary
blondes," all with a special relationship to the American 1950s: Anne
Sexton, Anne Parsons, and Sylvia Plath, but also Jean Harlow, Madonna, Betty Page, and Jayne Mansfield. These extraordinary women have
banded together within the virtual space of *BOOMING* to stage a
1950s-style game show. Their goal? They want to help Marilyn Monroe
(the ultimate 1950s blonde) better understand why she had to die when
and how she did.

BOOMING: A SYNOPSIS

Baby's Daddy died shortly after her birth in 1951. Mom thinks he was
murdered. It's Baby's job to use her capacity for Booming[1] in order to
figure out who killed him.

Baby's Daddy worked at Los Alamos after the war, but not on the
bomb. No, his was an even more secret project known as EPPAP: The
Eugenics Project for a Post-Apocalyptic Planet. This early bio-genetics
project was ostensibly funded by the World Health Organization, but
secretly by the Howard Hughes Medical Institute. Mom thinks that
Daddy was killed because of his work on viral cloning and DNA.
Baby's not so sure. What she does know is that there are shadowy
forces still searching for her Daddy's experiment write-ups. And these
forces seem to think she has them. She also knows that her own lack of a
belly button and her Mom's total dependence on TV in order to communicate are just plain weird and somehow intrinsically connected to
her Daddy's death.

Baby's quest to find out how and why her Daddy died leads her to

[*WSQ: Women's Studies Quarterly* 33: 3 & 4 (Fall/Winter 2005)]

the unsettling discovery that not only is her Daddy dead, but so is DADDY—the concept, the body, the purpose, the institution. She learns that his death has affected the Baby-Boom generation in ways that are not yet entirely understood. What is clear is that, for Baby-Boomers, the death of Daddy-The-Body has led to physical regression; the death of Daddy-The-Warrior to profound fearfulness; the death of Daddy-The-Provider to deep unhappiness; the death of Daddy-The-Hero to rampant paranoia; the death of Daddy-The-Husband to romantic cynicism; the death of Daddy-The-Lover to sexual dystopia; the death of Daddy-The-White-Master to ever more insidious forms of racism.

As Baby explores these historical consequences of the Father's demise, her travels take her from Paris, through Bangkok, to Serowe, Alexanderplatz, and Palm Springs. Slowly, Baby begins to put together the pieces of an exorbitant plot too horrific to believe. She learns of the project "Mr. Magico" and is terrified by its really bad guys (Roy Cohn, Desi Arnaz, Howard Hughes). She is also moved by the stories of the really good guys (Bobby Kennedy, Julius Rosenberg). She begins to put together the puzzle connecting EPPAP, the CIA, and of course DESILU. And as she listens to Bette Davis, Lucille Ball, Marilyn Monroe, and Ethel Rosenberg; to Ann Parsons, Anne Sexton, and Sylvia Plath; to Dian Fossey, Joy Adamson, and Jane Goodall; to Winnie Mandela, Lorraine Hansbury, Billie Holiday, and Bessie Head—Baby finally begins to hear . . . and to understand the incommensurate horror of Daddy's Death.

And, ultimately, at the huge Elvis Resurrection Concert held in Honolulu on the eve of the New Millennium, Baby sees the truth: it is she who murdered her Father. Not that Baby had any intention of killing him. But she's indisputably the murderer nonetheless. And now an entire generation—indeed, an entire civilization—has to pay for her crime . . .

THE GAME SHOW

Sylvia Plath: ATTENTION!! ATTENTION!! OUR FIRST CONTESTANT IS MR. PHILIP WYLIE, AUTHOR OF THE BEST-SELLING BOOK, *GENERATION OF VIPERS*, AND PRIMARY INVENTOR OF THE TERM "MOMISM."

Welcome Mr. Wylie. Now don't be nervous. Please have a seat right over here. Anne Sexton?

Anne S: Hello Mr. Wylie.

Philip Wylie: Where the hell am I? What are you madwomen up to?!

Anne S: Indeed. But don't worry. You're just fine . . . For the moment at least . . . Now, here is how The Game works.

Wylie: The Game? What Game? I demand that you let me out of here!!

Anne S: Now, now. This game is called "What's My Viper?" Now to your left are three curtains, behind which are three different opportunities for your self-betterment. Which one do you choose?

Wylie: OK. Door Number Three . . .

(APPLAUSE)

Anne S: Behind Door Number Three, our lovely JEAN HARLOW (WILD APPLAUSE) is showing the medium-sized gilded cage we will be using henceforth. Please step into it please. Yes, like that, now lock the door, Jean. Now, you will be asked a series of questions, Mr. Wylie. For each one you cannot answer, a newborn very ugly, dirty viper will be taken out of those large boxes that are an important part of your prize and introduced into your cage. If you get all of the questions wrong, of course . . . Your category is "Women in the 1950s"

Anne P: We'll help you when we can . . .

Wylie: Little Anne Parsons?????

Anne S: Quiet. OK. Question number one: What year was Aid to Families with Dependent Children granted to single female heads of household?

Wylie: Oh, I know that kind of stuff: 1958.

Anne S: Very good. Question number two: By 1960, what percentage of married women were working outside of the house?

Wylie: 32 percent, I think.

Anne S: Very, very good indeed. Now Mr. Wylie: Between 1960 and 1962, how many women had been talked into "surgical menopause"?

Wylie: Uh . . . Uh . . .

Anne S: Time's up!!! Five million women, Mr. Wylie!!! Hysterectomy as the answer to all that filthy, God and Country undermining Momism huh?? Did you take the test to see if maybe you are yourself one of these dreaded MOMS? Mr. Wylie, in 1953 some 80 percent of the hysterectomies performed in five major hospitals under study were shown to have been unnecessary—30 percent showing no disease at all in the womb; 39 percent open to criticism; and 12 percent "unfortunate". . . One male GYN put it like this: "Perhaps women live too long. Maybe when they get through having babies they have outlived their usefulness." (ADD A VIPER!)

Wylie: But wait. That's not my fault!!! Argghh. Get that thing away from me . . . !!!

Anne S: Mr. Wylie: Who wrote *The Natural Superiority of Women*?

Wylie: Why Mr. Ashley Montagu of course, in 1952 . . . I demand . . .

Sylvia P: What percentage of men and women were married after World War II?

Wylie: That's easy. 96.4 percent women and 94.1 percent men.

Anne S: Please identify at least twenty superior women—of world renown—who did important work in the 1950s.

Wylie: Uh, Uh . . .

Marilyn: Helene Deutsch and Karen Horney, for example . . .

Wylie: Oh, yes. Well . . .

Sylvia P: Grace Paley, Cynthia Ozick, Flannery O'Conner, May Sarton, Elizabeth Bishop . . .

Wylie: Uh, Ayn Rand? Oh yes, Margaret Mead.

Anne S: Good, good. Anybody else?

Audience: Rachel Carson, Hannah Arendt, Diana Trilling, Janet Flanner, Gwendolyn Brooks, Georgia O'Keefe, Martha Graham . . .

Wylie: Grandma Moses, perhaps . . . ?

Anne S: What do you think, you girls "who bend men like wire" according to Mr. Wylie?

In unison: A small, filthy viper!

Wylie: Ugh . . . HELP!! They're going to kill me!! This is murder!!

Anne S: Mr. Wylie, on what TV program in the early fifties did a lead character say: "Don't need no woman as long as I got my horse!"

Wylie: I have no idea!!

Anne S: Too bad, Mr. Wylie . . . (Another!) Oh, by the way, it was *Fury* . . . One of your favorite shows no doubt . . .

Marilyn: Mr. Wylie, in what year were American women finally able to get credit, buy their own houses, and make contracts?

Wylie: Heeeeeeeeeeeeelp . . .

Marilyn: Not until 1964, Mr. Wylie. Now what do you think of that!! (Another.)

Anne S: What were four of the common behaviors recommended to women in the fifties in order to keep their man?

Wylie: How should I know . . . Please help me. I'll do anything . . .

Anne S: 1. SMILE! OK EVERYBODY SMILE!! 2. FLATTER! WHY MR. WYLIE, YOU DO LOOK HANDSOME WHEN YOU'RE ALL WORKED UP LIKE THAT! 3. TEASE! NOW, MR. WYLIE, WOULD YOU LIKE FOR US TO GET THOSE HORRIBLE, POISONOUS, SLIMY THINGS OFF OF YOU? 4. ACT HELPLESS! I'M REALLY VERY SORRY, MR. WYLIE, BUT FINALLY I'M JUST TOO SCARED TO DO A THING!

LET'S HAVE A BIG ROUND OF APPLAUSE FOR MR. PHILIP WYLIE. Mr. Wylie? Mr. Wylie??

Well, let's at least show our studio audience what Mr. Wylie has won today—JEAN??

Jean Harlow: Why yes, Mr. Wylie, you have won: THIS KITCHEN OF TOMORROW!!!

(DELIRIOUS APPLAUSE)

This postwar kitchen includes the newest facilities for efficiency . . . and yet it's the most livable room in the home. Here is a room where dreams of easier living will come true, with air conditioning, a quick-freeze unit, and no-splash sink with sliding grill. Notice the dish secretary and food budgeteer, and the television screen above the combined fireplace-incinerator unit. A Venetian-type partition, electrically operated, separates the cooking section from the rest of the room. All yours, Mr. Wylie, your very own psycho-environment to inhabit in an abandoned Levittown house of your choice for all eternity.

(SOLEMN APPLAUSE)

ALL THE HONORARY BLONDES: MARILYN, THIS MAN HELPED KILL YOU, YOU SEE?

Marilyn: OUR NEXT CONTESTANT IS MR. HUGH HEFNER, FOUNDER OF PLAYBOY ENTERPRISES. Good evening, Mr. Hefner. And welcome to The Game "Balance Your Blondes."

Hefner: Well, hello Marilyn. Long time no . . .

Marilyn: Mr. Hefner, behind one of the curtains to your left is your . . . Please don't worry. You're just fine . . . For the moment at least . . . Now, here is how The Game works. To your left are three curtains, behind which are three different opportunities for your self-betterment. Which one do you choose?

Hefner: OK. Door Number One . . .

(APPLAUSE)

Marilyn: Behind Door Number One, our lovely MADONNA (WILD, WILD APPLAUSE) is showing the unique new spring mattress we will be using henceforth. Lie down upon it please, while our lovely Madonna secures you in place. Yes, like that. Now, Mr. Hefner. You will be asked a series of questions. For each one you cannot answer, a blonde and quite beautiful, nude and fun-loving female dummy will be thrown on top of you. Each dummy weighs approximately 150 pounds and has been carefully proportioned for your viewing pleasure. I guess I should mention that the standard coil springs in the standard mattress under you have been replaced by two-foot-long standard kitchen knives pointed straight up. If you get all of the questions wrong, of course . . . Your category is "Sex in the 1950s."

Hefner: This is outrageous!!

Marilyn: Mr. Hefner, let me begin by asking you to please name twenty-five of the sexiest blondes that have been through Hollywood: like Mary Pickford and Mae West . . .

Hefner: Oh!! Why, the Gish sisters, Marion Davies, Greta Garbo, Alice Faye, Joan Blondell, Jean Harlow, Carol Lombard, Betty Grable, Lana Turner, Veronica Lake, Jayne Mansfield, Kim Novak, Anita Ekberg, Brigitte Bardot, Mamie Van Doren . . .

Marilyn: Go on, please . . .

Hefner: Marilyn Monroe, of course. Michelle Pfeiffer, Glenn Close, Meryl Streep, Madonna, Julie Christie, Fay Dunaway, Jessica Lange, Cybil Shephard . . . uh, Shirley Temple . . .

(AUDIENCE APPLAUDS WILDLY!!)

Marilyn: Mr. Hefner, How many black market abortions were being performed every year in this country by 1962 and how many women died from them?

Hefner: Uh, uh . . .

Marilyn: Ten million Mr. Hefner. TEN MILLION ILLEGAL, BACK ALLEY ABORTIONS! WITH FIVE TO TEN THOUSAND WOMEN DYING PER YEAR!! One blonde, please!

Hefner: Ouuumf.

Marilyn: In what year did scientists finally figure out that mammals (e.g. females) had eggs?

Hefner: Oh my God!!

Marilyn: Not until 1936!! (Add a blonde!)

Marilyn: In what year did the FDA approve the commercial marketing of the birth control pill?

Hefner: 1960. I remember well. Hey, this isn't funny!! These girls are heavy!! This is a joke, right? Hey, I was the good guy—liberated sex for the next two decades, and it was all airbrush clean!!

Marilyn: Who invented it?

Hefner: What?

Marilyn: The Pill.

Hefner: Gregory Pincus!!

Marilyn: Good ole Goody Pincus!! On whom was it tested?

Hefner: On poor women in Puerto Rico, and the guy didn't tell the women that some of them had placebos and they got pregnant and some had abortions . . . How's that? Is that the kind of stuff you want??

Marilyn: Good. Good. You're starting to get the hang of it . . . OK, what were the three public service areas the U.S. government ascribed to Communist plots in the fifties?

Hefner: How the hell . . .

Marilyn: Fluoridation, day care, and SEX EDUCATION! (Add another blonde!) Mr. Hefner, what year was Lolita published?

Hefner: Oh no, I forget . . . please don't . . .

Marilyn: (Another please!) 1955.

Hefner: OOOOHHHH. Oh God, please, I can't breathe and I'm sinking fast . . .

Marilyn: Too bad. You should have thought of that before . . . By the way, according to the Kinsey Report, what percentage of businessmen had had extra-marital affairs as of the survey?

Hefner: Um, 40 percent?

Marilyn: No!! 80 percent!! (A blonde please!) In 1950, what was the legal status of cunnilingus in this country?

AUDIENCE: YEAH!!!!!!

Hefner (small voice)**:** I really don't know.

Marilyn: Well, that's a surprise!! It was illegal in all the states except

Illinois, Mississippi, Wisconsin, and Ohio. In Kentucky and South Carolina, it was OK if married; in New York, it was a misdemeanor. One more!! Mr. Hefner, what were the Kinsey figures on adultery?

Hefner (Tiny voice): No idea . . . AAAAHhhhhhh . . .

Marilyn: 50 percent of married men and 26 percent of married women . . . How about homosexual experiences, Mr. Hefner?

Hefner: (Silence)

Marilyn: More! 37 percent of the men and 13 percent of the women were willing to admit they had dallied, Sir . . . And—the big surprise for the American People—according to Kinsey, how many men and women masturbated regularly in the fifties?

Hefner:

Marilyn: Hello?? Uh, Mr. Hefner?? OK. So much for that. Oh, just in case you can still hear me, it was 92 percent of the men and 62 percent of the women . . . OK, let's see what Mr. Hefner has won . . .

Madonna: Mr. Hefner, why . . . you have just won your very own fifty-foot-tall, inflatable Betty Furness doll!!! Betty Furness, The Lady from Westinghouse, who helped make visiting model homes in the search for the fantasy kitchen a national Sunday afternoon pastime!! Bright, upbeat, neat, no-frills, confident, sophisticated but modest, and very modern, Betty Furness was the ideal fifties wife as glamorous hostess!! She was also gutsy: why, when the network told her they wanted her to be more like Betty Crocker, she flatly refused to wear an apron—eventually leaving the TV industry because of such unfair pressure and because, in her own words, "I had the feeling I was shrinking as the machines got bigger and people were being swallowed up by their refrigerators"!! And so, Mr. Hefner, you will exist forever alongside this model of fifties courageous wifeliness in a TV commercial of your choice. You can be sure if it's Westinghouse, Mr. Hefner . . .

(GENERAL APPLAUSE)

ALL THE HONORARY BLONDES: MARILYN, THIS MAN
HELPED KILL YOU, YOU SEE?

Anne P: OUR NEXT CONTESTANT IS MR. NORMAN VINCENT
PEALE, AUTHOR OF THE BEST-SELLING BOOK, *THE POWER
OF POSITIVE THINKING*, AND STAUNCH DEFENDER OF
THE REPUBLICAN PARTY, RICHARD NIXON, AND THE U.S.
MILITARY-INDUSTRIAL COMPLEX. Good evening, Mr. Peale.
And welcome to The Game "I've got a Government Secret."

Peale: Well, hello Anne. You're looking more and more like your
father every day . . .

Anne P: Mr. Peale, behind one of the curtains to your left is your . . .
Please don't worry. You're just fine . . . For the moment at least . . .
Now, here is how The Game works. To your left are three curtains,
behind which are three different opportunities for your self-betterment. Which one do you choose?

Peale: OK. Door Number Two . . .

(APPLAUSE)

Anne P: Behind Door Number Two, our lovely BETTY PAGE
(DELIRIOUS APPLAUSE) is showing the very sophisticated and elaborate sound and viewing system which is now yours to keep, Mr. Peale.
Please just sit there in the chair as Betty is indicating. Yes, like that.
Don't worry too much about all the leather paraphernalia—Betty is an
expert! Now, Mr. Peale, you will be asked a series of questions. For
each one you cannot answer—or for each question that you answer
untruthfully—the clean and squeaky words THINK POSITIVE will
be shot into your ears and eyes at an excruciatingly high decibel and
magnification level, audible and visible only to you while the set is on
your head. No, you are not allowed to take it off . . . Of course, the
human body can only take so many of these assaults . . . Your category
is "The Church and the State in the 1950s."

Anne P: Mr. Peale, what did you think of Anne Morrow Lindbergh's best-selling 1955 spiritual meditation, *Gift from the Sea*, with its fifties style liberalish feminism—especially given that her husband had supported the Nazis in the 1930's?

Peale: I thought it was silly . . . Oh no. . . . OW!

Anne P: Mr. Peale, in 1955, what was the breakdown in the United States among the major faiths?

Peale: 68 percent Protestant; 23 percent Catholic; 4 percent Jewish; 5 percent No Preference.

Anne P: Uh huh. That must have made you very happy!! Mr. Peale, in what year, after much resistance from the religious community, did the AMA begin to officially sanction contraception as a general principle?

Peale: 1959. Please . . . this is not worthy of you . . .

Anne P: Mr. Peale, what did the phrase "I'm in trouble" refer to in the 1950s?

Peale: Unwed pregnancy.

Anne P: What happened most often to young women who found themselves in that category?

Peale: I really wouldn't know . . .

Anne P: Let it rip!

Peale: AAARRRRRRGGGG! Why, this is a brutal torture—positively un-American!!

Anne P: Uh huh. So? Have you ever found yourself in a back alley abortionist's office? That REALLY FELT un-American!

Sylvia P: And then there were the young women who tried to convince their doctors that they were "mad" so that they could have a therapeutic abortion: "She was a borderline schizophrenic with homo-sexual and masochistic tendencies" was the magic sentence for these women, even if it meant . . .

Marilyn: And, Reverend Peale, do you know the famous study which showed that between 1941 and 1950, 75 percent of the legal, therapeutic abortions done in one midwest hospital included forced sterilization?? And how about all those unwed mothers who were diagnosed as neurotic—not to mention dominant, aggressive, narcissistic, and hostile because they must have been—to find themselves in this sinful state—schizophrenic, masochistic, psychopathic, or—worst of all—homosexual!!

Anne S: And, of course, as you well know, most unwed mothers in the fifties were sent away to "homes" where they were taught lessons in femininity and forced to give up their babies after birth . . .

Peale: This is all very impressive and I am aware there were abuses, but what's that got to do . . .

Anne P: Uh, Mr. Peale, wasn't the government that you supported so fervently in the 1950s engaged in widespread secret psychological research?

Peale: I've heard something about all of that too, but . . .

Anne P: Have you heard of MK ULTRA?

Peale: No. AAARRRGGGGGGHHH.

Anne P: Mr. Peale, what kind of psychological research were the Republicans you supported attempting at that time?

Peale: Well, uh, I hear that drugs and hypnosis and electroshock therapy and even lobotomy were being studied to close what was called "the mind gap". . .

Anne P: On whom were they being tested?

Peale: I don't know.

Anne P: THINK POSITIVELY MR. PEALE!!! NONE OF THIS NEGATIVE STUFF NOW . . . AFTER ALL, LIFE IS GOOD AND GETTING BETTER!

Peale: Uh . . . Well, I hear there was considerable testing performed in the fifties on stable—captive—audiences—prisoners, mental patients, soldiers . . .

Anne P: Orphans, college students, the seven hundred poor pregnant women who went to the Vanderbilt Health Clinic . . . many of whom received radiation directly into their food and water . . .

Peale: The government was just trying to . . .

Anne P: Radiation, LSD, nerve gas, electric shock, sensory deprivation . . . Have you ever heard of Dr. D. Ewen Cameron, Mr. Peale?

Peale: No. (Ohhhhhh . . .)

Anne P: Now, now. Yeah, you and Ron Hubbard are so innocent and pure . . . . Ewen Cameron was the one who developed something called "Depatterning"—essentially a combination of electric shocks and LSD—and "Psychic Driving"—essentially being subjected to repetitious tape recorded messages in a sensory deprived environment. There was a joke going around among government circles that if this worked perhaps the Politburo could be brainwashed, and eventually lobotomized. We tried to bring Mr. Cameron here today for our games, but he must have burned up in hell.

Peale: I wouldn't know about that . . . (OWWWWWW).

Anne P: Now, Mr. Peale, please think positively. Even if you didn't know about these things directly, don't you think that, somehow, given how inside the Republican Party and government you were, you might at least have tried to find out . . .

Peale: No more so than your own father, who, after all, worked with army intelligence and the State Department to recruit Russian-born Nazi collaborators to Harvard while pushing out faculty considered on the Left one by one. He wasn't so great on the topic of women, either, young lady!!

Anne P: You're not telling me anything I didn't already know. Why do you think I'm here? Hey girls, my father once wrote: "The woman's fundamental status is that of her husband's wife, the mother of his children." I'm convinced that's why he wouldn't let me out of the loony bin—I wasn't fundamental enough for him . . . But we're talking about you, Mr. Peale . . .

Peale: I can't hear you . . . my ear drums are about to explode. Please, take mercy on me.

Anne P: Bells are pealing huh?? Reverend Peale, have you ever heard of Robert Carter?

Peale: No.

Anne P: Ladies, Robert Carter was one of the many thousands of people in the western part of this country who were exposed to dangerous levels of fallout and radiation from nuclear testing in the Nevada Desert by the government Mr. Peale used every means at his disposal to support and encourage.

Marilyn: Mr. Carter was marched along with his buddies as close as possible to ground zero of the "Hood Shot"—this was a hydrogen bomb—in July 1957 at the Nevada Test Site. He remembers vividly the feeling of being on fire.

Sylvia P: He and many of his compatriots also remember seeing what used to be animals and even a human or two chained in cages near the detonation site. Of course, when he told that to the doctor treating him for radiation sickness, he was immediately "committed" and "deprogrammed" through "reverse brainwashing". . . . He had to let them do it—it was the only way they'd let him out. He's a very sick man today—along with hundreds of thousands of other "downwinders."

Peale: What's all this got to do with me??

Anne P: Don't you think you had a responsibility to find out what you were using your talents as a preacher, as a guardian of people's faith, as a representative of the clean and the good and the pure, to support?!

Peale: Not at all . . . Those were different times . . . How was I supposed to know . . . oooooooooooh . . .

Anne P: Sweet dreams, Mr. Peale . . . And now for your Grand Prize!! BETTY PAGE?

Betty Page: Why Mr. Peale, your prize is very special indeed! A life-sized, lifelike replica of—why, ME, Mr. Peale, dressed all in black leather and chains, with more outfits for you to change me into whenever you want. And that's not all!!!

(APPLAUSE)

You and "me" are going out to Ground Zero in Nevada to open up three chains of fast food: 1950s style Big Boys, McDonald's, and Holiday Inns. Only hitch is, you can only eat at these restaurants for all eternity and can never leave Ground Zero no matter what is happening to you.

(ECSTATIC APPLAUSE)

ALL THE HONORARY BLONDES: MARILYN, THIS MAN HELPED KILL YOU, YOU SEE?

Sylvia P: OUR LAST CONTESTANT IS MR. WALTER FREEMAN, INVENTOR OF THE TRANSORBITAL LOBOTOMY AND GREAT POPULARIZER OF THIS MODERN TECHNIQUE. Good evening, Mr. Freeman. And welcome to The Game "You Bet Your Beanie."

Freeman: Where am I?!

Sylvia P: Mr. Freeman, behind one of the curtains to your left is your . . . Please don't worry. You're just fine . . . For the moment at least . . . Now, here is how The Game works. To your left are three curtains, behind which are three different opportunities for your self-betterment. Which one do you choose?

Freeman: OK. Door Number One . . .

(APPLAUSE)

Sylvia P: Behind Door Number One, our lovely JAYNE MANS-FIELD (EXCITED APPLAUSE) is showing an exquisite array of "virtual" lobotomy instruments, copied exactly from those historical ones found in the Moniz Museum (named after the inventor of the frontal lobotomy, girls) and which will be used on your brain, along with your own handy dandy model ice pick twisted around in so many other people's brains with no success—this is what will happen to you each time you do not answer my question in a way that . . . Please lie down on the table now. Now, now. This is all virtual, so you can't really get hurt—and we will follow your directions with the ice pick method you so believe in. Now, if we do that, you can't get hurt, can you?? Your category is "Therapy and the 1950s."
INSERT VIRTUAL ICE PICK AND RODS!!
Now, Dr. Freeman, what were the most common forms of therapy in the fifties?

Marilyn: After all, Dr. Freeman, this was big business!! In the mid-fifties, it was determined that one out of twelve children would spend some part of their life in one of the 750,000 asylums in the United States.

Freeman: Uh—please be very, very careful there, don't wiggle them too much!! Uh, uh yes, ECT shock treatments, insulin shock therapy, sedatives, hydrotherapy, wet packs, straightjackets, implantation of silver electrodes, lobotomies . . . And of course Thorazine was introduced in 1954 . . .

Anne S: Tell me about it, you creep . . .

Sylvia P: Shhh!! Is it not true that the vast majority of patients subjected to electro-convulsive shock therapy were women—an experience that would send many of them—I know—into a state of terror for the rest of their lives?

Freeman: I guess.

Sylvia P: Can you please tell the audience what a borderline personality is?

Freeman: It didn't exist as a category in my day, although it should have perhaps—it refers to someone who hovers on the border between psychotic and neurotic behavior. It concerns patients who often lost one or both parents while children and have grown into adults who are often emotionally unstable, excessively impulsive, histrionic, seductive, needing constant external approval, loving the applause, unable to be alone, finally depressive, with crash-like reactions to rejection, and with a tendency to abuse alcohol and drugs, often ending with suicide attempts for attention. In my day, these symptoms—much more common in women—were lumped along with schizophrenia— which then led to delusions and hallucinations.

Sylvia P: Take note, girls!!

(GENERAL AUDIENCE HOOTING)

Sylvia P: And Dr. Freeman, is it not true that women (especially those who were not "submissive, dependent, emotional, and subjective" à la Farnham and Lundberg) were those who tended to be diagnosed as mentally disturbed, very often because of a "rejection of femininity"— a rejection indicated by such "symptoms" as dysmenorrhea, pain in labor, menstrual irregularity, infertility, or miscarriage? Is it not true that a large number of women were committed in the fifties simply for wanting to divorce her husband or for refusing something to her boss?

Freeman: Yes, I guess so.

(MORE GENERAL HOOTING)

Sylvia P: Dr. Freeman, why was the entire psychiatry establishment so against the Kinsey Report?

Freeman: I'm not sure it was . . .

Sylvia P: A LITTLE WIGGLE PLEASE! Oh yes, well they were very clear about it. It was the report's establishment once and for all of the dominance of the clitoral orgasm in the vast majority of women that got so many shrinks going, wasn't it??

Freeman: Uh, oh, esssss.

Sylvia P: Dr. Freeman, between 1949 and 1952—the height of your practice—how many lobotomies were performed just in the United States?

Freeman: Tens of thousands of psychosurgeries were performed around the world; about five thousand pre-frontal (that was different from mine) and trans-orbital lobotomies (mine) were performed in the United States per year during that period. By 1951, 18,608 lobotomies had been performed in the United States.

Sylvia P: What a good memory you have, Dr. Freeman.

Freeman: Uh, thank you, but could you please tell her to hold the "corer," but especially the ice pick, very, very still at this point . . .

Jayne Mansfield: Look, buster. I was decapitated when I died. This here thing don't mean nothin' compared with that, I can assure you!!

Sylvia P: Dr. Freeman, can you please tell us—generally speaking— how a lobotomy is performed??

Freeman: Well, yes, most generally, after drilling two or more holes in the patient's skull, a surgeon (not a blonde sex kitten!!) inserts into the brain any of a variety of instruments—some of which look like an apple corer, a butter spreader, or an ice pick—and then proceed to destroy lesser or greater parts of the brain by twisting these instruments around in various ways . . .

Sylvia P: I see. TWIST THE RODS A LITTLE, KITTEN!! Dear oh dear. Dr. Freeman, were you not jealous about Dr. Moniz having won the 1949 Nobel Prize for his invention of pre-frontal lobotomy when it was really you who has the honor of having popularized it?

Freeman: One not could say nothing. No!

Sylvia P: Uh huh, TURN THE ICE PICK TO THE RIGHT AND WAVE IT AROUND A BIT! Dr. Freeman, did you go on a kind of "lobotomy spree" during the summer of 1951, driving across the country in your station wagon, stopping in towns along the way to perform well-publicized lobotomies of under ten minutes each?

Freeman: Yes . . . no . . . up . . . down . . . you I hate them no . . .

Sylvia P: Maybe a couple of electric shocks at this point with a twist to the left??

(GENERAL AUDIENCE ACCORD)

Sylvia P: Dr. Freeman, I read a newspaper story yesterday about a young black woman who was committed, in 1956, to an asylum in Columbus, Ohio (an institution with thousands of patients and only three psychiatrists, and where only 4 percent of the patients were there voluntarily) by her live-in boyfriend. This was because she had screamed and yelled at him when he told her he was leaving her with their two kids. She told the doctors how she felt unloved and abandoned and how her man beat her regularly and how she had no money and how the only thing which kept her sane were the voices—those on a tape recorder she kept with her at all times.

Marilyn: The doctors would all look at each other meaningfully and then ask her what the voices on the recorder were saying. She sat silent for a long time; she seemed to gather herself; you could see her body tautening. "Women's rights! Women's rights, it says." She would then sink back in her chair wearily. The doctors diagnosed her as a case of acute undifferentiated schizophrenia with paranoid and catatonic features and locked her up. She never saw her children again.

Sylvia P: Does this story seem at all odd to you, Dr. Freeman?

Freeman:

Sylvia P: Well . . . JAYNE MANSFIELD, show Dr. Freeman how well he has done today . . .

Jayne Mansfield: Why, yes, Dr. Freeman, welcome to the friendly and cute world of fifties food!! For you have won . . . AN ETERNITY'S SUPPLY OF FIFTIES PREPARED CONVENIENCE FOODS, which—now that you've had your operation—you will be responsible for listing, out loud, in a predetermined order, each time before you get to put on your apron and cook any of it. And here's the list of goodies you have won: 10 million frozen TV dinners, 6 million cans of Jolly Green Giant peas, 5 million jars of Folgers Instant Coffee, 2 million boxes of Pillsbury Doughboy Rolls, 6 million boxes of Duff's Devils Food Mix, 1 million boxes of Swan's Down Fluff O'Mint Cake, 100 million boxes of Aunt Jemima's Pancake Mix!! But that is not all!! You have also won your very own set of Revere Ware . . .

Betty Page: Oh, I won some of those in a contest once!!!

Jayne Mansfield: . . . Pyrex and CorningWare in which to prepare these unforgettable feasts . . . all this in a solitary detention cell at the asylum of your choice.

(SUBDUED APPLAUSE)

ALL THE HONORARY BLONDES: MARILYN, THIS MAN HELPED KILL YOU, YOU SEE?

Baby: Um, excuse me, but I can't stay here much longer.

Sylvia P: OK, dear. There's just one more thing. Each of the Quatromavens gets to ask one last question—oh, not of these creeps. They're finished already anyway. But rather, she will be able to ask one last question of one man in her life, someone she loved and/or trusted with her life, and who left her with an incurable wound. I thought we'd proceed according to how long we've been gone, most recent first . . . So . . .

Anne S: Well . . .

Sylvia P: And remember, this is for Marilyn . . .

Anne S: Well, I guess I'd like to ask Dr. Orne—my most important and trusted therapist—something . . .

Dr. Orne: Hello Anne.

Anne S: Dr. Orne, how could you?! I mean, how could you give away to the public all those tapes we did?? They were so intimate, for no one else's ears but ours . . . How could you so deeply break my trust?

Dr. Orne: I have no excuse, Anne. Please forgive me . . .

Anne S: I guess. But if this were still part of The Game, I'd make you eat those tapes—every single one of them . . . chewing very slowly. And I'd make those who took away your privacy do worse, Marilyn . . .

(SILENCE)

Anne P: OK, I'm next I guess. I'd like to speak to my father for a minute . . .

Talcott Parsons: Hello, darling.

Anne P: Hello, Daddy. Daddy, how could you let them keep me locked up in the bin when you knew—better than anyone else in the world—that my only problem was that I was too smart for a girl back then . . .?

Talcott Parsons: I don't know, honey. I'm sorry.

Anne P: Well, I'm not sure I can find it in my heart or my head to forgive you . . . and if we were still playing The Game, I would seal you up in a small room and have it fill slowly and relentlessly with Russian library books until you were crushed . . . And I'd do worse to those who tried to put you in captivity, Marilyn . . .

(SILENCE)

Sylvia P: Ted, are you there?

Ted Hughes: Yes, I'm here. Hi.

Sylvia P: Hi. Ted. Tell me, why did you tell everyone that it was I who told you to gas our sick little bird when, actually, you were the one who broke my will and my spirit and indeed my sanity to get me to give up on its fragile little life just because you wanted the pleasure of killing it?

Ted: I don't know. It seemed inconsequential, really.

Sylvia P: That's what I thought. You know—just so as not to break the rhythm . . . You know, if we were still playing The Game, I would put an inverted bowl over your head and run a hose into it and when you talked to me like that I'd open the attached gas spigot just a little at a time until . . . And I'd do worse to those who tried to emotionally if not physically beat you into submission, Marilyn . . .

(SILENCE)

THE HONORARY BLONDES: Well, Marilyn . . .?

Marilyn: I don't have any more questions for men. None at all. I'd just like to talk to my mother for a few minutes please . . .

Baby: Well, why don't we leave you alone with her for a while, Marilyn . . . But before we go . . .

THE HONORARY BLONDES (STANDING ALL TOGETHER IN A CIRCLE WITH MARILYN, HOLDING EACH OTHERS' HANDS VERY, VERY TIGHTLY, SING TO HER IN A SOFT BUT STRONG AND UNIFIED VOICE):

Good-bye, Norma Jean . . .
From some women in the second row . . .
For you were something more than sexy oh . . .
More than just our Marilyn Monroe.

Seems to us you lived your life like a candle in the wind . . .
Never knowing who to cling to when the rain set in . . .
And we would have liked to have saved you . . .
But weren't we all just kids . . .
Candles burned out long before . . .
Our legends ever did.[2]

ALICE JARDINE is professor of romance languages and literatures and of studies of women, gender, and sexuality at Harvard University. She is the author of *Gynesis: Configurations of Woman and Modernity* (Cornell University Press 1985) and of the unpublished novel, *BOOMING: A Millennial Memoir*. She is co-editor of five volumes: *The Future of Difference*; *Men in Feminism*; *Social Control and the Arts*; *Shifting Scenes: Interviews on Women, Writing, and Politics in Post-68 France*; and, most recently, with Kelly Oliver, *A Surplus of Living Attention: In Honor of the Life and Ideas of Teresa Brennan*. Her new book in progress is *Prophetic Voices: The 21st Century 1950s Style*.

NOTES

1. "Booming" refers to Baby's ability to transform herself into an un-material cipher, and to how, as such, she is able to negotiate time and space effortlessly. As a virtual girl, Baby is capable of inhabiting/speaking/listening to those who have lived in other conjunctions of space-time, whether those historical conjunctions take place in books, movies or—most importantly for her generation—on 1950s TV. In her own words: "I am but a cipher, an antenna, a channel, surfing the alpha waves of my own virtual history."
2. Parody.

KINSEY, SEX RESEARCH, AND THE BODY OF KNOWLEDGE: LET'S TALK ABOUT SEX

KAREN WINKLER

In October 2004, I left my three-and-a-half-year-old daughter with her grandmother in New Jersey and flew to Indiana to talk about sex at the Kinsey Institute. Sex research, actually, which is not typically as sexy as sex. I had been invited as a postdoctoral fellow of the Sexuality Research Fellowship Program (SRFP) of the Social Science Research Council (SSRC) to The Kinsey Institute for Research in Sex, Gender, and Reproduction (KI) to participate in a five-day cross-disciplinary conversation with a dozen other fellows about the work we were doing in our fields—American studies, sociology, psychology, anthropology, education, and history.[1] A highlight of the conference was to be a screening of the not-yet-released film *Kinsey* by director Bill Condon (Coppola). The subject of sex is taboo between my mother and me, and I confess that I was deliberately vague to her about the nature of my trip—I said I was meeting with other fellows at Indiana University, covering over the sex part as I've covered my body in front of her since I was eleven or so.

Many women of my generation, who came of age in the 1970s, tended to think of our mothers as prudish and sexually reserved, domestic relics of that conventional decade into which we were born—the fifties. On a certain level, we bought into the popular constructions of the era as all *Ozzie and Harriet* and *Father Knows Best* and flattened out the complicating social and cultural forces represented by beatniks, Communists, and early civil rights struggles (not to mention Elvis Presley and Chuck Berry), as well as the sexual revelations of the "Kinsey reports." We were more comfortable viewing our mothers at a safe maternal distance from our own sexually awakening bodies and assuming their ignorance of what passions we were experiencing. My mother was just twenty-three, and her brief marriage to her first husband was already annulled, when the "Kinsey report" on women was published in 1953. I wonder now if she

[*WSQ: Women's Studies Quarterly* 33: 3 & 4 (Fall/Winter 2005)]

bought Kinsey back then, like so many women, hoping to learn the secrets of sex and marriage. Was it left behind, dog-eared and abandoned, in some small Brooklyn apartment, detritus of her sexual history? I don't recall its title in my preadolescent searches for my parents' secrets among their shelves of paperback novels, left-wing political essays, and my grandfather's books of Yiddish stories.

Growing up in the sixties, I became familiar with the naked bodies of women other than my mother through photos in the *Playboy* magazines that a third-grade classmate named Charlie sneaked into school and hid in the small compartment beneath his desk; boys and girls vied for peeks of the centerfolds to learn what sexy was. (*Playboy* began publication in 1953, the same year Kinsey's *Sexual Behavior in the Human Female* was released.) In the fourth grade, I'd discovered Masters and Johnson's (1960s heirs to Kinsey's pioneering sexology) *Human Sexual Response* (1966) covered with brown paper and hidden in my parents' bedroom bookcase on the second floor of their suburban house. I'd just learned the rudiments of sex from a dirty joke told in the cloakroom by a girl in my class, and I remember the joke and the book as mainly exciting but also unsettling. (Punch line: "Fa(r)ther! Fa(r)ther!" the girl called out for her dad [spoken with a thick, southern drawl]. "What do you think, I got a six-foot dick?!" said the man in her bed.) My image of my mother could not admit then, and can hardly more now, of a sexual life for her.

In preparation for our first separation of more than a day, my daughter and I made a calendar decorated with photos of us together, drawings of airplanes for Mommy's going and coming, and many farm animal stickers stuck in the center of a cut-out map of the United States: *Indiana.* Born at the tail end of the baby boom, I came to parenting late and single, influenced by the movements for sexual liberation and women's rights that were fed by Kinsey's research. At the baby shower for my daughter, I was given a book called *Bellybuttons are Navels* by Mark Shoen, by a friend who teaches sex education to children.

It's about a pair of rosy-cheeked, white, and wholesome-looking young siblings called Mary and Robert, who use the occasion of a bath together to name and discuss all their body parts. They make their way from eyes to nose, arms, fingers, and bellybuttons. Then Mary says, "' I have a vulva; only girls have vulvas." "Well, I have a penis; and only boys have penises,'" declares Robert. "'Oh! Well I have a clitoris just inside my vulva right above the opening of my vagina. That's what I have!'" Mary explains proudly. Their conversation moves easily from one part to another, without privileging anything—an enlightened and modern effort "to help children integrate healthy acceptance of the genitals into normal, confident acceptance of the total body," as the book cover advertises. I find little Mary and Robert oddly precocious (and the didacticism more strained) when they point out "anus," "scrotum," "urethra" (though Mary Calderone, a leading figure in sexuality education, argues persuasively in the book's foreword that it's empowering for children to have language for all these body parts [Calderone 7]). I read through the entire book with my daughter, but I've stuck to vagina, penis, and clitoris in our own conversations. For a time, she insisted on reading "Robert and Mary" over and over, fascinated. I wondered how my mother would react if my toddler asked her to read this favorite out loud during my absence.

SEX, SCIENCE, AND TRUTH

Alfred C. Kinsey ardently believed that science could help us learn and speak the truth about sex. (No ironic quotes around truth—he was a whole-hearted positivist.) Scientific knowledge about sexuality would set us free from oppressive moralizing, ignorance, shame, and inhibition, and it would liberate sexual pleasure. For Kinsey, it was a natural, ordinary, inalienable human birthright to know your body and to enjoy it sexually in whatever ways you like; he regarded all the variation in sexual desires and practices as a normal part of our species-life. The publication of his two remarkable volumes, *Sexual Behavior in the Human Male* (in 1948) and *Sexual Behavior in the Human Female* (in 1953), which were based on in-depth, face-to-face interviews resulting in what he called "case studies" or "sexual histories" of more than 18,000 individuals (Ericksen), were immediate bestsellers in the United States (and soon internationally) and shook the country "like an atom bomb," as headlines in the popular press proclaimed.[2] After an initially exuberant response, the *Female* volume quickly came under fierce attack for undermining America's moral fiber; critics were outraged by its findings that nearly 50 percent of all women had premarital affairs, and 26 percent had extramarital affairs, for example.

Kinsey set out to ask what people did, felt, and thought about sexually, and he described a remarkable variation in sexual experience that exploded then-current assumptions of premarital chastity, women's lack of sexual interest and experience, fidelity, heterosexuality, and vaginal orgasm. Kinsey reported that the majority of his subjects masturbated, that premarital sexual relations were common and tended to improve "marital adjustment" and satisfaction, that women took pleasure in sex, and that homosexual encounters were neither rare nor abnormal. He devised a homosexuality-heterosexuality scale to rate an individual's shifting desires and behaviors, and he argued that sexuality was more accurately represented by a continuum (ranging from 1, completely heterosexual in behavior and fantasy, to 6, completely homosexual in behavior and fantasy) than by a categorical, dichotomous designation of identity. Kinsey concluded that many problems in marriage would be avoided if women and men were equally free of constraints against sexual experimentation before marriage, and that the male's lack of skill in sexual relations contributed significantly to poor "marital adjustment." In the course of almost twenty years (1938–56), Kinsey personally collected more than 8,000 histories (approximately 40 percent of the more than 20,000 collected in all),[3] traveling across the country with his team of three interviewers. His work was not the first, but it was the most public and extensive research into human sexuality undertaken up to that time.

Kinsey spent the first part of his academic career (more than twenty years) as an entymologist and professor of zoology, specializing in taxonomy and writing the definitive monograph on the gall wasp in 1930. To research gall wasps and his 1943 field guide, *Edible Plants of Eastern North America*, he literally walked across the United States (as sex researcher John Gagnon remarked to the audience at a screening of *Kinsey* in October 2004 in New York City). His biographers (cf. Gathorne-Hardy; Jones) tell us that Kinsey was the son of a harsh and punitive Methodist minister and a loving but submissive mother; tended to be a loner who was rather socially awkward; found solace in nature and cherished his solitude there. He struggled with sexual feelings in his homosocial relationships as a boy (and later came to recognize and act on his homosexual desires), and he was an obsessive collector. When he married Clara McMillen (nicknamed "Mac" by her husband), a gifted and energetic graduate student in chemistry at Indiana University, they were both virgins, and they suffered mechanical (and, for Clara, painful) difficulties with penetration during sexual intercourse due to her thicker-than-usual hymen. The condition was finally corrected—much to their relief and pleasure—in a minor office procedure after consultation with a physician.[4] Kinsey attributed his own sexual suffering in childhood and his early marriage to the twinned social and religious scourges of ignorance and shame about sexuality that permeated even his beloved science, and his anger and sadness fed what became his brilliant enlightenment crusade to accumulate and spread sexual knowledge. In 1938 he began teaching what was for the time a revolutionary (in content) and hugely popular "marriage course" at Indiana University, in which he lectured explicitly about sexuality to his shocked but eager students. Kinsey became a self-styled sex counselor to the students, who increasingly approached him for advice and factual information, spilling out their urgent concerns about their bodies, desperate to learn whether their fantasies and desires were normal. Because so much was simply unknown about sexual response and behavior, Kinsey resolved to investigate the subject scientifically, and he began collecting the first of his sexual histories; by 1940 he was devoting himself entirely to the study of human sexuality (Gathorne-Hardy, 150).

On a *Kinsey 2004* film poster, fragments of typed questions, seemingly cut off at the paper's edge, give a glimpse into the intense and explicit encounter between sex researcher and subject:

How frequently do you fantasize . . .
How old were you the first time t . . .
Did you ever feel guilty about ma . . .
How much does your size change wh . . .
Are you ever aroused thinking abo . . .

At the bottom of the poster: *It always starts with a question.* Kinsey's sex interview was a "talking cure" for the subject, a two-person encounter that gave voice and narrative form to a lifetime of private sexual acts and desires. Multiplied by the thousands (then tabulated and published), the interview was an intervention into a culture mired in sexual secrecy and hypocrisy. James H. Jones, one of Kinsey's biographers, states that Kinsey broke "the conspiracy of silence" around sexuality enveloping 1940s and 1950s America (Allan). Kinsey's studies of sex made the private public and brought the previously taboo subject into the national conversation. Publication of his books made front-page news in all the major newspapers and magazines, and his work was celebrated in popular culture by the likes of Cole Porter ("It's Too Darn Hot": "According to the Kinsey report / Every average man you know / Much prefers his lovely dovey to court / When the temperature is low") and Martha Raye ("Oh! Dr. Kinsey!"). Claiming sexual diversity as the norm, his revelations opened the closet of American sexuality (and demonstrated that there *was* a closet) and fed what became the liberation movements for gay and women's rights and health.

In discussing my upcoming trip and the soon-to-be-released film with some younger friends who are academics and educators in their early thirties, I was surprised to discover that they had never heard of this monumental cultural and scientific figure of the twentieth century, or of his pioneering investigation of sex. That chapter of American sexual history was eclipsed by the sexier sixties and the "sexual revolution" (with our apparently expanding knowledge of sex enhanced by Masters and Johnson, Shere Hite, and MTV). I cannot remember how I first learned of him, but I know that Kinsey's name was somehow mixed up in the culture of my growing up. Later, working in various capacities as a sex researcher and sex educator, I became aware of Kinsey's long shadow in the field; as I prepared for the conference, however, I realized I didn't really know much about Kinsey at all. The Kinsey Institute was only a code, a sexual cipher, in my imagination—fixed in the 1950s, but with no real geographic location. I dusted off the original 1953 edition of Kinsey's *Sexual Behavior in the Human Female* I'd purchased as a curiosity some years ago at a used bookstore, but never looked at, and packed it to read on the plane to Indiana. The pages are yellowing and crumble easily, and I began to sneeze as I pulled it out to prepare for takeoff.

NAKED PICTURES, SEXUAL SCIENCE, AND POLITICS

Several of us from different parts of the country meet at the Indianapolis airport taxi office to share a cab to Indiana University in Bloomington. To our surprise, we are shown to a gleaming stretch limousine that has just been added to the taxi fleet and apparently needs a trial run. Three of us sit in the cavernous back. I've never been in a limousine before, and it feels weirdly incongruous—more suited to high-school seniors getting drunk and having sex on prom night, or businessmen downing martinis and cavorting with escorts, than to middle-aged academic types, tired and parched from traveling, sipping from water bottles and trying to intelligently discuss sex research. The drive to the campus takes us past dry mowed fields of straw-colored corn stalks and miles of strip malls. When we finally arrive at the campus center, I unpack, shower, dress respectably, and follow a winding path through red brick buildings and past parking lots, in search of the Kinsey Institute.

I am surprised to discover it is just a modest two floors within a traditional limestone classroom building. Lost and a little late for the early evening preliminary meeting, I ask several students heading into Morrisson Hall, the biology building, if they can direct me to a stairwell for the Kinsey Institute. None of them have heard of it, though it occupies the building's third and fourth floors. Another SRFP Fellow approaches, and I follow her into the elevator; we emerge chatting, our identification tags prominently displayed, and proceed down the corridor to our meeting room. On first glance, the institute seems very institute-like: quiet, modest, plain. Dull carpeting and fluorescent lights. Mild-mannered researchers walking about in bland, casual clothing. The usual. Until your eyes begin to focus on the art.

Vulvas everywhere. And penises. Cunnilingus, fellatio, anal sex, men with men, women with women, men and women in all positions of sexual intercourse. Photographs, pen-and-ink drawings, watercolors, etchings. Sex in China, in Italy, in Iran. A self-portrait of Rembrandt doing "it" in France with his lover, Hendrickje Stoffels, c. 1650. Delicate ink drawings and woodblock prints of Japanese couples copulating, their genitals visible under the mounds and folds of elaborate robes. Bawdy engravings from England by Hogarth. Photos of famous dancers, like Nijinsky, and a gorgeously naked and young Yul Brynner taken in 1942. A pen-and-crayon drawing from Germany (by Walter Kirchoff) called "The Bridegroom" (1940), depicting a nude woman in a bridal veil, being handed a penis on a tray by a nude maid with a serving towel neatly arranged over her bent arm. Postcards of Jack La Lane, in the nude (his perfect body like I'd never seen him on my childhood television screen when I watched my mother do her daily calisthenics on the living room carpet). A contemporary black-and-white photo of a woman's torso, breasts compressed within an elaborate iron device. Cartoons, film posters, fine art, and amateur sketches. Twentieth century, eighteenth century, and sixteenth century. The frames hang close together, with cards detailing date, medium, artist (many unknown), donation date, and informative historical and cultural explanations of the practices depicted or the sources of the art. There is no discernible order to the presentation of images; geography, century, medium, behavior, are all a-jumble (which seems to be the point). The visual collection is at first almost overwhelming: erotic, fascinating, unruly, beautiful, familiar and unworldly, creepy, funny, poignant. Walking down the hall, you pass by representations of pleasure, pain, arousal, humor, love, sensuality, mischief—the quotidian and the rare. It's all there. This is not your ordinary scientific institute, with a couple of modestly chosen and framed prints on the walls. Who knew? I feel like I've tumbled down Alice's rabbit hole.

It is difficult to settle down to discussions of research projects in the ordinary beige conference room we've been assigned, with all that fabulous (and valuable) art just outside the door. Later, the institute's art curator, Catherine Johnson-Roehr, takes us on a tour of a small internal gallery and explains that there are hundreds of crates and boxes of this

Unknown photographer, United States. Catalog page featuring unknown male model, 1950s. Gelatin silver print. KI-DC: 2693. Donated in 1962.[5]

Above: Unknown
photographer, United
States. Two women
kissing on a bed, c.1950.
Gelatin silver print.
KI-DC: 41347. Donation
date unknown.[6]

Right: Reamer Keller and
Percy Barker, United
States. *Sexual Misbehavior
in the Human Female*, 1953.
36 paper cocktail napkins
in original box. A630R
A398.1/ISR 400.
Donated in 1953.[7]

Attributed to Katsushika Hokusai (1760–1849), Japan. Asuma nishiki, or Brocades of the East, c. 1810. Woodblock print. E7`1 A25 v. 1. Donated in 1958.[8]

stuff—more than 80,000 items of art, photography, and artifacts—that Kinsey collected in the 1940s and 1950s, and that interview subjects and collectors continue to contribute all these years later. The boxes of photographs are sorted and labeled according to an elaborate taxonomy worked out by Paul Gebhard, one of Kinsey's team (for example: C ♀ PRONE DV means coitus, female prone, dorsal-ventral, an SDM ♀ on ♀ WRSTL means sadomasochism, female on female wrestling), but most of them remain uncatalogued and unaccessed. (The KI does not have a full-time archivist.) Kinsey was an obsessive collector, and his collection of erotic visual culture conveys something sexy (and obsessive) about sex that escapes Kinsey's exhaustive tabulations and statistics.[9]

Although the Kinsey Institute itself, in collaboration with the Indiana University School of Fine Arts Gallery, has mounted a number of small shows of the collection, it has not been shown in a major exhibition elsewhere.[10] As a recent Ph.D. accustomed to comparing dissertation topics and counting pages like a graduate student, I think: There are hundreds of potential doctoral dissertations in art history in that space! This is a hidden gold mine! I vow to come back to New York City to convince some art curator somewhere important to make a show from this massive historic collection of erotic art. It is perhaps not only lack of resources keeping the KI art collection from being exhibited much, however. Historically, the KI has been the focus of aggressive political attacks on its research, archives, and art collection, and the attacks have bred a deep protectiveness, along with some defensiveness, about its holdings. In a landmark case in 1950, the U.S. Customs office in Indiana seized a shipment of erotic materials headed to the Kinsey Institute from overseas, on the grounds that it constituted an illegal importation of pornography. Kinsey himself battled the Treasury Department over this landmark obscenity case for years, arguing that it was unconstitutional governmental infringement on academic and scientific rights. The case was finally decided in 1957, after Kinsey's death, in a victory for Kinsey and Indiana University—the ban on pornography did not apply to material collected for legitimate scientific and scholarly research (Gathorne-Hardy, 442). Today, however, although researchers providing proper credentials have tremendous access to the Kinsey Institute holdings, via the wonderful library and collections (and wonderful librarians and curator), Kinsey Institute staff members remain circumspect, if not downright secretive, about discussing the treasures of the institute's closed "vault." Kinsey and his team filmed hundreds of hours of people (including Kinsey himself, his researchers and their wives, and many volunteers) engaged in sexual activity, including masturbation, oral sex, and intercourse, in order to directly observe and document the physiological aspects of sexual arousal; the KI carefully guards the privacy and confidentiality of participants who are still living, along with families of subjects. These films are under lock and key, and what else is in the vault remains an intriguing and seductive mystery, known only to a privileged few.

The Sexuality Research Fellowship Program (SRFP) of the SSRC has completed nine years of its Ford Foundation–funded ten. According to Diane DiMauro, Director of the SRFP, "From its inception, the focus of the program has been strengthening and legitimizing sexuality research across disciplines within the traditional social sciences, but also encompassing work in the humanities, public policy, legal studies, and public health. We've fostered a cross- and interdisciplinary spirit that respects and appreciates serious scholarship involving a range of methodological approaches and theoretical frameworks, even extending the mantle of sexuality research to economics and language studies."

Kinsey's own tiny research team was interdisciplinary from the start, including an anthropologist and a psychologist (as well as a nonprofessional former student), in addition to Kinsey himself—a zoologist. The research of the current crop of sexuality fellows comprises work that would have fascinated Kinsey, I imagine, and delighted him with its scope.[11] There is a study of sexuality education in American public schools and an ethnographic study of vulvar pain syndrome. A psychology fellow is studying the effects of sex steroids on arousal and cognitive processing, and an ethnic studies scholar is writing about Cuban American gay Miami. I meet a demographer investigating whether cultural factors and healthcare access are key to cross-national differences in sexually transmitted disease rates in the developed world, and historians exploring sexuality and American citizenship (1900–65) and the impact of McCarthyism on American sexual identity (1945–65). In American studies, a fellow is writing a history of sexual minority activism against violence in New York City and San Francisco.

There are fifteen new fellows this year, and though space does not permit the mention of all their work, their research projects all sound fascinating and important. It isn't always easy to talk to each other across disciplines, however, and we bump up against the limits and challenges of interdisciplinarity: cultural critics and social historians (who have not tended to see themselves as part of a unified "field" of sex research) sometimes find themselves at odds with more traditional empirical sex researchers, who define sexuality through surveys and measurement. It should be noted as well that despite the energetic "targeted outreach" efforts of the SRFP, this year the researchers are mainly white, and the only African American at the conference is an invited guest—a previous predoctoral fellow in social welfare, Jeffry Thigpen, whose dissertation study of sexual behaviors in African American children in Chicago is the sole work presented that directly addresses sexuality among black people.[12] According to Diane DiMauro, the problem of representation of African American researchers in the SRFP is reflective of the field of sexuality research in general, though she points out that "it has been encouraging to see a growing diversity among junior-level researchers, and especially an increase in Latino and Asian sexuality scholars." This raises the question of whose work counts as "sex research" and what self-other definitions, academic allegiances, and disciplinary histories may work to exclude African American researchers and scholars from identifying themselves, or being identified, as part of the "field" of sexuality research.

When it is my turn to introduce my own postdoctoral research in clinical psychology and women's studies to the group, I try for a compelling sound bite: I'm developing feminist, psychoanalytic theory about the transformations of puberty for girls, locating the girl's pubertal body as key to the psychic (re)production of compulsory, normative heterosexuality and femininity. My work theorizes pre- and beginning puberty as "queer" developmental moments when gender and sexual flexibility hold sway, before the claims of culture foreclose girls' bodies, desires, and self-representations.

Currently, I am writing an article about Beauvoir's brilliantly embodied analysis of "the crisis of puberty" and the alienation and losses of girls growing up. In the course of the conference, I realize with surprised satisfaction that there is an interesting historical connection between Beauvoir's *The Second Sex* (1948) and Kinsey's *Sexual Behavior in the Human Female* (1953)—both were published in the United States in 1953 as radical explorations of women's sexual situation. As Deirdre Bair notes in an introduction to *The Second Sex*, Blanche Knopf, wife of the publisher Alfred A. Knopf, actually argued that the book should be translated and published in the United States because it was "a modern-day sex manual, something between Kinsey and Havelock Ellis" (Bair, xiv). Further, Mr. Knopf asked H. M. Parshley, who, like Kinsey, was a professor (emeritus) of zoology, to evaluate (and later translate) Beauvoir's book.

After the introductory impressions have been made over snacks and seltzer (Indiana University is a "dry" campus), most of us return to our rooms to watch the first presidential debate between Bush and Kerry. If the exhilaration of being hosted at the Kinsey Institute has threatened to go to some of our heads, the presidential debate brings us down to earth. The debate focuses our attention on the dire political and ideological context in which we work: these are dangerous times for science and scholarship, chillingly similar to conditions Kinsey faced in the 1950s.

The advance notice for the film *Kinsey*, which we are scheduled to see tomorrow night, has brought forth aggressive attacks from the Christian Right. Kinsey has become as much of a symbol of sexual radicalism now as he was in the 1950s. The Traditional Values Coalition, a conservative religious lobbying group, has called for a year-long boycott of all movies released by *Kinsey*'s distributor, Fox Searchlight.[13] Judith Reisman, leader of the contemporary anti-Kinsey movement, has for years crudely attempted to smear the field of sexology by discrediting Kinsey's scientific research, throwing around inflammatory and entirely unsubstantiated accusations of pedophilia and child pornography. Her incendiary anti-Kinsey campaign has helped to mobilize the right-wing troops amassing at the doors of the National Institutes of Health, determined to block government funding of sex research.

In a scary assault on academic freedom and scientific integrity, the Traditional Values Coalition was discovered in 2003 to be circulating a "hit list" to Congressional Republicans of nearly 200 NIH-funded researchers and their studies involving sexually transmitted diseases, prostitution, homosexuality, and substance abuse.[14] In July 2003, Rep. Patrick Toomey (R-PA) proposed an amendment to the annual appropriations bill that would have prohibited completion of five peer-reviewed research grants approved by the NIH and already underway. Among these grants was the Kinsey Institute's Dr. Eric Janssen's research on mood, sexual arousal, and sexual risk-taking. The amendment lost by only two votes, 212–210. *Only two votes.* In October 2003, conservative members of the U.S. House of Representatives continued the assault on government funding of scientific sexuality research by initiating a hearing on ten research grants funded by the NIH, demanding proof of their public benefit. The evidence of the sex research "hit list" prompted a new *unofficial* policy at NIH, according to *Johns Hopkins Magazine* (Hopkins public health researchers were among those targeted): research proposals using the words "sex worker, injection drug use, harm reduction, needle exchange, men who have sex with men, homosexual, bisexual, gay, and prostitute" in their titles or abstracts were to be sent back to the researcher to remove them, so they could not be flagged by conservatives in their witch-hunts-cum-database-searches (Keiger).

In response to news of the hit list, Rep. Henry A. Waxman (D-CA) protested what he termed "scientific McCarthyism" in a letter he wrote to Health and Human Services Secretary Tommy Thompson (Keiger). In December 2004, Waxman's office also issued a report on "The Content of Federally Funded Abstinence-Only Education Programs"— another priority of right-wing religious activist organizations like the Family Research Council. The report found that more than 80 percent of the abstinence-only curricula, used by grantees of the largest federal abstinence initiative (funded by the Department of Health and Human Services at $170 million in fiscal year 2005—more than twice the amount spent in fiscal year 2001), and reaching millions of adolescents and children each year, "contain false, misleading, or distorted information about reproductive health"; "blur religion and science"; "treat stereotypes about girls and boys as scientific fact"; and "contain scientific errors" (i-ii). The right-wing crusaders are determined to deny teens the same truthful and accurate sexual information that Kinsey made available to their grandparents.

In the face of this contemporary political interference in science and the bad science informing abstinence-only programs, it is important to remember that one of Kinsey's great contributions to the study of sexuality, and to academic freedom in general, was his insistence on the scientist's right to investigate. Kinsey passionately and vigorously protested the intrusions of religion, politics, and morality into research:

> There is no ocean of greater magnitude than the sexual function, and there are those who believe that we would do better if we ignored its existence, that we should not try to understand its material origins, and that if we sufficiently ignore it and mop the floor of sexual activity with new laws, heavier penalties, more pronouncements, and greater intolerances, we may ultimately eliminate the reality. The scientist who observes and describes the reality is attacked as an enemy of faith, and his acceptance of human limitations in modifying that reality is condemned as scientific materialism. (Kinsey, *Human Female*, 10)

Kinsey's major institutional funding source—the Rockefeller Foundation—withdrew its support in the wake of the controversy stirred by the publication of *Sexual Behavior in the Human Female* and the perceived threat posed by the House Committee to Investigate Tax-Free Foundations. This Congressional committee was convened in 1954 at the instigation of Kinsey's conservative critics; according to sociologist Julia Ericksen, the only issue addressed by the committee was the Rockefeller Foundation's funding of Kinsey, and the only witnesses called to testify were those hostile to Kinsey (59). Joseph McCarthy and his followers turned Kinsey's findings on their head to support the idea of a "moral decline" in America that left the country open to Communism. Kinsey himself was under surveillance by J. Edgar Hoover for many years, according to historian (and SRFP Fellow) Craig Loftin.

Today, according to *Johns Hopkins Magazine*, senior established sex researchers express their concern that newer researchers won't remain or even enter the field of sexuality studies, given aggressive right-wing tactics that threaten careers and necessary funding. "Long After Kinsey, Only the Brave Study Sex" was the title of a November 9, 2004, article in the *New York Times* science section in advance of the film's opening. When I approach the new Kinsey Institute director, Dr. Julia Heimann (yes, really), during the SRFP conference to ask her thoughts about the attacks on our field, she replies, "The best thing to do is just keep doing the work." I wonder if this represents the bunker mentality of a group trying to survive while steadily under siege or a stubbornly optimistic loyalty to Kinsey's belief in scientific reason over the forces of irrationality. (As the film *Kinsey* shows, Kinsey himself did not seem to believe in keeping his head down to avoid controversy—for better and for worse.) Meeting in small groups, many of the sexuality fellows talk about political activism as a basic career requirement as well as a moral imperative. Even as I write this essay, I am aware of feeling like I am looking over my shoulder, tempted to self-police. Will my work and potential funding as a researcher be limited by some key word search a right-wing zealot does on me someday? I want to title this article, "My Daughter's Clitoris," but I choose something less provocative, to stay under the repressive radar with my publications list.

WATCHING *KINSEY*

A highlight of this trip to Bloomington is a private screening of the film *Kinsey*, by Bill Condon, scheduled to open in theaters in November 2004. The fellows pile into a comfortable bus for the half-hour ride past the strips of highway shopping and service stations to an empty multiplex. We have the theater to ourselves, with a few Kinsey Institute staff and board members along for the show. At the movies, passing around popcorn and red licorice, the fellows and staff seem looser, even sexier. When the lights go down and the film begins, we are drawn into a grand romance of science: Kinsey is the hero in a just struggle to bring light where there's darkness, knowledge to ignorance, all that. Watching the film, I am surprised to feel a growing debt of gratitude: we see ourselves differently after Kinsey; his journey across America really changed the world.

Much has been written of the film, which Frank Rich, writing in the *New York Times* (12 December 2003) called "a bellwether cultural event of this year." As a psychotherapist, one of the things that interests me most about *Kinsey* is its portrayal of Kinsey's interview and the ways that producing a "sexual history" between a researcher and subject became a clinical and social intervention around shame. As a feminist currently writing about Kinsey's contemporary, Simone de Beauvoir, and her view of female embodiment and the "Other-ing" of girls, I was curious about Kinsey's relation to The Woman Question, and how women figured in the film's story.

The film begins with a black screen and Kinsey's voiceover (the actor Liam Neeson, in a brilliant and touching performance): "Don't sit so far away, anything that creates a distance should be avoided." When the image appears, we see Kinsey's research assistant, Clyde Martin (played by Peter Saarsgard), seated at a lab table, listening to Kinsey's stern, impatient voice, instructing how to ask about sex. Martin learns to take a sex history by taking Kinsey's (as do the rest of Kinsey's team); questions about religion and family cut away to Kinsey as a boy, listening to his puritanical and mean-spirited Methodist father preach to a congregation in a small church about the dangers of sex. "Lust has a thousand avenues. The dance hall, the ice cream parlor, the tenement saloon, the Turkish bath . . . Because of the telephone, a young woman can now hear the voice of her suitor on the pillow next to her." The device of cutting away from scenes of Kinsey's research assistants practicing the sex interview on Kinsey himself to flashbacks of Kinsey's life is used to elegant and smart effect by the director, Bill Condon. But this is more than a narrative device; the sexual history—Kinsey's amazing interview—becomes the compelling through-line of the film, as it was the brilliant intervention of his work.

Kinsey designed his sex interview to override the subject's shame and guilt, carefully structuring its sequence, pacing, and wording to elicit a person's sexual narrative. Kinsey seduced his subjects into deep person-al disclosure through plain-speaking and sympathetic, nonjudgmental listening—asking them to tell a story about themselves many longed to tell but had never done. For many, if not most, of the respondents, the interview was the first and only place they'd spoken of intimate details of their sexual selves, recited the whole sweeping narrative of their sexual history, from memories of early childhood to the present. The presence of a recognizing "other"[15]—a sexually knowledgeable scientist—authorized the teller to tell and recognized her as a "subject" with a narrative. The interview thus helped to confirm the subject's sexual subjectivity.

Most previous sex research had been conducted with written questionnaires, and no previous researcher had simply sat down face to face with so many people to talk with them about their sexual experiences and feelings. As the film shows, Kinsey and his team (all men—he thought people would refuse to talk about sex to women interviewers) took histories from waitresses, accountants, doctors, professors, truck drivers, housewives, actors, artists, prisoners, lawyers—attempting to capture all differences by sampling the entire spectrum of American society.[16] They met with people in bars, homes, offices. The researchers memorized more than four hundred questions, asking some and omitting others in semistructured interviews that typically took from one to four hours; they recorded their informants' responses on a single 8 1/2 x 11 sheet of paper, using an elaborate coding system that was also memorized, in an effort to ensure the strictest confidentiality.[17] Questions ranged from the sexually indirect: "How young were you when you no longer thought of your parent's home as your own?" to the sexually explicit: "How young were you the first time you had an orgasm while dreaming?" As the film shows, the interview method involved assuming that "everyone does everything," in order to give people "permission to report behaviors and experiences that are not generally revealed," even to a psychotherapist (Pomeroy et al., 10). (Instead of asking "Did you have intercourse before marriage?", for example, the interviewer would ask, "How many times did you have intercourse before marriage?") At a screening in New York City in October 2004, Dr. Anke Ehrardt, Director of Columbia University's HIV Center for Clinical and Behavioral Studies, commented that "Kinsey's chapter on taking a sex history is still one of the best there is. We assign it to our medical students today." The richness, flow, and emotion of the interviewee's story cannot be captured, of course, by Kinsey's coding method, and complex and intimate stories were reduced to discrete and detailed pieces of data for the purposes of statistical analysis. In their effort to collect vast quantities of data, the researchers also tried to keep the subjects "on track" by encouraging direct and brief answers wherever possible; they were also alert to the dangers of drawing their subjects too deeply into painful emotional waters. Yet "not infrequently," interviewees told long, detailed stories (Pomeroy et al. 20). As a clinical researcher it is painful to think of how much incredible qualitative data was lost because (in order to ensure confidentiality) Kinsey did not audiotape his interviews.

In a series of fictionalized interview scenes (with a script informed by the memories of research team members as well as study participants), the film helps us to imagine the thousands of face-to-face encounters Kinsey undertook. To capture the vastness of his interview project, there is also an (overly) long montage of talking heads superimposed in quick succession over a map of the United States—a nostalgic representation (in the style of a period travelogue film) of Kinsey's traveling team of researchers driving around the country in the Kinsey family Oldsmobile. In one deeply affecting scene, we see Kinsey and Martin sitting in a gay bar (in the Chicago area) late into the night, talking with a young man who tells the story of being branded and beaten at age thirteen by his brothers after his father caught him "messing around" with another boy in a haystack. "It's not that I mind being queer," he says, "'cause I don't. I just wish other folks weren't so put out by it." Later, in a moving (but evidently entirely invented) scene, Kinsey sits with his still belligerent but now elderly father, who has agreed to have his son take his sex history. After some impatient back and forth, his father responds to Kinsey's question about masturbation: "There was a problem. A chronic condition, the doctors called it . . . I was outfitted with a tight strap that I wore at all times. It kept me from coming into contact with my genitals . . . It was a highly embarrassing remedy, but, after, it proved effective. The condition was cured . . . I was ten." In Kinsey's sad and compassionate response, we read the intergenerational transmission of shame and sexual ignorance that drove his own work.

One of Kinsey's signal achievements in his two volumes is the documentation not only of tremendous variation, but of vast numbers of people with similar feelings, similar practices, and similar desires. Above all, many people wanted to know if they were like others, as they confided their deepest, darkest sexual secrets in a private encounter with a tolerant and accepting interviewer. Kinsey made it clear that no practice or behavior was "abnormal," only perhaps rare or unusual— statistically speaking. Telling one's sexual history functioned as a kind of confessional before a neutral but compassionate scientist-cum-priest, who could absolve a person's guilt and shame by conveying that there was nothing wrong with them, that their body and their sexuality were normal. Biographer Gathorne-Hardy makes a similar point, citing Foucault on the power of the confession, and agrees that the sexual interview could be "therapeutic," with subjects often experiencing something akin to "the transference" (178–79). Alongside the intimate power of the confessional or therapeutic bond, the interview provided the opportunity for a sort of social reparation for those who sought it: in telling all, the subject was helping science and doing a public good.

Toward the end of the film, Kinsey sits with a woman of around sixty (played by Lynn Redgrave), in a deeply affecting scene. By this time in his life, Kinsey was despairing of completing his work, exhausted from health problems and the unrelenting attacks from sexual and political conservatives and the withdrawal of financial support for his research. The woman tells him some of her own sexual history: that she was married but had a secret desire for a woman at her workplace, which led her to drink and lose her husband, become estranged from her children, and contemplate suicide. Kinsey responds sympathetically: "It's just another reminder of how little things have changed in our society." To Kinsey's surprise, the woman insists that things have gotten much better, "because of you." Reading the *Female* volume made her realize how many other women felt as she did and gave her the courage to confess her feelings to the woman she'd worked with: "She told me, to my great surprise, that the feelings were mutual. We've been together for three happy years now." "You saved my life, sir," she tells him.

The *Female* volume presented a dramatic challenge to conventional ideas of American womanhood, and through it Kinsey became a de facto spokesman for women's right to sexual expression and satisfaction. He found that women who had had premarital sex were more satisfied in marriage, and that women's orgasm (what he termed "sexual outlet") also added to "marital adjustment." Insofar as he believed that marital adjustment aided not only personal happiness but societal stability, Kinsey mobilized support for his research via the rationale that sexual freedom was good for marriage and therefore good for society. This fascinating tension between the unconventional and the conventional can be seen in Kinsey's own marriage to Clara McMillen, who is portrayed in *Kinsey* with great warmth and grace by the actress Laura Linney.

Clara is a compelling and contradictory figure in the story, and I wanted to know more about her than the movie offered. She is portrayed as centered, good-humored, and direct—a woman who was full of life, adoring and accepting of her husband, and unwavering in her support of his work. Early in the film, when Kinsey asks her to marry him, she tells him, "I've always considered myself a free-thinker. Frankly, I find you a little churchy." When they marry, however, she becomes in many ways a wife of the times—with a twist. Mac curtails her own career (as a scientist), and seems to take on the role of home-maker and mother with pleasure. She actively supports Kinsey's research even when it takes him away from the family for long stretches of time and brings personal attacks and intrusions into their lives. But she also becomes an apparently willing participant in the sexual partner-swapping Kinsey encouraged among his team.

After Kinsey begins a sexual affair with Clyde Martin (who, according to Gathorne-Hardy, was one of the great loves of his life), Clara and Clyde are seen in the Kinsey kitchen in a scene that perfectly captures Clara's contradictions:

> **Clara:** Would you like some pie?
> **Martin:** Rhubarb? (Clara smiles, opens the refrigerator. Martin sits.)
> **Clara:** You know, Clyde, . . . I didn't like you very much at first.
> **Martin:** I don't blame you. Most women would have had me murdered.
> **Clara:** Oh I considered it. But I hate to think of myself as conventional. (Clara pours a glass of milk.)
> **Clara:** But if this had to happen . . . I'm glad it was you. (Clara serves the pie and milk, sits.)
> **Clara:** And I'll admit there have been benefits. It's certainly sparked things up sexually. I suppose we'd both grown bored, without even realizing it.
> **Martin:** I think you've handled it remarkably well.
> **Clara:** I learned something a long time ago. Once Prok [Kinsey's nickname] has his mind set, it's no use trying to stop him.

Soon after, Clara and Martin begin their own sexual affair, with Kinsey's knowledge.

When Clara is seen in the film straightening up the bed for the filming of sex between one of Kinsey's researchers and a sixtyish female volunteer, there is something more sexy in her calm and economical gestures than in the wild thrashing that comes next. According to Gathorne-Hardy, Clara typed up the sex diaries of Kinsey's most sexually prodigious and controversial subject—a pedophile who claimed to have had sex with thousands of people and who recorded these encounters in great detail—which took her until 1956 (Gathorne-Hardy, 20). One pictures her deliberate and calm progress through the sensational and disturbing material. During this same period, Clara Kinsey became a leading figure in the Girl Scouts of Bloomington.

The wives of Kinsey's team—Agnes Gebhardt, Martha Pomeroy, and Alice Martin—remain on the margins in the film, seen only at the Martins' garden wedding and a group picnic, talking ironically about Kinsey's influence over their families:

> **Martha:** [to newlywed Alice] At least you passed the test.
> **Alice:** What do you mean?
> **Martha:** He took your sex history, didn't he? Well, he
> wouldn't have let Clyde marry you unless he thought you'd
> fit in.

Who were these women whose husbands spent their days talking about sex and who themselves defied all convention to participate in Kinsey's rarefied experiment in free sex during the forties and fifties? According to Gathorne-Hardy, the wives were involved in sexual activity with the different men of the team (including Kinsey) and in Kinsey's films (Gathorne-Hardy does not report whether they participated in homosexual encounters with each other, as the men of the team did), although Alice Martin—who fell in love with Gebhard after they'd begun an affair—remained resentful of what she perceived as Kinsey's pressure to participate.

In some fundamental way, despite his years of study, women remained "other" to Kinsey. In *Sexual Behavior in the Human Female*, Kinsey was at pains to establish that women were like men at the level of anatomy and physiology, that the female's sexual organs and pathways of stimulation were homologous to those of the male, her physical capacities equal, in order to dispel the myth that women were innately less sexual than men. Yet when he documents how different women appeared from men psychologically—in terms of sources of arousal,

levels of premarital sexual relations, sexual needs, patterns of masturbation, and role of orgasm in sexual satisfaction, for example—Kinsey
seems perplexed by differences he cannot explain, except by recourse to
hormones. It is as if he asks himself: Why can't a woman be more like a
man? Reading the *Female* volume, I found it at first quite confusing to
understand Kinsey's odd formulation that women are less often affected
by psychological factors as "[her] previous sexual experience . . . [her]
vicarious sharing of another person's sexual experience, or by [her] sympathetic reactions to the sexual responses of other individuals" (650).
Kinsey seems to mean that whereas men develop generalized expectations and physiological responses as a result of prior sexual experience
(according to a traditional model of psychological conditioning), women
tend to experience each encounter, each actual relationship, on its own
terms. Interestingly, Kinsey's statistical analysis leads him to conclude
that although women exhibit much more variety in sexual behavior than
do males, they are more similar to each other across educational background; in other words, educational differences (an indicator of class) do
not account for differences in sexual experience among women. Kinsey
takes this to mean that "females are not conditioned to the extent that
males are conditioned by the attitudes of the social groups in which they
live" (686). Beauvoir, Kinsey's contemporary, of course argued instead
that women *across* class and educational backgrounds experience themselves as "Other"—that it is women's oppression that conditions female
sexuality most profoundly.

Whatever Kinsey's weaknesses as a social or psychological analyst
of the data he gathered, his *Female* volume offered a profoundly new
and convention-shattering view of women as sexual beings, with sexual
bodies that were knowable.[18] For this, he was vigorously attacked in the
press, by psychologists like Karl Menninger and by religious fundamentalists like Billy Graham (Gathorne-Hardy). Some challenged the book
on the grounds that it must be biased toward prostitutes, because no
respectable, "normal" woman would have agreed to talk to Kinsey
about sex! Clara Kinsey is shown in the film bluntly confronting her
husband's bewilderment over the controversy stirred by the publication
of his *Female* volume:

Kinsey: I'm trying to understand why people hate this book so.
Clara: You told them their grandmothers and daughters are

masturbating, having sex with each other. What did you expect?

TOYS, TOTS, AND THE PRODUCTION OF SEXUAL KNOWLEDGE

The last evening of the conference, a large dinner reception for the fellows and the Kinsey Institute staff is held in the private back room of one of Bloomington's more upscale restaurants. Clusters of researchers form as everyone loosens up over some wine. After the meal, several women talk about a sex toy house party (an old-fashioned Tupperware-like gathering), one of the fellows (an anthropologist) recently attended in a suburb of Austin, Texas. She reenacts the sales pitch, complete with hand motions, to great gales of laughter from her audience of serious researchers. The performance relies on pantomiming progressively sized anal beads being deftly slipped into the unsuspecting anus of a woman's male lover as she strokes his hairy chest with her other hand and murmurs, "Ooh baby, you're so fine." Like backup singers in a 1950s girl band, we all mimic the motions, murmuring, "You're so fine, baby, you're so fine." Enjoying the irony of our "pleasing your man" act and the ludicrousness of the scenario being sold—anal seduction by stealth attack—we for the moment hold at bay the painful and complicated sexual and gender dynamics embedded in the performance. Like the fourth grader learning of sex from my more knowledgeable classmate's dirty joke, I am surprised to find myself embarrassed by my own sexual ignorance. Am I the only one here who's never heard of anal beads? I wonder (but don't ask). "Tell it again! Tell it again!!" we beg our storyteller as another woman joins us, drawn by our hysterical laughter. She does, and it's just as funny the second time. (And the third.) For a moment, we are just a bunch of women laughing about sex, as women sometimes do. (In a profound irony, I find myself somewhat uneasy writing that we were actually talking about "real" sex at a sexuality conference: sex researchers tend to be naturally defensive about "telling stories out of school," for fear of providing ammunition to the Right.)

Under the surface of the story, of course, are the kinds of questions an interdisciplinary group of contemporary sexuality researchers tend to think about. Who were the women at the sex party—professionals? working class? whites? African Americans? single or married, heterosexual or lesbian? mothers? monogamous? Did the products turn them on or please their partners or turn them on by pleasing their partners?

What fantasy was being produced, or stoked, by these sexual scripts? How were gender roles and sexual identities played into/with? Does the use of toys and lubricants, and the like, affect sexual arousal? Does it affect sexual risk or the practice of safer sex? What sort of homoerotic *frisson* circulated among the partygoers as they handled the products and imagined and showed each other how they'd use them? Is going to a sex toy party empowering for women? What was the legal context of the party? (On February 11, 2004, Reuters reported that a Texas woman, Joanne Webb, a mother of three, a Baptist, and a former schoolteacher who worked for a company that sells sex toys at house parties, had been arrested in November 2003, under a Texas obscenity law, for selling sex devices to two undercover police officers and explaining how to use them for sexual stimulation.)

Kinsey understood that there was something important to be learned about sexuality (and the human condition) by asking people about their sexual histories, fantasies, and everyday sexual practices, and observing them in their social contexts. He maintained an unshakable optimism in the idea that scientific knowledge would free us to experience and express our sexual desires without guilt or shame, and that we would be healthier and happier for it. He showed us not only the significance of simply describing the amazing variation in what people do sexually, but the power of telling sexual stories and having the words to talk about sex.

In the film, *Kinsey*, Mac and their teenage daughters sit in their yard at the picnic table, talking freely about sex. "Would you like to take my sex history, Daddy?" asks seventeen-year-old Joan. Kinsey replies with gentle interest: "Do you have a sex history, sweetie?" To her question about whether breaking the hymen hurts, he answers, "It helps if you spread the vulva to facilitate penetration." Their son, Bruce, complains bitterly that it isn't *normal* for a family to talk about such things over dinner and storms away from the table. The dinner table conversation still surprises, not because it was "advanced" for the fifties (it certainly was), but because it is still advanced today, more than half a century later.

A student I taught in a course on adolescence during the mid-nineties wrote anonymously that she was shocked and terrified when she began to menstruate (even in the 1990s, this was not uncommon among women at an urban public college); no one had ever taught her about her body. "I would never do that to my daughter," she promised. That our endless wonderment and curiosity about sex and our bodies is often punished, or foreclosed, and perhaps can never be fully satisfied, given all the limits imposed by culture, religion, family, science, politics, and psyche, is one of the lessons of *Kinsey*. Yet the film is wistful about the possibilities of knowing, and subversive in its insistence on our right to discover ourselves. What will I teach my own daughter that will help her love her body and feel confident in her sexuality as she grows? Last night before her bath, she sat on the cold white tile of the bathroom floor, separating her labia to examine her body. She tells me: "Mommy, my clitoris is pink. Why it's pink (sic)?" It always starts with a question.

KAREN WINKLER is a post-doctoral fellow in the Sexuality Research Fellowship Program of the Social Science Research Council. She writes about girls at puberty, and her research focuses on developing feminist, psychoanalytic theory about embodiment, gender, and sexual development. She is a psychotherapist in private practice in New York City.

ACKNOWLEDGMENTS

This research was assisted with a fellowship from the Sexuality Research Fellowship Program of the Social Science Research Council, with funds provided by the Ford Foundation. Many thanks to Catherine Johnson-Roehr, the Kinsey Institute's Curator of Art, Artifacts, and Photographs, for her generous help selecting images and providing descriptive labels (with permission to edit) for this article).

NOTES

1. Information on the Sexuality Research Fellowship Program of the Social Science Research Council can be found at http://www.ssrc.org/programs/sexuality.
2. For discussion of press reaction to Kinsey's books, see Gathorne-Hardy and Condon.
3. According to Ericksen, only approximately 18,000 of the total were used for the two books.
4. As represented in the film *Kinsey*, this scene makes much of Kinsey's supposedly extra-large penis and uncharacteristically mystifies the doctor's intervention. After their visit to the doctor, Kinsey and Mac are shown having wild, abandoned, and apparently gratifying sex.
5. The Kinsey Institute collection includes a large number of male physique photo cards and catalogue pages. Supposedly produced for artists and bodybuilders, these images of handsome, muscular males were popular with gay men, and

found an enthusiastic market in the post–World War II era. It was not uncommon for the studies of physique photographers to be raided by the police in the 1950s.Photographers sometimes painted g-strings on nude figures to avoid violating the obscenity laws—once the photographs reached their destination, the owner could remove the paint to reveal the nude figure underneath. Note the image of Groucho Marx on the television screen in the background, and the female pin-up photos on the wall. (Courtesy of The Kinsey Institute for Sex, Gender, and Reproduction.)

6. This image was among fifty photographs, prints, and paintings from the Kinsey Institute collections selected for a 1998 exhibit called *The Kiss* at the School of Fine Arts Gallery, Indiana University, Bloomington. "Simple lip kissing may be extended into a deep kiss (a French kiss or soul kiss, in the college parlance) which may involve more or less extensive tongue contacts, contacts of the inner lips, and a considerable stimulation of the interior of the mouth by the other individual's tongue" (Kinsey, *The Human Male*, 540). (Courtesy of the Kinsey Institute for Sex, Gender, and Reproduction.)

7. These cocktail napkins feature different cartoons illustrating statistics supposedly taken from the Kinsey Report. The cover of the box resembles the cover of *Sexual Behavior in the Human Female*. (Courtesy of The Kinsey Institute for Sex, Gender, and Reproduction.)

8. Many *shunga*, or erotic Japanese paintings, prints and illustrations, are among the KI collection. This *ukiyo-e* (the floating world) woodblock print is the first plate of a pillow book, an erotic medium meant to teach, entertain, and stimulate with images of couples in one of forty-eight standard positions of lovemaking. The calligraphic characters to the left of the lovers relates that the man pretends that his penis wants to see the woman's vulva. The text goes on to say that the woman is understandably dissatisfied when the man tries to ejaculate in the right place but misses. (Courtesy of The Kinsey Institute for Sex, Gender, and Reproduction.)

9. Elizabeth Grosz makes a similar point.

10. Recently the KI has generously lent some of the collection to the small but important Museum of Sex in New York City, and a few specialized exhibits of small parts of the collection have been organized, including a show of George Platt Lyons ballet photos in Purchase, New York, for example.

11. A complete list of postdoctoral and dissertation fellows and descriptions of their studies can be found at http://www.ssrc.org/programs/sexuality. The authors of the work listed here are (in order): Nancy Kendall, Christina Labuski, Lisa Scepkowski, Susana Pena, Kirsten Smith, Margot Canaday, Craig Loftin, and Christine Hanhardt.

12. In the tradition of Kinsey, Thigpen's research sets out to question assumptions about "normalcy" and "deviance" that have resulted in many African American children in foster care being labeled according to the vague and undefined term "sexually aggressive behavior" and then separated from siblings and peers and denied beneficial placements such as adoption. Kinsey himself declined to publish data on African Americans, deciding that he had too few middle-class

African American subjects "and did not want to confound class and race," according to Ericksen (51). This left his work open to criticism not only for statistical weaknesses but for social bias. Historian Estelle Freeman notes that concern among some African American women that Kinsey's research might be used to fortify stereotypes of black female sexuality was reported in *Ebony* magazine to have kept significant numbers from participating as subjects. She suggests (only partly in jest) that Kinsey could have called the *Female* volume "Sexual Behavior in the White, Non-Prisoner, North American Human Female." Kinsey himself addressed this limitation in his data by offering the following disclaimer in the *Female* volume: "This is a study of sexual behavior in (*within*) certain groups of the human species, *Homo sapiens*. It is obviously not a study of the sexual behavior of all cultures and of all races of man. At its best, the present volume can pretend to report behavior which may be typical of no more than a portion, although probably not an inconsiderable portion, of the white females living within the boundaries of the United States. Neither the title of our first volume on the male, nor the title of this volume on the female, should be taken to imply that the authors are unaware of the diversity which exists in patterns of sexual behavior in other parts of the world" (4).

13. See http://www.traditionalvalues.org for their call to boycott Fox Searchlight, along with other antisex, antigay, antiwomen news and initiatives from the religious right.

14. See the Coalition to Protect Research at http://www.cossa.org/cpr/scientificin-tegrity/html for more on the attacks on sex research and efforts to fight back.

15. See Benjamin for a discussion of this concept in psychoanalytic terms.

16. For a discussion of Kinsey's sampling methods, and criticisms that have been raised of his statistics, see Gathorne-Hardy; Ericksen, and Gebhard and Johnson.

17. See Pomeroy et al. for a detailed discussion of Kinsey's interview and coding methods.

18. Kinsey's section on anatomy provided the first detailed analysis of female sexual structure and sexual response and demonstrated that female orgasm was located in the clitoris, not the vagina.

WORKS CITED

Allan, Catherine, and Steve Krahnke (Executive Producers), Barak Goodman, and John Maggio (Producers/Directors). *Kinsey* [TV Film]. United States: Twin Cities Public Television and Ark Media, for American Experience, WGBH, 2005.

Bair, Deirdre. Introduction to *The Second Sex* by Simone de Beauvoir. New York: Vintage Books, 1989, vii–xvii.

Beauvoir, Simone de. *The Second Sex*. trans. Dierdre Blair. 1948; New York: Vintage Books, 1989.

Benjamin, Jessica. *The Bonds of Love*. New York: Pantheon Books, 1988.

Calderone, Mary. Foreword to *Bellybuttons are Navels* by Mark Schoen. Buffalo, NY: Prometheus Books, 1990.

Condon, Bill. *Kinsey: Public and Private*. New York: Newmarket Press, 2004.

Coppola, Francis Ford et al., (Executive producers), Gail Mutrux, and Richard Guay (Producers), Bill Condon (Director). *Kinsey* [Motion Picture]. United States: Fox Searchlight Pictures, 2004.

DiMauro, Diane. Personal communication, 2005.

Ericksen, Julia A. (with Sally A. Steffen). *Kiss and Tell*. Cambridge, MA: Harvard University Press, 1999.

Freeman, Estelle. "Toward Sexual Self-Determination: Female Sexuality in Historical Perspective." Keynote address to conference, *Women's Sexualities: Historical, Interdisciplinary, and International perspectives*, at the Kinsey Institute, Indiana University, Bloomington, IN, 13-15 November 2003.

Gathorne-Hardy, Jonathan. *Kinsey: Sex the Measure of All Things*. Bloomington, IN: Indiana University Press, 1998.

Gebhard, Paul H., and Alan B. Johnson. *The Kinsey Data: Marginal Tabulations of the 1938–1963 Interviews Conducted by the Institute for Sex Research*. Reprint. Bloomington: Indiana University Press, 1998.

Grosz, Elizabeth. "*Sexuality's Future*." Conference paper presented during closing plenary of the conference *Women's Sexualities: Historical, Interdisciplinary, and International Perspectives* at the Kinsey Institute, Indiana University, Bloomington, IN, 13-15 November 2003.

Jones, James H. Alfred C. *Kinsey: A Public/Private Life*. New York: Norton, 1997.

Keiger, Dale. "Political Science." *Johns Hopkins Magazine*, 2004. http://www.jhu.edu/~jhumag/1104web/polysci.html).

Kinsey, Alfred A. "The gall wasp genus Cynips." *A Study in the Origin of the Species*. Bloomingotn: Indiana University Press, 1930.

Kinsey, Alfred A., and M.L. Fernald. *Edible Wild Plants of Eastern North America*. A Gray Herbarium of Harvard University special publication. New York: Idlewild Press, 1943.

Kinsey, Alfred A., Wardell B. Pomeroy, and Clyde E. Martin. *Sexual Behavior in the Human Male*. Philadelphia: W.B. Saunders, 1948.

Kinsey, Alfred A., Wardell B. Pomeroy, Clyde E. Martin, and P. G. Gebhard. *Sexual Behavior in the Human Female*. Philadelphia: W.B. Saunders, 1953.

Loftin, Craig. Personal communication, 2005.

Masters, William H., and Virginia E. Johnson. *Human Sexual Response*. New York: Little Brown, 1966.

Pomeroy, Wardell B., Carol C. Flax, and Connie C. Wheeler. *Taking a Sex History*. New York: The Free Press, 1982.

Schoen, Mark. *Bellybuttons are Navels*. Buffalo, NY: Prometheus Books, 1990.

Thigpen, Jeffrey. *The Protosexual Behavior of African-American Children: An Exploratory Study*. Unpublished doctoral dissertation, The University of Chicago, 2005.

U.S. House of Representatives, Committee on Government Reform—Minority Staff, Special Investigation Division. "The Content of Federally Funded Abstinence-Only Education Programs," report prepared for Rep. Henry A. Waxman. December 2004. http://www.democrats.reform.house.gov.

THE CHICAGO POETRY GROUP: AFRICAN AMERICAN ART AND HIGH MODERNISM AT MIDCENTURY

LUBNA NAJAR

Most popular accounts of African American literature gravitate toward two brilliant explosions: the Harlem Renaissance of the 1920s and the Black Arts movement of the 1960s and 1970s. The decades between these two literary moments are conspicuous largely through their absence from the narrative of twentieth-century African American art. Though individual writers of the intervening years have been canonized, there is little sense of the type of literary community that might have existed among African American artists during the 1950s, for example. Yet it is implausible that such talents as Richard Wright and Gwendolyn Brooks emerged fully formed from the ether. Surely they had literary compatriots and institutions, organs of publication that influenced the subjects and modes of their art. Recent work has begun to shed light on the literary happenings of these lost years, often placing the work of Richard Wright at the center of a "Chicago Renaissance" that developed through the 1940s and 1950s. Such a portrait privileges the novel and Wright's particular project of a "new realism" as the characterizing aesthetic of this latter Renaissance.[1] Equally important to this period, however, were a variety of creative endeavors emanating from Chicago's South Side Community Art Center. Gwendolyn Brooks memorialized one such enterprise, the Chicago Poetry Group, in her autobiography, *Report from Part One*. Brooks fondly recalls the workshop as an early stage in her development as a poet, and thus has it been dutifully invoked in many critical discussions of her work.[2] As a pole of African American literary culture in the forties and fifties, however, the poetry group merits greater attention for what it can reveal about a lesser-known dimension of a little-known period.

The poetry group was more properly a poetry class, and only a drop in the bucket of classes taught at the South Side Community Art Center, most of which involved visual arts of some kind.[3] The center, born of the WPA's Federal Arts Project, matured into (and remains) a meeting place for community members interested in the arts, as well as a studio for up-and-coming black artists. The poetry classes were a natural extension of its focus on self-expression across media, including sculpture and painting. Taught by Inez Cunningham Stark, the Gold Coast art patron who sat on the board of *Poetry* magazine, the class was intended to "cultivate" poetic talent among the South Side's young black artists by training them in modernist aesthetics. Aside from Brooks, the student who arguably went on to make the most of her poetry instruction, participants included Margaret Burroughs, Robert Davis, William Couch, John Carlis, and Margaret Danner Cunningham. Though none of these figures achieved Brooks's level of fame, they all remained active in the arts throughout their lives. In the years immediately following the poetry class, almost all of its students were published, often in local African American publications such as *Negro Story*. Later in the 1950s, the members of the poetry group entered professional life, though not, in most cases, as poets. Margaret Burroughs, originally instrumental in founding the community center itself , went on to found the DuSable Museum of African American History. Though trained in sculpture and painting, she is best known as a printmaker whose work has been exhibited in many American museums. She also published several volumes of poetry over the course of her life (Mullen, 97). John Carlis became a noted painter and sculptor during the 1950s. Robert Davis, though he published only once—an autobiographical sketch in *Negro Story*—went on to a long career as a TV and film actor under the name Davis Roberts. William Couch published poetry regularly, though with little fanfare, in issue after issue of *Negro Story* in 1944 and 1945. He eventually taught college English and, in the 1960s, edited a volume of black playwrights. Taken together, the lifework of even the lesser-known participants in the poetry group represents a remarkably wide-ranging engagement across the artistic spectrum. Evidently, the group that formed in the poetry class, and the community center more generally, eschewed specialization in favor of interdisciplinary experimentation, a perspective one loses when regarding the era primarily as one of prose style.

In determining more precisely what happened in this class, a 1961 Smithsonian interview with John Carlis proves illuminating. Though the interview focuses on Carlis's career as a painter and sculptor, it also makes clear his attunement to developments in other areas of the art world. Gwendolyn Brooks, in particular, seems to have served as a kind of touchstone for his understanding of what it meant to be a black artist during this period. She emerges in his reminiscences of the poetry group:

> During the time I was at the South Side Community Arts Center a woman named Inez Cunningham Stark came and taught a class in poetry. She was a white lady from the North side who was a rather important art patron of the day in Chicago. We became friends—I mean, everyone in her class. Most of the people in her class became good friends. And Gwendolyn Brooks was in that class and Inez encouraged Gwendolyn a great deal. And she used to bring records of various poets which was rather new in those days. But she had recordings of Yeats reading and of Vachel Lindsay and Langston Hughes and various people. Langston Hughes visited the class. Peter de Vries who now writes for the *New Yorker* so often and is a wonderful novelist was a great friend of Inez's and he took the class on several occasions. And the girl he eventually married [Katinka Loeser] was a friend of Inez's and she took the class when Inez went to Europe or California or somewhere or other. (Carlis, 13)

Frustratingly, Henri Grant, Carlis's interlocutor, changes the subject directly after this fascinating recollection, just as Carlis is attempting to remember more about "the people who were connected with" the poetry class. Nevertheless, Carlis's brief comment gives a sense of the cross-fertilization that occurred between members of the group and a certain high literary tradition: the cultural landscape he sketches is expansive. Perhaps even more significant than Stark's tenure as president of the Renaissance Society (1936–40) and the *Poetry* associates she brought before the group is the list of poets Carlis recalls her making them listen to: Yeats, a cornerstone in the modernist pantheon; Hughes, whose reputation as a major voice in American letters was secure by 1941; and Vachel Lindsay. Hailing from Springfield, Illinois, Lindsay was a white popular modernist poet who had published frequently in *Poetry*, and who was deeply concerned with the problem of racial harmony. Black figures appear in some of his poetry, most infamously in

"The Congo (A Study of the Negro Race)," a poem whose representation of race has been controversial since its publication in 1914. W. E. B. Du Bois, among many others, criticized "The Congo"'s racism, suggested by its division into three sections: "Their Basic Savagery," "Their Irrepressible High Spirits," and "The Hope of Their Religion" (Van Wienen). Given Lindsay's problematic record on matters of race, it is fascinating to consider his poetry being "taught" to the poets at the Community Art Center: one wonders what uncomfortable discussions followed after Stark had played a Lindsay recording. But then, this may have been precisely the moment of opportunity for recasting the racism of modernism. Among other things, the relationship between high modernism and the construction of racial identity invalidates any arbitrary division between high poetic art and political poetry. The modernist potential for recording identity, particularly racial identity, resonates to some degree with James Smethurst's observations regarding Brooks's poetry:

> *A Street in Bronzeville* is obsessively concerned with the problems
> of literary representation of the individual African-American
> subject in an "authentic" manner that is also "literary" and of
> the relation of the "folk," "popular," and "high" discourses to
> social hierarchy and social power. (178)

Smethurst's description of Brooks's poetic project reads like the creative impulse behind "The Congo" gone terribly right. Though by identifying the dominant note of Brooks's modernism as "ambivalence," Smethurst saps her work of some of its political power; the fact is that viewed against the existing modernist problematic of primitivism, Brooks's ethic of racial inscription appears downright revolutionary. And yet, it is very much in the tradition of other black poets of the era, especially Langston Hughes, who was clearly an important influence on the Chicago Poetry Group (179).

In order to test whether the thorny interembeddedness of modernism and race influenced others in the group besides Brooks, we need look no further than the example of Margaret Danner Cunningham. Cunningham was a minor poet who continued to write through the Black Arts movement, during which period she achieved her greatest success, publishing a slim volume of poems in 1974. During the 1940s and 1950s, however, she was hard at work, publishing in *Crisis, Opportunity*, and *Negro Story*. She was also the member of the poetry group whose self-conception as a poet was most like Brooks's, as Brooks herself recalls in *Report from Part One*:

> How serious we were, how enchanted with each other and with ourselves! How diligently we learned from and taught each other. I remember long literary-inquisition walks about Woodlawn, for example, with Margaret (Danner) Cunningham, who was "just" Margaret Cunningham in those days and absolutely the member of the group most determined to improve herself. She would exhaustively examine me, to find out just how I achieved this or that effect: "Now how did you do *this*?—how did you get *that* effect?—why did you use *this* word instead of something else?" (67)

Indeed, Cunningham was the only other member of the class to submit poems to *Poetry* magazine, eventually becoming an associate editor there. Even before her contributions, though, *Poetry*'s record of publication bears witness to the modernist preoccupation with race. Not only did the magazine publish Lindsay's poetry but, in 1940, they published "The Defender," by none other than Katinka Loeser. Loeser, of course, took over the South Side poetry class from Stark and eventually became an associate editor of *Poetry* in 1943 and a contributing editor in 1946. As Carlis mentions in his interview, Loeser enjoyed a reasonably successful literary career; her short stories were published in the *New Yorker* and eventually in three book-length collections. Early on, at least, Loeser had an interest in racial identity, which surfaces in "The Defender." The poem takes up race (not least in its titular reference to the African American weekly), though more obliquely and less problematically than "The Congo," as the first two stanzas illustrate:

He shall be nameless.
Who can give to him
The strict and tender appellation due
To one whose birth provides an ample text,
Where precedent is garment for the new.

He shall go uncompanioned.
Where is friend
To risk the narrow hazards of this place,
Repudiate the standard color chart
Whether of reputation or of race.

Loeser's poem dramatizes the complications of forming an identity in which race and its attendant history of inequality are important parts. The language accomplishes this largely indirectly until the last line of the second stanza. The final line suggests at once the generative power of race (which has provided the oblique occasion for the entire poem), even as it conforms to an aesthetic imperative to discuss racial inequality only in the most abstract terms. Still, Loeser's interest in such matters even before her involvement with the Chicago Poetry Group suggests an ongoing conversation among black and white modernist poets about what race means to poetic expression.

This conversation continues in the poems Cunningham published in *Poetry* in 1952. One, eventually titled "Garnishing the Aviary" (originally "Far from Africa"), uses the extended metaphor of birds' plumage to discuss racial identity.[4] Over the course of four tercets, the poem traces African American distantiation from an original African identity through the metaphor of birds moulting their bright, exotic feathers. The final quatrain instantiates a hybrid African American identity, where colored "feathers,"

though still exotic
Blend in more easily with those on the wings
Of the birds surrounding them; garnishing
The aviary, burnishing this zoo.

The poem's intricate rhyme scheme and complex form bear witness to the lessons learned in Stark's class, while the poem ends on that note of modernist ambivalence to which Smethurst calls attention in Brooks's poetry. "Garnishing" carries positive connotations of African Americans' enhancement of the American population at large, as well as a negative sense of loss of an original African identity, and is thereby a thematically apt word to enjamb the next-to-last line of the poem. "Burnishing" similarly conveys the paradoxical sense of brilliance achieved through abrasion, and in this context, self-abrasion. Margaret Cunningham's work thus lies at the point of contact between a burgeoning African American arts movement and the tradition of literary modernism.

The history and literary production of the Chicago Poetry Group complicate the existing portrait of African American art at midcentury. Viewed through the lens of the poetry group, an overlooked dimension of the literature of the Chicago Renaissance emerges: the legacy of modernism. In particular, the interconnections between *Poetry* magazine and the South Side Community Art Center allowed for cross-fertilization between the famous organ of high modernism and the aspiring poets. Modernism influenced, in tone and form, the literary experiments of the South Side poets, and they, in turn, refashioned the commitments of the tradition in their own image. In fact, the strand of modernism that might be expected to most alienate the members of the group—its reliance on primitivism—became incredibly productive for such poets as Brooks and Margaret Cunningham. The South Side poets made use of modernism's much-vaunted potential for representing the individual consciousness, transforming the racial exotification of high modernism into racial self-expression. This intervention made its mark on *Poetry*, as well—an influence on that organization that has largely been forgotten. Further exploration of this cultural moment will help fill in the blanks of African American literary history and produce a more robust understanding of modernism.

Garnishing the Aviary

Our moulting days are in their twilight stage
These lengthy, dreaded suns of draggling plumes.
These days of moods that swiftly alternate between

The former preen (ludicrous now) and a downcast rage
Or crest-fallen lag, are fading out. The initial bloom;
Exotic, dazzling in its indigo, tangerine
Splendor; this rare, conflicting coat had to be shed.
Our drooping feathers turn all shades. We spew
This unamicable aviary, gag upon the worm, and fling

Our loosening quills. We make a riotous spread
Upon the dust and mire that beds us. We do not shoo
So quickly; but the shades of pinfeathers resulting

From this chaotic push, though still exotic
Blend in more easily with those on the wings
Of the birds surrounding them; garnishing
The aviary, burnishing this zoo.

—Margaret Danner

The Defender

He shall be nameless.
Who can give to him
The strict and tender appellation due
To one whose birth provides an ample text,
Where precedent is garment for the new.

He shall go uncompanioned.
Where is friend
To risk the narrow hazards of this place,
Repudiate the standard color chart
Whether of reputation or of race.

He shall be undeceived,
And being so,
And drenched in understanding, know the life,
Be unconfounded by infinitives,
To see, to breathe, to feel, to live, to die.

He shall be most bereaved.
Of usual
And dear prerogative he shall have none,
The magnitude of triviality,
The ardent apathy of sun to sun.

—Loeser Katinka

LUBNA NAJAR is a graduate student in English at the University of Chicago. She studies twentieth-century American literature.

NOTES

1. The masculinism of Wright's literary project, readily apparent in his master-piece *Native Son*, further particularizes this picture of the Chicago Renaissance in ways that obscure the literary contributions of women.

2. See Robert Bone's "Richard Wright and the Chicago Renaissance," in which Bone reproduces a paragraph description of Inez Cunningham Stark from *Report from Part One*—without quotation marks. Dubious as Bone's citational method may be, it at least testifies to the centrality of Brooks's account to any history of the Chicago Poetry Group.

3. I discovered this by looking through the community center's PR files in the Harsh Collection. Unfortunately, these did not contain internal records of the poetry class, and the community center itself lost its archives some years ago, according to archivist Michael Flug.

4. The University of Chicago's *Poetry* archives reveal that the magazine's editors convinced Cunningham to change the title from the elegant "Far from Africa" to the more unwieldy "Garnishing the Aviary." Questionable aesthetics aside, this is quite a telling revision. There is no concrete racial or political referent in the latter title, and the very abstraction of its metaphor says quite a bit about *Poetry*'s aesthetic and political gestalt in this period. The relationship between modernism-as-institution and the artists of the Chicago Renaissance, though productive, certainly bore the marks of a certain tension and, indeed, disjunction over racial politics.

WORKS CITED

Bone, Robert. "Richard Wright and the Chicago Renaissance." *Callaloo* 28 (Summer 1986): 446-468.

Brooks, Gwendolyn. *Report from Part One*. Detroit: Broadside, 1972.

Carlis, John. Interview. 1968. Smithsonian Archives of American Art. http:// artarchives.si.edu (6 June 2004): 1-29.

Couch, William. "Epitaph." *Negro Story* 1.2 (July/August 1944): 30.

———."To a Soldier." *Negro Story* 1.1 (May/June 1944): 60.

———. "Interment." *Negro Story* 1.6 (May/June 1945): 34.

———. "Love We Made, The." *Negro Story* 1.4 (December/January 1944-45): 22.

———. "O This Love." *Negro Story* 1.3 (October/November 1944): 46.

———. "River Road." *Negro Story* 1.5 (March/April 1945): 40.

Danner, Margaret. *Impressions of African Art Forms*. Detroit: Wayne State University Press, 1968.

———. "Garnishing the Aviary." *Poetry*. 81 (1952): 16.

Davis, Robert A. "This is the Way it Was." *Negro Story* 1.2 (July/August 1944): 55-6.

Hillyer, Robert. *First Principles of Verse*. Boston: The Writer, 1950.

Lane, James W. "Afro-American Art on Both Continents." *Art News* 40 (October 15, 1941): 25.

Locke, Alain. *The Negro in Art*. Washington, DC: Associates in Negro Folk Education, 1940.

Loeser, Katinka. "The Defender." Poetry. 52 (1941): 16–17.

Mullen, Bill V. *Popular Fronts: Chicago and African-American Cultural Politics*, 1935 Chicago: University of Illinois Press, 1999.

Smethurst, James Edward. *The New Red Negro: The Literary Left and African American Poetry*. New York: Oxford University Press, 1999.

Thomison, Dennis. *The Black Artist in America: An Index to Reproductions*. Metuchen: Scarecrow, 1991.

Van Wienen, Mark W. "Vachel Lindsay (1879–1931)," *Modern American Poetry*. University of Illinois at Urbana-Champaign. Accessed 12 May 2004. http://www.english.uiuc.edu/maps/ poets/g_l/lindsay/lindsay.htm

PAULA RABINOWITZ

I started thinking about this course in early 2002 as the Bush administration seemed intent on initiating a war on Iraq. As the March invasion and bombing campaign dragged on into 2003, I found myself searching American history for a precedent. Vietnam didn't seem quite right; its horrors began as a long slow process of assuming France's imperial mantle after its defeat at Diem Bien Phu. Despite efforts by the Bush administration to portray Saddam Hussein as a latter-day Hitler and the U.S. armed forces as liberators who would be greeted with flowers, World War II was clearly not a useful model. I then turned to the Korean War, about which, as a scholar of the 1930s and an activist from the 1960s born in 1951, I knew practically nothing. The more I looked into political, cultural, social, and scientific events surrounding the 1953 cease-fire of the Korean War, the more I found evidence that directions taken then, eight years after the end of the Second World War, were coming to fruition, often in perverse ways, half a century later. I started keeping a running log of "firsts" occurring during 1953; everyone I talked to had something to add: from the inception of the American Society for the Prevention of Cruelty to Animals (ASPCA) to the first publication of *Playboy*; from Frank Lloyd Wright's *Future of Architecture* to Saul Bellows's *Adventures of Augie March* and the American edition of Simone de Beauvoir's *The Second Sex*; from Robert Rauschenberg and John Cage's *Automobile Tire Print* to Fellini's *I Vitelloni* and Yasugiro Ozu's *Tokyo Story*.

It seemed that almost daily, newspapers were reporting on some golden anniversary or another. I decide that I did not want to teach a course on "the 1950s" as a whole, but instead to focus on this crucial year—1953. I'm fond of cutting what Foucault named "a synchronic slice" to allow students to think across disciplinary boundaries and begin to understand how a discursive field—accruing from a variety of influences—develops into a cultural consensus, even one fraught with national, racial, class, and sexual differences and divisions. The year

[*WSQ: Women's Studies Quarterly* 33: 3 & 4 (Fall/Winter 2005)]

stretched into what I found, following Raymond Williams's sense of the "long revolution" toward democratic socialism, to be the "long 1953." It began in November 1952, with the first aboveground test of the H-bomb, cementing the arms race to megadeaths; continued through the December 1952 Great Fog in London with air so black that people could not see to cross the street, leaving about 20,000 people dead from pollution and inaugurating, along with Rachel Carson's books, what we know as ecology; and ended in July 1954 with the CIA-sponsored coup in Guatemala overthrowing Jacobo Arbenz. Widely protested in Latin America (in fact, Frida Kahlo's last public appearance before her 1954 death was at a demonstration against U.S. intervention), the coup was a direct aftermath of July 26, 1953, when Fidel Castro led an unsuccessful armed attack on the Moncada army garrison in Santiago de Cuba, launching the revolutionary struggle to overthrow the Batista regime. It set the tone for U.S. interventions in Latin America that continue today, with efforts to unseat Hugo Chavez in Venezuela. Along the way, we would consider Stalin's death, the Soviet crackdown against a popular uprising in East Berlin, Sir Edmund Hillary's ascent to the summit of Mount Everest, Watson and Crick's elegant model of the structure of DNA, the execution of Julius and Ethel Rosenberg as "atomic spies," Marilyn Monroe's ascent to Hollywood stardom, Joseph McCarthy's hearings, and Dr. Seuss's books. And on and on. Besides, by the time I actually got to schedule the course it was the spring term of 2004, so a course entitled "50 Years After" was, by necessity, fluid.

But the bulk of the course, this being a senior seminar for English majors, would focus on literature and films that first appeared in 1953. As an Americanist, my interest was in how the rise to global hegemony of the United States manifested latent shifts in European avant-garde literature, American popular culture, and African American fiction. These three thematic areas were diverse enough, yet strangely interlinked, to offer some overview of how individual artists and the culture industry responded to social pressures as varied as the new visibility of lesbians, war-ravaged landscapes in Europe and Japan, new media and technologies, the rise of "Big Science," Cold War hysteria over Communism, and the rise of suburbia. Ideally, students would move from the readings and films to world events, large and small, and try to theorize, for instance, what Dr. Seuss's book *Horton Hears a Who* might have to do with McCarthyism, nuclear weapons, and the double helix.

I found students utterly fascinated with the materials and almost completely ignorant about most of them. People got stuck on one idea—say, comparing the anomie and humor of Beckett's *Waiting for Godot* to the despair and tortured language of Paul Celan's poems—only to drop it when they encountered the Rosenbergs' "death house letters" and Ivy Meeropol's documentary, *Heir to an Execution*, after reading *The Crucible*; or discovering Eisenhower's speech at Dartmouth University denouncing censorship while reading *Fahrenheit 451* and finding Ann Petry's novel about an interracial affair, *The Narrows*, listed as indecent by the National Organization for Decency in Literature (NODL).

Anyone who teaches interdisciplinary courses in women's studies or American studies knows that a semester is too short. It is simply not enough time to fully explore how Claire Morgan's (i.e., Patricia Highsmith's) lesbian pulp novel, *The Price of Salt* (considered the first mass-marketed novel sympathetic to lesbians), with its cross-country road trip as the lovers elude discovery by a private eye, was connected to Ida Lupino's homoerotic film noir, *The Hitch-Hiker*. Both reanchored a claustrophobic suburban domesticity displaced onto the geographical and social mobility that traveling the anonymous highway was supposed to unsettle. The automobile provided white middle-class Americans with a confined escape related to what the train—hurtling north and east attended by Pullman porters—afforded black men in *Invisible Man* and *The Outsider*. Nor could we really think through how science fiction—from the two versions of *Godzilla* (Japanese and American) to Ray Bradbury's novella (to the discovery by one student of Bernard Wolfe's nightmarish postnuclear tale of plastic surgery, *Limbo*)—retraced and forecast debates and discoveries within science, from genetics to nuclear fusion. Roland Barthes's *Writing Degree Zero* seemed a perfect elaboration of Maurice Blanchot's trancelike novel, *The One Who Stands Apart from Me*; but could Theodor Adorno, suspicious that all American popular culture presaged a new insidious form of fascism, read the *Los Angeles Times* horoscope column and discern anything about how pulp fiction was opening narrative space to female desire, homosexuality, and interracial intimacy?

When I described my course to Somali novelist Nuruddin Farah, before I got further than noting the date and a few of the juicier items, he nodded enthusiastically: "Yes," he said, "it takes me eight years from each of the traumas generating my books until I complete the novel."

As a novelist witnessing and recording the violent destruction of his nation under successive dictators and civil wars, Farah discerned immediately that eight years marked the necessary period between the end of collective trauma and its assimilation into culture and narrative. It takes some time before language cheapened and mutilated by totalitarian regimes can reassume its salience, its power, its sources of meaning. This is why I began the course with Ingeborg Bachmann's poems. These evocative and amazing lyrics by a woman from a remote corner of the Austrian mountains who wrote a dissertation on Heidegger wrested the German language from Nazism and retrieved an emotive valence that evoked the barren devastation fascism and the war had produced psychically as well as physically. Her poems, and those of Paul Celan, another native German-speaking "outsider," are credited with helping to rehabilitate their mother tongue, his own mother's tongue silenced in Auschwitz.

When I was a girl, my mother used to say that the execution of the Rosenbergs felt to her—a leftist second-generation American atheistic Jew—like the last installment of the Holocaust, an American coda to Europe's catastrophe aimed at those who had been safely ensconced by U.S. borders. Now firmly situated within the twenty-first century, we can begin to reassess the periodization of the twentieth. The year 1953 seems a more logical place to begin thinking about the emergence of a postmodern America than the traditional markers of either 1945 or 1975. It took a while for midcentury modernism, already an afterthought in the United States, to circulate widely enough to enter middle-class living rooms, whether in the form of Donald Pollard's curvy decanter and cordial glasses for Steuben Glass, or of Marilyn Monroe's undulating "Walk" in *Niagara*, or any of the 250 million paperback books flooding the market with fiction and nonfiction, prompting an investigation by the House Select Committee on Current Pornographic Materials in December 1952. Now that it's all back, this time as *style*, it feels utterly now.

For feminists, this period is usually construed as an abysmal retreat from the advances women made in education and employment during the Depression and World War II. However, in Bachmann's stark visions of love in ruins or in Gwendolyn Brooks's prose-poem novel about the aching frustrations felt by a sensitive, dreamy black girl-woman living in Chicago's South Side, glimpses of the "problem that had no name" appeared. Was culture anticipating politics that would break forth a decade later? Or were these stirrings residual responses to the collapse of Western culture—and with it masculinity and femininity—in the wake of millions of corpses strewn across the globe? Interdisciplinary scholarship eschews assigning causality; it is difficult to decide whether art and culture anticipate, reflect, or mediate history and politics. Students are sometimes frustrated by this lack of a clear-cut trajectory; yet when they get hooked on the methods of thinking that refuse to isolate and separate language from economics—or anything from anything else, for that matter—the classroom becomes a heady place. I got hooked like this thirty-five years ago in a seminar on American studies taught by the late Berkeley political theorist Michael Rogin. I wish I could say my class worked the same magic on my students—perhaps it did; their papers' execution did not live up to their initial outlines, much less their largest imaginings. Still, in their energetic searches through archives, attics, and Web sites, each one taught me something: unearthing self-published volumes of poetry devoted to memorializing the Rosenbergs; using optics and color theory to decode *Invisible Man*; retrieving military handbooks and diaries of nuclear testing. With the revival of so much of the detritus from 1953, we discerned how we carry its legacy in the arts and politics, and the curious ways in which desire and trauma are lived out as a working through of repetitions and reminiscences.

50 YEARS AFTER: 1953 IN LITERATURE AND FILM

Using Michel Foucault's construct of the synchronic slice, this course will examine how the "long" year of 1953 (from November 1952, when the first H-bomb was detonated, to July 1954, when the CIA-sponsored coup in Guatemala overthrew the government of Jacobo Arbenz), signaled the emergence of a new world order in politics that found expression in the arts. In Western Europe, artists and intellectuals began a retrospective acknowledgment of the horrors of the Holocaust; in Eastern Europe, with Stalin's death, rumblings of dissent within Communist countries became manifest. In Japan, monster movies focused on the aftermath of the atomic bombings of Hiroshima and Nagasaki. In the United States, lesbian pulp competed with *Ozzie and Harriet*; black writers anticipated *Brown v. Board of Education*; leftist playwrights took on McCarthyism, and Elvis, and bebop, and abstract expressionism, and film noir, and more. We'll be examining a small slice of work from that long—and

long-shadowing—year, looking for parallels to and divergences from
our own long post-9/11 era.

REQUIRED READINGS
Ingeborg Bachmann, selected poems from *Borrowed Time* (handout)
Samuel Beckett, *Waiting for Godot*
Maurice Blanchot, *The One Who Was Standing Apart from Me*
Ray Bradbury, *Fahrenheit 451*
Gwendolyn Brooks, *Maud Martha*
Paul Celan, selected poems (handout)
Ralph Ellison, *Invisible Man*
Graham Greene, *The Quiet American*
Patricia Highsmith (as Claire Morgan), *The Price of Salt*
Arthur Miller, *The Crucible*
Ann Petry, *The Narrows*
Robert Warshow, selected essays from *The Immediate Experience* (handout)
James Watson, *The Double Helix*
Richard Wright, *The Outsider*

OPTIONAL
Theodor Adorno, *The Stars Down to Earth*
Erich Auerbach, *Mimesis*
Roland Barthes, *Writing Degree Zero*

FILMS (subject to change)
Heir to an Execution
Atomic Cafe
Touchez Pas au Grisbi (dir. Jacques Decker, 1953) at Oak Street Cinema,
    1/30–2/5
I Vitelloni (dir. Federico Fellini, 1953) at Oak Street Cinema, 2/13–2/18
Godzilla
The Hitch-Hiker
The Big Heat
Pick-up on South Street
From Here to Eternity
The Seven Samurai
The Front

SCHEDULE
January 20: Introduction: Paranoia 1953: Pulp modernism, Science and the Avant-Garde (and other things)

War's Aftermath I/Europe
January 22: Borrowed Time: Reinventing a German Poetics: READING: Bachmann and Celan (handout)

January 27: Emptied Spaces I: Approaching Ruined Landscapes: READING: Beckett. Visitor: David Bernstein, Theater

January 29–February 3: Emptied Spaces II: Encountering the Other: READING: Blanchot; FILM: *Touchez pas*. Supplemental Suggested Reading: Barthes. Visitor: Thomas Pepper, CSDS

Political Pulp/Amerika
February 5: Permanent Subcommittee on Investigations: READING: Warshow, Hughes, Ethel and Julius Rosenberg, McCarthy [Mary, that is] (handout)

February 10–12: Book Burning: READING: Bradbury; FILM: *The Front*

February 17–19: Cold War Witches: READING: Miller; FILM: *Pick-up on South Street* and *I Vitelloni*

February 24–26: Metaphors of Containment: Exposing Homoerotic Desire: READING: Highsmith; FILM: *The Hitch-Hiker*

February 26: Research seminar with Reference Librarians at S30C Wilson

March 2–4: Aliens Within and Out: READING: Watson; FILM: *Godzilla*

March 9–11: Evil Empires: Part I: Imperialist Wars, Advice, and the Rackets: READING: Greene; FILM: *The Big Heat*. Supplemental Suggested Reading: Adorno; Supplemental Screening: Atomic Café, Heir to an Execution

SPRING BREAK March 15–19

War's Aftermath II/Integration and African-American Civil Rights
March 23–25: The Underground: Becoming Visible: READING: Ellison

March 30–April 1: Speaking of Kitchenette Folks: READING: Brooks

April 1: Tour Givens Collection, Andersen Library

April 6–8: Revenge Plots I: Competition and Communism: READING: Wright

April 13–15: Revenge Plots II: What's Black and White…? READING: Petry. Supplemental Reading: Auerbach

Fifty Years After
April 20–22: Some Conclusions: So What Else Is New? Elvis, Bebop, Abstract Expressionism, DNA, and the Bomb: FILM: either *From Here to Eternity* or *Seven Samurai*

April 27–May 6: Presentations: Your reports

REQUIREMENTS
Full participation in the class.
One presentation on week's reading/viewing.
One 500-word review of reading/film for week of your presentation.
One 20-page typed double-spaced research paper.
One 10-minute presentation of your work for "conference" panels.
Learn something new.
Complete all requisite abstracts, drafts, bibliographies, revisions, etc.
Have fun while you're doing all this. It's the end!

WORKSHOP SCHEDULE
February 5, topic due (50 words)
February 12, annotated bibliography due (20 entries, 10 annotations)
February 19, abstract due (250 words)
March 25, first draft due (20 pages)

April 27– May 6, oral presentations (10 minutes)
May 6, final paper due

In order to receive a grade of "C," you must complete all of the requirements. For information on expectations for grades of "B" or "A," please consult "Information for English Students" on department Web site.

Partial and ever-expanding list of ("long") 1953 events (in no particular order):

Senate Committee on Government Operations' Permanent Subcommittee on Investigations (McCarthy)

Playboy

ASPCA founded

I. F. Stone's Weekly

DNA's double helix discovered

Sir Edmund Hillary climbs Mt. Everest

Joseph Stalin dies

The Korean War ends

The Rosenbergs executed as "atomic spies"

Uprising by citizens of GDR (East Germany)

Frantz Fanon, *Black Skin, White Masks*

James Baldwin, *Go Tell It on the Mountain*

First H-bomb tested (November 1952)

Veteran's Day

CIA-sponsored coup in Iran ousts Mohammad Mosaddeq and installs Reza shah Pahlavi

Salk Polio vaccine

Cuban revolution begins at Moncada

CIA-sponsored coup in Guatemala (July 1954)

London Fog (December 1952)

Brown v. Topeka [Kansas] Board of Education (May 1954)

French defeat at Diem Bien Phu (May 1954)

Eisenhower inaugurated president

House Select Committee on Pornographic Materials (December 1952)

PAULA RABINOWITZ (Ph.D. American Culture, University of Michigan, 1986) is professor of English at the University of Minnesota, where she teaches American studies, critical studies in discourse and society, and women's studies. Her research, teaching and training are in the areas of American materialist feminist cultural studies. A feminist cultural historian, her many books, including *They Must Be Represented: The Politics of Documentary* (Verso, 1994) and *Black&White&Noir: America's Pulp Modernism* (Columbia, 2002), and articles in *NY Arts*, *PAJ*, *Social Text* among others, consider the interlocking roles of cinema, photography, literature and space in the formation of nineteenth- and twentieth-century American social history. She has been the recipient of numerous awards including a Mellon Fellowship, a Rockefeller Residency at Bellagio, Italy, and a Fulbright Professorship in Rome.

WHEN SEX BECAME GENDER: MIRRA KOMAROVSKY'S FEMINISM OF THE 1950s

SHIRA TARRANT

Prof. Mirra Komarovsky, ca. 1940. Credit: Barnard College Archives/courtesy of Dolly Cheser; neg. 9.2

This essay focuses on Mirra Komarovsky's early interest in sex roles—a concept that came to be termed "gender" in the 1970s. Contrasting conventional accounts of a feminist dry spell after World War II, Komarovsky's theories provide evidence of the constrained yet continuing feminist project that endured throughout the 1950s. Komarovsky's theoretical perspectives enable us to understand the continuities connecting the postwar era with the second wave and beyond. These continuities rejuvenate our understanding of feminist theory's long tradition and suggest that our current conceptualization and categorization system of assigning waves to particular eras limits, in certain ways, feminism's emancipatory potential.

[*WSQ: Women's Studies Quarterly* 33: 3 & 4 (Fall/Winter 2005)]

Claiming that feminism died in the 1950s is overstating the case; but neither was this an active feminism like we know it today. The postwar period is instead better understood as a time of constrained feminism, a paradoxical, transitional era that was challenged by the limits of Cold War ideology and functionalist social science methodology. After World War II, the pervasive model of thinking within Western social sciences was a war model, or a weapons model, and social science became a form of social weaponry. Much of the political unrest that emerged in the 1960s was about a struggle to destabilize the military-industrial complex of which social weaponry—via the social sciences—was now a part. But even though the years leading up to the civil turbulence of the 1960s were not a time of widespread organized radical action (feminist or otherwise), feminist thinkers in the margins of the mainstream questioned the academic predominance of conservative ideology and its underlying assumptions.

Throughout the 1950s, domestic ideology and American Cold War concerns about security and containment reinforced each other and infused the rest of the West (May 1988). This blending of ideological perspectives encouraged private solutions to social problems, even though this approach ultimately failed to bring about dramatic change. Instead, postwar reconstruction, pronatalist welfare state policies, and domestic ideology combined to form a transnational climate that discouraged overt political activism. The feminine mystique, combined with the popularity of Freudian psychology, defined and attempted to dismiss critical feminist objections in the 1950s as a sign of neurosis. During "the politically troubled climate of the early 1950s, dissent of any kind required courage" (Rosenberg, 205).

Remarkably, despite the formidable hurdles of various Cold War constraints, feminist theorizing continued throughout the putative dry spell of this era. Elizabeth Wilson argues in her study of postwar British feminism that it would, in fact, seem unlikely "that a powerful social movement and political crusade . . . should suddenly have withered away only to reappear as suddenly, and—as it seemed—as if out of nowhere around 1970" (2). Leila Rupp and Verta Taylor's perspective is that feminism managed to survive the doldrum years mainly because it endured as an elite-sustained, academic enterprise. Most feminist-minded thinkers of the 1950s agreed that discrimination against women was based on crude ideas of masculine superiority—ideas that would have to be eliminated. The challenging question, and one that remained unresolved, was precisely what women's role *should* be. In looking at Mirra Komarovsky's work on sex roles, our attention is directed toward an emerging modern feminist perspective in the West that focused, in particular ways, on the social construction of womanhood.

Born in Russia in 1905 or 1906 (sources differ), Mirra Komarovsky moved to the United States in 1922 and became a pioneering scholar in the field of sociology.[1] Komarovsky's five decades of published research range from comprehensive studies on unemployed men and their families (1940) to the dilemmas of masculinity (1976) to women in college (1985). Her detailed analysis of stable working-class families in *Blue Collar Marriage* (1964) remains one of sociology's forty best-selling books. The 1953 publication of Komarovsky's *Women in the Modern World* coincided with the English translation of Simone de Beauvoir's *The Second Sex* in 1953, and predated by ten years Betty Friedan's *The Feminine Mystique* (considered by some as the kick off to the second wave) Uniting Komarovsky's work is her thematic focus on three central scientific objectives: "(1) revealing the functional significance of sex roles, (2) locating cultural contradictions, and (3) assessing possibilities for change" (Komarovsky, "Functional Analysis of Sex Roles," 509). It was her choice of gender as a central subject matter and her consistent challenge to claims made about the biological roots of women's nature that enable us to understand Komarovsky's research as specifically feminist.

KOMAROVSKY'S TWIST ON FUNCTIONALIST METHODOLOGY

Mirra Komarovsky was one of the earliest social scientists to use the term "sex roles." In a paper titled "Functional Analysis of Sex Roles" that Komarovsky read before the 1949 annual meeting of the American Sociological Society, she explained why sex roles presented so much social and mental conflict. The sociological approach Komarovsky used in answering this core question relied on deliberately and systematically placing sex roles in their structural context, an approach that Komarovsky explained was readily identifiable in the field as "functional analysis" (509). However, even if structural-functionalist methodology influenced Komarovsky's social science, she diverged from her more traditional academic colleagues in one extremely important way: she focused on change rather than on order.

Komarovsky took the traditional project of functionalism and subtly, if not brilliantly, shifted the emphasis of functionalism from "looking at societies as organic systems to understand how they achieved equilibrium" (Rosenberg, 196) to spotlight instead how conventional expectations "created deep contradictions, especially in gender relations, which, in turn, had negative effects on society" (194). Contrasting Talcott Parsons's widely influential model interpreting sex-based family divisions as instrumental functions for micro- and macrolevels of society, Komarovsky described existing conditions, suggested reasons for these conditions, and—most important—provided ideas for change. Her goal was to anticipate the needs of life and to suggest plans to educate women accordingly.

Many of Komarovsky's explanations for social dissent focused on the problems of time lag and changing norms concerning sex roles. Simply put, Komarovsky identified how behavior, sociopolitical conditions, and opinion or belief systems trailed behind changing sex-role conditions. Attention to this malfunctioning aspect of the social system enabled Komarovsky to describe not only the women who were subjected to it, but also the men who stood to benefit from such regressive social arrangements. Komarovsky recognized that gender conflict resulted not only from impersonal "system malfunctioning" but was created by interpersonal power or politics. Perhaps, though, because of her mentorship by traditional academic scholars like William Ogburn and Paul Lazarsfeld, combined with her own tendencies toward emotional understatement, Komarovsky preferred the language of malfunctioning and slippage in describing gender conflict rather than terms such as "oppression" or "patriarchy."

For Komarovsky, functionalist methodology was a tool that provided the structure for her research on women—itself a bold move in a time when research about women could herald a professional death knell for academics. Komarovsky's empirical and theoretical work stressed the significance of role theory while at the same time "incorporating the criticisms made of it, namely neglect of individuality and of social change" (Reinharz, 386). It is therefore clear that even if Komarovsky's postwar research stopped short of envisioning revolutionary sociopolitical change, Komarovsky was willing to ask far more questions about women and sex-role ideology than traditional Parsonian structural-functionalism ever did.

As a result of women's changing social and political situation, rigid sex-role expectations relaxed to a small degree during the postwar years. More easily now than ever before, women could wear pants, play sports, and earn wages. In fact, a central paradox of the postwar years was the coexistence of both rigid and less-rigid patterns of sex-specific behavior (Komarovsky, "Functional Analysis"; Breines, 1986). The problem was that new social goals emerged without parallel developments in the social machinery that might enable women to actually attain these goals. Sex-role norms persisted that were no longer functionally appropriate to the social situations to which they applied (Komarovsky, "Functional Analysis"). In this postwar context of changing social climates, the meanings of being female were breaking down. However, these newer concepts of womanhood conflicted with preexisting and long-sustained ideological predilections and sex-role expectations. Anticipating subsequent arguments about the double-bind of oppression (e.g., Frye), Komarovsky observed in the 1950s that women exhibiting aggressive or assertive behavior in cultur ally sanctioned "female" enclaves such as the PTA or neighborhood groups were exonerated, while these same traits displayed by women in the professions or academic endeavors were frequently denounced.

In the late 1940s and early 1950s, when women were completing their university studies in increasing numbers, Mills College President Lynn White boldly accused women's colleges of educating women as if they were "men in disguise." Komarovsky wrote *Women in the Modern World* in part as a response to White's specific accusation, as well as to ward off other conservative arguments that more broadly exemplified what Komarovsky termed neo-antifeminism (*Women in the Modern World*, 318).

Among the ideas influencing Komarovsky's work on sex-role socialization and women's education were Margaret Mead's theories on sex difference and cultural expectations. Komarovsky explicitly identified Mead's *Sex and Temperament* (1935) and *Male and Female* (1949) as having laid the foundation for utilizing a blended or dialectical approach in accounting for the ways in which biology and environmental forces contribute to the production of culture. Komarovsky regarded Mead as a primary model for her own choice in taking what she perceived to be the intellectual middle road; that is to say, neither antifeminist nor anti-maternal.[2] Antifeminists such as Ferdinand Lundberg and Marynia Farnham (1947) exemplified the era's conservative argument that women's "natural" disposition was maternal. Feminists were commonly denounced for being man-hating extremists. There was thus limited support or precedence for those who, like Komarovsky, promoted a pro-woman agenda while rejecting the perceived militancy character-izing feminism.

Although Komarovsky refused to label herself a feminist during the postwar era, she dedicated her life's work to feminist activism through her writing. Between 1945 and 1965 Komarovsky published popular articles on women's issues including features in *Harper's* and the *New York Times*. She presented academic lectures on the problems women faced and participated in Eleanor Roosevelt's televised program, *Prospects of Mankind*. In so doing, Komarovsky provided a connecting link between her predecessors who brought women's issues to public attention and those who followed.

In 1953 Komarovsky's interest in the issues of womanhood and education led to her publication of *Women in the Modern World: Their Education and Their Dilemmas*, a book that Komarovsky herself described as "polemical" ("Women Then and Now," 9). Komarovsky argued that paradoxical representations of womanhood were not rooted in women's biological traits or in collective psychological maladjustment, but, rather, in the conflict resulting from the increasing overlap between masculine and feminine spheres. Instead of focusing on the individual woman and her personal shortcomings, the primary task for Komarovsky was to explore the *social roots* of gender problems and maladjustment. She determined that women's economic, legal, psycho-logical, and political positions were not derived from biological fact but were largely the result of social fiction. By making this argument, Komarovsky produced "the first popular critique of Freud's 'Anatomy is (her) Destiny'" premise (9).

WOMEN'S EDUCATION AS A TOOL FOR SOCIAL CHANGE

Komarovsky attempted to achieve two goals in writing *Women and the Modern World*. First, she sought to describe middle-class, college-educat-ed women and the inconsistent social expectations imposed on them; and second, she aimed to explore specific plans for women's education that might eradicate the dilemma between the educated mind and the limitations of a housebound life. The underlying impetus for Komarovsky's research on educational policies was her belief that conflicting gender expectations and socially constructed meanings of womanhood severely hampered women's progress, opportunities, and well-being. Komarovsky was curious to discover the causes in contemporary society that were leading to such "widespread uneasiness in women and tensions in the relations between the sexes" (viii–ix). Komarovsky believed that studying women's schooling was important because the turmoil over educational policy was merely "a reflection of the larger confusion and the contradictions in the status of women" (47). The question of how best to educate young women was difficult, she suggested, because the status of women in society was fraught with conflict.

On the one extreme, feminists glorified masculine values without valuing women's own unique talents. On the other extreme, antifeminists associated publicly active women with neurosis. But women's aggressive, competitive, or outward-directed activity was not the culprit, per se. "Activity," argued Komarovsky, "becomes suspect *only when* it is found in spheres which a given society considers the domain of men" (41).[3]

Society adds to the confusion over sex roles by confronting girls with powerful challenges and strong pressure to excel in certain circumscribed lines of endeavor. Then, quite suddenly, traits that are defined as "assets" in one role become "liabilities" in the other. Again identifying the double-bind of oppression, Komarovsky notes that we train a girl to become the leaven of their families and the pillars of their communities while simultaneously defining the capacity for decisive action and executive ability as "unfeminine traits," thereby generating widespread confusion and conflict from these contradictory pressures and psychological somersaults (66).

Modern womanhood became a "social problem," explained Komarovsky, when, beginning in the early nineteenth century, technological and social changes disturbed an old equilibrium between the sexes without replacing it with another. Since the economic and social conditions of the past no longer existed, then neither should the sharp demarcation between masculine and feminine spheres. Hence, the notion of male superiority no longer made sense. Society, Komarovsky argued, must allow a woman to explore the wide range of life choices that might best suit her, and neither the professional woman nor the homemaker ought to be denigrated. Educating women in exclusively "male" courses (e.g., physics, medicine, microbiology) could not possibly prepare them for their social roles as wives and mothers. Yet if forcing women to imitate men violates their nature, then "women's nature" would also be violated by being pressed into a strictly female curriculum of nutrition, food preparation, and courses in child crafts such as those proposed by conservative antifeminists. Komarovsky understood that imposing domestic limitations on women's potential contributed to what she termed "the poignant signs of discontent" (52)—an insight she brought to the table a decade before Betty Friedan described the "feminine mystique."

Conservative educational reformers in the 1950s demanded a specifically "womanly" curriculum—one that encouraged the pursuit of family values, human relations, creative arts, and aesthetic appreciation. The argument put forth was that women educated in these "naturally feminine" areas could best heal the nation and bring out its most civilized qualities. Komarovsky agreed that the basic concepts of these courses were, in general, sound. The ability to choose sensibly between the purchase of two toasters, to prepare a well-marinated shish kabob, or to parent children is, of course, important, she wrote. "But life presents choices on a different plane, too, such as choices between political allegiances, economic and non-economic values, [and] competing cultural interests" (260). Critical insights gleaned from the social sciences and the liberal arts encourage a change in the student toward a more complex mode of thinking. The ability to discern and decide things for oneself is necessary for good citizenship and is a skill that, therefore, ought to be properly taught to *all* people, she stated.

Although some critics of women's higher education might suggest "that we leave 'the lofty and abstract structures of ideas' to men because they 'seem to arouse an architectonic enthusiasm in women less often than in men,'" Komarovsky wrote, these structures of ideas are more properly the domain of both men and women. Reserving theory for a handful of "born scholars" lowers the cultural level of the whole community, and proposing that women could simply be removed from education in masculine fields would be deeply repugnant to democratic values (265). Couching her argument in terms acceptable in the 1950s, Komarovsky proposed that a strictly "feminine" curriculum for women's education ran counter to the purpose of educating for citizenship, and to the principles of democratic theory.[4]

Flipping the conservative biological argument for separate spheres on its head and exposing its flaws, Komarovsky reasoned that if biology is destiny and men are destined for greater authority, then why not inaugurate "female" courses in men's colleges "on the theory that the prestige of the dominant sex should launch the needed changes more effectively!" (268). The gender problem was not a matter of women's natural inferiority to men, but a problem of conflicting, rigid, and socially constructed sex-role expectations. Given that framework, why not simply relieve men of the need to assert superiority over women in intellectual aptitudes and thereby alleviate the conflict, Komarovsky suggested.

Unless the educational process and, by association, society at large recognized and encouraged equally women's competence in the home and the professions, women's role as citizens could only be hampered. "The main emotional block to citizenship," Komarovsky wrote, "is not ignorance of democratic values . . . but the feeling that even one's supreme effort on behalf of the good society won't make a difference" or will not be valued (281). Postwar conservatives who argued that women's education ought to be geared toward the nurturing domestic arts—to the exclusion of broader training—"with one hand give to women the mission of redeeming a conflict-torn society, and with the other, take away the means necessary to carry [this] out" (268).

In one notably clear-minded article published by the *American Political Science Review* in 1948, Robert A. Walker, like Komarovsky, argued that "liberal education needs to be a required, not an optional, part of every college student's program. The colleges have, above all other institutions in our society, the responsibility for insuring that our future professional, business, and political leaders are liberally educated men and women, with the moral and intellectual qualities which that involves" (78). Still, it was a minority of academics who explicitly acknowledged the intellectual need and the democratic right of women to have access to unbiased liberal education. Breaking down the barriers of what it meant to be male and female in the community, the professions, education, and the home was, to Komarovsky, the first step in remedying the gender-role problem and could only make for better citizens overall. Komarovsky challenged existing ideology by stating that since it was difficult to know for sure how much men's and women's roles converge or diverge, it was important to establish new gender roles that matched the changing times, and it was necessary for education to both reflect and teach along these lines.

Komarovsky exposed how society makes formidable attempts to develop certain potentials in women while at the same time accepting outmoded traditions that partially defeat this purpose. She cautioned, however, that identifying the social roots of personal maladjustment must not be mistaken for absolving the individual for taking responsibility for her own life. Although Komarovsky thought traditional feminists erred in disparaging the homemaker, she condemned the unreflective housewife for risking "a self-abased subjection to tyranny and a deterioration of personality." However, finding creative solutions for these bewildering situations required an understanding of how these dilemmas came about. Recognizing the social odds one faced in aspiring to an Aristotelian good life put one "in a better position to define his [sic] dilemmas and to search for constructive remedies" (*Women in the Modern World*, ix). Armed with knowledge and understanding, some might even be inspired to improve society for future generations, Komarovsky added.

Komarovsky's theories on the topic of sex equality were, in many ways, finely tuned. She wrote at length about the inherent ethical contradictions in striving for new gender ideals during a time of social uncertainty and change. Komarovsky held both men and women accountable for their tendency to want a double dose of privileges while avoiding new responsibilities and leaving the added obligations to the other sex. Gender equality demands that as new opportunities present themselves, privilege and responsibility must change in equitable ways. In short, if women demand the right to drink at the bar with one foot planted on the brass rail they must also be willing to say, "The next round is on me." A husband who accepts his working wife's financial contribution must be prepared to accept her absence from the kitchen.

Nearly forty years after writing *Women in the Modern World*, in an article titled "The Concept of Social Role Revisited," Komarovsky wrote that "since gender stratification still characterizes our society, one would expect that in its slow restructuring, men, more frequently than women, would continue to be in a position to enjoy the double benefits" (304). Komarovsky thought this double-dipping was an ethical issue; one that was compounded by self-interest and resulted in men reaching out "for a double set of privileges, leaving the opposite sex the double dose of obligations" (304). Nothing we can do will resolve the ethical contradictions overnight, wrote Komarovsky, but clarifying public opinion "can help us recognize their existence and new social patterns can gradually redress the imbalance" in distribution of duties and rights for each sex (*Women in the Modern World*, 91).

Komarovsky apprehended the subtle shift in sex roles—and how we conceptualize gender—that was taking place throughout the 1950s and acknowledged that while husbands of wage-earning wives were beginning to share in domestic duties, wives were also learning to accept the new responsibilities that complemented their newly won opportunities (*Women in the Modern World*, 91–92). Still, in spite of her farsighted observations about changing gender roles, Komarovsky's functionalism caused her to stop short of conceptualizing a staunch, progressive, and transformative vision of parenting and household labor. Her thesis that eliminating sex bias from education would best serve both men *and* women contained one peculiar caveat: while woman might become many things, she would always remain wife and mother. Thus, argued Komarovsky, "women must be prepared to follow a pattern of economic and domestic activities which will, in general, differ from the masculine sphere . . . [We must] rear women so that they will be capable of mate love and mother love" (298).

We must therefore conclude that while Komarovsky expanded the boundaries of gender potential by openly writing about women's increasing educational and work experience, she was not willing to advocate a total overhaul of the private aspects of patriarchal authority, and she did little to resolve either the practical or theoretical tensions between women's heightened status and opportunity and the basic demands placed on women in their roles as wives and mothers. The limited conceptual approach of identifying prevailing sex-role ideologies did not provide adequate tools for revising or displacing the underlying assumption that womanhood equaled motherhood. Komarovsky's successors criticized her for relying on the concept of social roles, an approach they argued was an inadequate explanation for the subjugation of women. They also objected to Parsonian sociology because of its emphasis on the functional differentiation of instrumental (male) and expressive (female) roles (Komarovsky, "The Concept of Social Role Revisited," 303). Betty Friedan was one such outspoken critic.

BRIDGING THE FEMINIST ERAS: FROM KOMAROVSKY TO FRIEDAN

On the cusp of the second wave, Betty Friedan wrote in *The Feminine Mystique* that despite Komarovsky's brilliant social analysis of "how girls learn to play the role of women," Komarovsky was unable to escape the rigid framework imposed by functionalism and Freud. This suggested to Friedan that Komarovsky's theories were overshadowed by a tendency to explain, accommodate, or even promote the status quo. Friedan chided Komarovsky for what she felt was advocating women's adjustment to an imperfect society at any cost. In Friedan's analysis of Komarovsky's contribution to women's cause, she concluded that although functionalists such as Komarovsky "did not wholly accept the Freudian argument that 'anatomy is destiny,' they accepted whole-heartedly an equally restrictive definition of woman: woman is what society says she is" (135).

Nearly thirty years after *The Feminine Mystique* was published, Komarovsky responded to Friedan's critique, writing that *Women in the Modern World* was not a book intended to summon rage at the injustices women faced. That said, Komarovsky felt that some readers—Friedan among them—failed to appreciate her frequent sarcasm and outright indignation that was muted by her deliberately "cool" literary style. For example, Friedan explicitly critiques Komarovsky for writing that the best-adjusted college women were probably capable enough, but not so brilliant and ambitious as to get all A grades. In later reflection on Friedan's critique, Komarovsky said that she "assumed that the reader would see this as an indictment of a society that in various ways penalizes a female achiever" ("The Concept of Social Role Revisited," 313).[5]

Friedan, however, overlooked one of Mirra Komarovsky's particularly important contributions to the feminist canon—a concept on which Friedan herself based the whole of her book *The Feminine Mystique* and much of her subsequent fame. Ten years after the publication of *Women in the Modern World*, Friedan popularized the concept of "the problem without a name," which was essentially an adaptation of Komarovsky's phrase "the poignant signs of women's discontent." Cribbing from her academic predecessor in a process Robert K. Merton called "obliteration by incorporation" (Epstein, 4), Friedan made the "woman problem" both a readable and a palatable topic for the masses, and she struck a chord of women's discontent at just the right historical moment. Despite Friedan's criticism of Komarovsky's sociological methods, Friedan owed Komarovsky an enormous (if unacknowledged) intellectual debt.

Explaining what she meant by the phrase "women's poignant signs of discontent," Komarovsky wrote that "not every woman experiences these problems with equal intensity, if at all." Indeed, a social order can function only because the vast majority have somehow adapted themselves to performing the functions expected of them in society. This applies to men and women alike. But in the case of women, if the picture should appear "unduly dark" it is because the purpose of academic inquiry is precisely to portray the disturbed areas of life (*Women in the Modern World*, 52). Komarovsky's keen insight was that society only functions if we "adapt" to our prescribed roles, yet it is this very same adaptation that leads to women's discontent. Betty Friedan focused on this function of adaptation only insofar as it served her purpose in staking a claim for a political argument about women's discontent. Without crediting Komarovsky's theoretical and methodological wisdom, Friedan did not hesitate to critique her for her functionalist research paradigm. Responding to Friedan's methodological objections, Komarovsky pointed out that a functionalist concept of social role as applied to gender emphasized consensus, stability, and continuity. It was precisely this concept of consensus that, in turn, served as a sociological window of insight in determining which problems women faced during the postwar years—and why.

Komarovsky later clarified this point, writing in 1992 that to many of the postwar sociologists interested in then-contemporary women's problems, "the concept of social role, far from being tied to 'consensus, stability, and continuity,' proved to be an important construct [in the 1950s] for locating dissensus, discontinuity, and change." The macrosociological context for Komarovsky's analysis in *Women in the Modern World* was the sluggish pace at which patriarchy was weakening in American society, "and the slow improvement in the status of women in economic, legal, familial, and other social institutions and contexts." Within this framework, piecemeal improvements often failed to resolve existing problems and even generated new ones.

This "lead-lag" pattern meant that interrelated structural and cultural elements were not changing at an equal pace. In her 1950 paper titled "Functional Analysis of Sex Roles," Komarovsky asked a core feminist question: "Why do sex roles today present such an arena of social and mental conflict?" Komarovsky explained that her approach to the question was both sociological and functional and sought "to interpret social and mental conflict and the institutional malfunctioning which constitute the social problem in question" (508).

While it was one thing to quote anecdotal testimony of home life and conflict, it was quite another step for Komarovsky to set forth the conclusions that she did. "My brother is two years younger than I am," stated one female subject of Komarovsky's study:

> When we started going to school my father would always say as he saw us off in the morning, "Now, Buddy, you are the man and you must take good care of your sister." It amused me because it was I who always had to take care of him. (512)

A second student recalled that "when her brother refused to help her with her 'math' on the ground that no one was allowed to help *him*, her mother replied: 'Well, she is a girl, and it isn't as important for her to know 'math' and to learn how to get along without help" (512).

Komarovsky concluded that training girls into generalized dependency made it easier for them to transfer from a sheltered existence to life with a husband, while keeping intact a ready acceptance of a role as wife in a family that "still has many patriarchal features" (1950, 512). But rather than leave the issue at that, Komarovsky pried a bit deeper. If women were raised to develop "infantile" submissiveness and dependency in their family of origin, it was then assumed that this characteristic of female submissiveness would transfer to satisfactory marital relations, with each sex taking the "proper" role. But "woman's lesser emancipation from her family of orientation" was also found to be a factor in marital discord. How, then, might one have it both ways?

Although she gave no conclusive answer to this question, Komarovsky's research allowed her to suggest future agendas for investigating this peculiar double-bind. Komarovsky firmly believed in the benefits of empirical work, and she thought that her attention to theory enhanced this research. Data can be refined, but they are only meaningful when contextualized by theory, she commented. Although Komarovsky would later write that role analysis—like any conceptualization of gender—could not be an all-inclusive tool for understanding the historical dynamics of women's social transition, she maintained that the concept of gender roles had been an intellectually important one for understanding "dysfunctional structural and value patterns that are not inherent in the human condition but are potentially remediable by social reorganization" ("The Concept of the Sex Role Revisited," 304). Notwithstanding her later caution with regard to sex-role theory, Komarovsky believed that her theories of gender as published in *Women in the Modern World*, and the conclusions of her early research, had withstood the test of time.

KOMAROVSKY AND THE SECOND WAVE

Several key points Komarovsky initially made after World War II became central ideas for second-wave feminist theory. What later came to be known as "personal politics" had been earlier identified in the 1950s by Komarovsky in her studies of the malfunctioning aspects of gender roles within the social system. The uniqueness of Komarovsky's perspective was that she recognized that conflict was not only macrosocial and systemic, but it was also a deeply individual matter arising from personal and interpersonal power and politics. The overlapping of women's frustrations and psychological sex differences (despite the differential socialization of males and females) resulted from *social* and not personal problems, "and the increasing difficulty of maintaining a system of values 'for women only'" combined to make matters worse. In 1992 Komarovsky reiterated the observation she had originally made in *Women in the Modern World*: "If men believed for a moment that rearing children was as important and creative as building bridges and writing books, they would demand more of a hand in it too" (312–33).

While Komarovsky's method of social analysis stressed the significance of sex-role theory, it also incorporated criticisms focused on the dynamic stresses between individuality and social change, a concept Talcott Parsons's widely accepted functionalist methodology neglected. Whereas Parsons believed that the family's division of expressive and instrumental functions worked well for the whole society, Komarovsky used an alternative theoretical premise, one that acknowledged conflicts within families as well as within society at large.

As a theorist, Komarovsky recognized the contradictions and conflicts embodied by postwar gender norms, and she identified woman's role in relation to existing sociopolitical structure as a core component contributing to women's oppression, but these elements are not reduced to one essential element. Like Simone de Beauvoir's philosophical arguments in *The Second Sex*, Komarovsky's discussion of sex roles uses the language of gender ideology and identifies the cultural forces that construct it. Komarovsky (1) focuses on sex roles and the need for change, and (2) she identifies how these roles are socially constructed. Thus, this is the moment when sex becomes gender. As such, Komarovsky's is an early and provocative contribution to gender discourse. By conducting her academic scholarship in this manner, Komarovsky contributed to the emancipatory project that radical feminists Ti-Grace Atkinson, Shulamith Firestone, Kate Millett, Valerie Solanas, Juliet Mitchell, et al. would continue in the second wave, and that other feminist theorists would continue in subsequent, more contemporary ventures in the social construction of gender identity (e.g., queer theory, third wave feminism, postmodern feminism).

What comes to the forefront in reading Komarovsky's sociological research are the similarities between her work and the subjects and methods of her successors in the study of gender. It is remarkable that Komarovsky wrote about women at all, since doing so in the 1950s scarcely ensured professional advancement or success in the academic world. But nevertheless she did, and her research in the substantive areas of marriage, family, and gender opened doors and paved the way for others who would later do the same.

Twenty years before the women's liberation movement, Komarovsky's 1946 paper "Cultural Contradictions and Sex Roles" analyzed the "incompatible sex roles" that society imposes upon college women (184). The main thrust of this article was to point out the conflict and discontinuities in women's sex roles and socialization processes. She stated that "playing dumb" was a coping mechanism that some women used to succeed in college without being penalized for this success in their interactions with men. "Playing dumb" was a way to deal with the paradox that intellectual, academic, or professional success could penalize a woman and get in the way of interpersonal and emotional interactions (with men). This was an extraordinary idea for its time, and one that became a central focus in second-wave literature and consciousness-raising.

Komarovsky identified early on that the personal is indeed political. But she also recognized that in contrast to work of the second wave (e.g., *Scum Manifesto, Sexual Politics*, or *The Feminine Mystique*), her writing style did not appeal to women's sense of outrage. In 1982 Komarovsky remarked of her own work:

> I have to record that *Women in the Modern World* did not re-ignite the women's movement the way a decade later, Friedan's *Feminine Mystique* deservedly did. The time was not ripe, but, much more importantly, my book was written in tones of sweet reasonableness; it was friendly to men. It did not, as a revolutionary tract must, summon the reader's rage. (9)

Komarovsky was certainly no radical. But her description of existing sex roles, and the discomfort that would befall those who strayed too far, was exactly that: a description of, not a prescription for, stasis. Komarovsky challenged the "neo-antifeminist cry" that family values, and especially the status of child rearing, had to be reaffirmed (9). Her goal, though, was to turn this argument around from the traditional postwar domestic ideology, coopting the concept of sex roles for a positive agenda, and expanding the terms of debate to include men in order to establish a more transformative methodology and praxis. Komarovsky said of her plans that "we could no longer succeed in convincing women that child rearing was a most valued social task unless men believed it too; unless, that is, our whole society became oriented towards values that cherish strength and compassion, nurturance *and* creativity" (9). Komarovsky anticipated by more than a decade the second-wave argument that parity for women could not be realized as long as traditional role segregation was maintained within the family with no available alternative.

Komarovsky's focus on change and disagreement enabled her to develop a model of the family that contrasted with Parsons's functionalist paradigm. Where Parsons saw instrumental, functional sex roles, Komarovsky recognized conflicts, or what she termed "dissensus." Komarovsky's ability to point out women's dissatisfaction with familial roles predated and anticipated the major issues that the women's movement would make public. Komarovsky's comment that "cultural norms are often functionally unsuited to the social situations to which they apply" sounds an awful lot like Shulamith Firestone's later reference to "sex class" that runs so deep it is invisible. But Firestone, like her contemporaries, was either unaware of or unwilling to cite Komarovsky's research in her writing or to attribute to Komarovsky her early observations about sex roles, society, and conflict.

Generally speaking, social scientific work on the sexes in the 1950s was used to explain the functionality of existing arrangements. On the upside, using a Parsonian functionalism enhanced by incorporating Ogburn's theory of cultural lag enabled Komarovsky to identify areas of gender-role discomfort in the first place. This identification of gender roles as a legitimate focal point of concern moved the discussion about women's rights forward in immeasurable ways and established (unacknowledged) theoretical foundations for subsequent conversations about gender as a social construction. However, Komarovsky's functionalist research paradigm meant that she could never quite confront the problems of gender roles through a political lens concerned with power, conflict, control, or domination. Komarovsky instead remained trapped within a set of gender problematics defined as ethical rather than political dilemmas. Where we might expect Komarovsky's attention to structural and cultural elements of gender roles to propel us from psychological dimensions of personality toward a critique of institutions as conduits and purveyors of masculinist modes of power, this interest was not immediately achieved. Not until the 1960s was the climate right for research that was far more critical of the status quo and much more impatient with existing inequities and discriminations. Komarovsky's work, however, contributed to this transition by modifying the complacent acceptance of a functionalist domestic ideology.

TRANSCENDING FEMINIST DIVISIONS

We have been warned against creating simplified chronologies and categorizations of women's movements. It is misleading, if not incorrect, to hypothesize clear divisions between different women's movements, whether they promote individualism and equal rights or emphasize maternalist, relational, welfare, or social forms of feminism (Bock and Thane, 3).

Since 1968, however, the literature has divided feminist tradition into competing schools. This parsing into different epistemologies and distinct historical waves has invited, if not created, controversy rather than political unity. Although these multiple conceptual approaches are useful, they are also limiting. The division into a first-, second-, and third-wave construct has identified some important historical differences, but it has also led to some significant historical omissions and an understatement of important similarities. Much like the limitations of the hyphenate model of feminism (i.e., Marxist-feminism, liberal-feminism, cultural-feminism), feminist waves owe their existence to a model of comparison, contrast, and even opposition. With these precedents, each new school of feminism gives the distracting appearance of theoretical discontinuity and innovation. This is at odds with the goals and historical realities of feminism's rich heritage. When "new feminist theorists act as if they are isolated people or isolated generations," history is erased. When contemporary feminists "separate themselves from their own rich traditions," this diminished feminist work "erases each feminist generation's ties and continuities" (Deegan, 23).

In this time of so-called third-wave, no-wave, or postfeminism, and with (re)emerging theoretical scuffles often hinging on the notion of a feminist generation gap, exploring feminist thought in the 1950s is instructive. Mirra Komarovsky's contributions, made during a time perceived as anti- or nonfeminist, are vital in this regard. Not only are Komarovsky's ideas from the decade of the 1950s explicitly feminist, they sustained, anticipated, and predated debates about gender roles and emancipatory politics in later years. Her theories reappear thematically, if unattributed, throughout the second wave and into current times. Komarovsky's sociological insights into sex roles are concepts that invent the notion of gender and enable us to pose questions about the problematics of masculinity and femininity. We owe her a great deal for asking, "How should we educate our daughters?" (*Women in the Modern World*, vii), even though we have yet to find the answer. Like Komarovsky, we continue to struggle over the problem of women's role in society. Today, as Komarovsky pointed out in 1953, there are those who would incorrectly blame our current predicaments on the "feminist movement for sex equality" (vii). I am optimistic that the problem of gender is not intractable. Although we have achieved some tactical and material successes, what it means to be male or female in our society is not yet resolved in ways that remove the penalties of gender. We are indebted to Mirra Komarovsky for the project she articulated more than half a century ago.

SHIRA TARRANT, Ph.D., is assistant professor of women's studies at Goucher College in Baltimore, where she teaches in the areas of feminist political theory, women and the law, and contemporary feminist issues. Her current research interests focus on the theoretical connections between feminist eras. Her book on post–World War II feminist thought, *When Sex Became Gender,* will be published by Routledge in April 2006. Tarrant is editing a collection of manifestoes highlighting the links between the second and third waves. She received her doctorate in political science from the University of California, Los Angeles.

NOTES

1. Claiming to be "bored with the past and to live for the future," Komarovsky declined to establish any archives and turned down publishers' requests that she write her autobiography. What we do know is that Komarovsky's professional career began at Skidmore College (1928–29), after which she was a research assistant at Yale University (1930–31), then a research associate at Columbia University (1931–33) where she received her Ph.D. in 1940, and subsequently a full professor at Barnard College in 1954. Komarovsky passed away in 1999.

2. Margaret Mead was the teaching assistant for a sociology course Komarovsky took at Barnard during the 1920s (Rosenberg, 192).

3. And, as Ruth Milkman later wrote in her analysis of labor during World War II, what is considered men's domain, or how labor is divided between the sexes, shifts over time. In a 1966 lecture on "Women and Creativity" presented in Japan, Simone de Beauvoir similarly explained that "a boy who wants to be a sculptor or a painter rarely gets much family support . . . but for a woman the situation is even worse; people think she is mad; she is told to do something more lady-like, typing or dress making for instance" (21).

4. Carole Pateman writes that citizenship "has been developed around this inter-pretation of sexual difference" in both theory and practice: "'The citizen' has been constructed as a masculine figure, engaged in activities for which men alone are fitted. 'Women' stand opposed to 'citizens,' and motherhood is the womanly capacity that, above all, symbolizes what citizenship is not. Paradoxi-cally, women have never been excluded from the political order. That is to say that even when women were not citizens, 'women were subject to law, public policies were directed at them, and their lives, not least as mothers, were sub-ject to regulation by government.'" (Pateman, 6)

5. Komarovsky added that, had she written *Women in the Modern World* in the 1990s, it would no doubt have been a more radical feminist text, thus asserting an unequivocally feminist stance regardless of any semantic softening of feminist allegiance found in her earlier writings.

WORKS CITED

Beauvoir, S. de. *The Second Sex*. Trans. H. M. Parshley. 1952; New York: Vintage Books, 1989.

———. "Women and Creativity." 1966. In Toril Moi, ed., *French Feminist Thought*. New York: Basil Blackwell, 1987.

Bock, G., & P. Thane. *Maternity and Gender Policies: Women and the Rise of the European Welfare States, 1880s–1950s*. New York: Routledge, 1991.

Breines, W. "The 1950s: Gender and Some Social Science." *Sociological Inquiry* 56, 69–92, 1986.

Deegan, M. J. *Women in Sociology: A Bio-Bibliographical Sourcebook*. New York: Greenwood Press, 1991.

Epstein, C. F. "Colleagues Remember Mirra Komarovsky." *The American Sociological Association Footnotes* 27:5, (1999): 4.

Firestone, S. *The Dialectic of Sex: The Case for Feminist Revolution*. New York: William Morrow, 1970.

Friedan, B. *The Feminine Mystique*.1963; New York: Dell, 1983.

Frye, M. *The Politics of Reality*. Berkeley: The Crossing Press, 1983.

Komarovsky, M. *The Unemployed Man and His Family*. New York: Dryden Press, 1940.

———. "Cultural Contradictions and Sex Roles." *The American Journal of Sociology* 78, (1946): 184–89.

———. "Functional Analysis of Sex Roles." *American Sociological Review* 15, (1950): 508–16.

———. *Women in the Modern World: Their Education and Their Dilemmas*. Boston: Little, Brown and Company, 1953.

———. *Blue Collar Marriage*. New York: Random House, 1964.

———. *Dilemmas of Masculinity: A Study of College Youth*. New York: Norton, 1976.

———. "Women Then and Now: A Journey of Detachment and Engagement." *Barnard Alumnae* (Winter 1982), 7–11.

———. *Women in College: Shaping New Feminine Identities*. New York: Basic Books, 1985.

———. "The Concept of Social Role Revisited." *Gender & Society* 6, (1992): 301–13.

Lundberg, F., & M. Farnham. *Modern Woman: The Lost Sex*. New York: Harper and Brothers, 1947.

May, E. T. *Homeward Bound: American Families in the Cold War Era*. New York: Basic Books, 1988.

Mead, M. *Sex and Temperament in Three Primitive Societies*. 1935; New York: Morrow Quill, 1963.

———. *Male and Female*. New York: William Morrow & Company, 1949.

Milkman, R. *Gender at Work: The Dynamics of Job Segregation by Sex During World War II*. Urbana: University of Illinois Press, 1987.

Pateman, C. "The Political Incorporation of Women." *UCLA Center for the Study of Women Newsletter* (Winter 1992), 6–7.

Reinharz, S. "Finding a Sociological Voice: The Work of Mirra Komarovsky." *Sociological Inquiry* 59 (1989), 374–95.

Rosenberg, R. *Changing the Subject: How the Women of Columbia Shaped the Way We Think about Sex and Politics*. New York: Columbia University Press, 2004.

Rupp, L., & V. Taylor. *Survival in the Doldrums: The American Women's Rights Movement, 1945 to the 1960s*. Columbus: Ohio State University Press, 1990.

Walker, R. A. "Citizenship Education and the Colleges." *The American Political Science Review* 42 (1948), 74–84.

Wilson, E. *Only Halfway to Paradise, Women in Postwar Britain: 1945–1968*. New York: Tavistock Publications, 1980.

MIRRA KOMAROVSKY: ANOTHER APPRECIATION

NATALIE BOYMEL KAMPEN

Sociology class with Prof. Mirra Komarovsky at center, ca. 1962. Credit: Barnard College Archives

Mirra Komarovsky is one of the important protagonists in Rosalind Rosenberg's new book, *Changing the Subject*, and the author has dedicated the book to her.[1] The Eastern Sociological Association gives an annual Mirra Komarovsky Prize for the best book in the field. And Mirra Komarovsky's books, including *Blue Collar Marriage, Women in the Modern World*, and *Women in College*, remain in print many years after their first publication; four have been reissued in 2004.[2] She is hardly a

[*WSQ: Women's Studies Quarterly* 33: 3 & 4 (Fall/Winter 2005)]

forgotten heroine in need of rescue, but a decade after her death, it seems a good time to think again about how important a figure she was in women's studies as well as in sociology. I also want to think about her in more personal and local terms. A famous scholar in her own time and a pillar of the field of sociology, Mirra Komarovsky was also a pillar of Barnard College and a source of sustenance to a huge circle of colleagues and friends. In my mind's eye, I still see her striding up Broadway in her sensible laced shoes, on her way to teach a class at Barnard, her eightieth birthday a receding memory.

Others have written about Mirra as a scholar, a teacher, and a model, but we have not yet said enough about her contributions to women's studies; that is my goal here, along with adding another voice to the chorus of those who keep her alive in memory. Two main issues deserve note, although other people have spoken about them already. The first is Mirra's position as one of the earliest scholars interested in gender as it related to class and to economic relations in the United States in the twentieth century. From the earliest moments of her work, she was pointing to the interaction of gender and class in the formation of behavior and attitudes on domestic as well as broader sociopolitical levels. For example, in *Blue Collar Marriage*, Mirra looked at such previously unexplored questions as how the subtle differences of status and education between working-class partners in heterosexual marriages affected power relations in the couple. Unlike the majority of early Anglophone feminists, Mirra brought to her scholarship the sense, explicit in much Eastern and Central European class-based politics and academic theory, that gender always exists in a complex relationship with other social variables. This meant that she did more than make gender visible—a big and difficult struggle in itself in the universities of the 1930s, 1940s and 1950s, when gender was either a "bourgeois diversion from the real struggle" (class) or a concern of women, always already devalued minds and topics. She showed that gender could never be understood in isolation, a lesson sometimes neglected by political feminists in the early years of both the first and second waves of the movement, in the United States at least. Whether in *Blue Collar Marriage* or *The Unemployed Man and His Family*, or in her pathbreaking work on gender and education, Mirra insisted that class modulated gender and gender modulated class at every stage in the life cycle of both women and men.[3]

The second crucial contribution of Mirra's work to women's studies, beyond even her ability to reveal the variables that helped to construct social identity, was her interest in the fissures and gaps between social expectations and daily practice. Like Ruth Benedict and Margaret Mead, her colleagues in anthropology, Mirra looked for the places where realities didn't meet. From the start of her work on unemployment and its relation to men's self-image, she demonstrated that rapid social changes revealed not only the "cultural lag" that left expectations in place after they had been damaged or destroyed by economic and social actualities, but that unrealistic expectations had roots that went far deeper than social conservatism. The ideological underpinnings of such expectations continued to be propagated in suprapersonal contexts such as legislation and media. Her studies of education, first in *Women in the Modern World* and then in *Women in College* and *Dilemmas of Masculinity*, contributed further to our comprehension of what Althusser would later call "ideological state apparatuses" as she explored the discrepancies between what men expected of women and what women's and men's lives actually demanded of them. As *Women in the Modern World* (1953) demonstrated, modernity constructed expectations for middle-class women that social realities obstructed. When an educated young woman gave up career aspirations, for example, in order to stay at home to raise children, the personal malaise she experienced became part of an ideology of "the private" that constrained her psychological and social resistance. The way ideologies fostered cultural lag in the context of gender became an implicit element in all of Mirra's work and provided feminists what Althusserian theory could not: the missing variables and their relationality.

Here is a brief but apposite quote from *Women in College*, published twenty years ago, to give the flavor of her serene but probing intelligence:

> For all the wider opportunities to participate in the public spheres and the more egalitarian values now enjoyed by women, female undergraduates face many dilemmas, inconsistencies, and outright contradictions. They are inspired to reach toward new (for women) levels of achievement in a society that fails to provide the means necessary for the realization of these goals. The problem of combining careers and motherhood is an

illustration of such a dilemma. These young women often receive conflicting messages from their parents, who are proud of their daughters' high aspirations even as they keep reminding them about the probable costs of such choices.[4]

I knew a bit about Mirra's thought when I came to Barnard College in 1988 to chair the Department of Women's Studies, but I didn't realize how much of the theoretical frame I used came from Mirra. Mirra was the author of *Blue Collar Marriage*, a book I'd read and adored in college. I don't know how I found the book, especially since I loathed my required sociology course at the University of Pennsylvania and had vowed never to read a sociologist again. Yet the title of this book attracted me, the baby Marxist, to its class concerns. Devoid at that point of any proto-feminist consciousness (it must have been 1961 or 1962 and I hadn't heard of *Women in the Modern World*, already a classic by then), I found in *Blue Collar Marriage* something new to me. First, it was a sociology I could care about; more than statistics or Talcott Parsons–Edward Shils abstractions and impersonal dictates, the book had real people talking about their lives in all their dailiness. Second, it didn't assume that societies were dominated by a desire for equilibrium or that social behavior was normally functional in the sense that it stabilized and maintained social order. It allowed discontinuity and conflict, as the passage I quoted reveals. Third, the book did something I'd never seen in scholarship before. It told me how gender and class came together in my own America rather than in Emma Goldman's. It gave me insight into a world that existed around me but that was either invisible in my academic work or abstracted to such a degree that working-class people became instrumental. Of course, there were rich veins of scholarship that did what Mirra did, but I didn't learn about them in college sociology.

As I think back on it, Mirra's book formed one of the essential building blocks for the dissertation I wrote a decade later on gender and social status among workers in the ancient Roman Empire. Although there were a small number of Italian archaeologists working on Roman art and culture with a Marxist theoretical perspective in the years after World War II, none showed any interest in gender. Their studies of rank, status, and social differentiation failed to notice the specificity of representations of women, nor did they ever compare the ways of representing women and men beyond noting the emphasis on beauty in the depictions of women. To ask sociological questions about how artists made men and women alike as well as different in their images and about why difference and similarity occurred when and where they did had little precedent in the field, or for that matter in most of art history at the time. Studying workers, like studying women, involved cataloging the images, listing the activities, perhaps relating them to the textual citations, and assuming that neither had much psychic or social autonomy. The evidence proved otherwise, but only because I had at my disposal both the Marxists and Mirra to frame and inform my burgeoning feminism. At the time I didn't realize how powerful an influence Mirra's writing had been for me, but as I look back, I realize how once more I have such reason to be grateful to her.

Coming to Barnard in the late 1980s, I felt I had stepped into a world of great distinction, and a lot of that was due to the fact that Mirra Komarovsky had spent her career at Barnard. At the same time, that world possessed certain qualities, political and intellectual, that were important and familiar to me personally, again in large measure because of Mirra. Not only was her background similar in many ways to that of my own mother—they were both from prosperous Jewish families, both educated, and both dispossessed by historical events and shifted to a very different life in America—in addition, and equally worthy of admiration in my eyes, Mirra had refused to stay silent during the McCarthy years when her colleagues were under attack and losing their jobs because they had been Communist Party members or had been too close to such dangerous people. The change from a state university in a rural environment to a liberal arts college in a city was a little bit easier for me in many ways because Mirra was here.

As everyone says, Mirra was a very private person, although as she got older she had less need for reserve and opened up more often. She told me a bit about her growing up, her career, and her successes, but, interestingly, she never mentioned the fact that she hadn't taught graduate courses or sponsored dissertations through the Columbia University Department of Sociology. I learned about it from a reminiscence by Alice Rossi, former president of the American Sociological Association and eminent feminist scholar, who wrote:

> It was difficult for any graduate student in sociology at Columbia to have contact with Mirra Komarovsky. Unlike C. W.

Mills, whose primary academic appointment was in Columbia College, Mirra's appointment was in Barnard College. It seemed to be a taken-for-granted fact of academic life that Mills gave graduate seminars and sponsored doctoral students, but Mirra did not.[5]

I shouldn't have been surprised. As late as the 1980s some Columbia departments had longstanding traditions of restricting graduate teaching to the upper ranks of the faculty, which were populated in the vast majority by men. By the same token, for many years women faculty were not permitted to teach the undergraduate men in Columbia College (Carolyn Heilbrun experienced this particular form of internal discrimination for many years.) And some Barnard departments had, and still have, minimal interaction with their Columbia correlates, and thus the faculty in those departments did little or no graduate teaching. No matter how eminent a researcher or how gifted a teacher (and sometimes regardless of the individual's actual gender), a Barnard faculty member often remained a girl in the world of boys.

That Mirra had so important a position in the United States in the field of sociology and in education as a whole made the discrimination she experienced ludicrous as well as obvious. She seems to have refused both discouragement and embitterment and to have enjoyed thoroughly the rewards that came to her. Her presidency of the American Sociological Association and the ASA's lifetime achievement award gave her real joy. Her publications on women and men in college helped to shape the understanding of post–World War II educators on gender as the era of coeducation and feminist consciousness arrived (late, as usual, to elite enclaves). And the young women who took her classes at Barnard and, like me, read her work, often became scholars of the sort she would have produced, had that been permitted her. Even as a number of feminist sociologists recall having to write dissertations on topics approved by their male thesis advisors, and having feminist topics turned down just as readily as topics about women had earlier been rejected, they also mention Mirra's influence.[6] To have had so major an impact on a field, given the constraints imposed on her by her moment and academic situation (being a Jew and an immigrant also counted against her in her early years), suggests just how powerful a scholar she actually was.[7]

The real delight about Mirra at Barnard, from my own point of view, was her position as first head of women's studies in 1977. What a godmother for a baby—especially one with so many fractious and attentive mothers! Mirra gave women's and gender studies cachet, stability, a sense of academic heft that, even after seven years of organizing, it still needed in order to find institutional support. Mirra made it clear that women's studies was a field built on a grand and solid foundation of engaged scholarship. She gave it seniority from the start.

I came along a decade later, inheriting the operation from Nancy K. Miller, the first tenured member of what had become, by the late 1980s, a department and no longer a program. Not that this development came without struggle. Resources were often hard to come by and every gain involved a battle in those years. Relationships with Columbia continued to be uneasy, but Mirra regularly offered wise counsel, and without it the struggles would surely have ended in a number of significant defeats. The most striking problem in the first years of my being department head involved hiring a scholar for a second tenure line; getting the line had taken several years of work and argument before I arrived at Barnard. We searched for a year and didn't hire. We searched for a second year and, recruiting seriously, I found someone I really, *really* wanted . . . and I ran head-first into a wall. The wall was Columbia University, which played a major role in the final stage of Barnard appointments because it held significant power over who would receive tenure. Our candidates couldn't be asked to take a dead-end position, and that would be the outcome unless they were received with enthusiasm by one or more Columbia departments. At the time there was no women's studies program or department at Columbia, and the existing departmental structure there guaranteed a certain resistance to interdisciplinary candidates. To hire someone who, in the early 1990s, was clearly a women's studies scholar, rather than a trained art historian or a specialist in area studies or some other traditionally recognizable type, was extremely problematic.

In order to protect the privacy of all those involved, I pass from the mess to my ensuing tantrums, and then to Mirra's quiet and glowing apartment on a late afternoon in spring. I sit before her, cup of tea in hand, whining my head off. Finally, she looks into my eyes and says with that lovely Russian accent, "You certainly dislike not getting what you want."

The next year, chastened and saner, I accepted the experienced guidance of my colleagues and hired someone not only wonderful but seen as such by several departments at Columbia. Afsaneh Najmabadi now heads the women's studies program at Harvard, but her years at Barnard brought us the kind of luster that surrounded Mirra, and brought me the kind of understated but always trenchant counsel that Mirra offered. I'll bet there were plenty of others who benefited from Mirra's well-chosen and gently thrown buckets of cold water . . . ego-shrinkage without a drop of cruelty.

Everyone speaks of Mirra's beauty, her dignity, her intelligence. I add my voice to echo all that and to suggest that she continues to live not only in her books and articles and her impact on the fields of sociology and women's studies, but in individual lives. My work on Roman art would be less useful without her, as would my work in women's studies. Barnard and women's education would be poorer, and so too would feminism itself. She showed us how to be engaged intellectuals, how to do research that helped to change the way we understand the world, and how to do it with unfailing generosity.

NATALIE BOYMEL KAMPEN is an art historian specializing in Roman art as well as a longtime teacher of women's studies. She has published *Image and Statues: Working Women in Ostia* (1981), *Sexuality in Ancient Art* (1996), and *What is a Man: Manliness in Late Antique Art* (2000) and she is just completing a book on the depiction of families in Roman art. She teaches women's studies and art history at Barnard College, Columbia University, in New York.

NOTES

1. Rosalind Rosenberg, *Changing the Subject: How the Women of Columbia Shaped the Way We Think about Sex and Politics* (New York: Columbia University Press, 2004).
2. In 2004, four of her books were received as part of the Classics in Gender Studies Series, edited by Michael Kimmel (Walnut Creek, CA: Altanta Press): *Women in College: Shaping New Feminine Identities* (1985); *Dilemmas of Masculinity: A Study of College Youth* (1976); *Women in the Modern World: Their Education and Their Dilemmas* (1953); *The Unemployed Man and His Family: The Effect of Unemployment upon the Status of the Man in Fifty-Nine Families* (1940). Also in print are *Blue Collar Marriage* (1964; New Haven: Yale University Press, 1987) and *Common Frontiers of the Social Sciences* (Westport, CT: Greenwood Press, 1978). *A Women's College as an Agent of Socialization for Women's Roles* is out of print.

3. *The Unemployed Man and His Family*, *Women in College*, *Dilemmas of Masculinity: A Study of College Youth*, and, of course, *Women in the Modern World*.

4. *Women in College*, 4.

5. "Colleagues Remember Mirra Komarovsky," *ASA Footnotes,* May/June 1999, 4.

6. For example, Shulamit Reinharz's recollection, "Colleagues Remember Mirra Komarovsky," 4.

7. Rosenberg, 198. It is worth noting, however, that in her reminiscence of Mirra, Cynthia Fuchs Epstein asserted that Komarovsky's name and citations of her work were rare in the literature on the sociology of gender ("Colleagues Remember Mirra Komarovsky," 4). Yet her contributions to formulating basic principles of feminist sociology predate Simone de Beauvoir's *Second Sex* and Betty Friedan's *Feminine Mystique*.

REVIEW:

OUR KIND, A NOVEL IN STORIES, BY KATE WALBERT.
NEW YORK: SCRIBNER'S, 2004. 195 PAGES.

RACHEL M. BROWNSTEIN

In "Sick Chicks," the sixth of the ten mordant, moving stories that make up *Our Kind*, Kate Walbert's dead-on novel about women at the end of their lives, there's a book-group meeting in a hospice, in the Sunshine Room. Some of the members are "guests" for life in the "state-of-the-art facility"; the others are visiting Judy. "Bring a different perspective." Judy says: "Can you imagine if it were just us sick chicks?" Judy might be making that nice distinction with irony: irony is the mode of choice for these women, required by their circumstances. *Our Kind* is narrated in the present time, in the first-person-plural voice of ten women (including Judy) who "were married in 1953. Divorced in 1976. Most of us excel at racquet sports." Detritus of the 1950s, they are washed up together in old age in their rich Connecticut suburb, "in the same boat," ruefully rifling their memories to identify the beginning of their end. ("The Beginning of the End" is the title of the unforgettable final story). To "us," the still enterprising and finally dry-drunk Canoe and her buddies, Judy's fellow hospice residents are immediately familiar, "like all the women we had ever known, their faces slipping past in the silver-plated coffee urn, in the sugar bowl, the salad fork, the butter tong." Elegant outmoded accoutrements of the well-born, prosperous, proper-tied class: nice things like the women themselves, if cold and hard and (some of them) pointed ones, "not used to unpleasantness."

Viv, who is running the book group, is among the nonresidents; *Mrs. Dalloway* is the assignment of the month. Viv sets up the discussion by explaining it is about "us," that is, "women of a certain age" ("we" Americans don't of course mention class; and Clarissa, who invites the prime minister to her party, is of course English). Too brightly, Viv asks the teacher's standard question, "Did she peg us? How many of you

[*WSQ: Women's Studies Quarterly* 33: 3 & 4 (Fall/Winter 2005)]

identified with Clarissa?" Total silence. Then, "I've always been fond of
the name Clarissa," Barbara says. "You don't hear it anymore." You
know just where Barbara's coming from, and so does everyone else,
poor deflated Viv included: wittily or stupidly, these women cling
desperately to words. ("*Intervention*," half-crazy Esther says, when she's
asked to make one in the first story [called "Intervention"], "is not a
word of which I am particularly fond." In another story, Barbara
remembers that when her ex-husband called to tell her that their
daughter Megan committed suicide in his garage, she had to stop herself
from correcting him: not *hung* but *hanged*.) So Viv battles the depression
and distraction endemic to the Sunshine Room and her own regretful
nostalgic memories of more focused attention to books, when she was a
star student at Smith College; she soldiers on through the fine points of
Mrs. Dalloway. But Betsy Croninger says the phrase "the hour irrevoca-
ble" makes her think of the word *cancer*, then plaintively observes that
she would rather not die. Stalwart, formal Mrs. William Lowell continues to insist that Virginia Woolf's novel is "intentionally confusing":
she prefers a good story, she says, and wants them all to read *Pride and
Prejudice* next. The women agree. But Mrs. Lowell dies before the next
meeting, and the group misses what, "given her own pedigree," she
would have said about Darcy and Elizabeth and their social problems
("there was a First Lady in her background"). And as they think of her,
Mrs. Lowell is suddenly vivid to them, or rather her former self is—"a
spry Mrs. Lowell in pearls and mules, carrying the conversation as she
no doubt once carried the conversation at dinner parties. 'I like a good
story,' she would offer. 'A beginning, a middle, and an end.'"

You gather the beginnings and middles of these women's stories
from painfully sharp shards: Gay Burt terrified in the closet on her
wedding night, group excursions with daughters, a collective recollected pang for the sexy nameless real estate man who is "our" common
"past encounter." As in Clarissa Dalloway's story, fragments of the past
keep welling up. "It is not the materials in isolation that form a garden,
but the fragments in relation," reads the epigraph to Walbert's earlier,
very different, novel in fragments of time, *The Gardens of Kyoto* (2001).
The beauty here is more in the relationship among the fragments than
in the relations among the women—and in the pitch-perfect tone
between heartbreak and heartlessness with which the "we" confront
the collective end of life: "We are not cruel, understand. Nor are we

anything other than who our daughters will become. But we wish it over, this display; we'd like it gone. Because there's nothing to be done, we could tell them; because death comes to all the living; because they think us heartless and we are, somewhat, our hearts worn down by the slow drumming of our blood" (71).

"We think back through our mothers, if we are women," Virginia Woolf wrote memorably. Dedicated to the author's mother, *Our Kind* looks back through the scrim of the present at women who came of age in the fifties. They see themselves, in a metaphor drawn from their lives as fifties girls, as "yellowing pearls on a taut string: valued once but now too fussy. Grit when crushed, we could tell them; we were fakes all along" (173). Would their lives have been different and better if they had been women of another place and time, or if they had profited from what the moralizing women novelists of the eighteenth century called a "proper education"? (Viv, who went to Smith, is exceptional among the women of *Our Kind*: "Most of us had studied to be secretaries or teachers' aides—it was the highest we could reach: girls who substituted, who took dictation from war heroes in gray suits. We enrolled in the colleges that specialized in this instruction, studying from the spiral-bound notebooks that covered what our teachers referred to as the three Gs: Grooming, Grammar, and Grace. Some of us dropped out before Grace . . . " [44].) *Our Kind* is a satire on compliant materialistic snobs in what by common consent was an awful moment for women—on timid, shallow, lazy upper-class girls who feared disapproval and lived to regret the marriage made too early and easily and the fellowship not taken. (Full disclosure: I am not of the social class of the women of *Our Kind*, but I remember a classmate of mine being turned down for a fellowship in the late fifties because she was married and would have children and drop out of graduate school.) While it portrays in devastating detail American women of a particular time and place, it quite as convincingly and even more terrifyingly evokes the way most of our lives come to an end now—for the most part, in the company of women. Resisting and yet yielding to the coercive but exclusionary first-person-plural narrative voice, we take in the collective narrator of Kate Walbert's stories as not our kind at all yet, nevertheless, on the deepest, saddest level, as our kind.

Is it the current repressive regime and the consequent fear of losing the gains of the sixties and seventies that is provoking anxious glances back toward the fifties? Does the new fashion for stay-at-home moms (and perhaps the resurgence of pearls) remind one of how deadly that decade was for middle-class American women? Or do we look back apprehensively to the fifties right now because we have, in these perilous times, a sharpened sense of the brevity and fragility of human life, and therefore of the truth that so much depends on contexts and circumstances, choices and details? Such an apprehension of the world is, of course, traditionally the novelist's. In *The Wife* (2003), Meg Wolitzer, another witty writer of fiction who came of age well after the fifties, also looks back at a woman of that period. Like Viv in *Our Kind*—and like Betty Friedan and Sylvia Plath in real life—Wolitzer's Joan went to Smith College; like poor Viv and all her friends, she got trapped in a conventional marriage. Like Virginia Woolf's Clarissa, who wonders mildly at "this being Mrs. Richard Dalloway," she is aging and looking back, but her strongly and ingeniously plotted story has the beginning, middle, and end that Mrs. William Lowell requires. A WASP from New York's Park Avenue, Joan belongs to something like the social class of Walbert's suburban women, but personally she is more like a woman of today. Even as a college girl she wanted sex and success, respect and recognition, and she is still attractive and energetic at sixty-four. Like Austen and Woolf and most women writers in the great tradition of the novel, Meg Wolitzer invites her reader to "identify" with a single and singular heroine, as Kate Walbert refuses to do. And Joan's story is, in the end, in its wry way inspiriting. Read alongside *Our Kind*, it invites one to reflect on how only the better part of a lifetime ago, false assumptions about what women can and must be and do shaped and warped the selves and self-images of people who might have been very different.

RACHEL M. BROWNSTEIN is the author of *Becoming a Heroine: Reading about Women in Novels* (1982) and *Tragic Muse: Rachel of the Comedié-Française* (1993). She has been teaching English and women's studies at Brooklyn College since the seventies, and, since the eighties, at The Graduate Center, City University of New York.

ARIEL AND AFTER: REVIEW

ARIEL: THE RESTORED EDITION: A FACSIMILE OF PATH'S MANUSCRIPT, REINSTATING HER ORIGINAL SELECTION AND ARRANGEMENT, BY SYLVIA PLATH. WITH A FOREWORD BY FRIEDA HUGHES. NEW YORK, HARPERCOLLINS, 2004. 201 PAGES

HER HUSBAND: HUGHES AND PLATH—A MARRIAGE, BY DIANE MIDDLEBROOK. NEW YORK: VIKING PENGUIN, 2003. 361 PAGES.

ALICIA OSTRIKER

"The blood jet is poetry, / There is no stopping it," wrote Sylvia Plath in one of the many biting poems of *Ariel*, published in the United States in 1966, with its foreword by Robert Lowell and its organization— though we did not know this then—the work of Plath's estranged husband, Ted Hughes. Plath had died a suicide in 1963, at the age of thirty. With the publication of *Ariel* she became, and has remained, a myth; there is no stopping that.

I remember feeling the top of my head coming off, as Emily Dickinson said it should in the presence of poetry, when as a young mother I read *Ariel* while the rest of my family slept. There was the thrillingly idiomatic yet intense language, the incantatory repetitions, the surreal imagery, the slant rhymes, the cackling wit, the pure rage at all that I was supposed to hold holy, including love, marriage, children. "Kindness" was the ironic title of the poem with the blood jet in it, and the poem's opening lines establish its tone of mockery: "Kindness glides about my house. / Dame Kindness, she is so nice." Kindness is helping with a crying child, declaring that sugar can cure everything, offering a cup of tea, and threatening to anesthetize the poet—who responds with her antithetical fluid. I was awed by this, as I was by the poet's suicide. *She did it,* I kept thinking as I read, and I could not have said whether "it" referred to her death or her language.

Was I then being manipulated? Lowell's introduction identifies the poetry with the death: "Her art's immortality is life's disintegration."[1] For years, for decades, this was both the popular view and the view of

[*WSQ: Women's Studies Quarterly* 33: 3 & 4 (Fall/Winter 2005)]

most critics.[2] The arrangement of *Ariel* supported such a reading, as its poems of rage tend to come early in the book, the death-and-rebirth sequence of bee poems comes two-thirds through, and the final poems include its most seductively passive lyrics—"Totem," "Paralytic," "Poppies in July," "Kindness," "Contusion," which ends

> The heart shuts,
> The sea slides back,
> The mirrors are sheeted,

and "Edge," in which "The woman is perfected. / Her dead / Body wears the smile of accomplishment."

But the book I read was quite different from the manuscript entitled *Ariel and Other Poems* that Plath left behind at her death. Plath's manuscript opened with the word "Love" and ended with "spring." Its overall trajectory was one of triumph rather than self-destruction. She had rejected the titles *The Rival, A Birthday Present,* and *Daddy*—all taken from poems ripe with gender-inflected anger—for *Ariel,* with its allusion both to Shakespeare's blithe androgynous spirit in *The Tempest* and to the ecstasy of a wild dawn ride. In his capacity as literary executor as well as widower, Ted Hughes cut twelve of the poems out of that manuscript, added fifteen new ones, and altered the order. Many of Plath's readers and critics for whom an essential piece of the myth had been that Hughes, by his infidelity, killed Plath, had been further incensed to learn that Hughes (by his own statement) burned Plath's last journal and ostensibly lost the next-to-last one. When in 1981 Hughes published Plath's *Collected Poems,* his notes listing the contents of the original manuscript explained that the published version "omitted some of the more personally aggressive poems from 1962." Since several omitted poems, including "The Rabbit Catcher," "The Jailor," and "Purdah," were fairly transparent attacks on Hughes himself, he was once again widely attacked.

Is it possible to make an artistic judgment about the two versions? The restored edition, published to great fanfare and selling nicely despite its hefty price, will allow readers to decide for themselves. A case can be made that Hughes's *Ariel* was not merely self-serving and opportunistic, but esthetically superior to the manuscript. Some of the excluded poems, such as "Magi" and "Barren Woman," are relatively weak. Most of the newly included ones were composed during Plath's final spurt of white-hot writing in the weeks before she died. Had she lived, she might well have included them.[3] What this volume offers is the chance to experience the work as Plath left it. The foreword by Plath's daughter Frieda is informative about the book's history, justly irritated at the death-cult surrounding her mother, and defensive about her father:

> He was well aware of the extreme ferocity with which some of my mother's poems dismembered those close to her—her husband, her mother, her father, and my father's uncle Walter, even neighbors and acquaintances. He wished to give the book a broader perspective . . . He felt that some of the nineteen late poems, written after the manuscript was completed, should be represented. . . . "I simply wanted to make it the best book I could," he told me. (xv–xvi)

The volume also includes facsimiles of four handwritten and six typed drafts of the title poem, showing its development from scrawl to masterpiece, plus a corrected proof sheet in which the poet at the last minute scrupulously changed five exclamation marks to commas and periods. Anyone curious about the creative process of a great artist will find this the most valuable section in the book. On the other hand, including every *Ariel* poem twice—once in print form, once in typescript facsimile—makes the book fatter and thus more expensive, but not twice as interesting.

After all the accusations and counteraccusations, Diane Middlebrook's biography of the Plath-Hughes marriage is deeply refreshing. Savage commentary by supporters on either side frames Plath as the victim of patriarchy in general and of Hughes in particular, or of Hughes as the victim of a harridan in particular and of feminism in general; that the marriage was a disaster is essential to the myth. All's ill that ends ill is the basic view. Middlebrook's perfectly intelligent, yet perfectly original, contrary view is that the marriage was, for most of its duration, "one of the most mutually productive literary marriages of the twentieth century" (xvi). Indeed, she goes further. Where Frieda Hughes simply describes her father as having "a profound respect for my mother's work in spite of being one of the subjects of its fury"(xvii),

Middlebrook argues that Plath's and Hughes's art came into existence through a passionate synergy, and that they continued to create each other beyond the grave. Using the two-and-a-half-ton archive of Hughes's papers made available at Emory University after his death, along with previously published and public works by the two of them and extensive interviews with their friends and acquaintances, she effectively delineates the myth they themselves created—not merely a *folie à deux* (though it was that), but a story like something out of *Wuthering Heights*.

Well before Plath met Hughes, her journals were constructing a literary persona: "Make her a statement of the generation. Which is you" (15). Her aims were to fall passionately in love with someone "huge enough for me" and to become a great writer. Before Hughes met Plath, he was already a wild Yorkshireman, a believer in shamanism, astrology, and fate, and an aficionado of Robert Graves's *The White Goddess*, which claims that the true poet taps the primitive unconscious and needs "experience of a woman in whom the Goddess is to some degree resident" (33) with all her fearsome and erotic power. Plath was that woman. Both of them found violence sexually arousing. At their first meeting, Middlebrook points out, "when he kissed her, when she bit him, they were acting out a scene of primitive impulsiveness" straight from D. H. Lawrence, whom they both admired (5). Plath recorded the event immediately, imagining making "crashing, fighting" love with Hughes, "my black marauder, oh hungry hungry" (20). For his part, Hughes in *Birthday Letters*, the book of poems to Sylvia's ghost that he published shortly before his own death, remembers being knocked down by the panther that sprang from her eyes at their first meeting. Two years into the marriage, Plath enthusiastically records an agreement to fight every Friday and concludes "we had a very good f.ing. Enormously good, perhaps the best yet" (95). Ted and Sylvia both associate eroticism, poetic inspiration, and smell, as in Hughes's famous poem "The Thought-Fox," with its "sudden sharp hot stink of fox." Both want to protect the animal selves in themselves and each other as primal sources of creativity.

Hughes believed that he and Sylvia "shared a mind" that each accessed by telepathy (156). They showed each other all their work, riffing off each other's writing year after year. They worked side by side early on, and after the children were born they shared childcare and housework—Plath always had, according to Hughes, her morning hours free to write. Moreover, anecdote after anecdote makes clear that he tolerated in Plath behavior that others considered inexplicably antisocial or crazy. In a letter to Anne Stevenson, one of Plath's more critical biographers, Hughes defended his wife's jealous fits and insisted that he felt it his task to ride them out with her. Hers was the "mannerless energy" of the fox (103).

Her Husband stresses the "avidity" of the pair, individually and together, for love and sex, for art and fame. What then caused the breakup? Middlebrook ominously quotes Graves observing that the Goddess may reside in a particular woman "for a month, a year, seven years, or even more," but not forever (35). One thinks, eerily, of the lines near the end of Plath's "Daddy":

> The vampire who said he was you
> And drank my blood for a year
> Seven years, if you want to know.

Plath, very early on, had decided, "I shall be one of the few women poets in the world who is fully a rejoicing woman . . . my songs will be of fertility" (26). Middlebrook feels that Hughes never shared his wife's enthusiasm for fertility, and although he became besotted with Frieda, he apparently experienced a classic male resentment of Sylvia's besottedness with their son Nicholas. Sylvia must have become restless at Ted's superior fame, despite having swallowed the "fifties idea that a husband should be stronger than a wife. Her possessiveness rankled; domesticity and 'the strangling quality of our closeness'" (162), as he described it in a letter to Sylvia's mother shortly after her death, presumably chafed his wilder self as well as hers; and when Assia Wevill set her hooks, he bit. Plath's fury, their separation, her burst of writing in the following months, and her suicide in February 1963 during the coldest winter England had experienced in decades is a twice-told tale. His life post-Plath would be one in which no woman commanded his fidelity. Assia killed herself and their four-year-old daughter after he was unfaithful to her. The White Goddess found numerous avatars, while Hughes continued to pursue his animal self.

Middlebrook records some little-known facts. Despite their separation, Hughes did a fair amount of babysitting as well as supplying child-support money, and he was so broke at Sylvia's death that his father had to pay for the funeral. He claims that they considered a reconciliation (Middlebrook doesn't think he would have gone through with this) and told one friend that their relationship had been "almost completely repaired." But he later told other friends "It was either her or me" (208, 213). He did not tell the children their mother had killed herself until years later.

Why did she do it? Did she expect to be rescued? Speculation has plowed this ground thoroughly. Middlebrook is at pains to claim that Plath had been growing artistically and emotionally independent of Hughes before the breakup and that the separation was in fact energizing for her. In an early poem called "To Ariadne, Deserted by Theseus," Plath inscribes the agony of abandonment, but Middlebrook points out that Ariadne after her desertion is swept off by the god Dionysus, who makes her his bride and gives her immortality. She goes on to claim that Plath "cannot imagine a creativity that is not somehow a compensation for desertion" and sees Sylvia as thriving during her final free months— a condition shattered less by the ongoing separation than by her rereading *The Bell Jar*, which came out in January. Did reliving the story of her youthful suicide attempt send her into a downward spiral? Hughes blamed that "accursed book" (210). Another possibility is that the depression medication she was taking had not kicked in yet or that she was allergic to it. Middlebrook lays out the possibilities and concludes, fairly if sadly, "Depression killed Sylvia Plath" (211).

Middlebrook's nonjudgmental stance is a pleasure and a relief. She understands poetry and understands poets, and *poetry* is what this book is about. Many may decide she lets Hughes off too easily, forgives him too much. Others will think she gives him enough rope to hang himself. It seems to me there is a third, rather more subtle, strategy at play here. The whole last section of the book treats Hughes the womanizing married man as a bit pathetic—he is simply *caught* by a string of women as he was caught first by Plath, then by Assia. At the same time we watch Hughes the poet continuing to be fueled in his career by his need to come to terms with Sylvia. We see him editing her writing, communicating with her mother over Aurelia Plath's decision to publish *Letters Home*, reading her voluminous letters and journals, being shocked by what he finds, writing *Birthday Letters* in response, writing a poem he called "The Offers" in which the ghost of Sylvia appears to him three times, finally leaving him with the words "This time, don't fail me." For Middlebrook, this line defines his whole career. It is the voice of Poetry speaking to him. The last poem Hughes published in his lifetime, "The Offers" appeared in *The London Sunday Times* on October 18, 1998, ten days before his death.

The story Ted tells in *Birthday Letters* is that Sylvia was doomed to kill herself, that she was obsessed with her father, that he tried to help her but failed. Of his affair with Assia as the immediate cause of their split he says almost nothing. Middlebrook does not discuss his self-exculpatory stance but persuasively concentrates on his erotic obsession with Plath as the embodiment of Poetry. As for "The Offers," it is not a very good poem—it is far too long and far too lugubrious—but it does demonstrate that at the very end of his life Ted saw himself as still entangled by Sylvia. Sympathetic as she may be to Hughes, even-handed as she appears, I think Middlebrook has given Plath the subtlest sort of revenge. *Her Husband* respectfully reduces Ted to the role of consort.

ALICIA OSTRIKER has published eleven volumes of poetry, most recently *No Heaven*, and has been twice a finalist for a National Book Award. As a critic she is the author of *Writing Like a Woman*, and *Stealing the Language: the Emergence of Women's Poetry in America*. She is professor emerita of Rutgers University and teaches in the New England College M.F.A. Poetry program.

NOTES

1. Sylvia Plath, *Ariel* (New York: Harper & Row, 1966), viii.
2. An early exception was Judith Kroll's *Chapters in a Mythology: The Poetry of Sylvia Plath* (New York: Harper & Row, 1976).
3. Excluded poems were "The Rabbit Catcher," "Thalidomide," "Barren Woman," "A Secret," "The Jailor," "The Detective," "Magi," "The Other," "Stopped Dead," "The Courage of Shutting-Up," "Purdah," "Amnesiac," and "Lesbos" (which was excluded from the British but included in the American edition). Added were "The Swarm" and "Mary's Song" (only in the American edition), "Sheep in Fog," "The Hanging Man," "Little Fugue," "Years," "The Munich Mannequins," "Totem," "Paralytic," "Balloons," "Poppies in July," "Kindness," "Contusion," "Edge," and "Words."

REVIEW:

BEYOND THE GRAY FLANNEL SUIT, BY DAVID CASTRONOVO.
NEW YORK: CONTINUUM INTERNATIONAL PUBLISHING GROUP, 2004. 207 PAGES.

SARAH GLAZER

After reading *Beyond the Gray Flannel Suit,* which trumpets the 1950s as an era of "breakthrough literature," I had one question: Where are the girls?

David Castronovo, a professor of English at Pace University, makes a good case that the best novels of the 1950s rebelled against what they saw as the conformity of middlebrow America. He has chosen "the books that I consider . . . to be in a quarrel with the accepted values of their time and place." By puncturing the values of orderly life and the material aspirations of the postwar middle classes, he argues, the best of the break through novels sought "ecstatic transcendence or dark interiority."

I am willing to accept that most of the books discussed here had a quarrel to make with the status quo—at least for their times. But I'm dubious as to how many achieved ecstatic transcendence—Allen Ginsberg's "Howl" is one example cited—or dark interiority, at least in a way that satisfies this reader. One reason for my dissatisfaction is that their quarrel was a largely male struggle. In most of the novels discussed here, women never reach the status of fully formed characters; they are shadowy figures who exist mainly to satisfy the male sex drive.

Castronovo makes a reasonable argument that the books he has chosen were antiestablishment in a variety of ways: Salinger's *Catcher in the Rye* gives us the adolescent's alienation from grown-up conformity; Jack Kerouac's *On the Road* rejects the settled life for a sensuous odyssey of drinking and one-night stands; Nabokov's *Lolita* casts a satirical eye on American middlebrow culture; Ralph Ellison's *Invisible Man* dramatizes not only racial hypocrisy but also the conflict between the reasoning individual and ideological groups like the Marxist and black power precursors of the 1950s.

[*WSQ: Women's Studies Quarterly* 33: 3 & 4 (Fall/Winter 2005)]

But how do those books come across today? Holden Caulfield's view is that of a romantic adolescent—one who might get sent off for therapy today. Kerouac's journey involves "digging" girls in brief encounters and then dumping them after his male characters have had their fill. Sal, the Kerouac-like protagonist of *On the Road*, settles down for fifteen days of life in a tent with "the cutest little Mexican girl in slacks" and her child in what Castronovo aptly calls a "parodic version of family life." Then he leaves her with the casual adieu, "See you in New York, Terry."

Did he leave Terry pregnant with his child? We'll never know. And Kerouac doesn't seem to care. Compared to Dean Moriarty, a carousing philosopher and memorable personality, "Sweet Laura," another of Sal's romantic interests, is a pale figure, just "one of the babes that pass into the night," Castronovo writes.

Reading this, I was reminded of the poignant story of Kerouac's only daughter, Jan, whom he met only twice and spent most of his life denying was his. When his ex-wife tried to get child support from him, he first denied paternity and then he fled. How does a daughter who was never acknowledged by her father make sense of a man for whom each moment was to be lived for its pleasure alone—never for its consequences? (Not well, judging from Jan Kerouac's autobiographical tale, *Baby Driver*, which recounts her life of drinking, drugging, and prostitution.) And where's the story of the women on the other side of these relationships?

Then there's *Lolita*. On a recent rereading, Nabokov's arch humor struck me as dated and narcissistic. "But let us be prim and civilized," Humbert Humbert opens the paragraph in which he describes how he "tried hard to be good"—not to act on his lust for little girls. That sexual taste comes across as more repellent than humorous to many of my female peers today. But in 1955, when the book first came out, my mother tells me she would have been viewed as a philistine for expressing repulsion over what today would be roundly condemned as pedophilia. Modern readers may side with Vera Nabokov's interpretation of Humbert as "monstrous," but in the 1950s Lionel Trilling was among the prominent critics who viewed the story as a great love affair.

Americans, especially those who considered themselves intellectuals, were bowled over by Nabokov's European Old-World taste and sophistication; they felt humbled by his satire of the United States as kitschy and "culturally debased," in Castronovo's words. For example, Castronovo cites Nabokov's sardonic send-up of a movie Western in which the cowboy hero emerges from a table-throwing fistfight with nothing but a "becoming bruise," the scene ending sappily in an embrace with his frontier bride. But that example made me question the whole put-down of American popular culture as middlebrow vacuity. Today we understand the Western cowboy as our iconic version of the noble Samurai, the basis of the way we like our heroes, and a reflection of our respect for individualism, unhampered by European class rigidities.

In the 1950s, my aunt, who broke career barriers by becoming one of the few women archeologists, forbade her children from watching sitcoms like *Leave it to Beaver*, which relegated women to domestic straitjackets. By contrast, we were allowed to watch Westerns until our eyes gave out. Although she never explained her policy, I now think it was because Westerns like *The Lone Ranger* taught the more profound lesson of the individual's struggle against evil in the face of society's resignation. Think of Gary Cooper single-handedly fighting the bad guy in *High Noon* as the townspeople cower.

Castronovo summarizes how some of the towering intellectuals of the time—Lionel Trilling, Clement Greenberg—taught the American public to look critically at the popular fiction and art of the time and divorced it from high art. Greenberg's devastating critiques classed popular art as "kitsch." Dwight MacDonald's critiques condemned as "middlebrow melodrama" the best-selling *By Love Possessed*, by James Gould Cozzen, a novel about a lawyer who discovers rampant hypocrisy in his town. Today we're less likely to draw such a sharp division between the lowbrow and the highbrow, which seemed so important to these 1950s writers. We understand that the lowbrow culture of TV, for example, reflects who we are, even if it is refracted through lenses different from our own; we seem less afraid of popular culture as an alien force that will swallow our individuality.

The 1950s books discussed here often ignore the intricacies and struggles of family, marriage, and other aspects of domestic life that will make up the lives that most of us will live. Very few of us will continue a Jack Kerouac road adventure past adolescence. Even some of the most subtle books discussed here, such as *Invisible Man*, posit an individual against a social structure, rather than someone embedded in a family or a believable love relationship.

From Oedipus to Freud, our understanding of the struggle to be in the world has been embodied in the struggle between fathers and sons, notes Vivian Gornick in *The End of the Novel of Love*. "It's the ambiguity that belongs to the women," she writes. "Nowhere in literature is there a female equivalent of the protagonist locked in successful struggle either with the father or the mother, for the sake of the world."

Perhaps it's that complexity I miss in these books. Men seem locked in a struggle against society, but society often seems equated with domesticity and family—which in turn are equated with women. In railing against domesticity as the equivalent of deadening conformity, have Kerouac and 1950s giants like Norman Mailer, Philip Roth, and Saul Bellow thrown women in with the dish towel?

Historically, I'd have to say yes. In *In the Hearts of Men*, Barbara Ehrenreich pinpoints these novels of rebellion as part of the cultural progression toward the male flight from domesticity during the 1950s and early 1960s. At the opening of the 1950s, a man's failure to marry and support a family was seen as evidence of psychological immaturity and social maladjustment. But by the end of the decade, it became socially accepted as "healthy" to avoid the trap of financially support-ing a wife and child—a viewpoint helped along by new psychological formulas emphasizing personal fulfillment, *Playboy*'s idealization of bachelorhood, and medical concerns about the deleterious effect of work stress on men's health, she argues.

Male protest novels of the 1950s contributed to the collapse of the breadwinner ethic expected of men by painting women as oppressors and bringing a nascent contempt of women's home labors into the open, according to Ehrenreich. Where Castronovo sees inspiring rebellion, Ehrenreich sees bad news for women. What most Americans got from the Beats was their rejection of the pact on which the family wage rest-ed, she says. Here were men "who refused to undertake the support of women and seemed to get away with it," Ehrenreich observes.

When women of my generation (I was born in 1950) read Bellow's *Herzog*, about a middle-aged professor whose main connection to females involves coupling with pretty young things, we're struck by the lack of fully realized women characters. In many ways, these male writers of the 1950s don't seem to have moved beyond Hemingway's allegorical view of life, which "idealized women as the means of spiritual salvation, then condemned them as agents of subversion," in

Gornick's words. John Updike's and John Cheever's male characters seem to meet Castronovo's standard for subversive individualism mainly by having extramarital affairs.

The best novels of the 1950s, Castronovo argues, charted new stylistic territory. In breaking from the naturalistic blockbusters of the 1950s, they were veering away from Dreiser-style social realism and toward the psychological introspection we associate with Henry James, he suggests. Among the books he says broke out of this mold were Bellow's *Adventures of Augie March*, Flannery O'Connor's *A Good Man is Hard to Find*, Ellison's *Invisible Man*, and Bernard Malamud's *The Magic Barrel*. Those books are so much a part of our collective literary unconscious now that it's hard to recognize how different they were from 1950s bestsellers like *The Man in the Gray Flannel Suit*. (In fact, I would have liked to see a more compelling exposition of the stylistic changes.)

Sloan Wilson's *The Man in the Gray Flannel Suit*, published in 1955, revolves around a suburban husband haunted by the wartime past he has been denying. Tom Rath, the central character, has hidden from his wife the fact that he killed seventeen men in the war and fathered a child by an Italian woman. Once Tom confesses his past to his wife, the book resolves, rather unconvincingly, into a sense of contentment between husband and wife and "collapses into a bundle of clichés about a brighter future and being at peace," Castronovo writes. Nevertheless, Castronovo praises Wilson's ability to chronicle life in the 1950s, including the painful war memories and stalled careers. With all the fifties-bashing that goes on now, it's easy to forget that it followed closely on the heels of World War II's horrors, hardships, and separations; the domestic vale of the 1950s must have been welcomed by many men and by women as well. That rouses my curiosity as to whether there weren't some insightful observers out there at the time who have more to tell us about the postwar mentality of the 1950s and its turn toward domesticity.

Oddly, aside from Flannery O'Connor, one of the only woman writers discussed in any detail in this book is Patricia Highsmith, whose *The Talented Mr. Ripley*, published in 1955, is treated more as a genre novel that helped kick off the "noir" thriller tradition in American writing than a report from the homefront. Comic novelist Dawn Powell, who also gets detailed treatment, is "no Nabokov," Castronovo hastens to tell us.

It isn't until we get to the afterword that we get some hint that we may be missing something. Castronovo tells us he decided not to include Mary McCarthy's autobiography and fiction despite its "wonderful social history." Jean Stafford's "doom-filled novel of adolescence" doesn't make the cut, either. He argues that the works of McCarthy and Stafford were not among those "that gave modernism its second wind after the war."

In both his catalogue and his interpretation, Castronovo seems to be caught in something of a time warp. In recent years, feminists have been rediscovering 1950s novels by women that give us a whole new insight into the homefront—as well as stylistic experimentation. Gwendolyn Brooks's gem of a novel, *Maud Martha*, almost startlingly modernist in style, is a moving look at the interior life of a young black woman entering a bad marriage. Ann Petry's *The Narrows*, a black/white love story set in a New England town, and Grace Metaliovs's *Peyton Place*, about social hypocrisy, are also, in their own ways, about rebelling against social constraints. The stories of Grace Paley, who started out in the 1950s, continue to speak to us.

What do we really know of what women were thinking in the 1950s? *Ozzie and Harriet* is held up by contemporary feminists as the mirror informing us as to what stifled real-life women; we know that by 1963, Betty Friedan discovered that educated suburban wives and mothers were suffering from the problem that "had no name," puzzled by their lack of fulfillment as homemakers. At the same time, movies like *Kinsey* suggest that private life was not as conformist, at least sexually, as some of the common caricatures would have us believe. For those of us wondering how the other sex lived through the fifties, there's a book still waiting to be written.

SARAH GLAZER is a journalist who lives in New York. Her articles on feminism, women, and family have appeared in the *New York Times Book Review*, the *Washington Post*, *Congressional Quarterly* and in the book *Research in Science and Technology Studies: Gender and Work* (edited by Shirley Gorenstein, 2000).

WHAT DID THE WOMEN WANT?: REVIEW

DE KOONING: AN AMERICAN MASTER, BY MARK STEVENS AND ANNALYN SWAN.
NEW YORK: ALFRED A. KNOPF, 2004. 732 PAGES, ILLUSTRATED.

DIANE MIDDLEBROOK

In the 1950s, the loose group of downtown painters who later became
known as "the New York School" began making a little money. They
abandoned the Waldorf Cafeteria, where a nickel cup of coffee could last
for a whole night of shoptalk, and began gathering at a workingman's bar
called the Cedar Tavern. The painters, all men, sometimes brought
women with them. In 1956 the most eye-catching couple was Jackson
Pollock—already the most famous of the New York painters—and his
flamboyant young girlfriend Ruth Kligman. Later that year Pollock
drunkenly crashed his car against a tree and died instantly. But Kligman
was thrown free of the car and, once her injuries healed, she began showing up at the Cedar Tavern again—with Willem de Kooning. *He* was
now the most famous painter in New York. *De Kooning: An American Master* pursues many questions about these artists and their world, and one of
the most interesting is, what did the *women* want?

Willem de Kooning, born into a working-class Dutch family in Rotterdam in 1904, was raised in poverty and squalor. His ferociously
aggressive mother, Cornelia, dominated the home, scolding, screaming,
slapping. "That's the person I feared most in the world," de Kooning
said shortly before she died. His father took the highly unconventional
action of divorcing Cornelia when Willem was two years old, and
Willem grew up shuttling between the parental households, welcome in
neither. He left school at twelve, like most boys of the working class,
but a talent for drawing won him an apprenticeship in an upscale Art
Nouveau decorating firm in Rotterdam, where he learned to build furniture and mix paint, among other skills that later proved useful. His
employers rewarded his talent by paying his tuition for night classes in
Rotterdam's academy for fine and technical arts, where he trained for

six years in the draftsmanship that was to become a notable feature of his style as a painter. At age twenty-two, he stowed away on a ship bound for New York. Soon afterward he had settled in the bohemian artists' community of Greenwich Village, holding a well-paid day job and painting during his spare time. Then, in 1930, de Kooning formed a friendship with the immigrant Russian Arshile Gorky, whose example of total commitment to modernism set de Kooning on a path from which he never veered. In 1935, during the height of the Depression, de Kooning quit his job and bet on his talent; he was thirty-one years old. For the next sixty years, he lived mainly in his studios; he lived for painting.

One of the great strengths of this long, marvelous book is the clarity with which it historicizes de Kooning's changing aims as an artist and explains the technical strategies by which he struggled to accomplish them. But equally impressive is the biographers' shrewd understanding of de Kooning's character, including his resisting relationships to women.

There were two kinds of women in de Kooning's life. First, there were those who never doubted they had legitimate claims on him and whose efforts to press their claims aroused him to cruelty and flight, and when all else failed, to drunken oblivion: Cornelia, his mother; Elaine, his wife; Joan, the mother of his daughter Lisa; and Lisa herself. Then there were the numerous "other" women, whose intimacy with de Kooning lasted only as long as they did not behave as though intimacy gave them any rights at all.

By far the most interesting woman in this story is Elaine, who had a way of talking "as though history would be listening," the biographers tell us. She met de Kooning through a fellow artist when she was twenty, attending art school; de Kooning was thirty-four. A chestnut-haired beauty with the lithe body of an athlete, Elaine was also a talented painter in her own right—her most important commission would be a presidential portrait of JFK in 1962—and she had an utterly compelling gift for expressing herself: in ardent conversation, in physical daring, in having fun. At first sight, de Kooning fell madly in love.

Elaine, too, fell in madly in love, for a while. But for Elaine, the connection to de Kooning was above all a connection to a world she craved and could not enter on her own. When they met, Elaine Fried was commuting from her family home in Brooklyn, immersing herself in the art milieu, attending classes, earning a little money as an artist's model. She was ambitious, competitive, hardworking, and savvy. From the time she left high school, she had seen that she would get nowhere except through some kind of affiliation with an established artist. Someone had told her that de Kooning was "going to be the greatest painter in the country." She later said that the moment she met him she decided to marry him.

Despite the fourteen-year difference in their ages, Elaine quickly made herself a member of the circle around de Kooning, where she easily held her own as a quick-witted participant in the men's conversations. De Kooning became her tutor in European techniques of drawing, skills that buttressed her talent for portraiture. Under the influence of de Kooning's friends Rudy Burckhardt and David Denby, she also acquired a sophisticated grasp of avant garde music and ballet. Eventually she became a respected critic and reviewer of the arts.

De Kooning, for his part, was besotted with Elaine; and the biographers attribute to Elaine's presence a definitive turning toward the female figure in de Kooning's work: "[H]is palette seemed to stir, then awaken . . . Soon a powerful erupting pink would belong to de Kooning the way a certain blue belonged to Matisse." The paradox of de Kooning's sexually passionate attachment to the woman's femininity, and his equally strong responsiveness to her aggressiveness—her witchy glamour—began to emerge in 1940 and remained a distinctive subject in his art for many years. The color pink was a kind of code: shortly after meeting Elaine he surprised her by painting the bedroom in her apartment pink; and before he married her in 1943, he renovated a loft for them to live in, with a freestanding bedroom painted white on the outside and pink within, the pinks he was using in his paintings.

It's clear why Elaine had decided to marry de Kooning: she wanted his name. But it's not at all clear why de Kooning decided to marry Elaine. The biographers, noting that by 1943 de Kooning had made a successful career and a home for himself in New York, suggest that marriage to "a beautiful American who considered him a genius" was the completion of the arc that had ejected de Kooning roughly out of his family home in childhood. But de Kooning was already married—to his work—and it didn't take long for either him or Elaine to discover that another person in the house interfered with the productive rhythms each had developed while living alone.

Moreover, it would have been clear that housewifery was not going to be an aspiration of Elaine de Kooning. She was a partner, and she fully shared the acute discomforts of their hand-to-mouth existence. But during the couple of years they lived together as man and wife, she didn't learn to cook, though she was very good at cadging meals. Nor did she clean the house; it was Bill who knocked off early every Saturday to scrub it down. De Kooning had noticed this; as the biographers put the matter, tactfully, "he had a Dutch workingman's appreciation for the comforts of home"—that is, a home in which the man of the house is master. Shortly before their wedding, de Kooning told one of their friends, "You know, I loved Elaine and if she had married me last year I would have been so happy. But now, I tink [sic] I've been had."

Then, only two years into the marriage, catastrophe struck: the loft de Kooning had rented and rebuilt was sold, and they were evicted. Elaine said later that "devastating poverty seemed the most important thing in our lives together" at the time; since neither had been receiving any pay, they were almost destitute. They had to settle for a cold-water flat in a wretched tenement, where neither had room to work. When an opportunity to acquire another inexpensive studio arose, de Kooning sold a painting that covered the rent, moved in, and began living there. Elaine stayed on in the tenement.

Once de Kooning took possession of the studio that became his home, Elaine leaves center stage in this book; we see her continuing adventures only in tantalizing glimpses. But her ongoing role as Mrs. de Kooning gives the biographers' story of de Kooning's life a firm narrative structure. For one thing, Elaine cleverly designed what might be called the *persona* of the relationship, as they began to harvest advantages that, for each of them, lay in remaining married after they ceased to live together. Elaine always talked about "Bill" as if she had just seen and spoken with him, no matter how much time had passed between visits (it could have been years): the relationship was always present-tense, in her mouth; his name was her claim to status in the world of art. For de Kooning, marriage to Elaine meant that he would never have to marry anyone else; he could live as he pleased, in his studio, where the women would come and go but never get seriously in the way of his work. Nor would there be any question of a commitment to any of them: he could indulge in the refreshing emotional power of infatuation and conversation; when the rapture dissipated, he could ease them out of his life, no harm done.

So the de Koonings stayed married. During the mid-1940s they even continued to share a private life, when it suited them. None of the artists had telephones; when Elaine wanted to see Bill she would stand outside his studio and holler at his window. When she took up reviewing, she began reading philosophy and would sometimes bring her books to de Kooning's studio, to read him select passages—as she knew, de Kooning thrived on ideas; they made him want to paint.

By the late 1940s Elaine had become a well-regarded critic herself: she had an unusual talent for turning her vivid speech into lively prose. She made sure that de Kooning received the benefit of her professional influence. They regularly appeared together in public, at gallery openings and other art events, and together they accepted invitations to spend summers away from New York at the homes of affluent friends from the art world. Her written comments on de Kooning's work show that she thoroughly understood what he was after and how hard it was for him to achieve it—how much gorgeous imagery he sacrificed in his restless effort to "blast away" what had come too easily to his skillful brush. Elaine also greatly admired de Kooning's idiosyncratic talk about art and found a way to get his voice into print, literally; for one public occasion she jotted down his remarks and he edited them into a speech ("A Desperate View") that he could deliver and that could be published afterward. When Elaine undertook simultaneous affairs with two of de Kooning's most powerful admirers (Thomas Hess, her boss, the editor of *ArtNews*; and the influential critic Harold Rosenberg), some of de Kooning's friends gossiped that these were strategic interventions aimed at promoting de Kooning's marketability. But this seems dubious; Elaine never needed a secondary reason to be interested in sex, and splendid talk was her aphrodisiac.

By the early 1950s, de Kooning had finally achieved the success that insiders had been predicting for him. The milestones were the purchase of *Excavation* by the Art Institute of Chicago after its exhibition at the Venice Biennale and his show *Women* at the Sidney Janis gallery in which his radical use of the female figure was received as an advance in the history of painting, referencing precursors from Rubens through Ingres to Picasso.

Meanwhile, his private life took a wholly unexpected turn, when he became a father. The woman who bore de Kooning's only child was Joan Ward, a young commercial artist who began showing up at the

Cedar Tavern in 1951–52 with her twin sister Nancy. Joan was immediately added to de Kooning's pool of girlfriends. In 1953 she became pregnant and had an abortion, like the other women who had been close to de Kooning. (Elaine had numerous abortions and eventually underwent a hysterectomy.) Joan recovered physically but remained depressed long afterward. When she again became pregnant, she told de Kooning she meant to raise the baby, though it would mean giving up a job she loved. De Kooning did not help her much, either before or after Lisa was born in January 1956. Nonetheless he was powerfully attached to his "little angel" and proudly kept her picture tacked to his studio wall.

Joan hoped to lure de Kooning into acting like a family man. She began wearing a wedding ring and calling herself "Mrs. de Kooning." Elaine—who remained very publicly Mrs. De Kooning—turned the situation into a quip: "Bill and I always wanted a child," as though Joan had been commissioned to produce one. Joan tried to trump Elaine by moving with baby Lisa to Martha's Vineyard the summer after Lisa's birth and persuading de Kooning to join them. But de Kooning "fled from his suffocating family at the first opportunity," the biographers note; by the end of the summer, he was back in New York, and painting had once again commandeered his whole attention. Painting and beautiful young women, that is. Discouraged, Joan moved with the baby to California in 1959, found work, and stayed for two years, until de Kooning persuaded her that he could not bear to be separated from Lisa.

Not that he intended to live *with* his daughter. It was not until de Kooning became deeply alcoholic, in the mid-1960s, that he again made himself a part of Joan and Lisa's home life, but this was episodic, mainly for the purposes of drying out after an alcoholic binge. He would convalesce in complete silence, while making "blind" drawings—sketching with his eyes closed or with his eyes focused on the TV set. Strikingly, there was no conversation whatsoever in the family life de Kooning conducted with Lisa and Joan, as Lisa remembered it. Not until Lisa was in her teens, attempting to become an artist herself, did she form a mutually satisfying relationship with her father, and so did her artist friends; but that was in his studio or over the telephone. The account of de Kooning's interest in Lisa's art school peers—it was not a sexual interest—is among the most fascinating in the story of his life.

Success made de Kooning a wealthy man, but it also increased his concern about remaining productive and original as a painter. As a way to soothe the incessant throb of anxiety that painting caused him, de Kooning began drinking heavily in the 1950s. Alcohol also diminished his shyness and made him freer in the after-hours conversations that he loved and needed. Coming down from one or another horrifying binge, during which friends would sometimes see him lying in a gutter, he would frequently check himself into a hospital for detoxification, and he regularly went to a doctor for shots of vitamin B, to diminish harm to his liver. In 1962 he decided to escape the self-destructive patterns of his life in New York and build a studio—his dream house—in Springs, the artists' quarter of Long Island, a short but useful distance from the house where Joan and Lisa lived at the time.

But he did not escape; and it was alcoholism that brought the lives of de Kooning and Elaine together for a final act. Not long after de Kooning's move to Springs, Elaine also bought a house there. Always short of money, Elaine had begun taking teaching jobs that increasingly removed her from de Kooning's physical orbit for much of the year, but she returned to Long Island as her home base. She was a superior teacher, by all accounts, and her association with the New York art world enhanced her authority. As de Kooning's fame increased, however, he began resenting the way Elaine cashed in on their marriage—both literally, because she was always asking for money, and figuratively, in her professional self-descriptions—and he came to regard her as unserious. Still, no one could convince him to divorce her. Though the murky domestic arrangements that prevailed in his life greatly perplexed his legal and financial advisors, de Kooning seems to have felt completely at home in the ambiguities.

Then, in 1977, Elaine found a new usefulness in her position as his wife. Elaine too had been a heavy drinker, but she broke her own addiction in 1974, by disciplined participation in AA. She began cautiously monitoring de Kooning's state of health by dropping by the studio every day, paying neighborly visits. She decided that de Kooning needed full-time attendance by men who could serve as studio assistants but who could not be conned into supporting his alcoholism. By 1979, she had handpicked a crew, and de Kooning stopped drinking.

Once Elaine had taken control of de Kooning's studio, she attempted to restructure his social life to meet the ideal she had always lived by. They would, as a married couple who continued to live in different homes, dwell at the center of an artist's world, making de Kooning's studio into a salon to rival that of Gertrude Stein. This was not to be. By the early 1980s de Kooning had begun slipping into dementia, though Elaine managed to conceal his condition from the world until her own death in 1989. De Kooning died in 1997.

Now, back to the question: what did the women *want*? Obviously, each wanted something different, and different things at different times, but if the conditions provided by de Kooning's career can be generalized, one of its attractions was the severe isolation to which he condemned himself. De Kooning lived by example the loneliness of the existentialist. He had a great talent, and he understood that his obligation was to painting: that the severest challenge in his life was what he called "the anxiety of possibilities." By this he meant that no single brushstroke lay outside the history of painting itself, every action had to be performed with utter consciousness of its significance for the past and for the present. De Kooning's long, pensive silences, standing immobile before the easel, his furious pacing as he looked and worried with a pounding heart, his flight from the studio for midnight walks in the street, were all testimony to the severe purposefulness with which he conducted his life. No human relationship whatsoever was permitted to impinge on his demanding occupation.

This abdication of conventional domestic relationships was a model of freedom not easily found in the 1950s, except among artists, for whom "the important life was lived in the studio and the bar, not in the home." The women in de Kooning's life benefited in two ways. First, they were free from the expectation that they were destined to bear children. This was welcome to them, we gather. As de Kooning's first serious girlfriend told the biographers, when she became pregnant the first time, in 1930, de Kooning thought they should marry. (This was before his conversion by Arshile Gorky.) It was she who chose otherwise: "I'd seen too much poverty." She had three abortions during the several years she spent with de Kooning, sparing herself, she believed, the destitution that had ruined her own mother's life.

The second benefit to de Kooning's women was their heady admission to the milieu of artists' talk, a free-floating but exclusive seminar. De Kooning loved gab, he loved exploring any and all ideas with brainy girlfriends such as Ruth Kligman; the excitement of talking with them was compensation for the extreme solitude of the studio and for the many years of deprivation that had preceded his fame. The biographers speculate that de Kooning used women as social assets, but it's clear that being "used" as a social asset suited these women to a tee. Ruth Kligman, like Elaine, had the disposition of a salonnière (before attending a dinner party she would acquaint herself with the work of the guests, and like most of the women de Kooning preferred, she was adept at self-dramatizing eloquence). She had a knack for getting invited to the best parties, the best summer cottages, the best vacation spots. She drew out de Kooning's social personality, fed his vanity, and dressed him up. Partly because she resembled Elizabeth Taylor, with her on his arm he looked like the star he had become.

Yes, he was a good lover, too, but as one of them put it, the women were "looking for a great soul, not just great power or great sex." De Kooning had his last important affair when he was sixty-six, with Emily Kilgore, a wealthy married woman who was half his age. She and her husband and their large family lived in Houston and summered in East Hampton, so de Kooning conducted his side of their relationship mainly through love letters that offer wonderful commentary on the role his emotional life played in the dynamics of his painting. Reflecting on this later, Kilgore observed that the arrangement had been ideal for de Kooning: "he could have me the way he wanted me, in his head."

If no woman, no matter how clever, could ever impose on de Kooning a claim of obligation, how could any woman ever partner him? The answer appeared, to some, to be modeled in the relationship of Simone de Beauvoir with Jean-Paul Sartre. To be free and also bonded to one another, as de Beauvoir and Sartre were bonded: this was the aim of the women who entered de Kooning's life and stayed for years.

The name of de Beauvoir reminds us that 1950s existentialism, along with many other cultural movements, was gendered. Women's access to the New York art scene required the passport of sexual attractiveness: talent was not enough. So if we want to look for the way women drawn to the arts experienced new ideas about "freedom" and "choice" that were attaining currency in the 1950s, we probably have much to learn from the subjectivities preserved in the kinds of memoirs and interviews that form the basis of this biography.

Suppose, then, that we can position ourselves in the receptive state of mind of a young woman who has fallen into conversation at the

Cedar Tavern with Willem de Kooning. She has come with a vague purpose—to find out what it's all about, this world of the artists, and to get away from the world in which she feels herself to be a misfit—and suddenly de Kooning focuses the purpose. He listens; he doesn't talk about himself; he finds out what interests her in painting, music, popular culture, design, ideas. He is comfortable with long pauses, and he laughs a lot. He is not seductive, but he is undisguisedly attracted, and he invites her to visit his studio. Beforehand, she asks a lot of people about him and maybe she even reads some things about him; she learns that he is married and has many girlfriends. When she arrives she falls back under the spell of his conversation, and that becomes the core of her experience: his receptivity to her inner life, his low-keyed, canny recognition of where her talent might go. They make love eventually. Probably she came looking for a soulmate, and possibly his responsiveness makes her hope to be the exception to the de Kooning rule: no more wives. She finds instead the other half of what she sought: not a mate but a soul, one whose solitude presses on her with unavoidable questions about her . . . well, call it "authenticity," the word a 1950s existentialist philosopher would choose. And as the biographers comment with a faint tone of surprise, once the relationship ended, as it always did, the woman "might speak of him ruefully, but none of them regretted" the time she had spent getting to know herself under the attentions of Willem de Kooning.

DIANE MIDDLEBROOK is a professional writer and professor emerita of English at Stanford University. Her *Anne Sexton, A Biography* (1991) was a finalist for the National Book Award and for the National Book Critics Circle Award. Middlebrook's latest book is a biography of the creative partnership of the English writer Ted Hughes and the American writer Sylvia Plath, titled *Her Husband: Ted Hughes and Sylvia Plath, a Marriage* (2003).

REVIEW:

COLD WAR ORIENTALISM: ASIA IN THE MIDDLEBROW IMAGINATION, 1945–1961,
BY CHRISTINA KLEIN. BERKELEY: UNIVERSITY OF CALIFORNIA PRESS, 2003. 316 PAGES.

*AMERICAN THEATER IN THE CULTURE OF THE COLD WAR: PRODUCING AND CONTESTING
CONTAINMENT, 1947–1962*, BY BRUCE MCCONACHIE. IOWA CITY:
UNIVERSITY OF IOWA PRESS, 2003. 363 PAGES.

STACY WOLF

Christina Klein's *Cold War Orientalism: Asia in the Middlebrow Imagination, 1945–1961*, and Bruce McConachie's *American Theater in the Culture of the Cold War: Producing and Contesting Containment, 1947–1962,* both participate in and expand the conversation around the ideological work of U.S. culture in the mid-twentieth century, and both are excellent, welcome additions to the field. The two books also speak to each other, either directly (McConachie cites Klein's dissertation, on which her book is based), or indirectly, through their readings of the same texts. In addition, both authors explore the relationship between U.S. public policy and the construction of "American" identity at the time, and both are primarily concerned with the operations of middle-class, middlebrow culture on predominantly white theatre spectators, film-goers, and readers. Finally, both authors organize their projects in relation to the idea of containment, but from entirely different perspectives.

Since the 1988 publication of Elaine Tyler May's *Homeward Bound: American Families in the Cold War Era,* scholars of mid-twentieth century U.S. culture have developed illuminating analyses of Cold War politics in the context of domestic issues. May's groundbreaking book observed how politics played out as thoroughly gendered both on the home front and in the home itself, with women's bodies being portrayed as bombers, and the "good mother" preserving not only the family but also the entire country. By analyzing how government policies inflected everyday practices, May joined political and cultural histories, showing how "containment" pervaded every aspect of daily life.

Klein's *Cold War Orientalism* takes on May's thesis to assert that while containment was indeed a prevalent aspect of Cold War policies and culture, integration was an equally powerful objective. Without rejecting the "containment" thesis, Klein instead focuses on the United States' effort to promote a universal understanding and tolerance of Asia and the Pacific. She sees this project originating with the U.S. government, being articulated through U.S. public policy, and then being affirmed through popular magazines, novels, travel writings, and Broadway musicals. These texts, as Klein writes, "performed a certain kind of cultural work: they helped to construct a national identity of the United States as a global power" (9). Taken together, these representations ultimately "generated . . . a wide-ranging discourse of racial tolerance and inclusion that served as the official ideology undergirding postwar expansion" (11).

In her introduction and first chapter, Klein lays out the terms of this integrationist project: orientalism and the middlebrow. Crucial to her understanding of "the middlebrow imagination" is sentimentality, which dominated U.S. writers' construction of Asia's otherness. By historicizing both the "middlebrow" and the "sentimental," Klein recuperates their current negative valences. Postwar middlebrow writers and intellectuals were self-consciously so, and they aimed to render Cold War politics as "something that ordinary Americans could take part in, as a set of activities in which they could invest their emotional and intellectual energy" (7). (For more critical readings of "middlebrow," see Joan Shelley Rubin, Janice Radway, and David Savran.) They articulated global connections in "personal terms," in sentimental narratives that portrayed the "self-in-relation," that emphasized how "bonds are forged across a divide of difference" characterized by "reciprocity and exchange," and that foregrounded emotions "as the means for achieving and maintaining this exchange" (8, 14). The very project of sentimentality was feminized and feminizing, with an image of the good mother at its center.

Other chapters look closely at a range of cultural texts. One explores two magazines, the left-leaning *Saturday Review* and the conservative *Reader's Digest*, which both constructed Asians as children to be cared for by U.S. citizens, even while urging their readers to accept cultural difference. Another examines travel writing, including James Michener's *The Voice of Asia* (1951), which assured readers that well-behaved Americans were welcome in Asia, and, in contrast, J. Saunder Redding's *An American in India* (1954). In Redding's book, the author, an African scholar, portrays his visit to India as a failure, since his lecture audience wanted to align with him on the basis of race and "did not believe" that Americans were truly sympathetic to Indians. In the book's second half, Klein presents extended readings of Rodgers and Hammerstein's "oriental" musicals—*South Pacific* (1947, film 1958), *The King and I* (1951, film 1956), and *Flower Drum Song* (1957, film 1961).

While elegant and persuasive readings of magazines, novels, travel writing, and Broadway musicals provide the evidence for Klein's incisive cultural analysis, she constructs an equally rich and lively historical context for the production and reception of each of these texts, whether written or performed. Each text converses with public policy—from Eisenhower's People-to-People exchange program, to the Children's Christian Fund adoption program, to economic support of Thailand—and Klein traces their connections in fascinating ways.

Although many figures appear in both books, and although McConachie gives a passing nod to the importance of national and global integration, his project, with extensive and detailed evidence, supports the containment thesis. *American Theater in the Culture of the Cold War* begins not with a discussion of U.S. history (or even theater), but with an argument for the usefulness of cognitive psychology in understanding theatre audiences. Citing the work of George Lakoff and Mark Johnson, McConachie asserts its value for historians "because it encourages them to discover cultural patterns in embodied actions centered on primary metaphors, including dramatic performances on the stage" (10).

From the 1947 National Security Act until the mid-1960s, the cognitive metaphor of containment dominated U.S. culture. For McConachie, Lakoff and Johnson's schema of containment facilitates a series of metaphors that organized almost every element of politics, society, and theatrical production and reception, and his array of examples is impressive. In the first chapter, after his initial discussion of Lakoff and Johnson, McConachie compares Clifford Odets's *Awake and Sing* (1935) with Arthur Miller's *Death of a Salesman* (1949) to illustrate the shift from a photographic culture to a radiophonic one, from realism to metatheatricality, and from history to allegory.

McConachie organizes the three chapters that follow according to figures of containment: the "Empty Boy," the "Family of Man," and the

"Fragmented Hero." After astutely outlining key political events and vibrantly recounting their social and cultural contexts, McConachie moves among several performances in each chapter. "The Empty Boy," for example—"a mixture of innocence and independence, vulnerability and strength"—emerged in relation to the threat from without and from within both the country and the person (57). McConachie finds this type embodied in the characters of Johnny Pope in Michael Gazzo's *A Hatful of Rain* (1955) and Richard Sherman in George Axelrod's *The Seven Year Itch* (1952), and also in Tennessee Williams's *A Cat on a Hot Tin Roof* (1955). Audiences could interpret such a figure because texts and representations that used related metaphorical schemas pervaded the culture, including the star persona of Montgomery Clift, Freudian psychology, and popular texts such as David Riesman's *The Lonely Crowd* (1950).

Furthermore, all elements of Cold War–era theatrical practice—both production and reception—relied on similar metaphors of interior and exterior, of restraint and compulsion, of self-possession and abandon, and extended the literal into *allegoresis*. In each of his extended examples, such as William Inge's *The Dark at the Top of the Stairs* (1957), Archibald MacLeish's *J.B.* (1958), Martha Graham's *Night Journey* (1947), Miller's *The Crucible* (1953), and Lorraine Hansberry's *A Raisin in the Sun* (1959), McConachie expands the containment schema's relevance beyond a study of theatrical representations to analyses of theatrical space, set and lighting design, and acting and directing techniques. His evocative explorations of Elia Kazan's directing, Lee Strasberg's acting techniques, and Jo Mielziner's set designs—to note some of the key theatrical players of the time—underline the pervasiveness of the containment schema. Such attention to the multiple ways that theatrical performances are constructed is surprisingly rare in theatre histories. Thus McConachie's new book joins his *Melodramatic Formations* as a key text in theatre history as well as theatre reception studies.

Richard Rodgers and Oscar Hammerstein II, composer and lyricist of *Oklahoma!, South Pacific, The King and I, Flower Drum Song*, and *The Sound of Music*, occupy central roles in both Klein's and McConachie's books, as they were the creators of extremely influential and pervasive middlebrow, middle-class culture, as well as intentional supporters of global humanitarianism and accidental perpetuators of liberal racism. Klein's and McConachie's excellent work on the musicals of Rodgers and Hammerstein contributes to musical theatre studies in important and original ways. Interestingly, their different readings of *The King and I* foreground the distinction between these two books and illustrate how, taken together, they offer a rich and complex perspective on Cold War culture.

Klein locates the musical as an educational arena for both the non-white characters and the presumptively white Broadway (or film, she assumes) theater audience. After summarizing the U.S. political and economic support of Thailand, she maps a narrative of "sentimental modernization" through three musical numbers: "The March of the Royal Siamese Children," "Getting to Know You," and "The Small House of Uncle Thomas." Anna's education of the Siamese people is "figured in cultural—as opposed to military or conventionally political—terms: the embrace of Western, specifically American, cultural forms marks the successful modernization of the country" (207–88). By the end of the musical, Anna, the white woman, is the only adult left. Through emotional attachment, mimicry, and analogy, Anna, the quintessential American middlebrow intellectual, teaches Asians to act civilized, to act modern; that is, to act American.

Klein's reading of *The King and I* follows an analysis of the almost-erotic polka "Shall We Dance?" with speculation about audience response: "Just as the King is drawn in to Anna's liberal political ideology by joining her in song and dance, so we are led to embrace the ideals of international integration and Third World modernization by our own sense of participation" (211). Klein's use of first person plural in this example is unexpected. Throughout the book, Klein admirably accounts for white readers' likely interpretations by creating an identifiable context with particular horizons of expectations. Although not explicitly invested in reception, Klein's analysis of historical audiences is superb. In this instance, then, while I agree with her model of how a musical works to interpellate its audience, I find the presumed "viewer" surprisingly ahistorical.

McConachie, in contrast, first offers a history of representation of bad mothers in the immediate postwar period to chart the representational shift to good mothers. He then examines the influence of Method acting practices on musical theatre (which was a star-driven enterprise), and reads Yul Brynner (as the King) and Gertrude Lawrence (as Anna) through questions of surface and depth. He stresses the King's harsh exterior and childish interior, Anna's feminine exterior (made more complex by the hoop skirts that the language-lacking Siamese women find so amusing) and masculine interior, and the utter lack of continuity between the races of the nonwhite actors and their Siamese characters. As McConachie argues, costume and makeup are necessary to construct Siameseness, which becomes "a performance in itself" (159). McConachie also finds Mielziner's set reminiscent of suburban houses of the time. For McConachie's spectator, *The King and I* offers the empathetic positions of mother or child, or an experience in which "shifting between the pleasures of mothering and being mothered effectively creates a third position—empathizing with a mother-centered family" (145).

Both Klein and McConachie see Anna as the good mother and the musical's overall objective as a pedagogical one, but Klein's larger context is international politics and McConachie's is the American family. Still, both authors are fundamentally concerned with an American ideological project: with how white, middle-class spectators might make sense of this oft-repeated story and be persuaded (or reminded) that U.S. expansion (cum capitalism) is a good thing because, underneath, Asians are (or can be made to be) "just like us."

McConachie's model of containment metaphors is at once thoroughly persuasive and useful and also occasionally seems to fit his examples so well that I wonder if there are limits to this schema. If everything fits, then how does it illuminate differences and distinctions among texts? In the end, though, McConachie's history and historiography offer much more than his application of Lakoff and Johnson's theory of metaphors. Still, the theoretical model—cognitive psychology's use of metaphors—will no doubt prove immensely useful to theater historians studying audiences.

Given his attention to detail and to the nuances of acting, directing, design, playwriting, and criticism, I was surprised that McConachie incorrectly credits Julie Andrews with creating the role of Maria in the Broadway production of *The Sound of Music*. Not insignificantly, Mary Martin, one of the two queens of the Cold War Broadway musical, actually debuted in the role, after acquiring the rights to Maria Von Trapp's autobiography and convincing Rodgers and Hammerstein to write the role for her. No doubt Andrews now (and forever?) occupies the role of Maria in our cultural imaginary, as she played the role in the

1965 film version, but Martin originally created the character of tomboy-mother Maria. Martin, a middle-class dancer from a small town in Texas who became a rich and powerful Broadway star, would have made another interesting subject for McConachie's already exhaustively researched book, insofar as she embodied contradictions of surface and depth in her portrayals of Nellie Forbush and Peter Pan.

Both Klein and McConachie create rich, nuanced, and thoroughly engaging books, but their different disciplines weigh their projects differently. Klein's primary concern is culture's relationship to history and especially to public policy. In terms of reception, she doesn't interrogate the distinctions among reading a magazine, reading a novel, listening to a lecture, or seeing a Broadway musical. McConachie, on the other hand, wanting his work to serve as a model for historical reception studies, focuses on the influence of radio, of visuality, of the proscenium space of the Broadway stage. For both authors, the imagined audience of these texts and performances is white, middle-class, and middlebrow. I wonder how nonwhite U.S. audiences might have read them.

Overall, Klein and McConachie have made impressive and groundbreaking contributions to the fields of American studies, gender studies, and theater studies. Each book is a terrific, engaging read, and placed side by side, they create an extraordinarily animated sense of U.S. culture during the Cold War.

STACY WOLF is associate professor of theater and dance at the University of Texas at Austin, where she teaches in the Performance as Public Practice Program. She is the author of *A Problem Like Maria: Gender and Sexuality in the American Musical*. Wolf has written essays on musical theater, theater audiences, and feminist pedagogy. She also works as a dramaturg.

ALERTS AND PROVOCATIONS: A FEMINIST PUBLIC SPHERE FOR DEBATE AND ACTION

ACADEMIC FROSTBITE (A CAUTIONARY TALE)

ANAHID KASSABIAN

This fall, I'm starting a new position at University of Liverpool. I thought I'd never leave New York—except, maybe, for a job in San Francisco—but many events conspired last year to show me it was quite simply time to go.

Chief among them was the incredible erosion of academic freedom, nationally and at my own institution, Fordham University. As recently as August 12, 2005, *The Chronicle of Higher Education* carried a three-page story on Amina Wadud, a faculty member who was asked by her university to stay off campus for safety reasons. An African-American Muslim, she led a group of women and men in prayer, violating a taboo against women leading men in prayer. In response to the threats against her, did her university, Virginia Commonwealth, stand up for her? No. Instead, they asked her to stay off campus and teach her courses by video-link from home.

The September 2005 issue of *Harper's* offers another bleak moment in this debate: a roundtable on whether or not there should be a concern for political diversity in faculty personnel decisions. And by diversity, they don't mean feminists or critical race theorists; they mean conservatives. There is much to say on this matter, of course. For now, let it suffice to point out that the prevalence of Democrats in the academy does not make it a left institution that requires balancing through the hiring and retention of more Republicans and Christian fundamentalists, as the article could be seen to be suggesting.

Our national commitment to academic freedom has been seriously derailed. Clearly, without carefully protected academic freedom, there can be no thought and no learning; we obviously need to hear every well-argued perspective, no matter how uncomfortable. But in the current

[*WSQ: Women's Studies Quarterly* 33: 3 & 4 (Fall/Winter 2005)]

climate, certain values—in particular those associated with Islam, the political left and feminism (often uncomfortable bedfellows in their own rights)—are not respected or protected. I offer you the following list of attacks (from academic 2004–05, compiled only from my own place as someone teaching at a Jesuit university in media studies, women's studies, Middle East studies) on that cornerstone of our project and our existence, in hopes that you'll share my deep worry for our future:

The Cardinal Newman Society reported on Catholic college and university faculty donations, posting them on a website with individual faculty members' names and accusing them of being out of step with American Catholics more generally.

The David Project, a group from outside Columbia University, produced a documentary called *Columbia Unbecoming* on faculty in Middle East Studies at Columbia that alleges inappropriate and hostile anti-Israeli teachings (and, by implication, though never overtly, anti-Semitism). The students who make these allegations are anonymous, and none of them had filed complaints through regular university procedures. This attack was part of a long-standing, well-calculated and well-funded effort to undermine pro-Palestinian faculty, especially at prestigious universities. Over the course of several years, but most clearly this year, the lives of several faculty were torn apart, and permanent damage may well have been done to the career of an untenured and well respected professor, Joseph Massad. Moreover, largely in response to this attack, university president Bollinger has put the Department of Middle East and Asian Languages and Cultures (MEALAC) in receivership, despite the findings (by an ad hoc committee of his formation) in favor of the faculty in question.

There is a continuing campaign to remove Indian activist Ward Churchill from his tenured position in Ethnic Studies at the University of Colorado, Boulder. In an essay initially published on September 11, 2001 titled "Some People Push Back: On the Justice of Roosting Chickens," Churchill argued that the victims of the Twin Towers attack were not innocent. An inflammatory view, no doubt, but a position on the role of capitalism in Middle East politics that deserves hearing, whether or not one ultimately agrees. But because of response to this essay, he has stepped down as chair of Ethnic Studies, has been uninvited as a guest speaker at colleges around the country, and has been investigated by his university for possible research misconduct.

Tariq Ramadan was appointed as Luce Professor of Religion, Conflict and Peacebuilding at the Joan B. Kroc Institute for International Peace Studies at the University of Notre Dame, but his visa was revoked by the U.S. Department of Homeland Security. They allege that he has ties to terrorist organizations, which he denies. He eventually had to resign the position.

The Solomon Amendment, which permits the federal government to withdraw funding from schools that refuse to host military recruiters, is in front of the Supreme Court; many universities, in particular law schools, argue that it violates their First Amendment rights.

Alan Dershowitz has threatened to sue the University of California Press for publishing a book by Norman Finkelstein critical of his support for Israel despite its documented human rights abuses (*Chronicle of Higher Education*, 22 July 2005, Volume 51, Issue 46, Page A1).

Rep. David Baxley of Florida has introduced legislation substantially written by conservative activist David Horowitz that would allow students to sue faculty for unbalanced teaching, including, for example, the absence of creationism and intelligent design on biology syllabi. Such legislation is being proposed and discussed in many states and by a member of the Board of Trustees of the State University of New York.

Oneida Meranto of Metropolitan State College in Denver has been accused (and found innocent) of having a liberal bias and intimidating conservative students. Along with these accusations she has received death threats and hate mail (*Chronicle of Higher Education*, 26 November 2004, Volume 51, Issue 14, Page A8).

But these attacks on academic freedom are not just happening on the national academic scene, they have local forms as well at campuses across the country. At my own university, Fordham College at Lincoln Center, there have been a number of chilling incidents. In addition to the listing of Fordham faculty members' donations on the Cardinal Newman Society website, as mentioned above.

The Office of Student Affairs refused to fund a student production of Eve Ensler's widely acclaimed "The Vagina Monologues." While to my mind the play is artistically uninteresting, it is politically important, and the Office of Student Affairs' response amounted to a kind of tacit censorship, apparently with the approval of the university's president. In addition, student leaders' and residence hall staff members' jobs were unofficially threatened if they participated in the production in any way, including hanging posters.

A young woman published a beautifully written, frank but polite "Urban Cocktail," the campus student newspaper's sex and relationships column, in which she argued that college is a time for women to learn how to find and expect sexual pleasure. She was subjected to a widespread gossip fest and required to meet with the Dean of Students, who questioned her morality and judgment and threatened to inform her parents of the column. The column was anonymously sent to her parents.

As these events were taking place, there was an ongoing debate—three College Council meetings and two stories in the student paper—about the silencing of conservative students.

A quick review: progressive faculty and students, among others with oppositional views, are having our political donations made public, having fake documentaries made about us, risking our jobs, losing our visas, being forced to allow military recruiting on campus, and possibly laying ourselves open to lawsuits. But the main academic freedom topic of last year on my campus? Conservative students' speech.

Don't get me wrong—I think it's an important issue. I worry about making room for conservative voices in the classroom all the time. I answer avowedly conservative students more gently than I do students with whom I agree, and when I grade students with whom I disagree, I err on the side of generosity to compensate for my unconscious biases. And then I worry about how that sounds, and what it means about the academic freedom of students who agree with me. None of this is simple. I really do think we all—faculty and students—need to work hard to make classrooms a space of open, generous, respectful, productive debate and discussion. And I think most of us DO work very hard at precisely that task.

The debates in Fordham College at Lincoln Center's College Council were remarkably like the roundtable in *Harper's*. They pretended that the biggest threat to the pursuit of open intellectual inquiry on college campuses today is the restriction of conservative ideas. When a piece related to this one appeared in the student newspaper last year, I got exactly one response—from a former Fordham Law student who explained to me in very ungenerous language how little I understood about the situation at Columbia. Having had dinner with a former chair of the department in question a week earlier, having read everything I could on the topic (including the David Project's website, film transcripts, and published excerpts from the committee's findings), having close friends in and associated with the department, and knowing some members of the task force that looked into the film's allegations, I couldn't imagine he was better informed than I. But he could. It didn't occur to him that someone with whom he disagreed could be well informed and thoughtful. To his mind, there was only one right and true position on the question.

This sort of one-note response is precisely the problem facing politically engaged academics in the U.S. at the moment. We've somehow become the bad guys, through duplicitous and disingenuous campaigns orchestrated by well-funded conservative think-tank hacks like Lynne Cheney and David Horowitz. It's a big part of why I left for the U.K., where there are ample problems (including racial profiling in random stop-and-searches on the London Underground and Tony Blair's vile new anti-terrorism initiatives) but not this one. In a world in which Muslims like Tariq Ramadan and Amina Wadud are wrong before they start, in which lawyers feel free to make baseless accusations against writers, in which some faculty and students are being asked to self-censor, we are in very serious trouble. The chill in the halls of Fordham, and of American academe more generally, is not nipping at the earlobes of conservative students. It's biting the lips and tongues of leftist, anti-imperialist, feminist, and anti-racist faculty who dare to speak out in a very dark political night frost.

Virginia Woolf and the Bloomsbury Avant-Garde
War, Civilization, Modernity
Christine Froula

Froula traces the emergence of Woolf's art against Bloomsbury's public thinking in a period marked by two world wars and rising threats of totalitarianism.

"The best reading of Woolf's total oeuvre I have ever seen."—Marianne DeKoven, Rutgers University

Modernism and the Architecture of Private Life
Victoria Rosner

This study draws on a host of previously unexamined archival sources and reveals the many personal and aesthetic connections among modern British writers, interior designers, and architects, elegantly synthesizing modernist literature with architectural plans, room designs, and decorative art.

"A book of enormous interest, refinement, and originality."—Terry Castle, editor of *The Literature of Lesbianism*

Cool Men and the Second Sex
Susan Fraiman

Fraiman identifies the "cool masculinity" of academic superstars and bad boy filmmakers, deciphering the gender codes and baring the contradictions implicit in their work.

"With wit, guts, and the kind of critical crankiness that can give left critique what it really needs, Susan Fraiman dissects the celebrity culture of academic masculine cool. Required reading for anyone unafraid of being a bad girl!"
—Robyn Wiegman, author of *American Anatomies*

Hamlet's Mother and Other Women
Carolyn G. Heilbrun

Now in a new paperback edition with a new preface by the author, this collection explores feminism in literary studies during the last three decades, demonstrating the consistency and clarity of Heilbrun's vision and her deep respect for the lives of women who write.

"A wonderful, living book for those who love to read and to think. It is engaged, fervent, good-humored; it is wise and intellectually substantive and a real pleasure to read."—Andrea Dworkin

Pursuing Privacy in Cold War America
Deborah Nelson
A Choice Magazine Outstanding Academic Title for 2002

This book explores the relationship between confessional poetry and constitutional privacy doctrine, situating both as part of a far wider anxiety about privacy that erupted across the social, cultural, and political spectrum during the late 1950s.

"An elegant and ambitious book."
—Diane Middlebrook, author of *Anne Sexton: A Biography*

But Enough About Me
Why We Read Other People's Lives
Nancy K. Miller

"In her poignant, mesmerizing new book, Nancy Miller presents the definitive defense of memoir…Her clear prose, brimming with ironies, gives unadulterated pleasure; blending narrative and analysis it sets a stylish new standard for innovative critical writing."—Wayne Koestenbaum, author of *The Queen's Throat*

☰ COLUMBIA UNIVERSITY PRESS

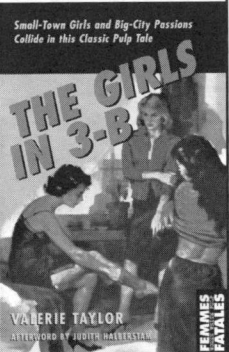